Politics, Religion, and Society
in Latin America

Series

Religion in Politics and Society:
Dynamics and Developments

Politics,

Religion &

Society in

Latin America

Daniel H. Levine

LYNNE
RIENNER
PUBLISHERS

BOULDER
LONDON

Published in the United States of America in 2012 by
Lynne Rienner Publishers, Inc.
1800 30th Street, Boulder, Colorado 80301
www.rienner.com

and in the United Kingdom by
Lynne Rienner Publishers, Inc.
3 Henrietta Street, Covent Garden, London WC2E 8LU

Library of Congress Cataloging-in-Publication Data
Levine, Daniel H.
  Politics, religion, and society in Latin America / Daniel H. Levine.
      p. cm. — (Religion in politics and society)
  Includes bibliographical references (p.) and index.
  ISBN 978-1-58826-852-5 (alk. paper)
  1. Latin America—Religion. 2. Religion and politics—Latin America.
3. Religion and sociology—Latin America. I. Title.
  BL2540.L48 2012
  200.98'09051—dc23

                                            2012014909

British Cataloguing in Publication Data
A Cataloguing in Publication record for this book
is available from the British Library.

Printed and bound in the United States of America

        The paper used in this publication meets the requirements
 ∞   of the American National Standard for Permanence of
        Paper for Printed Library Materials Z39.48-1992.

    5 4 3 2 1

For my family

Contents

Preface

When I first went to Latin America (to Caracas, Venezuela, in 1967) the movie houses still showed newsreels along with advertisements before the main feature. A lot of footage was taken up with official events—cutting ribbons on public works, opening factories and businesses, inaugurating athletic competitions, and so on. Each of these occasions, big or small, was presided over by a trio representing state, church, and military, accompanied as appropriate by the smiling owner of the business, the athletes, or the happy residents of some new housing complex. The politician would make a speech and cut the ribbon, the priest would say a blessing, and the officer would look on in solidarity, providing by his presence a silent guarantee of order. The joint presence of these three figures was a powerful and tangible representation of the alliance of powers that had been immemorial in Latin America.

In this age of twenty-four-hour cable news stations, newsreels are no more. The same can be said for the automatic alliance that I witnessed those evenings at the movies. The unquestioned relation of religion to power was shattered decades ago by the appearance of new ideas and movements that challenged the established order of things—in religion as in politics and society at large. That such change should have arisen within religion, and particularly within Latin America, was a surprise to most social scientists and observers, who were in the grip of theories of modernization and secularization according to which religion was a conservatizing force that would inevitably decline and disappear in the face of education and progress. This has not happened, and the question before us is why. In the search for answers, I examine in this book politics, religion, and the evolving relation between them that have characterized the experience of Latin America in the past fifty years.

I strive to understand and explain how and why these changes arose and what gave them lasting social power. This means identifying the major lines and moments of change, while at the same time accounting for variations across countries, between specific churches, and among the social movements linked to religion that proliferated in these years. This is an ambitious program, more ambitious still when we remember that Latin America is part of a larger world. Because the religious and political forces of this period also have powerful links to global trends and transnational movements, the effort to understand and explain change in Latin America also requires us to situate the experience of the region in a broader comparative and theoretical context.

There are several ways to organize an effort of this kind. A common solution is to begin with a general overview, noting key events and critical moments in the region as a whole that link different national and group experiences together. This could be combined with a series of national case studies, striving to cover as many cases as possible. Such case studies typically start out with a historical narrative and make an effort to link each specific national experience to an overall view of regional patterns. An alternative approach would be more analytical, organizing the material before us not in terms of time lines or national experiences, but rather in terms of the importance of particular issues selected for their theoretical relevance, that is, for the extent to which they fit within an overall explanation of the process.

The logic and organization of this book combine these approaches. I offer an overview of the major dimensions and trajectories of change that mark the past half century of the Latin American experience of politics and religion. This period has been one of intense and continuous change accompanied in many parts of the region by significant violence, a violence that has deeply affected churches and the movements and individuals linked to them. The violence at issue includes civil wars (El Salvador, Guatemala, Peru, Colombia) and massive and extended state repression (Chile, Argentina, Brazil). It also encompasses what we might call a violence of daily life: the violence that comes with domestic abuse, poor health, unemployment, alcoholism, crime, personal insecurity, and the impunity of police and other security services. Much of this story has been told in detail elsewhere; here I provide indications and a summary where possible, but of course this history continues to be created all the time, so there is always new material to consider.

Beyond describing events and actors and locating points of change, I work at constructing an explanation for what we see. In a purely epistemological sense, there is no explanation without theory. It is not possible to describe or to name anything at all without having at least an implicit theory of reality that tells us what to look for, identifies likely connections, and gives us tools with which to weigh competing explanations, judge how well they account for reality, and make accurate and reliable predictions about the future. To this end, early on in the book I examine general accounts of the place of religion in society and politics, along with competing theories and methods of study that have been advanced in recent years to identify and account specifically for change in Latin America.

There is a temptation built into our language to consider politics and religion as separate in practice as in theory and therefore to view mutual influence as untoward. Thus, it is common to hear about the (presumably undue) "politicization of religion" and also (although less so) about the "religionization of politics" as if these relations could be measured by some kind of religious-political thermometer where too high a reading would indicate a feverish, and therefore undesirable, condition. This is reinforced in common usage by traditions of separation of church and state, which are often conflated with separation of politics from religion, but which are not the same thing at all. It takes less effort now than twenty years ago to convince students that politics and religion are deeply and permanently intertwined in North American experience as in the experience of much of the world. The surge of fundamentalist and evangelical movements in US politics, the bitter campaigns over abortion, and the renewed political activism of many religious groups have surely put to rest the notion that religion and politics are separate in the United States (even our currency has "In God We Trust" on its face). But the expectation remains in other parts of the world, often framed as a goal on the way to "modernization."

The perspective I take in this book requires us to see the boundaries between "politics and religion" or "politics, religion, and society" or "religion, society, and culture" less as walls to be maintained and defended than as porous border zones where mutual influence and interchange are normal and continuous. I argue here that what we see in Latin America, in the United States, and in much of the world beyond is neither secularization in its crude form (the decline, privatization, and disappearance of religion), nor a massive politicization of religion, but rather a continuous renegotiation or recomposition of what being religious and being political mean in these societies in the past, present, and future.

Religion has played a major role in the social, cultural, and political transformations of Latin America since the 1960s. Transformations within religion have been central to the ability of churches, religious groups, and individuals to contribute to the building of a different kind of society. Through all this, Christianity remains utterly dominant, but this is not the Christianity of fifty years ago. It is much more diverse, and it has a much more plural and varied presence in public life. The creativity and vitality of religion in Latin America are likely to remain, shaping the world in ways as yet unknown. If this book provides reliable guidelines for understanding the past and making sense of likely futures, it will have more than accomplished its goals.

* * *

This book is the interim conclusion to what has been a long journey. I became seriously interested in the relations among politics, religion, and society in Latin America in the early 1970s after reading the late Ivan Vallier's pioneering work. My interests have evolved through my work in several books based on field research in Venezuela and Colombia, several other edited books, and a long series of articles, chapters, and monographs on issues ranging from religion and democracy to the relations among religious change, violence, and social movements. Working with generations of students at the University of Michigan, the Universidad de Salamanca, the Pontifical Catholic University of Peru, and the Universidad de Buenos Aires has helped shape my focus. Spurred by their questions, I have been pushed to open new and exciting areas of inquiry.

This academic journey has also been a personal journey. I began my studies of religion from a standpoint that is conventional in the social sciences: objective, neutral, skeptical, and disinterested. My encounters with religion as lived and experienced in Latin America, and with countless people who give voice to new ideas and whose actions give them social presence and staying power, made me question these positions. From skeptical observer I became sympathetic and (I hope) empathetic, and from there a believer.

Along the way I have incurred many personal and professional debts that I want to acknowledge here. I am grateful to all the people I have met in Latin America, whose generous sharing of their experiences has enriched my life and made my work better. I hope I have been faithful to their experiences. I have a great debt to friends and colleagues who have read my work over the years and been generous with observations, reactions, and criticisms: Said Arjomand, Philip Berryman, Thomas Bruneau, José Casanova, the late Edward Cleary, Humberto Cucchetti, Michael Dodson, Paul Freston, Bryan Froehle, Paul Gifford, Frances Hagopian, David Lehmann, Scott Mainwaring, Fortunato Mallimaci, José Enrique Molina, Enzo Gustavo Morello, Robert Pelton, José Raúl Perales, Catalina Romero, David Smilde, Brian Smith, Timothy Steigenga, David Stoll, and Alexander Wilde. I never got to meet Ivan Vallier, but I benefited greatly from his example and from correspondence with him, even though I ended up disagreeing with many of his conclusions. Bryan Froehle provided invaluable help with the organization and display of quantitative data in Chapter 3. I gratefully acknowledge the helpful comments and observations made on all or parts of the manuscript by Joaquín Algranti, Miguel Carter, Maria Soledad Catoggio, Humberto Cucchetti, Michael Dodson, Luis Miguel Donatello, Juan Esquivel, Bryan Froehle, Fortunato Mallimaci, Damian Setton, David Smilde, Alexander Wilde, and two anonymous reviewers. Sandy Thatcher and Lynne Rienner provided valuable help and feedback at all stages of work on the book.

I am happy to acknowledge the support I have received over the years from the Department of Political Science and the College of Literature, Science, and the Arts of the University of Michigan, which have provided a stimulating and collegial environment. I benefited greatly from the opportunity to present parts of this work in seminars and panel discussions at the Harvard Center for International Affairs, the Helen Kellogg Institute for International Studies at the University of Notre Dame, the Berkeley Center for Religion, Peace, and World Affairs at Georgetown University, and the Woodrow Wilson International Center for Scholars, as well as at various professional meetings of the American Political Science Association, the Latin American Studies Association, the Spanish Association of Political Science, and the Society for the Scientific Study of Religion. I am grateful to all those institutions and associations. I am particularly grateful for the precious gifts of time and support that I have received from appointments as a Security and Development Faculty Fellow of the Center for International and Comparative Studies at the University of Michigan, a visiting fellow of the Helen Kellogg Institute for International Studies at the University of Notre Dame, and a Luce Foundation Fellow at the Woodrow Wilson International Center for Scholars.

—Daniel H. Levine

1

Politics, Religion, and Society in Latin America

If anyone interested in politics, religion, and society in Latin America had had access to an accurate crystal ball in 1959 or 1960, they would have been astonished by what they saw. The world in which they had grown up, and whose norms and social arrangements appeared to be part of the natural order of things, was about to be turned upside down. The solid relation of the Catholic Church to power and privilege, its long-established monopoly of religious authority and moral voice, and its uncertain stance to democracy would all experience a series of shocks. Instead of Catholic monopoly they would see religious pluralization and competition with a proliferation of Protestant churches. Protestantism itself would not only expand but also diversify, with multiple churches claiming the allegiance of up to a quarter of the population in many countries. The focus of much religious practice would shift as well, as the expansion of Pentecostal Protestantism made the direct experience of divine power a core element of the practice and the presence of these churches in public life. Even the Catholic Church would not look the same. New and sometimes radical voices would emerge to claim the authority of faith for the initiatives. Something like a real civil society, with deep and often public debates, began to consolidate within the church. Civil wars would be fought, repressive military regimes would take power, often in the name of Western Christian ideals and the fight against "subversion," with the Catholic Church a determined opponent in some cases, a complicit ally in others. Democracy would return, and with it an open and plural civil society.

Long assumed to be the unchanging and unquestioned bulwark of established power and privilege, religion has diversified and flourished

1

while taking on a new social and political presence in more open and competitive societies. Understanding these changes requires analysis to reach beyond conventional categories like church and state to include the impact of violence and new ideas about rights, the realities of pluralism and competition, the creation of new forms of power, and the changing encounter of religion with democracy and social movements. Why did churches in Latin America take up new ideas about rights, sponsor social movements, and become advocates for democracy? Why at this time, in this way, and with what implications for the future? What explains the spectacular growth of Protestantism, and what implications does it have for politics and social life?

To answer these questions, this book examines the past and future of politics, religion, and society in the search for keys to the dynamic and direction of change in the future. It is always risky to write about the future. There is a tendency to speculate, to be excessively optimistic or pessimistic, or to fall back on simple extrapolation, believing that what has been will continue in some form in the future. But our subject is a moving target, and there is too much creativity in both politics and religion for continuity alone to serve as a guide, and too many interlocking forces at work from too many levels for simple models of any kind to be of much use. In the words of Peruvian theologian Gustavo Gutiérrez, "At present we are in the position of those trying to decide whom a newborn child resembles. Some will say the father, others the mother. Some will even find that the child has this grandfather's nose or that aunt's eyes, whereas still others will be of the opinion that the child does not remind them of any family features known to them. Better to photograph the child and decide later on whom it resembles" (Gutiérrez 1984: 92). A photograph I took more than forty years ago may be a good place to start.

The photograph records my first encounter with an evangelical street preacher in Latin America, which came in 1968, in the Guatemalan market town of Solalá. The market was in full swing, and in the midst of people buying, selling, and bargaining, a Protestant preacher was working the crowd. The majority of Guatemalans are Indians, the audience was entirely made up of Indian men and women, and the speaker, I remember, was preaching the Gospel in Kakchiquel, the language of the region. Holding a Bible in his hands, he illustrated his sermon by pointing to a hand-painted canvas that depicted heaven, hell, the judgment of the nations, the temptations of this world, and the ways of the righteous and of the sinner. I found the scene stirring enough to save

the slide for more than four decades, but at the time it seemed little more than an interesting sideshow. The religious experience was new, as was the leadership: ordinary, often nonwhite and barely lettered men using a popular language, who recall the circuit-riding preachers of nineteenth-century North America (Hatch 1991). The signs were there, but they slipped by most observers. None of it fit into the accepted scheme of things at the time.

One decade into the twenty-first century, it is easy to see this preacher as a precursor of the wave of Protestant and Pentecostal religion that swept Guatemala, along with much of Latin America in subsequent years (Garrard-Burnett 1998; Martin 1990; Stoll 1990, 1993). He and others like him have since gone on to transform the religious landscape and the public presence of religion throughout the region. Particularly in the big cities (and Latin America is heavily urban), the religious scene is a blooming cacophony of churches, chapels, street preachers, and television and radio evangelists competing for attention and vying for members and a share of public goods and public space.

The photo tells us a lot, but as with many images, the questions we bring shape the kind of answers we seek and the meaning we give to what we see. Excessively strict dichotomies between religious and secular, public and private, will not help us to capture this dynamic. The issues are not well understood in terms of an isolated phenomenon (religion) suddenly springing into political action. Religious institutions, activists, and believers are simultaneously members of and affected by the society and political order in which they live. There is a continuous and wholly normal exchange of ideas and models of appropriate and possible behavior between these two areas of life. Every day, ordinary people and ordinary experience put together what academic convention and ideas about the separation of politics from religion often hold apart.

The problem that religions present to the social sciences is only in part a matter of empirical predictions. Studies of religion also bump up against a persistent unease that many scholars—nurtured on ideas of objectivity, rationality, and the need for empirical verification—experience in the presence of institutions and sets of beliefs and practices where the suprarational, supra-empirical, and nonverifiable play so central and compelling a role. The urge to reduce all this to more familiar and easily manageable categories (for example, of class interest or preference) is often difficult to resist, but it should be resisted. If we are to understand the relation between religion and politics, we must be willing to engage religion on its own terms. This means striving to make sense of how religious people and institutions understand themselves and their place in the world as a foundation for explaining why and how they organize to act in and on that world. In other words, we must take religion seriously if we are to have a serious chance of understanding its role in society and politics. Taking religion seriously means paying close attention to religious ideas as motivators and legitimators and to religious institutions and religiously sponsored social groups as spaces for social innovation.

As we study the relations between politics and religion, it is essential to recognize the relative autonomy of each. Each brings something to the table, each generates a presence in the public sphere, and the interaction and mutual influence that follow form the core of our study. The approach pursued here conceives of the boundaries between "politics and religion" or "society, culture, and religion" less as walls to be defended and maintained than as porous border zones where mutual influence and interchange are normal and continuous. What we see in Latin America, in the United States, and in much of the world is neither secularization in its crude form (the decline, privatization, and disappearance of religion) nor a massive "politicization of religion," but rather a continuous renegotiation or recomposition of what being religious and being political mean in these societies in the past, present, and future.

Into the Twenty-First Century

Latin American Catholicism entered the twentieth century in control of the religious field, but to borrow the language of economics, the church was a lazy monopolist, its power and position guaranteed by law, custom, and elite links. Lazy monopolists have little incentive to keep day-to-day operations vital, and as a result the church was vulnerable to new challenges and competitors—including innovative religious expression—that began to appear with growing force as the twentieth century passed its midpoint.

The past was marked in many countries by multiple images and symbols of religious-civic fusion, such as Te Deums with the presence of political and ecclesiastical "authorities" at the highest level or the repeated joint presence of politicians, clergy, and military officers at the inauguration of public works, the opening of stores or factories, the initiation of athletic events, and so on. This omnipresent triad provided a public affirmation of the identification of "the church" (only one was recognized) with political and economic power and social hierarchy. The world of Catholic monopoly seems a distant memory today. The public face of religion and the ways in which religion is present in the public sphere have been utterly transformed. New churches proliferate, and new voices jostle for space and attention. Street preachers abound, often working public spaces with little more than a Bible, a loudspeaker, and something to stand on (see Smilde 2004b, among many). Where there was monopoly there is now pluralism, where a limited number of spaces were once officially reserved for religious practice (with a limited number of authorized practitioners) there is now a rich profusion of churches, chapels, and mass media programming, not to mention campaigns and crusades that carry the message to hitherto "profane" spaces like streets and squares, beaches, sports stadiums, jails, bars, and nightclubs.

This new landscape challenges the traditional role of the Catholic Church as *the church*—the officially acknowledged wielder of moral and social authority within the boundaries of a defined national territory. In José Casanova's terms, the church is no longer *the church*—a religious institution with an official or semiofficial monopoly in a given territory—but rather one actor among many in an open civil society (Casanova 1994: 217). Making this change work is no easy task, and learning to live in a world that no longer can be defined by *one church* in mutual alliance with *one state* can be unsettling. Institutions long accustomed to public support may find competition and cultural openness to be less opportunities for growth than signs of decay, cultural peril, and disintegration.

One way to appreciate the extent of change is to consider how the world looked to the region's Catholic bishops when they met in 2007 at Aparecida, Brazil, for their Fifth General Conference (Pelton 2008; Levine 2008). This was the latest in a line of conferences that have set an agenda for Latin American Catholicism and provided a new moral vocabulary with which activists and believers could understand the world (Gutiérrez 2006; Cecilia Tovar 2007). From an earlier landmark conference at Medellín, Colombia (1968), came the idea that sin can refer to more than individual moral failings—whole social structures can be sinful if they are built on and continue injustice. Medellín also articulated a concept of institutionalized violence—that unjust societies condemn many to needless early death through poverty and disease, and that this is sinful. The next conference, at Puebla, Mexico (in 1979), made famous the commitment to a "preferential option for the poor." Given a choice, church resources should be placed at the service of the poor and vulnerable, and church people (clergy and lay activists) should side with the poor and accompany them in their struggles.[1] By the time of Aparecida, the great conflicts that were punctuated and in some sense legitimized by Medellín and Puebla had passed from the scene. Aparecida reflected an effort by Catholic leaders to chart a course that would allow their church to survive and prosper in the newly plural and competitive environment of the twenty-first century. Aparecida can also be understood as an effort by Pope Benedict XVI to continue the policies of his predecessor John Paul II, while placing his own mark on them and becoming acquainted with and open to what is, after all, the major Catholic region of the world.

In the run-up to Aparecida, the world that Catholic leaders saw around them was like night and day compared to the one in which most had been born and raised. Statistical reports (including national census data and a series of surveys and studies) confirmed what they could see every day. The proportion of men and women identifying themselves as "Catholic" was in steady decline, while those declaring affiliation with Protestant (especially Pentecostal and neo-Pentecostal) churches had grown, along with a smaller but still notable segment that affirmed no connection to any church or religion. Surveys also regularly report a substantial sector that declares itself *católico en mi manera* or *cuenta propista* (Catholic in my own way or on my own), picking and choosing the kinds of issues on which they adhere, or even listen, to "official teachings" (Parker 2005, 2009; Mallimaci 2005; Mallimaci and Villa 2007).

The decay of monopoly and the growth of pluralism in religious expression and organization have been accompanied by processes that have moved religious groups, issues, and leaders off center stage of public debate, contestation, coalition formation, and political discussion. This is an inevitable consequence of the transformations that have accompanied the democratization of civil society and politics of the past two decades. In a plural environment, church leaders can no longer monopolize the public expression of religious comment, nor can they count on being king makers or critical veto players. The effort is, in any event, bound to run into others who are working the territory. There is simply a lot of competition out there.

The convergence of these multiple pluralisms means that simple reference to church and state, much less exclusive attention to the institutional Catholic Church (or to the statements of its official leaders and spokespersons), no longer suffices as a guide to understanding religion or its place in society and politics in Latin America today.

Since the mid-twentieth century, Latin America has been the scene of innovation and intense, often violent, conflict centered on the proper relations between politics and religion. There have been notable theological and ideological debates, debates that were closely related to significant mobilizations and to the creation of religiously linked social movements. All this was well under way long before public and scholarly attention was focused on such questions by the Iranian Revolution, and long before the global surge of fundamentalisms and Islamist movements made the revolutionary potential of religion into the daily stuff of television news (Marty and Appleby 1992; Appleby 2006). Religion became a focal point of cultural and political innovation in Latin America after the middle of the last century because of the ways in which changes within religion narrowly conceived—theologies, liturgies, church structures, church schools, and a range of groups linked in some way with the churches—intersected with transformations in society and politics in ways that altered the life situations of masses of people, creating spaces in which these initiatives could gain a foothold, acquire resources, and reach an audience. To use the language of contemporary social movement theory, changes within religion created a new cognitive frame for action, demographic and social changes provided hitherto unknown resources and leaders, and the opportunity structures of politics created openings and made action possible.

The Terms of Debate:
What We Mean by Religion and by Politics

Religion may be universal but its expression is anything but uniform, and the very attempt to define *religion* is risky. In this book, I use a commonsense definition that points to beliefs, practices, and affiliations that group people together in an effort to make sense of how they fit into the universe and what their existence means. Religions involve supra-empirical (I prefer this to supernatural) explanations and connections that are key to this effort to make sense of one's life and its meaning. They are supra-empirical because the appeal is ultimately to evidence beyond our rational senses and beyond the ordinary apparatus of verification that we use every day—touching this, testing that. Religions are the public and organized expression of this repeated personal search for meaning and understanding.[2] But more is involved than contemplation of the meaning of life. The lived experience of religion is closely linked to ways of managing ordinary life: coping with tough times, overcoming alcoholism or disease, working on relationships. Religious ideas are often depicted as "otherworldly," but like many social science definitions, this misses the point. A sense of the otherworldly is intimately intertwined with actions and commitments in everyday life. The fact that religious experience is simultaneously personal and collective is the foundation of the social and cultural power religions have long possessed to move people and motivate and legitimize behavior. The power of religious ideas and experiences to motivate and legitimate comes from the ability of religion to set proximate and personal acts in contexts of ultimate significance.

Definitions like these can be helpful, but like much social science work on religion, they sidestep or miss entirely much of what makes religion such an enduring and compelling part of human experience. For those who believe, faith involves more than a statement of preference, a discrete and separable part of life. It is not just that religious beliefs spill over from neatly confined church spaces to infuse action in other parts of life. On closer inspection, the distinction between otherworldly and this-worldly, between committed and spiritual, does not hold up very well at all.[3] Speaking of his work on Christians in the Central American revolutions, Philip Berryman states that

> much of what is important and deepest in religion is of course beyond the scope of this work. I have in mind that sense of ultimacy, the deep personal relationship of the believer to the ultimate, the mystical sense of wonder and awe that even nonmystics occasionally experience, the

sense of groundedness and purpose that words can express only haltingly and indirectly. Much of what is said here may be quite secondary
to religion in that sense. Yet to the extent people have been willing to
die for a faith-based vision of a more just society, their struggles are
not really foreign to what is deepest in religion. (Berryman 1995a: 3)

Taking a commonsense view of religion (it is basically what people call it, what they experience as religion), I also take a commonsense view of the variations that present themselves to us. Christianity
came to Latin America with the conquest and settlement of the region
by Spain and Portugal, and its social and political positions and connections have long been marked by that original tie with power and domination. Although religious minorities and heterodox movements exist
and in some cases take a prominent role, the core focus of this book is
on Christianity, which has been the dominant form of religious faith and
practice since the formation of what we now call Latin America. For
present purposes, the basic distinction within religions and among
churches in Latin America is therefore between Catholics and non-
Catholic Christians, which for all practical purposes means Catholics
and Protestants, above all Pentecostal Protestants. To put things in this
simplified way is not to undervalue the plurality of positions and the
diversity of voices in either grouping or to ignore the presence of other
faiths, but simply to acknowledge a core reality. Chapter 3 presents
extensive detail on nuances and distinctions within the overall categories of Catholics and Protestants, and on trajectories of growth and
institutional consolidation.

Although the 500-year Catholic monopoly of religion (at least public religion) in the region has pretty much disappeared, the Catholic
Church remains everywhere the single largest church and the one with
the most elaborate and continuing links with state and political power.[4]
One of the central dramas of the past fifty years has been to observe the
gradual loosening of those ties. The hierarchical structure and monolithic look of Catholicism mask a great deal of internal diversity and
sometimes open conflict between positions and groups. This can take
the form of ideological and theological dissent; of open, even armed,
conflict (as in Argentina in the 1970s); or simply the emergence of a
series of organizations with autonomy that is jealously guarded from
control by the church's hierarchy and its most visible representatives,
the bishops. For its part, Protestantism has always been characterized by
internal diversity. A great variety of churches with very different ideas
and styles of organization share this label if nothing else. For our purposes, historical Protestant churches (Baptists, Methodists, Lutherans,

Anglicans, Presbyterians) and fundamentalists as well as Pentecostal or neo-Pentecostal churches are all Protestant as distinguished from the Catholic Church, albeit with notable differences among themselves in terms of how they are organized, their public ideologies, and their presence in the public sphere.[5]

The meaning of *politics* has also expanded and changed. There is more than one kind of political power, more than one way to sway publics as well as those who hold official office. Conventional politics linked to the presence and impact of states and public institutions of course remain important, but there is also a kind of politics that is expressed in new forms of organization, new sources of leaders and followers that have brought hitherto silent or ignored voices into the political arena. The consolidation of democracy, the expansion of social pluralism, and the lowering of barriers to access to the public sphere have had a notable impact on religion and religious actors. New ideas and models of organization make themselves felt within the churches as they develop strategies for action in the altered circumstances of democracy. Pluralism and social change also bring groups with new experiences into the churches, making their presence felt both in the new megachurches and in the altered quality of membership in ongoing Catholic movements.

Because religions are not easily confined to what is said or done within the formal framework of institutions, and because politics is not easily confined to what governments or state agents say or do, the relations between them are necessarily broad-ranging and diffuse. This suggests that it is important not to reify any particular set of arrangements. There are many possibilities, all are historically contingent, and actors and goals are continually evolving. Throughout history, religious institutions and groups have supported or identified with just about any political position that imagination can devise—from staunch conservatism to reform or revolution, from accommodation with states to persistent demands for autonomy, from traditions of toleration to identification with ethnic nationalism, from liberation theology to contemporary fundamentalism. It is difficult to disentangle religion from politics, if only because religious people live in a social and political world. They work, vote, play sports, join groups, and tie their shoes much as their neighbors do. As Nancy Ammerman (1994a) puts it, religious people have not learned the lesson that they are to keep these areas separate. Without necessarily campaigning for explicitly religious goals, they are influenced by values and connections and bring these to bear on a wide range of issues.

The general and diffuse social presence of religion, as part of civil society and through groups and coalitions, however fragile, has another consequence that will be important here. In the past, the churches, especially the Catholic Church, relied on formally articulated and clerically controlled networks of organizations as a way to make their case known, and as a basis from which to mobilize pressures and contacts for the pursuit of particular goals. But as we shall see (in Chapters 3 and 5), these networks no longer have the power to convince and mobilize that they once had. Organizations may continue to exist on paper, but they have lost their ability to move people like pawns on a chessboard. This reality presents a dilemma for church leaders trying to devise strategies for the future and also for political analysts.[6] They need to learn how to adapt to the realities of a plural society in which strategies focused exclusively on mobilization through existing organized movements are unlikely to fare well.

Because Latin America is part of a larger world, and because the religious and political forces of this period have powerful links to global forces and often to specific transnational movements, the effort to understand and explain change in Latin America must situate the region's experience in a broad comparative and theoretical context. Globalization is of course nothing new for Latin America, which has been the object of global forces at least since 1492. What is different now is not the fact of globalization, but rather the way in which the quickening pace of mass communication heightens the salience of influences and linkages among levels, keeping ideas, publications, people, and resources in creative motion. Churches are transnational organizations par excellence, and their ability to move ideas and human and material resources across national boundaries has played an important role in recent years in everything from education to human rights. Once mainly an object of global forces, be they economic, cultural, political, or military, Latin America has now become a source of notable and much emulated changes on issues ranging from education and theology to the defense of democracy and human rights and creative uses of religious media as stepping-stones to broader social and political influence (Cleary 2009; González and González 2008). The relation of the churches to violence and their role in the aftermath of violence (including the defense of human rights and participation in truth commissions) have also been a model for much of the rest of the world (Borer 1998; Sikkink and Walling 2006).

In this book, I advance an explanation of the dynamics of change that rests on a combination of three elements. First is the generation of new ideas in the churches, ideas that inspired and legitimated innovative ways of understanding and engaging in social change. Attention to ideas is particularly important in the case of religion because ideas and the symbolic repertoire that accompanies them are often at the heart of what distinguishes religious groups from others. The choice of religion is specific and has specific impacts. The connection with religion matters not only because of the resources that churches control, but also and in particular because of the legitimacy and the connection to something larger that religious ideas give to people as they pursue their goals. It is common lately in the social sciences to find the power of ideas downgraded in favor of a focus on supposedly harder evidence of interest and influence. The premise of this exclusion is that ideas and motivations are "soft data," difficult to identify and harder still to quantify. But this is an impoverished view of religion, which limits our understanding by leaving out much of what explains loyalty, motivation, and commitment. Ideas are not some kind of disembodied mental stuff. They appear to real people in real social contexts, and they have a social history that can be traced, for example in pamphlets, books, or audiocassettes. The task before us, therefore, is to understand why and how new ideas arise, who articulates them, and how they reach an audience. Frances Hagopian (2009: 46) states that it is incumbent on theories that stress the independent role of ideas to "explain from where these beliefs emanate, how they evolve, why old ones lose credibility and new ones arise to conform to new realities, how they are reproduced or recycled in new guises, and why certain ideas can prevail and guide church responses to religious and political pluralism in some contexts but not in others."

It is not evident to me why such explanation should be more incumbent on those arguing for the power of ideas than for, say, class or institutional interest, but setting that aside for the moment, three points can be made, all of which are taken up in greater detail in later chapters. The first point is to underscore the fact that at any given moment, ideas are always being created. An irreducible element of human creativity has to be acknowledged. A further and more interesting question is how these ideas find voices and an audience, and why and under what circumstances issues succeed one another in setting an agenda for action in public space. They make sense to people and thus acquire agents and an audience when they in some way fit with the circumstances of their lives. Max Weber (1948a) referred to this as *elective affinity*, noting that ideas can fit the routines and expectations of particular groups. He had in mind the model of how emerging Protestant ideas about the relation of individuals to God fit notions of contract that were beginning to form in social and economic life. Finally, it is essential to acknowledge that these ideas and those who advance them commonly compete for space and voice. Who gets heard and which ideas shape the agenda of groups and institutions cannot be determined only by looking at the content of the ideas. To understand their social presence and political reach, ideas have to be set firmly in a social and political context. The ideas and projects that are carried to society by activists meet up with groups bringing their urgent needs and their potential new intellectuals to the churches. When initiatives find a hearing, it is because of the way that social and political changes of the time create groups and make them available and make these ideas seem more relevant than ever before. What is at issue is a marriage of interests, followed by a struggle to shape and hold discourse in public space. It is the intersection of new ideas about authentic faith, practice, and how to organize, with needs coming from society and models that encourage activism and leadership by ordinary people that create these new realities.

Periods of intense social transformation are always throwing up new intellectuals, voices that in some way articulate the meaning of new situations (Beinart and Bundy 1987). These are what Antonio Gramsci (1971) meant by "organic intellectuals," figures who emerge as part of the changes under way and whose ideas reflect and reinforce those changes. The multiplication of voices that comes with urbanization, education, and access to mass media, and the general loosening of older ties that accompanies social transformations, make it more possible for the ideas that are always bubbling up to find organized social expression. Another way to think of these intellectuals is as prophetic figures. Prophets—like Isaiah, Jeremiah, or Amos—are religious leaders who by word and example mount a critique of injustice. Prophets do not arise suddenly out of nowhere determined to put a new and decisive stamp on the social order. They appear and articulate a message and gain an audience in ways that resonate with what is going on in the societies around them (Kselman 1985).

Scholars of Islamist movements, often mislabeled *fundamentalist* (a term that comes out of North American Protestantism), have argued in different ways that if we look at instances in which such movements have either achieved power (which are rare) or in which they have managed to persist in time and consolidate a strong base, we find successful alliances among what they term the pious middle classes, entrepreneurial lay intellectuals, and an available mass base. They argue that the incorporation of the pious middle classes is the key to the consolidation and long-term impact of these movements (Arjomand 1995; Eickelman and Piscatori 2004). The role of the pious middle classes in Latin America is played by key elements in the churches who provide the resources, legitimation, and in many cases the political cover needed for the alliance of lay and clerical intellectuals with grassroots sectors in need. When such movements were able to consolidate, they left an important legacy of new ideas, new organizations, and a sense that activism is legitimate (John Burdick 2004; Miguel Carter 2012). Where and when they did not survive (as in the case of Argentina in the 1970s and 1980s), the result was groups shattered by a repressive and often bloody alliance between dominant groups in the church and security forces in the state. In cases where support is first given and then withdrawn, or where initially sympathetic groups and leaders are replaced by others—as has been general in the region over the last few decades—movements lose material and ideological resources, are cut adrift, and activists often burn out when they are not co-opted by political parties or governments.

The second core element in our story is the encounter of religion and the churches with pluralism. This encounter has transformed the relations of religion with society and politics while bringing new concepts of activism and equality into the churches. However they are defined, politics and religion are linked in an ongoing process of mutual influence, borrowing, and exchange. What is borrowed and exchanged includes material resources, support and alliances, norms of leadership (the authoritarian leader vs. the democratic leader, for example), ideas about activism and participation (as good or limited), and norms that delineate what is right, wrong, possible, and necessary.

A third and final factor is the impact of violence, and the recovery from violence, that has reshaped the relations of many churches and religious people to politics, putting new issues (such as rights or accountability) on the agenda of politics and society over the long term. The point that drove this connection home was the effects of violence, which put new groups in connection with the churches, bringing their urgent needs to the newly open institutions. Because multiple ideas are always in play, as circumstances change, the salience of particular ideas in the churches is also likely to vary. The decline of violence and the restoration of democracy have meant in many churches the return to center stage of more conventional concerns about sexuality and the family and the moral ordering of public life, replacing concepts of justice and participation that had been so prominent in the 1970s and 1980s.

When I began my studies of politics and religion in Latin America, several paradigms dominated scholarship on those issues. A well-established older tradition of research on politics and religion defined the topic in legal and institutional terms. Analysis centered on church and state and the basic units of analysis were treaties, laws, and documents. This was mostly the field of historians. In the social sciences more generally, theories of secularization and modernization set the agenda of discussion. The general expectation was that religion was destined to dwindle in both its public presence and its power to shape private lives as urbanization, literacy, health, and other indicators of modernity took hold. Religious institutions would gradually yield ground to secular, public forces in key areas of the life cycle such as the registration of births, the management of cemeteries, the affirmation of marriages, education, and health care.

Much of this theorizing came wrapped up in functionalist assumptions according to which the coherence of societies and their ability to manage issues depended in fundamental ways on the existence of a prior normative consensus. According to this view, societies would collapse without some agreement on basic values. This makes sense in some cases, as for example in the idea of contracts, whose very validity depends on all sides accepting one another as valid participants and agreeing on the rules of interaction. But when it comes to entire societies and political systems, the problem is much more complex. Societies hang together for all kinds of reasons, including at some moments force, others compromise. Apart from basic agreements on who belongs to the nation, which itself has to be constructed (Van Cott 2008; Yashar 2005), thorny issues arise. Whose values will provide the standard? Where will they come from and how will they become known? For many scholars, religion was a likely provider of such values, but to fulfill this role in the twentieth century, it was first essential for the churches to resituate themselves in social and political space, withdrawing from their historical involvement with power and politics in Latin America, and convert themselves into general moral guides for the society. In this vein, Ivan Vallier argued that for Catholicism to retain influence and a capacity to shape Latin American culture, society, and politics in the future, the *institutional church* had to withdraw from politics. Breaking the mutual dependence with power and privilege would free the church to provide the kind of cultural and ideological consensus that in his view was a prerequisite to modernization (Vallier 1970).

Vallier's work was both empirical and normative. He believed that the path he outlined was measurable and already in progress, and he also argued strongly that it was a good thing, an essential element in the process of development and modernization. Setting aside the evident functionalist predilections of this sort of analysis (the notion that social order and "modernization" require cultural consensus), Vallier also ran up against a practical difficulty. At the very moment that he called for withdrawal from politics in the pursuit of unified cultural leadership, new tendencies were emerging in Catholicism. Political engagement was demanded, but now it was not with established power or existing institutions, but rather in opposition to dictatorship, in pursuit of social justice, and with a view to creating a new kind of politics. These ideas and movements also inspired many activists, who went out to form innovative social and political alliances (French 2007; Levine 1992; Christian Smith 1991).

The developments reveal not so much a search for influence as Vallier understood it, but rather a new sense of the proper mission of the church, now centered on ideas about social justice, and a new openness to initiative and leadership by laypersons. The evolution of these new positions brought elements in the churches along with related groups and activists to the very center of the political conflicts that Vallier hoped to supersede. Conflict, not consensus, dominated the relation between politics and religion in the decades after Vallier wrote. These conflicts carried high costs: many lost their lives. Surely there must be an easier way to retain influence.[7] The concept of influence articulated by Vallier and those who followed his lead (Bruneau 1974, 1982; Gill 1998) turned out to be too undifferentiated: influence for what?

Beginning in the 1960s and with growing force in later decades, these approaches all lost their capacity to make sense of, and in a basic way even to see, the changes taking place on the ground in Latin America. Here, as in much of the southern half of the globe, there has been a surge of religious innovation, a proliferation of new churches and groups linked to them, and a continuing presence of religious actors and voices and institutions in the setting and management of public policy (Jenkins 2002, 2006). Given the presumptions of secularization and modernization theory, change arising from within religion was a surprise to most social scientists and was all the more startling in Latin America, a part of the globe where for so long the monopoly of the Catholic Church seemed secure, if never wholly unchallenged.

The power of presuppositions and intellectual blinders cannot be denied, but there are also *facts* that break through our concepts, inconvenient facts that force themselves on us and make us reconsider the foundations of our approaches. What are the facts that have broken through in Latin America to remind us of the power of religion, not just to sustain itself but also to change itself as part of a changing world? A prime fact is the explosion of multiple churches and religious spaces. It is not that Latin America is "turning Protestant," to cite the title of David Stoll's important early book. Rather, it is becoming pluralist for the first time in its 500-year history (Stoll 1990; Levine 2009a, 2009b). Religious pluralism has been accompanied by a new and more diverse range of political stances on the part of the churches. Another fact that presses itself on our attention is that with rare exceptions all the churches now support some form of political democracy and open civil society. This is a cultural shift of prime significance, with roots in debates within the churches as well as in the end of the global Cold War which loosened once immutable religious-political alliances. The relation of churches to civil society (both the idea and the reality of independent groups) is a third fact. Over the past half century, Catholic and Protestant churches have sponsored and protected a range of social movements—land leagues, housing coalitions, neighborhood groups, or human rights organizations to name a few. This entailed serving as a conduit for resources and information, training leaders, bringing church-inspired activists together with grassroots groups, and providing legal and other aid as needed. With the restoration of democracy and the decline of many of these movements, churches continue to shape civil society through less mobilizational civic networks along with institutions such as schools, new media outlets, cooperatives, and health centers.

These new facts and the eye-catching changes in the public face of religion are undergirded by long-term social, cultural, and political transformations that provide the raw materials and the dynamic of the process. The past fifty years have seen significant migration, mostly rural to urban but also intrarural, accelerated in cases like Peru or Central America by extremes of civil war and violence, but present everywhere. Cities have grown, and bigger cities have everywhere grown faster than smaller cities. Two related facts are expanded literacy and access to mass media along with drastically reduced barriers to organization and public participation. The most recent waves of democratization, which got under way in the mid-1980s, had a significant impact on social life by bringing an end to civil wars and massive political violence and lowering barriers of access to civil society. Together with the growth of cities, these facts create the audience and set the scene for competition among churches and between churches and other groups, and provide both means and targets for those seeking to gain or hold members, acquire resources, and get a public hearing.

The preceding discussion lays out the bare bones that define the situation of religion in Latin America today. These are the facts that together broke through the intellectual blinders of ideas about secularization and forced scholars and observers to come to grips with the new experiences of religious practice, meaning, and community being created on the ground in Latin America. These new facts spur us to create new ways of understanding how these related transformations have created a very different world from the unquestioned monopolies of the past. The transformations outlined here evolved over the last half century in a continuous process of innovation, conflict, and resistance. The next section locates these changes in time.

Marking Historical Periods

For present purposes it is possible to identify a series of critical moments and historical periods that mark turning points in the evolving relation among politics, religion, and society and that left enduring legacies for the future. The first period runs from the end of World War II until 1959. The second is bracketed by two revolutions and runs from 1959 when Fidel Castro took power in Cuba to the victory of Nicaragua's Sandinista Revolution in 1979 and its aftermath. This period is noteworthy for the role played by two popes, John XXIII and John Paul II (elected, respectively, in 1958 and 1978), and coincides with the rise of revolutionary violence in Central America and repressive regimes elsewhere in the region. The final period, from the mid-1980s to the present, has brought the emergence and consolidation of democracies, the decline of massive violence, continued expansion and consolidation of Protestant and Pentecostal churches, and the inauguration of a new pope, Benedict XVI (elected in 2005), who has continued many of the policies and orientations of his predecessor. Figure 1.1 identifies key religious and political "events" of these years that shaped the agenda of politics and religion and notes the predominant theme of the major conferences of Latin American Catholic bishops in these years.

Postwar to 1959

The postwar period was a time in which the churches in Latin America gradually (albeit with notable resistance in some cases) adapted to evolving political circumstances, including growing democracy and the pressure of social and political populism. The form that these responses

Figure 1.1   Religion and Politics in Latin America: Essential Points

1959	Cuban Revolution
1962–1965	Second Vatican Council (Vatican II) Aggiornamento
1964	Military coup in Brazil
1968	Meetings of Catholic bishops at Medellín, Colombia. *Key themes:* institutionalized violence, structural sin
1971	Liberation theology
1973	Military coup in Chile
1976	Coup in Argentina
1979	Meetings of Catholic bishops at Puebla, Mexico. *Key themes:* preferential option for the poor and ecclesial base communities (CEBs)
1979	Nicaragua Sandinista Revolution
1979–1990s	Central America wars
1980–1992	Peru Civil War
1980s–1990s	Transition to democracy: democratic restorations
1992	Meetings of Catholic bishops at Santo Domingo, Dominican Republic. *Key themes:* 500 years of evangelization
1998	Pope visits Cuba
2007	Meetings of Catholic bishops at Aparecida, Brazil. *Key themes:* missionary disciples
2007–	Democracy and open civil society

took varied from country to country, but one key issue to examine for clues to the tone and direction of responses is what happened to a group of social movements organized by the Catholic Church and generally known as Catholic Action movements. A wide range of organizations gathered under this general label were sponsored by the church in many countries in the decades following World War I in order to reach Catholic groups (students, workers, professionals, women, journalists, trade unionists, and so on), to insulate them from the influences from the left and liberalism, and to use them as a base for political mobilization. The traditional model of Catholic Action entailed close integration with the institutional church in the form of clerical supervision of what the group did and said and control of how it was organized (Levine 1992).

I discuss Catholic Action in further detail in Chapter 5. The point I want to make here is how this effort to engage politics and society worked out in different countries. Some movements evolved into or were absorbed by the Christian Democratic parties that sprang up after World War II and became the reformist/developmental expression of Catholic accommodations to democracy. The intent to oppose the Left was still there, but now the goal was not to create sheltered networks of organizations but rather to construct a broad social and political appeal. The Christian Democratic strategy was most successful in Chile, Costa Rica, and Venezuela. In other cases, such as Peru and Brazil, Catholic Action took a very different turn, generating groups and activists with a social change agenda that took them well beyond the limits of what the institutional church had in mind, leading groups and individuals into open alliances with others on the left and in the grassroots (Mainwaring 1986). Student, agrarian, and labor groups established under this program became key elements in the emergence of liberation theology and of a wider range of social movements. This evolution is especially visible in the Catholic student and worker movements in Peru and Brazil, which had considerable influence in subsequent engagements of urban and rural poor, and in Chile with the later development of Marxists and Christians United for Socialism, with subsequent influence on the positions that church leaders took to protect and sustain opposition to the military regime of Augusto Pinochet.

In Argentina, the impulse to address politics and society in more direct ways led many of those originating in Catholic Action to engage with Peronism, which controlled the terrain of the working classes. This engagement was more than matched by fears in the Catholic hierarchy of competition from Peronism, which in its later years increasingly took on the form and discourse of a secularized religion (Michael Burdick 1995; Caimari 1994; Ghio 2007). These fears reinforced a longer-term alliance of much of the Catholic hierarchy with the military, as both claimed to "represent authentic national values" (Donatello 2008; Mallimaci, Cucchetti, and Donatello 2006; Morello 2003, 2011a). These tendencies were reinforced by the overthrow of Peronism in 1955 by a military with close affiliations with conservative Catholic nationalism and tight relations with the Catholic hierarchy. Tensions between these two veins of Argentine Catholicism surfaced repeatedly in the quarter century following the overthrow of Juan Perón and form the backdrop to the role played by the Movement of Priests for the Third World and related Catholic leftists before the military coup of 1976 and after, when they became prime victims of the military's internal war. (See Chapter 6 for more details on the Argentine case.)

From 1959 to the Mid-1980s

The period beginning in 1959 marks the start of important transformations both in politics and in religion. The effort to work out the consequences of these changes dominated the relations between them, and shaped the presence of religion in Latin American public space over the next half century. As this period began, the Catholic Church was dominant throughout the region as it had been for the previous four and a half centuries. Only a minuscule proportion of the population of any country defined itself as anything other than Catholic, and no competitor had yet appeared to challenge the church for access to and influence over government and the popular masses. Catholic dominance was reinforced by a series of laws, treaties, official subsidies, and institutional protections that with rare exceptions (e.g., Mexico and Uruguay) provided the Catholic Church with a privileged position as the national faith. Legislation and public policies commonly reflected Catholic positions on issues central to the church, including registry of births, marriage and divorce, family law, and education. Whatever its legal and institutional position in formal terms, however, the Catholic churches of the region had many weaknesses that would soon appear. As a lazy monopolist, accustomed to relying on official support and subsidies to get its work done, the church remained structurally weak and unable to reach large elements of the population in a regular and effective way or even to keep up with population growth (Cleary and Stewart-Gambino 1992, 1997).

In the broader social and political arena, the 1960s began in Latin America with widespread optimism about the possibilities of progress. The political atmosphere would darken soon enough, but in political terms the period opened with considerable hope and notable social and political opening in many countries—a new democracy in Venezuela, democratic continuity in Chile and Brazil, and a period of relative peace in Colombia. Of course, democratic reformism was not the only path available to activists at this time. The victory of the Cuban Revolution in 1959 reinforced established trends of opposition between the churches and the Left, and sparked a backlash among conservative governments and church elites throughout the region. In a longer-range perspective, it also opened new possibilities of accommodation, not so much between the Cuban regime and its church but rather between insurgent and change-oriented groups and their own leaders, as well as in their engagement with political and social forces. This was soon visible in intellectual and practical rapprochements between Christian and Marxist groups and ideas in numerous cases, among them Colombia, Chile, Argentina, and Peru.

The choice of 1959 as the starting point of a new period also acknowledges the importance of the election of Pope John XXIII one year earlier and his convocation of the Second Vatican Council (Vatican II), whose deliberations began in 1962. The influence of the council was directly felt in Latin America in the deliberations and documents of the Latin American Bishops Conference, which met at Medellín in 1968 and whose documents opened new perspectives of social and political engagement for the region's Catholic churches.[8] The portrait that is commonly painted of this time has Vatican II sparking change in Latin America, which in turn generated a series of new ways in which the church and religious people understood and engaged with society and politics. This is correct but incomplete. A fuller account would show that in country after country, the reforms of Vatican II (and later deliberations at Medellín) engaged with currents of thought and organization that were already gaining a foothold. Despite resistance and conflict over change within some churches, in much of the region the effect of Vatican II was to legitimize initiatives already under way.

The impact of Vatican II, Medellín, and Puebla in Latin America has been amply documented, and only a brief summary is possible here (Levine 1992). I would note the following. The move to local languages and local references in religious liturgy and in the general life of the church opened participation to a much wider audience. At the same time, there was a clear encouragement of the laity—lay organizations and lay action—to create initiatives with much less direct clerical control. There was also a notable turn to the social sciences for guidelines for action. Church leaders found themselves facing societies that were deeply divided and unequal, realities that challenged conventional bromides of social harmony and charity, and many turned to categories of class and conflict to make sense of things. Finally, these years witnessed a substantial upgrade of the organizational capacity of the churches. Regional and national conferences were created and staffed, and many new dioceses and parishes were established, putting the church into much closer contact on a day-to-day basis with the faithful. The same phenomenon of greater organization and capabilities came also to the Protestant community, but not until the next historical period. (See Chapter 3.)

This period closes with the victory of the Sandinista Revolution in Nicaragua, a process that took place amid a general upsurge of revolutionary activity throughout Central America, much of it with notable links to churches and to grassroots religious movements and activists (Berryman 1984, 1995a). These alliances were more fully developed in the next period, but there were noteworthy precursors who argued that authentic faith required consistent effort to create justice, and that in the real existing situation of Latin America, this was not possible without taking up arms. The means of violence and the destruction they caused could be redeemed by the ends of justice and the creation of a better world. Among these precursors, which I discuss in more detail in Chapter 6, were Colombia's Camilo Torres (the first and still the most famous of Latin America's guerrilla priests) and elements of the Movement of Priests for the Third World (MSTM, Movimiento de Sacerdotes para el Tercer Mundo) in Argentina who acknowledged Torres as an inspiration. As things turned out, these cases inspired fewer followers than other options (such as those linked to liberation theology) who, although equally committed to change, opted to work through peaceful means of consciousness raising, education, and popular organization.

This period closes with the Sandinista Revolution and Puebla meetings of the region's Catholic bishops (both in 1979), and with the appearance on the scene of a new pope, John Paul II, whose influence would reshape the public position of the Catholic Church and its leadership in subsequent years. There is a sense in which Puebla and the Sandinista Revolution were high-water marks for the involvement of the churches in contestational politics and for the alliance of Catholic groups with those advancing a radical agenda of change (e.g., John Burdick 1993). This position has some validity but is too narrow. The Sandinista Revolution did have important elements of support from what came to be known as the "popular church" and counted a few priests among its first public leaders and its first group of ministers. But if we extend our analysis beyond activism in the context of repression and resistance to include participation in the beginnings of the transitions to democracy, which have their origin in the early to mid-1980s, and we include a range of less confrontational social movements of religious inspiration, then the impact of radicalization is broader and, well, less single-mindedly radical. Many of these initiatives were less visible, flying as far as possible under the radar of church and government. This is also the period of gestation for the energies that would soon make themselves felt in the spectacular growth of Protestant and Pentecostal churches, laying the basis for religious competition and for the continent's first real experience of religious pluralism.

Two elements that are of particular significance to our story also emerged in the years following 1979. This is a period in which violence in the form of open war, repression, and the everyday violence associated with migration and city life made itself felt most sharply. The churches were affected by this violence in several ways. The ideological and theological changes of the previous period, along with new ideas about the proper mission of the churches, and the injunction to side with the poor and powerless led many in the churches to adopt positions (accompanying the poor, defending rights) that put them squarely across the path of power. As a result, churches and church-related groups and individuals often became targets of violence and identified with its victims. The churches also took on a major role in engaging and opposing authoritarian regimes. This has been amply documented, and I discuss the process more fully in Chapter 6. The point to underscore here is how much this engagement was driven by a new sense of mission and a new set of social and political connections made through and supported by the churches, both Catholic and Protestant.

The decades that followed 1979 were also a peak period for the role the churches assumed in promoting and protecting social movements of all kinds. The promotion of social movements by the churches drew strength from more general trends, including political closure, which drew activists to the churches because they often provided the only open spaces available in authoritarian societies where any meeting of more than a few people was subject to surveillance and control. The counterpart of this attraction to the churches was a deliberate effort by clergy and lay activists, inspired by the ideas outlined earlier, to reach out to sectors in need and play an active role in the creation of movements. The marriage of interests between a church with a new mission seeking to create initiatives and groups in need lies at the heart of many of the most important social movements of the period, including peasant organizations like Brazil's landless movement (MST, Movimiento Sem Terra) and rural initiatives in other countries, settlements of new migrants to the cities throughout the region, and movements to define, extend, and defend human rights.

Protestant growth also took off in this period. Protestant churches gained strength all across the region, but the spike of growth is particularly notable in combination with the elements of violence, internal migration, urbanization, and media exposure noted earlier. Protestant growth is associated with violence in several senses. The devastating effects of violence led many to seek a way out, a way to navigate a threatening world. In Guatemala, where the dynamics of conflict for a while made the Catholic Church and its agents and activists into prime targets of the government, Protestant churches offered a way to step laterally out of the conflict and into a supportive community of the saved. One could leave a violent and crisis-ridden world behind by making something of a forward contract with God, in which belief and commitment were exchanged for help and support. This dynamic is also visible in the recruitment activities of the churches among the urban poor, who in similar ways may choose to step out of a world of violence, drugs, and domestic abuse into a supportive community (Chesnut 1997, 2003; Garrard-Burnett 1998, 2010; Smilde 2007; Steigenga 2001).

No account of politics and religion in this period would be complete without acknowledging the influence of Pope John Paul II, elected in 1978, whose twenty-seven-year reign did much to reshape local Catholic hierarchies. Pope John Paul II made many visits to Latin America and devoted considerable attention to appointments of new bishops in the region. He worked hard to push and pull them into closer alignment with the Vatican. He also insisted on greater control of social and political stances within the church and initiated a vigorous response to the growing strength of Protestant churches in the region, whom he famously compared to "rapacious wolves" preying on the (Catholic) flock.[9]

The Current Period

In contrast to the violence and the visible, often spectacular, changes of the previous three decades, the period that begins in the mid- to late 1980s has been marked by the return of democracy, the emergence of a more open civil society, and the accommodation of the churches to these developments. Civil wars in Central America and Peru came to an end, and democracy returned to Chile, Brazil, Argentina, Uruguay, and Paraguay after years of military rule. This particular wave of transitions to democracy is of course not the first in Latin American history, but it has proven to be one of the most durable (Levine and Molina 2011;

Peter Smith 2005). The sharp curtailing of political violence is perhaps the most notable feature of this period. The consolidation of democracy has been accompanied by an opening of civil society in the sense of lowering barriers to organization and making it easier for multiple groups to get started, gain access to the public sphere, survive, and in some cases flourish.

For many churches, the recovery of democracy and the opening of civil society represented an opportunity to abandon exposed and costly positions of confrontation with states and political groups and direct resources instead to rebuilding church structures and reasserting authority. Many of the social movements sponsored in earlier years were cut loose or shut down, as Catholic Church leaders turned their attention to competition with expanding Protestant and Pentecostal churches for adherents, resources, and a place on the public stage. For many newly confident Protestant churches, this was a time to return to the basic business of growing the church and spreading the Gospel; for the Catholic leadership this was a time to preserve and defend the region's Catholic heritage. Church leaders strove to move away from the contestational stances and the stress on social or political issues of the previous years to a position that emphasized institutional consistency and a return to more conventional issues and tactics, including lobbying for official subsidies (to schools or for welfare initiatives), the exercise of moral controls (e.g., through combating objectionable material), and resurgent campaigns centered on issues like abortion, divorce, sexuality, or same-sex marriage. Many of the groups that emerged in the years of struggle to create or restore democracy fragmented or disappeared, but this does not mean that civil society has been eliminated or suppressed. To the contrary, throughout the region, groups of all kinds remain active, if more fragmented and less united in movements with explicitly political projections.

For the Catholic Church, it is fair to say that if Medellín and Puebla epitomized a move to challenge social and political injustice and called for a preferential option for the poor,[10] more recent conferences at Santo Domingo and Aparecida projected something quite different. The meeting at Santo Domingo underscored the idea of 500 years of Catholic presence and of evangelization in the region (Santo Domingo was Columbus's initial landfall in 1492). The emphasis was on preserving and protecting this core Catholic heritage. For their part, the documents and discussions of Aparecida are dominated by a pervasive fear of change and loss of control. Both conferences fit within a broad effort to reinforce authority within the church, counter dissidence, and gather resources for competition with Protestants and for protection against the inroads of a globalizing culture that threatened to undermine core religious values that are defined above all in terms of general moral standards, gender roles, sexuality, and the family.

Legacy for the Twenty-First Century

However one reads the historical record, Latin Americans have crammed a great deal of change, conflict, and sacrifice into relatively little time. Politics saw the collapse of democracy, the creation of new and more powerful authoritarianisms, a rise to revolution and civil war in Central America, and the restoration (in some cases the creation) of civilian rule and democratic political arrangements throughout the region. Religious life was transformed, with Catholic monopoly replaced by pluralism and competition, and vigorous debate and diverse positions within all denominations. In social and economic terms, the last half century brought expanded literacy and access to communications, a general decline of agriculture, intense migration from countryside to cities, and the growth of new megacities. Despite instances of macroeconomic growth, for most people these have also been years of economic decay and decades of loss. A word like *crisis* applies in every sense of the term. The crisis experienced by Latin Americans of all classes and conditions has brought economic decay, social dislocation, and danger, with a constant threat of violence.

But crisis can mean more than decay. One can also imagine a kind of crisis of the old order that brings opportunity. Crisis in this sense crystallizes as existing institutions and political formulas lose the moral and social force required to contain behavior and give it meaning acceptable to communities. At such historical moments, societies are particularly open to the articulation of new moral codes and to innovative ideas about social organization. Religions share in change not only when leaders and activists take new positions. Social change also brings new issues into the churches, as members and leaders grapple with reality, making choices about what to do and grounding these choices in their understanding of what faith says about what is right, wrong, necessary, and possible.[11]

The patterns of change and conflict reviewed here have left a legacy in the lived experience of politics and religion, in relations between them, and in how scholars and observers make sense of these developments. Not so long ago, religion seemed to have a secure, established, and unchanging place in Latin America. Religion meant the Roman Catholic Church, and its messages legitimized existing social arrangements and its institutions and agents meshed with them in mutual support. Although the nineteenth century had witnessed bitter and occasionally violent conflicts over church-state relations in some countries, by the early decades of the twentieth century, church and state had reached a broad accommodation almost everywhere, open conflicts had ebbed, and the church had settled into a relatively comfortable conservative role as an established, if lazy, monopolist. Religion was no longer a threat but rather a supporting element of the way things were. But for decades now, uniformity and stability have been replaced by variation and conflict. Religion can no longer be assumed to support the established order of things, and no single voice can now be taken to speak in the name of religion. If we think of the past as *then* and the present as *now*, it is clear that in Latin America as now in much of the world, expectations have changed so that many now look to churches and to religion as a source of innovation. In contrast to what David Voas (2009) finds for Europe, religions in Latin America have not merely remained in place. Underlying trends of pluralization, pluralism, and competition continue, with notable expansion of the presence of multiple churches throughout civil society. This presence extends beyond the churches, worship spaces, and congregations to encompass a wide range of expressions, from schools and social clubs to publications and mass media.

The Book to Come

This book is organized thematically. Chapter 2 examines and evaluates alternative theories and methods for studying the relations among politics, religion, and society, and assesses the relevance of debates about secularization. The two chapters that follow are devoted to the main groups of religious actors. Chapter 3 addresses long-term transformations in Catholicism and Protestantism, with particular emphasis on demographic trends, ideas, and organizations. The next four chapters take up the core empirical dimensions of change and conflict outlined here in summary fashion. Chapter 4 explores the relation of the churches to pluralism and democracy. This relationship involves protection and support of democratic spaces and initiatives during authoritarian rule, the extent to which the churches can accept equality and democratic practices within, and the ways in which churches and religious groups engage in political activism. Chapter 5 looks closely at the experience of the churches as sponsors of social movements. I examine the extent to which new movements empower members and create social capital, and consider the strengths and weaknesses of churches as promoters of social movements. Chapter 6 addresses the mutual impact of violence and religious change. This includes analysis of how the churches react to and explain violence, how church people at some times have sanctioned and engaged in violence for political ends, and how the churches have operated as mediators and brokers of truces and political transitions. I also consider examples of religiously motivated and sustained nonviolent action. Chapter 7 details the emergence of a vocabulary of rights in religious discourse. I examine the impacts of this new discourse on the culture and practice of politics and consider the involvement of churches in efforts at postviolence reconciliation, including truth commissions.

Latin American experience is shaped by its own particular history, but it is also part of a larger world. The particular features, strengths, and weaknesses of the process of change in the region become clearer when set against other historical and contemporary experiences. I therefore close with two chapters that set Latin American experience of politics and religion in a general comparative context and raise questions about the future. Chapter 8 draws the threads of comparative evidence together with specific reference to the issues of interest here: pluralism and democracy, civil society and social movements, violence, rights, and reconciliation. I pay particular attention to materials from the United States, Eastern Europe at the end of communism, Africa, and South Asia. Chapter 9 considers the likely future of politics, religion, and society and asks how we can best know about that future. These are matters of considerable debate and conflict within the churches and between churches and other institutions. These are dynamic processes, and they are the subject of efforts by competing groups, inspired by different ideological and theological projects, to shape the future. What we can be sure of is that religion will not fade from the scene, as much early theorizing predicted. Religion and the churches will remain important, creative actors well into the future.

Notes

1. Although conservatives have regularly insisted that this preferential option is not socially exclusive and embraces attention to the poor in spirit, the

documents have generally been taken as intended to focus attention on the materially poor, the oppressed, and the excluded.

2. Cf. Bruce (2010: 1): "I will define religion substantively as beliefs, actions, and institutions based on the existence of supernatural entities with powers or agency (that is, Gods) or impersonal processes possessed of moral purpose (the Hindu and Buddhist notion of Karma for example) that set the condition of, or intervene in, human affairs."

3. As Warner notes, "the special potency of religious institutions comes from answers they give to a group's need for faith in the justice of their cause and the inevitability of triumph. Such faith depends on the conviction, misleadingly called 'other-worldliness' of the existence of a religious reality. If one assumes a sacred/secular dichotomy, supernatural beliefs can seem at best irrelevant to this-worldly action. . . . [But] to insist that rebels be iconoclasts is to deprive them of one source of their courage" (Warner 1993: 1069–1070). See also Harris 1999 and Harris-Lacewell 2007.

4. This status carries with it assumptions that the Catholic Church has a presence in public life. Despite the disappearance of a formal establishment of religion, the Catholic Church is often exempt from laws that require religions to register with the state (e.g., Catoggio 2008a), a requirement enforced on all others. In Peru, evangelicals struggle to get similar access to public space, as Catholic church buildings (but not Protestant churches) are maintained at public expense (Castro Aguilar 2001; Muñoz 2001).

5. The common umbrella term used in Latin America is *evangelical (evangélico),* which as in the United States connotes an emphasis on personal salvation and the born-again experience. Pentecostals and charismatics differ by virtue of their belief that the gifts of the spirit described in the Bible (Acts 2) are not simply of historical interest but are available and viable for all believers in all times. I discuss these in more detail in Chapter 3.

6. A good example is Hagopian 2009, in which the author insists on the notion of the churches (in this case the Catholic Church) moving to the reconquest of social space through its networks of organizations despite compelling data by other contributors to the same book (Blancarte 2009; Loaeza 2009; Parker 2009; Romero 2009), showing that the ways in which believers relate to their church have multiplied and loosened.

7. A notable counterexample is Argentina, where the Catholic hierarchy collaborated with and legitimated the military's war on what it labeled "subversion" through the 1970s (Bonnin 2010; Catoggio 2006, 2008b, 2010, 2011; Mallimaci 2005; Mallimaci, Cucchetti, and Donatello 2006; Mignone 1988; Morello 2011a; Verbitsky 2005, 2006, 2007, 2008, 2009).

8. The English title of the Medellín documents is *The Role of the Church in the Present Day Transformation of Latin America in the Light of the Council.*

9. In 1992 at the CELAM meetings in Santo Domingo.

10. Debate continues within the churches over the proper way to define "the poor": does this primarily refer to the materially poor and marginalized groups (which would include women, indigenous groups, ethnic minorities, and

the disabled), or should it more properly encompass the poor in spirit or those in need of spiritual assistance?

11. The example of Eastern Europe, where the decay of communism was spurred by forces as different as blue jeans, western rock music, new information technologies, underground unions, and "catacombs churches," is illustrative (Ryback 1990; Bartee 2000).

2

A Note on Theory and Method

Conventional writing on politics and religion is shaped by two assumptions that need to be made explicit, and explicitly rejected. The first views the social and political role of religion in terms of domination and control. Following Emile Durkheim (2008) and the later functionalist tradition in sociology, religion is taken to be essential to social order. Religions constitute social order by providing a floor of normative consensus, a basic set of understandings and mostly tacit agreements that make life in common possible. These norms are bound up with existing social order: part reinforcement, much reflection. The perspective is profoundly conservative. A second assumption takes a different path and sees religion and religious involvement in politics as a secondary reflection of supposedly "harder" and more durable forms of interest, such as class, race, or lately, gender. This second assumption leads many to see the political involvement of religion and religious groups as something of an aberration, a survival, most likely transitional (until more "normal" channels take over), and in most cases explainable in light of the failure of other forms of action. There is a Wizard of Oz quality to this point of view, a commitment to pulling back the curtain to reveal the supposedly more real interests manipulating the levers that appear as religion.

The net effect of these two pillars of the conventional wisdom has been to give scholars a set of conceptual blinders that make it difficult to see emerging patterns of change and to hear voices advancing new ideas about religion, politics, and the space where they meet. Making order primary obscures the origins of change within both religion and politics. It also makes it hard to see how religion and politics nourish one another, exchanging problems to solve and models to follow on a regular basis.[1] For its part, reducing religion to an epiphenomenon of other social interests ignores sources of change within religion and confines us to an impoverished view of the world and of human beings as agents within it. Ideas and commitments of all kinds (including religious ideas) move people just as much as class, racial, and gender identities, or political loyalties.

Religion is always involved with politics, which is not at all the same as relations between church and state. In the United States, which has a long legal tradition of separation of church and state, currency carries the motto "In God We Trust," chaplains serve in the armed forces and in prisons, and the Pledge of Allegiance to the flag speaks of "one nation, under God." Since the 1960s, religiously inspired groups and issues have also been increasingly prominent in US politics, inspiring campaigns and empowering mobilizations. Those who complain about an undue politicization of religion all too often do so only when their particular interests are threatened. During the civil rights movement, African American pastors were criticized by white churches and southern white leaders for being "involved in politics"; antiabortion campaigns by churches have been criticized by liberal groups as an improper politicization of religion; the US Catholic bishops' pastoral letters on nuclear war and the economy were derided by conservative economists and politicians. This is not a productive way to proceed. Serious analysis has to get beyond questions of whose ox is being gored. We need to put the specter of "politicization of religion" to rest once and for all, recognizing that religion influences politics and politics influences religion in a continuous relation. The particular form this relation takes, the vehicles through which it works, and the specific issues that are engaged can and will change, but the relation itself is constant. The heart of the matter is not to discover *whether* religion is involved with politics or to develop guidelines about when and how religion *should be* involved with politics (or vice versa). Since believers act both in religion and in politics, they regularly cross the lines that theory erects between the two. In this light, what is often called a "resurgence" of religion in politics around the world is less a resurgence than a restructuring or reorganization of a continuing relation. There is no resurgence because religion never really left public life. The heart of the matter is to understand how this relation came to be, how it works, and why and how it persists—with what guiding ideas, through what vehicles, to what ends, and with what consequences for politics, for society as a whole, and not least, for religion itself.

Thinking about religion and politics in this way helps distinguish what we might call a politics of the system from a politics of transformation. The first hinges on an exchange of ideological and institutional support between religion and what Emmanuel Mounier called the *established disorder* (John Hellman 1981). At the heart of the second is a kind of politics that generates new forms and new images of power. Activists create new vehicles, mobilize hitherto unrepresented groups, tap new leadership strata, and create a new vocabulary for understanding and acting on the world. The effort to create new kinds of power is risky and subject to frequent failure, but the fact that initiative passes to different hands says a great deal about what power can mean, and how religion can be lived and understood, in a changing society.

It can be difficult to disentangle religion from politics. There is no single location, no unitary axis of conflict or dimension of ideas that we can examine for clues. They are engaged with one another and in multiple locations throughout the social order: among elites, between institutions, in neighborhoods, and in movements that may cut across conventional social categories. One way to bring order to this collection of possibilities is to center attention on three sorts of social locations that are likely contexts for the articulation of a relation between religion and politics. There are, of course, situations in which institutions (formally organized collections of leaders, ideas, resources, and routines) such as churches or states or their agents bump up against one another, sometimes in conflict, sometimes in mutual support. Issues of politics and religion are also joined at points where social movements meet up with institutions. Examples include anything from lobbying about public policy on war, peace, immigration, or reproductive rights to campaigns for educational subsidies. The experience of religiously linked social movements offers prime examples.

A third way to identify likely points of contact between religion and politics directs attention to sites where global forces come in contact with national and local groups and contexts. Religions are transnational organizations par excellence. Institutional religions and related groups regularly move material and human resources across the formal frontiers that states establish and strive to maintain (cf. Byrnes 2011). Change emerges at the intersection of social levels. José Casanova states that religions are likely to assume public roles when their transnational identity is reinforced by their actual situation in local and regional terms. "In the case of Catholicism," he writes,

> the interrelated dynamics of globalization and public involvement of
> the various national churches in their particular societies has been

obvious since the 1960s. Vatican II, the first truly global council, made
the Roman church aware of its global reach and induced it to think
globally. Simultaneously, the aggiornamento promoted by the Council
led each national church to greater involvement in its own society and
to translate the universal Catholic message both literally and figura-
tively into the vernacular. This combination of globalization, national-
ization, secular involvement and voluntary disestablishment led to the
change of orientation from state to society and permitted the church to
play a key role in processes of democratization. The national churches
stopped viewing themselves as integrative community cults of the
national state and adopted a new transnational global identity which
permitted them to confront prophetically both the national state and
the given social order. (Casanova 1994: 225–226)

A few pointers follow from this injunction to seek connections. One
is to locate critical social spaces, venues for repeated encounters of individuals with others, as individuals or groups. Such spaces provide arenas in which important events play out, are remembered, and in some
form are reproduced. This is where abstractions of "human agency" take
concrete form in work by men and women who, by their actions, make
and remake culture: real people, not "the people." One such critical
space is created when, in whatever physical setting and social context,
people get together regularly for worship, Bible study, or any social
activity connected with "religion."[2] Other such "spaces" are provided
by repeated rituals, such as masses, processions or funerals, or events to
remember a particular event (Peterson 1997; Berryman 1984, 1995a).
Another way to ask the question is to examine why certain issues come
to center stage at a given moment and to explore precisely what that
stage is. We need to ask who articulates and carries the issues, how an
audience is created, and who the audience is. Considering Latin
American experience in this light yields some insights that are of particular interest. To begin with, it is important to acknowledge the sheer
power of creativity present within religion (Parker 1996). These have
been years of great innovation in ideas and organization. The transformation of ideas involved reconsideration of what would make faith
authentic and what the relation of the churches should be to the societies in which they found themselves. The transformation of organizations entailed the creation of new ways to turn these ideas into regular
and routine kinds of religious practice.

The evolution of conflicts around politics and religion has been
matched by an evolution of ideas, with diverse and often sharply contrasting concepts of what faith means and requires in ordinary life taking the lead in shaping discussion and motivating and giving legitimacy

to organized social action. Ideas acquire organized social power to the extent that they can convince key actors that they are a correct and necessary expression of faith. People make a wager of faith (Berryman 1995a), betting that the God they believe in wants them to have a better life and putting that belief to work in action that can range from cleaning up the neighborhood and combating alcoholism to militant political commitment. This process cannot be reduced to the simple defense of interests or the exercise of preferences. As Joshua Mitchell put it, "Religious experience is of a different order than having preferences. . . . Religious experience cannot be understood as a 'preference' because the God who stands before man is not among the plurality of scalar objects among which he prefers this or that" (Mitchell 2007: 351).[3]

Ideas are important, but who gets heard and which ideas shape the agenda of groups and institutions cannot be determined only by looking at the content of the ideas. To understand their social presence and political reach, ideas must be set firmly in the contexts (ecclesial, social, and political) in which they compete with one another for space and voice. When initiatives find a hearing, it is because of the social and political changes of the time, which created groups and made them open to ideas and influences, and made these ideas seem more relevant than ever before. The ideas and projects that are carried to society by activists meet up with groups bringing their urgent needs and their potential new intellectuals to the churches. At issue is a marriage of interests, followed by a struggle to shape and hold discourse in public space.

Among the ideas that have set the agenda for religion and politics in the years of interest to us, the following are of particular interest here: liberation theology, concepts of institutionalized violence, structural sin and the preferential option for the poor, concerns about rights, alliances of religion with militarized nationalism, and the spread of Pentecostal ideas and practices. I examine these and others in subsequent chapters. Here I want to comment specifically on liberation theology.

Liberation Theology

Liberation theology arose as part of a broad effort to rethink the proper role and mission of the church in Latin America in light of changes in Catholicism since the Second Vatican Council (1962–1965). Theologians and activists identified with this body of thinking share a concern with change, insist on the necessity and primacy of action to promote justice, and look to everyday experience—above all, the experience of the poor—as a source of religiously valid values. These necessarily brief comments underscore two key points about liberation theology: the centrality of the poor and the insistence on mixing faith commitments with action, above all collective action in the public sphere (Berryman 1987; Christian Smith 1991; Sigmund 1990; Levine 1988).

The centrality of the poor explains a great deal about liberation theology: its concern with history and sociology (as tools for understanding poverty), its engagement with Marxism and Marxist groups, its characteristic emphasis on the need for accompaniment (sharing the experiences of the poor and vulnerable, standing with them), and the relative ease with which religious positions mix with social and political conflict. Leonardo and Clodovis Boff (1986) insist that discussing liberation theology without seeing the poor misses the point, because liberation theology is not theology in a traditional sense, but liberation. El Salvador's Archbishop Oscar Romero put it plainly:

> The church's option for the poor explains the political dimension of the faith in its fundamentals and in its basic outline. Because the church has opted for the truly poor, not for the fictitiously poor, because it has opted for those who really are oppressed and repressed, the church lives in a political world and it fulfills itself as church also through politics. It cannot be otherwise if the church, like Jesus, is to turn itself toward the poor. . . . Let no one take it ill that in the light of God's word that we read in our mass we enlighten social, political and economic realities. If we did not, it would not be Christianity for us. (Oscar Romero 1985: 179, 182–183)

As intellectuals and activists, liberation theologians helped focus the church's agenda on issues of poverty, violence, injustice, and activism, with a view to legitimizing calls for fundamental change. They shaped many church documents, but it is important to realize how much their actions reached beyond formal church institutions. Gustavo Gutiérrez argues that the writing of theology is always "second act." In this view, theology is not a deductive system, working off established axioms, but rather a way of talking about God (a *logos* of *theos*) that takes shape in response to specific historical conditions. "The theological moment," writes Gutiérrez, "is one of reflection from within, a moment of open and historical praxis in confrontation with the living word of God that is accepted in faith, the faith that comes to us through multiple, ambiguous historical mediations, a faith we remake every day" (Gutiérrez 1984: 103).

Like Gutiérrez, most liberation theologians have insisted on the need to learn from experience, indeed, to be part of that experience. The result has been a theology that from the beginning has resisted being confined by seminary walls or limited to library shelves. Schools and social movements have been founded, alliances brokered, leaders identified and trained, and an enormous pamphlet literature created, all directed at putting ideas into the hands of ordinary people and into practice through their activism. Mixing faith commitments with action is often depicted as requiring a move *from faith to action,* but from the vantage point of liberation theology such dualisms and dichotomies misread the situation. There is only one history, and building the Kingdom of God is a task for here and now, and for everyone. Faith and action join in the living of human life.

The churches as institutions, and religion as a set of ideas and symbols, have been so deeply intertwined with power for so long in Latin America that it should surprise no one to find them providing grounds for critical reflection on power and what makes power just. It will not do to dismiss such reflections as no more than ideas. Ideas shape action; ideas are taken up and used by people in light of their own circumstances. One often hears that "talk is cheap," but this is at best a half truth. The contemporary experience of Latin America shows how costly talk can be, above all when the talk is about justice and equity in unjust and inequitable societies. Over the past thirty years, many lives have been lost. No complete accounting exists of the deaths or disappearances, let alone acts of torture, physical abuse, or intimidation, inflicted on religious activists or their allies in these years.[4] Their status and institutional connections ensured that attacks on clergy, sisters, and missionaries were recorded, but of course they are merely the tip of the iceberg. The main body of the iceberg, which holds countless victims of violence whose names we do not know, remains hidden.

The heart of the matter is not just that words can be costly. The heart of the matter lies in the new meaning people like these gave to notions of testimony and witness. The two are distinct but also related. In the familiar legal sense, giving testimony and being a witness means telling the truth. A witness commits her- or himself to reporting what is seen, faithfully and without distortion. A witness in court swears to "tell the whole truth, and nothing but the truth." The religious sense of witness has a more active and reflexive meaning. To give testimony and bear witness, or to be a witness, is not only to observe and tell others what you have seen, but also, and more importantly, to share the experience, to express solidarity through that sharing, and often to be transformed in the process. One witnesses to the worth and truth of values by living them.[5] The murders of clergy, sisters, and lay activists reflect the meaning of witness in all these senses. As witnesses, these men and women saw objectively and reported fully on what they saw. Seeing with new eyes and in new ways made it imperative to be different and to connect in new ways with society. That is how phrases like "preferential option for the poor" (made famous at the Catholic bishops' meeting at Puebla in 1979) get worked into day-to-day routines of choice and action. Religious speech can be costly indeed, and clerical status, once a shield against physical abuse of any kind, became more likely to turn priests or sisters into prime targets for official suspicion. Those who share the lives of the poor often share their fate as well (Noone 1995). Those who died lost their lives because they put themselves in places where there was great risk.

The risk was taken and the cost paid as a core part of their witness. Anna Peterson reports that when she asked why people were killed in El Salvador a common response was for telling the truth *(por decir la verdad)*. "Speaking the truth means denouncing injustice and oppression, pointing out structural violence, naming killers and describing a more just alternative. Announcements of the truth awaken people to the oppressiveness of the economic and political system and often provoke resistance to it, which the elites seek to crush at all costs. For progressive Catholics, this is the link between truth and martyrdom" (Peterson 1997: 125). The very word *martyr* comes from the Greek for "witness," and the verbal form is "to bear witness." In classic usage, a martyr is someone who suffers persecution or death for refusing to renounce a belief, and in Christian tradition, someone who bears witness to the truth and suffers death in the cause of Christ.[6]

Alternative Theories and Methods

Despite the academy's pretensions to objectivity and neutrality, scholarship is never separate, much less isolated, from the objects of its inquiries. The very effort to insulate scholarship misreads what objectivity is all about. The rich experiences of religion and politics renew and refresh scholarship, engaging it directly with the hopes, dreams, fears, and concerns of ordinary people. Like activists anywhere, those involved in religion and politics in Latin America resist being reduced to mere objects of academic study. These are active and creative subjects, and their efforts have opened new fields of inquiry and pushed scholarship to take new issues seriously. Despite otherwise enormous differences among them, African Americans, Shi'ite and other Islamic activists, North American Christian fundamentalists, and the Latin Americans who concern us here (leaders as well as ordinary women and men) advance a common claim to legitimate voice and activism in society and politics and root that claim in a new understanding of what religious faith calls them to accomplish in this world. If it is to have any hope of identifying the sources and dynamics of change, scholarship has to listen to these voices and incorporate what they say and do into explanations. Objectivity requires clarity and fairness in the collection of evidence and a balanced approach to evidence in the first place, not isolation imposed in the name of neutrality.

The effort to understand and explain the evolution of religion and politics in Latin America has been taken up by scholars working with a highly varied set of theories and methods. Any review of the issues must begin with the work of Ivan Vallier, who was one of the first scholars to move the study of religion in Latin America beyond attention to narrowly defined church-state conflict. As we have seen, Vallier argued that keys to understanding the possible role of the church in Latin America were to be found not in its religious message or political ideology, but rather in the regular and routine ways in which church structures are tied into those of the surrounding society. He believed that *as an institution,* the church was always in search of influence. The precise strategies that church leaders selected in their pursuit of influence determined the overall character of the institution's social role. He wrote:

> I place first emphasis on the structural changes that are occurring between the Church (and its immediate institutional extensions) and the wider society. . . . It is not so much a question of the individual's religious orientations, but the kinds of implications corporate structures of religious control hold for the functioning of the secular power structures, for the integration of social groups, and for the stability of the general ground rules that impinge on everyday exchange and role systems. (Vallier 1970: 157–158)

This concern with integration, stability, and order is highlighted in the title of Vallier's major book, *Catholicism, Social Control, and Modernization in Latin America.* Vallier looked to renovation within religion as a source of the common values that he believed were necessary for social order to be possible. Articulating such a core of common values, and thus providing a floor of normative guidelines for the whole society, would allow the churches to "get out of politics." Others could address political tasks; the churches would provide socio-ethical leadership and thus ensure the broad social consensus that Vallier believed essential for modernization and development.[7]

The assumptions underlying this position led Vallier to focus his empirical work on Catholic elites and the strategies of influence that they pursued. Elite control and continued Catholic monopoly are taken for granted. The central question was how church elites could reposition their institution and the groups they "controlled" so as to make the contribution to progress and development that only they could provide. Vallier saw the church moving from extrication (taking the church out of politics) through insulation (rebuilding the community, articulating new values and leadership) to reentry, where free of old entanglements, the church could at last provide the kind of generalized moral and ethical leadership that was essential to getting a society together behind common goals of development. On this basis, he distinguished politicians and papists (wedded, respectively, to old state elites and intrachurch strategies) from pastors and pluralists. Neither papists (those who focused on rebuilding the formal structures controlled by the church) nor pastors (focused on the church as community) could accomplish what Vallier had in mind. Politicians would also not do. They were too identified with the status quo and too easily roped into partisan conflict. The solution was found with pluralists, who abandon the effort to dominate society and reach beyond elite manipulation to articulate generalized moral and ethical leadership in the world. Note that despite the differences among them, all four types operate within a frame of reference in which the institutional church gives values to society. None of Vallier's options contemplates the possibility of a world where the church does not give authoritative guidance to society, culture, and politics, but acts instead as one of many voices in a pluralist world. Politicians and papists see social transformations above all as threats to the position of a weakened church. Their solution is to insulate the ecclesiastical institution and the Catholic community as a whole. Pastors and pluralists renew the church through liturgical renovation and the promotion of lay initiatives, including the formation of small communities. Even pluralists seek to turn the church to the promotion of change rather than to work for change with available tools and allies.

Vallier's work sparked a generation of studies of politics, religion, and society, but few of his specific expectations have been confirmed. There has been more conflict than consensus, more direct involvement in politics than withdrawal, more innovation from "the base" than control by institutions. He assumed that what elites say and do remains a sufficient guide to the direction and impact of religion and missed the central dynamic of change being created at the time. He failed to see the emerging reality of popular movements and their claim to voice and autonomy. He also failed to contemplate the possibilities of a genuine religious and social pluralism. In the long run, the differences among his leadership types turned out to be less important than the fact that they all operate within an elite-driven model, in which action is confined within the institutional framework of the church.

Vallier's analysis was also plagued by confusion about the scope and meaning of politics, and about the proper relation of politics to religious thought and action. He looked for a separation of religion from politics in practice that would be comparable to the theoretical separation that was central to his perspective on the issues. But these distinctions are filled with difficulties. Individuals and groups breach these neat lines every day, joining private and public life, fusing sacred and secular with an ease that seems to escape many scholars. In any case, there is no reason to believe either that social integration is primarily normative (rather, than, for example, grounded in coercion) or that the Catholic Church is somehow uniquely fitted to provide such integration. The distinctions to which Vallier looked for guidance and solutions were about to be exploded by the events of the time, as emerging debates, innovations, and conflicts all over Latin America put religion and politics together in new and, for the most part, unanticipated forms.

Subsequent scholarship on the issues has taken a few different paths. Working with Vallier's core concept of influence, scholars like Thomas Bruneau (1974, 1982), Warren Hewitt (Bruneau and Hewitt 1992), and Philip Williams (1989) have underscored the central role played by institutional dynamics. In this view, the ongoing effort to maintain influence is what makes churches reach out in new ways to changing populations. A second body of work highlights the other side of the equation. Identifying closely with popular causes and insurgent groups, and inspired by Gramscian ideas about hegemony and counterhegemony, writers like Otto Maduro (2005) or Philip Berryman (1995a) situate religious change firmly in a context of social conflict. The churches cannot be understood apart from their involvement in society and politics. The ideas they espouse, the models they present, and the kinds of organizations they advance make sense in light of who they represent. Dominant institutions project a view of the world that leads people to accept subordinate status as inevitable and natural. That is what hegemony is all about. In the same way, counterhegemonies emerge as the new ideas created by what Antonio Gramsci (1971) called "organic intellectuals" are brought to emerging social groups and make sense to them. From this perspective, the central question is to identify these counterhegemonies and the organic intellectuals who advance them.

Religion and politics are assumed to be always linked in some form: strict distinctions between the two are dismissed as misleading when not simply hypocritical. The process is dynamic and dialectical. New ideas and organizations are tried out, and changing dynamics of conflict and class formation lead people to "erupt into the churches" in search of allies, moral support, and legitimacy. Those who "erupt" into the churches are not a passive audience: they receive ideas, adapt them to experience, and generate and project new understandings. A central norm of liberation theology is that subordinate and long-ignored social groups have important and religiously valid values and experiences to offer. Identifying with them, taking their side, and drawing models from them were not only legitimate—they were imperative. Whatever position one takes on liberation theology, the ideas it articulates and the intense conflict and polemic that have surrounded it require us to acknowledge that who churches ally and identify with makes a substantial difference to the positions they advance, and hence to the very meaning of "influence."

A third perspective, which in other work I call *phenomenological*, directs attention neither to bases nor to elites and institutions but rather to the mutual influence of changes in the churches' sense of identity and mission (which can be discovered through documents and interviews) and the needs and desires of populations coming to the churches. I call this perspective phenomenological for its neo-Weberian emphasis on the autonomy of religious categories and the need to reconstruct the logic of these categories as a basis for understanding commitments and actions. It is *neo*-Weberian because, although it is grounded in Weber's great work on the sociology of religion with his characteristic emphasis on the elective affinity between ideas and forms of association—for example, between the idea of contract and the emergence of Protestant individualism (Weber 1948a, 1978b, 1978c)—emphasis is placed here on the history of the ideas, tracing their social origins and the way they find voices and an audience. Attention is directed to how changes in religion (beliefs, organizations, and practices at various levels) are linked in recognizable patterns with institutional and ideological conflict, and with relations between religious and other institutions.[8]

The preceding comments notwithstanding, concepts of influence can be useful and should not be wholly abandoned. After a quarter century of profound change and challenges to elites of all kinds, the character of church leadership remains vital to determining the public position taken by ecclesiastical structures and how the resources they command are put to use. For its part, the notion that change comes "from the people" and that the "people erupt into the churches" has taken an empirical as well as a theoretical beating. The rise of Pentecostal Protestantism, the fall of socialism, and the perceived decline of liberation theology and its allies have undermined confidence that "the people" were in fact behind the surge of new groups and committed to their agenda (Levine 1990a, 1990b). Cases that at first sight appeared to be prime examples of independent popular initiative regularly turned out to have their origins in deliberate efforts by some church agents (priests, sisters, or lay activists) to test the waters, start a group, and encourage activism of some kind (Miguel Carter 2003, 2012; French 2007). What is happening here is not a simple "eruption of the people" into the churches, but rather a complex encounter of people in need with churches taking on new missions and roles in changing contexts. This suggests that the orientations and efforts of pastoral agents (lay as well as clerical) have as much as if not more impact on the character of grassroots groups and the beliefs of members than the social traits or political connections of members themselves. Whatever the specifics, the impacts are tangible and traceable and suggest that continuity is as much a part of the picture as change. There is in any case considerably more division within popular groups than theories that rely on concepts of resistance allow for. The problem is not simply that groups are not of one mind. The political commitments of observers and activists often lead them to project their own desires onto the people they study, blinding them to nuance and division. Sherry Ortner finds this to be a general problem in studies of resistance, which too often gloss over or just refuse to address divisions and complications among the oppressed. "The impulse to sanitize the internal politics of the dominated," she writes, "must be understood as fundamentally romantic" (Ortner 1995: 179; see also Judith Hellman 1992).

Beginning in the mid-1990s, a new generation of scholars advanced a critique of earlier work and an argument about how to extend and reformulate the issues of religion and politics to fit the new social, political, and religious context of the 1990s. This work shares an emphasis on four points: the urgency of situating research in the context of religious competition; the need for new criteria for selecting groups for study; the importance of systematic attention to transnational groups, and to their connections with national and local initiatives; and concern over how best to tap into popular religious culture.[9]

John Burdick (1993) argues that students of religion and politics give excessive attention to liberation theology, and to changes within the Catholic Church. In so doing, they weigh the scales too heavily with texts, words, and literacy and ignore the role played by liturgical and symbolic representations. He suggests two correctives. The first is to select groups for study with reference not to churches but rather to categories of people, looking not at Catholics or Protestants, but rather at blacks, youth, and women, and thus building religious choice and competition into the analysis from the outset. He makes a convincing case for systematic attention to race and gender elements hitherto ignored or simply subsumed under the general headings of church, denomination, community, and class (see also Drogus 1997a; French 2007). In later work, Burdick (2004) eases his criticism and provides detailed evidence of the continuing influence of liberation theology on grassroots groups, manifest in organizational patterns, in the legitimating power of symbols and common rituals, and in the way activists are recruited and motivated.

A recent and theoretically distinct attempt to reformulate issues of religion and politics brings the matter back to influence and church-state relations, but through the lens of rational choice theory. The rational choice tradition stresses individual choice and microeconomic models of competition. Work in this vein has made important contributions to the study of religion and society in the United States and Europe by underscoring the importance of deregulation, a growing supply of religious goods in the market, and competition as elements in the growth and character of churches (Iannacone 1995; Iannacone and Stark 1994; Iannacone, Finke, and Stark 1997; Finke and Stark 2005). This perspective attracts many because it seems to offer a model that is simple and portable (that is, applicable without modification to many different contexts), specifies concrete data, and provides explanations tied to general propositions about how individuals pursue interests. Arguments about the impact of ideas or assertions of commitment to the community are dismissed as romantic illusions based on unreliable "soft" data.

At the same time, work in this tradition has a number of difficulties, ranging from an impoverished view of human motivation (which is reduced to individual calculations of self-interest) to faith (no other word will do) that economic or seemingly economic data are more reliable than data about motivation and values. There are also problems addressing the impact of belief and dealing with long-term commitments to a community or an organization. The ups and downs of commitment and the fate of movements are depicted almost exclusively in the context of the "free rider problem." Members are assumed to be along for the ride and to leave as soon as short-term interests are satisfied. The experience of organization, and the sociability and sense of mutual support and empowerment that come with membership, have little value in this view. Belief is set aside in the search for more instrumental rationales. Steve Bruce points to a basic problem: "Our difficulty is not that rational choice theory is wrong (though it usually is); the greater problem is that, beneath the brittle veneer of hypotheses and equations, there is a sea of vagueness that allows almost any outcome to be claimed as support for rational choice" (Bruce 2010: 147). He goes on to point out that "the economistic model requires that we be able to assess costs and returns from some neutral or consensually agreed standpoint, before we make a commitment to one religion rather than another. But the nature of religion does not allow such comparisons and measurements" (Bruce 2010: 147). Peterson comments that "in El Salvador and in many other places, religious engagement and political struggle have not been contradictory but mutually reinforcing. Further, both are often sustained by rational analysis and a commitment set within a narrative framework and nurtured within the believing community, rather than by strategic-institutional calculations or calls for revolutionary commitment from afar" (Peterson 1997: 166).

The record of rational choice–based scholarship on religion, society, and politics in Latin America is mixed. Anthony Gill has argued for an "economic model of church state relations" that explains opposition to authoritarian rule by particular Catholic hierarchies as a response to competition from Protestantism. An expanding supply of religious goods creates fierce competition for clientele, and competition makes clergy and church leaders more responsive to parishioners' needs. Competition provides "the wake-up call the Church needed to realize that poverty and repression were serious problems that demanded more than temporary acts of charity. More than just a wake-up call, however, Protestant advances also provided the motivation to do something about these problems" (Gill 1998: 120). The search for hard data and a more "rational" logic leads Gill back to the Catholic bishops' sense of institutional self-defense. The institutional church, more precisely the public positions of the episcopal conferences of each country (the unitary actor in this scheme), serve as Gill's basic units of analysis. The dependent variable is church-state conflict, read in terms of support for or opposition to military governments. The effort suffers from lack of historical depth, conceptual confusion, and unexamined assumptions about the proper unit of analysis. Gill asserts that "there has always been a relatively high demand for both social justice and religion in Latin America" (Gill 1998: 48), but he pays little attention to how needs are defined, how those definitions change, or how competing visions of need are brought to a mass clientele, which is, after all, how social justice issues came to center stage in the first place. Gill works with an economic model with demand held constant, but demand can grow and its specific implications can change with changing political and social contexts. Conceptual confusion is also apparent in the way in which proper relations of religion and politics are defined. That religion and politics mix at all is taken as something in need of explanation. "Even in the United States," Gill writes, "the constitutional separation of church and state cannot keep the religious and political realms apart. The intertwining of religion and politics is even more pronounced in Latin America—the focus of this study, where the issue of church-state separation remains far more ambiguous" (Gill 1998: 2).

Gill's comments are not a good way to begin the search for a new approach. Ties between religion and politics have been a conspicuous part of the history of the United States, are visible in all cultures and traditions (by no measure "even more pronounced in Latin America"), and evolve continuously everywhere. The issue is not to keep these realms apart, either in theory or practice, but to understand who brings them together, for what purposes, and with what consequences. Gill treats the unit of analysis as "the church," which in effect means the pronouncements and decisions of the top hierarchy, but despite their formal and sometimes hierarchical structure, like all complex organizations churches are not well understood as undifferentiated wholes. They are neither monolithic nor univocal. Competing currents of thought and action are always present, and competition is often intense and sometimes linked to violence.

Competitive Spirits: Latin America's New Religious Economy by Andrew Chesnut is a more successful effort at using rational choice theory and economic models to understand how religion and politics interact. Chesnut works with market analogies that help him address both the supply and the demand of what religions offer: connection with divine power, healing, companionship, community, and support in the organization of daily life. In his working model, competition in an open market promotes supply by attracting leaders and groups who see the possibility of gaining adherents. Competition generates its own dynamic of growth and adaptation to changing clienteles. New and more effective organizations and innovative techniques of preaching and reaching a clientele are introduced. Chesnut works with the terminology of microeconomics. Founders of new churches are described as religious entrepreneurs, proselytizers and pastoral agents as sales representatives. He speaks of new religious products (healing services and innovative uses of the media) being brought to market and considers the competitive effectiveness of the organizational structure of different churches. He also examines differentiated advertising that tailors religious messages or music to the tastes and needs of specific audiences. This kind of language makes many who study religion very uncomfortable. The great debates of the 1970s and 1980s over liberation theology, justice, political change, and democracy rarely appear, although democracy is subtly present as a concomitant of openness and competition. By setting aside elements of belief and motivation in favor of a simplifying focus on competition (for the religious groups) and "comparison shopping" (for religious consumers), Chesnut's analysis feels reductionist, but it is effective in its own terms.

What makes Chesnut's work an advance within the rational choice paradigm is how Chesnut combines the core issue of competition with a specific focus on why spirit-centered religions like Pentecostals have popular appeal.[10] Systematic attention to spirit-centered religions is welcome in a social science environment that has problems with phenomena many have been trained to regard as little short of fraud and hokum (spirit possession, faith healing, and casting out demons, to name just a few). These phenomena are something like the ghost in the machine: it is there to be sure, but no one knows how to find or much less understand it. These *pneumacentric* movements are contrasted to *virgophilic* (devoted to the Virgin Mary) Catholic groups. Pentecostals, in contrast, are described as *virgophobic*, their energies directed to conversion through commitment to Jesus Christ and openness to the Holy Spirit. A focus on healing of physical and emotional illness, including domestic strife, is also characteristic of new ministries, who thus can be said to favor the "soma over the psyche."[11]

Frances Hagopian identifies three schools of thought: (1) a focus on institutions (hinged on the interest of churches in self-defense and institutional maintenance); (2) concern with the church's changing sense of mission; and (3) her own view, which she calls a "theory of the embedded church," that explains variation in the positions taken by Catholic leaders in different national churches by setting the extent of church hegemony against the relative autonomy of grassroots groups. She argues that the greater the church's monopoly and control over its base, the more defense of institutional interests will shape leadership positions. As monopoly erodes and the autonomy of the grassroots expands, the hierarchy will pay more attention to such groups in shaping its policies. There are problems here, not least determining precisely what grassroots interests are, or mapping political dimensions (of left and right, for example) directly onto disputes about church doctrine. The effort also runs into difficulties when it comes to assessing the control that church leaders can in fact exercise, which is quite different from what they aspire to. Much of what church leaders see as "their groups," and which Hagopian (2009: 443) refers to as the church's "eyes and ears on the ground," is more loosely linked to the institutional church and for that reason much less subject to control and direction than this point of view allows for.

Each of the perspectives outlined here derives its logic from a theoretical and conceptual framework that defines the field of politics, religion, and society according to its own central precepts. Some frame the issues in terms of the relation among institutions, motivated by the goal of maintaining influence and securing goods and advantages for the institution. Others conceive of them as a process of social and political transformation that generates new ideals and new actors. This has the advantage of extending the field of study beyond the formal boundaries of institutions. Those working within the conceptual framework of rational choice see the relations among politics, religion, and society as a field in which rational actors seek to advance their own interest and sell their religious product in an open and competitive market. A fourth group concentrates on cultural and institutional change that generates new ideas, capacities, and forms of action. This places the process of transformation of ideas, values, and beliefs at the heart of the inquiry. Hagopian tries to combine the first and third of these, but with much less stress on ideas.

I want to offer more extended comment on the phenomenological approach, which has inspired most of my own research in this area (Levine 1992, 2003). Work in the phenomenological tradition operates with a very specific logic. To understand a process from the point of view of the social impact of ideas, we need to construct a valid and reliable qualitative methodology. In the social sciences today, it is common to understand qualitative methods less in terms of what they do than as a function of their not being quantitative. But this will not do. The use of qualitative methods responds to a theoretical framework in which a central task is to explain the meaning of actions and the meaning-filled character of social relations. The choice of such methods reflects acceptance of the power of ideas and of the centrality for society and politics of efforts to construct a moral vocabulary that can orient and legitimate action. A perspective of this kind is all the more important in dealing with religion, where the formation, expression, and transmission of values and beliefs play an evidently central role. A telling example from outside of Latin America comes from the experience of peace marches in Leipzig, Germany, in the last year of Communist rule. Marches and demonstrations began with prayer meetings for peace in the churches of the city and soon grew as massive numbers of citizens and groups joined, often waiting outside the churches for services to end and peaceful candlelit marches to begin. As the marches grew and spread, the ability of participants to defy the regime and its secret police, the Stasi, undermined the authority of the regime, which fell not long after these marches got under way. The attractive force and social power of this process cannot be understood without taking into account the moral force of the demonstrations, grounded in a consistent, principled nonviolence and situated in the churches of the city, which provided legitimation, places to meet, resources and connections, and some political cover. The study of those marches illustrates very well how qualitative techniques—including interviews and organizational histories—can be combined with structured opinion surveys to highlight the power of values and situate them in the normative life of a particular time and place (Bartee 2000; Steele 1994).

The distrust of qualitative methods that is so common lately in the social sciences rests on doubts about the possibility of creating systematic and reliable data about the formation and transmission of ideas and values. These are commonly depicted as "soft data," compared to supposedly more reliable economic statistics or variables of personal interest. But information about values is as real and concrete as any other kind of information and can be identified and measured with a range of techniques, including surveys, content analysis, and symbolic analysis (of music or visual images). All these provide means for getting to the interpretation of values. This is the core of the matter. A qualitative method works with the assumption that *the task of explanation is itself a task of interpretation.* Since all human behavior has meaning (given to it by the actors themselves), a meaning that is not necessarily shared by external observers, it is indispensable to disentangle the logic of the process as experienced and understood by participants (Weber 1978b).

There is a tendency in discussions of culture to act as if culture were simply a matter of ideas and values. But ideas never come in the abstract; they are not some disembodied mental stuff. Ideas come to real people in concrete, historical circumstances. Just as we allow room for human agency as people create new ideas and understandings, we also need to set these changing ideas against what seems possible and realistic in any given situation. There is a social and material structure to ideas, a net of institutions, connections, and arrangements by which they are produced, transmitted, and delivered from one place to another. These are very specific realities: the production and distribution of pamphlets or cassettes, arranging transport or housing for a meeting, and so forth. Tracing the social structure of religion and politics in these terms means looking closely at competing efforts to transmit ideas, create and sustain groups, and commit groups and their members to specific activities. It also means following the career of ideas and groups, working back and forth between "ground level" and the agendas and agents of big structures like churches or governments. Working with this kind of methodology is not easy. It cannot be done from the library, the data bank, or the office. One is commonly required to go to remote areas, and to travel in uncomfortable and difficult circumstances, in minimal conditions of health and security. My personal experience has taken me to remote villages and to urban neighborhoods where (I was repeatedly warned) "no one ever goes," and I have gotten interviews that "cannot be gotten." I have swallowed clouds of dust, waded through muddy roads, and spent countless hours on rural buses only to find that the people I was supposed to meet were not there. It is not easy and it requires a lot of time and sometimes considerable discomfort, but the payoff can be very great. One learns, for example, what it means to say that "ideas come from below," ideas that despite lacking a voice in official texts nonetheless can move people and communities to sustained action in common (Levine 1993b). In light of the problem of so many studies of religion now and in the past, which is to confuse texts and official documents with the attitudes and commitments of the population as a whole, qualitative methods of the kind outlined here offer a promising solution.[12]

How can we best assess the evidence of ideas and action? Making sense of the issues requires a conscious, *sympathetic* effort to situate them in the context of the hopes and fears, the opportunities and the dangers in which they emerged, found carriers and audience, and began to push and pull behavior into new paths. A better vision of religious change and its meaning has to be a more sympathetic vision. In part, this calls for a systematic effort to distinguish "between the conceptual apparatus of the social scientist and the lived experience of social actors, to see things 'through their eyes'" (Wuthnow 1992: 145). But more is at issue than empathy. Sympathy is also required, sympathy in the ordinary language sense of understanding and seeing the value of what others are thinking and doing. Having a sympathetic ear and looking at things from the point of view of those involved (and not only in terms of what happens to interest the academy at any given movement) are an essential part of any intellectual strategy that enjoins us to listen to others as a first step to making sense of who they are and what they do. Analysis is not set aside but rather enriched with the product of sympathetic listening. Insulating scholars from "involvement" with those they study makes it hard to hear, much less make sense of new voices and see new realities.

Secularization

I noted earlier how contemporary Latin American experience challenges many expectations derived from classical theories of secularization. There is more to the story than the simple persistence of religion, or even the demonstrated vitality and creativity of religion in the teeth of theoretical expectations. The evolving reality of secularization, in the form of plurality and pluralism in religion and civil society, has important implications for the relation of religion to democracy. The facts of pluralization and secularization reflect the existence of autonomous subjects who create new ways of relating to one another in an open and accessible civil society. How religions make a place for themselves in this newly plural public sphere, working with groups that are no longer subject to automatic control, is at the heart of the relation between secularization and democracy. Secularization in this sense should not be confused with secularism. The first refers to the consolidation of a plural and competitive environment in which no particular religious group has a predetermined monopoly of institutions or practices. The second points to a deliberate policy of "de-religionizing" states and public spaces. The anticlericalism of the French Revolution or of elements of the Republic in the Spanish Civil War are cases in point. The issues were joined in Latin America in numerous civil conflicts of the nineteenth century, but militant secularism of this kind acquired enduring public presence only in Mexico and Uruguay, where it has faded—particularly in Mexico—in recent years (Camp 1994, 1996, 2008; Da Costa 2003, 2009).

Theories that anticipate an inevitable secularization of culture and politics and corresponding decline, privatization, and ultimate disappearance of religion are of little help in Latin America, where the evidence affirms the enduring vitality and force of religion as a source of change in society, culture, and politics. Religion's continuing presence on the public stage forces us to rethink the conventional wisdom of secularization theory and to search for sources of change within religion, and in religion's ongoing encounter with "the world," a world of which it remains, as ever, an integral part. The question is also not well addressed in terms of a "resurgence" or "politicization" of religion. Religion has never really been absent from politics and society in Latin America. At issue is less resurgence or politicization than a change in who speaks, what social connections they have, and what they have to say. The issue is also not captured by theories that see the new social presence of religion as a direct response to the failures of rationalism and secular modernity.[13]

The new role played by religion and by the churches in these years caught most scholarly observers and many political activists by surprise. Civil and military elites accustomed to unquestioned backing felt betrayed when they encountered criticism and opposition from the churches. Scholars accustomed to a narrow view of religion, or to seeing religion as epiphenomenal (secondary to the "hard" and supposedly more basic facts of interest and class position), were also caught by surprise, unable to fit these developments into their view of the world. Until recently, the prevailing narrative about religion (as about religion and politics) would have made this book hard to imagine. Scholars and most observers writing on the subject were invested in a story about religion whose guiding line was that religions everywhere were in long-term decline. Present-day decline was contrasted to a view of the past in which religions thoroughly penetrated and dominated cultures and institutions. The past was assumed to have been more religious, with a wide range of behaviors and institutions organized on religious principles, guided and directed by religious ideas and religious leaders.

The common view of secularization points to a broad process of decline of religion in private life and above all as a presence (much less a determining presence) in the public sphere (Casanova 1994; Bruce 2010). This decline is manifest in indices of belief, belonging (affiliation), and religious practice, and in the assumption by other private groups or by public agencies of roles once filled by religious institutions, including registry of births, arrangements for education, certification of marriage, health care, and management of death (cemeteries and death certificates). Bruce (2010) rightfully insists that this is a simplistic depiction of a complex and multifaceted social process. In his view, two elements are central to secularization: the loss of control by religious institutions and leaders in the public sphere, and an intergenerational decline in practice, belief, and belonging, "a slow process of generational change in which people gradually lose interest in things that mattered to their parents and in which the possibilities for belief and practice expand while the salience of any of those beliefs and practices declines" (Bruce 2010: 19).

There is no question that the data for Europe show a steady and consistent pattern of intergenerational decline in belief, practice, and affiliation beginning in the early twentieth century, particularly in Europe (Bruce 2010; Voas 2009).[14] Ronald Inglehart and Pippa Norris (2004) extend the argument worldwide, with data that show a close relation between the decline of religiosity (in all the senses indicated here) and the rise of what they call *existential security*. The bottom line is that richer, more educated, and more secure nations are likely to be less religious; and richer, more educated, and more secure persons within any nation are also likely to be less religious. The continuing religiosity of the United States is explained with reference to high levels of inequality, and the authors account for the continuing vigor of religion in much of the world by reference to demography and tradition. The birthrate is higher in poorer and more religious countries, and religious tradition (often identified with nationality and language) limits the pace of religious decline in some areas, like the territories of Orthodox Christianity in Eastern Europe. In later work specifically on Latin America, Inglehart (2009) sees the Latin American situation as paradoxical. Latin Americans combine continued adherence to religious values with growing demands for self-expression and personal freedom. The paradox disappears if, as I have suggested, we take a view of secularization that allows for religious diversity precisely within a secularizing society.

Although general debates about secularization are suggestive and the findings often powerful, they do not exhaust the questions of interest. Along with concern about measures of religious belief and practice, we also want to know how people relate to the institutions of religion, and how these institutions, and the collection of groups and movements associated in some way with them, position themselves in public life. The growing pluralism of society, culture, and politics in Latin America makes its presence felt not only in how churches position themselves in public life but also in the internal life of the churches and in the debates, discussions, and initiatives that take place there.

What has happened in much of Latin America is not undifferentiated religious decline but something much more complex and interesting. A surge of religious innovation and diversification has developed in environments no longer dominated or controlled by religion, and certainly not by *a church* in the classical sense. The whole process can be understood as secularization with religious vitality. Growing urbanization, education, and access to media have combined to generate not so much an undifferentiated decline as a reorganization of relations with the churches and with religion as a set of norms, one that suggests patterns of affiliation and obedience that are much less automatic than in the past.[15] This is not secularization in the ordinary language sense of decline, privatization, and ultimate irrelevance but rather secularization in the sense of a greater autonomy of groups (contested, to be sure, but very present), an autonomy that changes the relation of individuals and groups to the churches, and alters the stance that churches can assume and have in fact assumed in what is now a decidedly plural public space. These transformations have direct bearing on the role churches play in the public sphere. They confirm that there will be multiple voices and multiple actors and that therefore an effort at the reconquest of public space by the churches is likely to fall short, if not implode on itself. They also make it clear that what is at issue is less a "return" or "resurgence" of religion (as much commentary has it) than a renegotiation of an ongoing relation.

The connection of secularization with democracy deserves a closer look. In a recent dialogue (or to be more precise, a juxtaposition of views), German philosopher Jürgen Habermas and Joseph Cardinal Ratzinger (now Pope Benedict XVI) reflected on the meaning of secularization in terms that are relevant here (Habermas and Ratzinger 2006). For Habermas, the political culture of democracy is not something that can be imposed but emerges rather as "the fruit of a socialization in which one becomes accustomed to the practices and modes of thought of a free political culture" (Habermas and Ratzinger 2006: 30). The uniting bond is the democratic process itself, a communicative praxis that can only be exercised in common. Here, as in much of his work, Habermas insists on the power of moral values and looks for ways in which explicitly religious norms and institutions can be incorporated into the operations of a postsecular state. The expression "postsecular," he writes, "does more than give public recognition to religious fellowship in view of the final contribution they make to the reproduction of motivations and attitudes that are socially desirable. The public awareness of a post secular society also reflects a normative insight that has consequences for the political dealings of unbelieving citizens. In the post secular society, there is an increasing consensus that certain phases of the modernization of the public consciousness involve the assimilation and the reflexive transformation of both religious and secular mentalities" (Habermas and Ratzinger 2006: 46). He goes on to state that

> when secularized citizens act in their role as citizens of the state, they must not deny in principle that religious images of the world have the potential to express truth. Nor must they refuse their believing fellow citizens the right to make contributions in a religious language to public debate. Indeed, a liberal political culture can expect that the secularized citizens play their part in the endeavor to translate relevant contributions from the religious language into a language that is accessible to the public as a whole. (Habermas and Ratzinger 2006: 51)

Cardinal Ratzinger advances three points that are relevant to our discussion. The first concerns the continuing importance of natural law as a basis for assertions of human rights. Second, he recognizes that neither the culture of Christianity nor that of secular rationality is universal but rather is a particular contribution of the West to world culture. Finally, he points out that along with pathologies of religion, it is essential to recognize the historical fact of pathologies of reason that have overridden rights and treated individuals as ciphers (Habermas and Ratzinger 2006: 71, 75, 76).

The Habermas-Ratzinger discussions on secularization bear directly on the core themes of this book. They are relevant to the relation of religion to democracy because they raise the question of how churches and religious groups and individuals understand their role and situate themselves in open and plural social and political contexts. They also highlight grounds for the religious legitimation and defense of democracy and point to the ability of religious norms and groups to play active roles in a secularized and democratic political order. Finally, they are directly relevant to the emergence of ideas about rights in the churches and to the way these ideas have framed the actions of churches in the defense of rights, their relation to the human rights movement, and in counterexamples, their support in some cases for the abuse of rights (Chapter 7).

Recent empirical work by Latin American scholars (Parker 1996, 2005, 2009; Blancarte 2009; Loaeza 2009; Mallimaci 2005; Mallimaci and Villa 2007) affirms that the evolution of pluralism has altered the relations of religious believers to institutions. As noted earlier, growing numbers now define themselves as "Catholic in my own way," which means that although they may continue to identify as Catholic, such an identification no longer translates (if it ever did) into automatic political adherence or social mobilization in support of policies articulated by church leaders. The emergence of autonomous citizens and groups in a secularized and open milieu changes the ways in which politics is open to the churches and raises serious doubts about the viability of ecclesiastical strategies founded on the idea of reconquering social and political space for religion. Religious values and ideas are more likely to be served by persuasion in a competitive marketplace.

There are ironies here, for as Tocqueville recognized in the 1840s, it is precisely where religions have been separated from other institutions (where no official faith exists) that religious practice has flourished and diversified the most. Tocqueville recognized that the very effort to prolong the existence of Christendom did grave damage to institutional religion in Europe. "So long as religion derives its strength from sentiments, instincts, and passions which are reborn in like fashion in all periods of history," he wrote, "it can brave the assaults of time or at least can only be destroyed by another religion. But when a religion chooses to rely on the interest of the world, it becomes as fragile as all earthly powers. Alone it may hope for immortality; linked to ephemeral powers, it follows their fortunes and often falls together with the passions of the day sustaining them" (Tocqueville 1967: 298).

The experience of the United States bears directly on this issue and has long presented a puzzle to the theory of secularization. US society is modern, highly educated, urban, and industrialized, with institutions, laws, and a high culture that are secular in tone and content, but the United States is also a highly religious culture, now perhaps more than ever. To use an economic metaphor, the absence of established religion in the United States meant a deregulated market. This was the foundation for what proved to be a highly competitive and democratic religious arena (Finke and Stark 2005). In the plural and open context of the United States, religions have provided critical spaces for social and cultural pluralism and, along the way, have adapted to a general US model of congregational organization (Warner 1993). North American society was and remains both highly religious and highly pluralist, a combination that fits poorly with classic models of secularization.

Rereading the theory of secularization from a perspective rooted in the history of the United States, Stephen Warner (1993) sees the US "paradox" of religious modernity as no paradox at all. The central thread running through US history is not the decay of a previous religious-political unity, but rather a consistent pluralism reinforced by marked religious populism. As Nathan Hatch puts it, "Following the long tradition of democratic Christianity in America, Fundamentalists and Pentecostals reject modernity as it is expressed in high culture, but remain stalwart defenders of modern attitudes as they build popular constituencies with the most innovative techniques. They will not surrender to learned experts the right to think for themselves" (Hatch 1991: 219).

These aspects of North American experience are relevant to religious change more generally. Elements of social and cultural populism have been prominent in Latin America, as grassroots groups seek autonomy and press for equality, while new leadership strata emerge to claim a place in the sun. The populism at issue here is more than demographic. There has also been a notable transformation of language, as preachers and tract writers strive to appeal to ordinary men and women who now have access to reading and to mass media (cf. Eickelman and Piscatori 2004 on Islam). North American experience also suggests that if we are to understand the evolution of religion and politics, religion has to be distinguished from culture in general and must, in any case, be seen as dynamic, not static. Religion is not well understood as an unchanging whole, transmitted in toto from one generation to another. Religions provide spaces for the creation of human ties and organized social life for a mobile and changing population, spaces in which older ties are breaking down and new solidarities are arising in their place.

The conventional story of secularization is not so much wrong as incomplete. Ammerman points out that although it pretends to be universal, the secularization story is really the particular story of particular groups of people. It is a story written by elites and intellectuals, a story composed from the perspective of the center. If we read history from a different angle, and listen at the margins, quite a different pattern emerges (Ammerman 1994a). On the basis of her study of US congregations, she affirms that most ordinary people have "simply not learned the ideological lesson that if they believe in promoting social justice they should place less emphasis on witnessing, or—at the other pole— that if they believe in witnessing they should be wary of calls for social justice. They are perfectly willing to affirm that both social justice and evangelism are important, or perhaps that neither of those things is as important as a life of prayer, Bible study and high moral standards"

(Ammerman 1996: 297). She points out that secularization theory presumes a unique and definitive path to modernity but other possibilities exist.

> While modernist social theory took pains to relegate religious gatherings to the margins and to "private" social life, a newer paradigm can include religious communities as among the "publics" present in a complex society. Just as the either/or dichotomy of communal versus urban life is better described as both/and, so the either/or dichotomy of a single "common good" versus warring particularisms is better described as a both/and web of multiple publics collectively constituting the whole. (Ammerman 1996: 357)

Conclusion

The way we ask the questions does a lot to shape the answers we are likely to find. This is no mere matter of investigative technique, a puzzle that can be solved by new or different statistical methods. Method should always be subordinate to theory, and the working theories that we employ make a substantial difference in how we set about the project of asking questions and finding answers. A full account of the transformations of politics, religion, and society in Latin America requires us to be self-conscious about theory and method. It also requires us to think beyond issues of the short-term success or failure of any particular group or program. That they may not have succeeded as they hoped does not mean that the effort is without value or legacy. New voices were created and the terms of debate in society and politics were altered in fundamental ways. Nathan Hatch has described the surge of religious populism in nineteenth-century North America in terms that are relevant to Latin American experience. He speaks about "storming heaven by the back door." "The fundamental impetus of these movements," he writes, "was to make Christianity a liberating force: people were given the right to think and act for themselves, rather than depending on the mediations of an educated elite" (Hatch 1991: 11). Hatch's insight directs attention to transformations in culture, and in the vehicles through which culture is shaped and transmitted day to day, that enhance the ability of ordinary people to think and act for themselves and make the effort legitimate. Changes of this kind also create possibilities for religious institutions to reposition themselves in the public sphere, providing legitimacy to different kinds of social and political arrangements, including pluralism and democracy, and to develop new relations to organized social life and to social movements of all kinds.

Notes

1. This is as true now as it was in the past. In Western Christianity, concepts of rulership and proper forms of organization derived from Roman and medieval experience made for a pattern of organization challenged first by the Reformation and later by arguments that authority has many sources and can be shared as much as imposed.

2. Nancy Ammerman speaks of congregations in these terms. Congregations, she writes, "provide an arena in which people can organize effective strategies of 'public' action, but they can also retell the story of their individual lives—without discernible institutional boundary drawing—in terms they think their God would recognize. They ask for prayers and advice and they organize to get things done. It is that combination of meaning-making and practice-creating that makes congregations such a powerful arena of social action" (Ammerman 1996: 294–295).

3. Mitchell states further that "our understanding of the phenomenon at hand is liable to seriously underestimate the amplitude of what is likely to transpire. The common failure of social scientists to anticipate, let alone predict the Iranian revolution, for example, may have been due, in no small part, to the terminology that was used. In American politics, it is difficult to imagine Martin Luther King standing on the steps of the Lincoln Memorial saying, 'I have a preference today.' He did not have a preference, he had a dream. In both cases, rendering what happened in terms of preference or choice would have led to a serious underestimation of what actually transpired" (Mitchell 2007: 360).

4. Anna Peterson (1997) states that between 1968 and 1982, Latin American governments and armies imprisoned, exiled, or killed close to a thousand priests, nuns, and bishops. In Central America alone, at least forty nuns and priests were murdered between 1971 and 1990. More than half of those killings occurred in El Salvador, the smallest country in Latin America. See also Lernoux 1982. An early sign of violence against clergy in El Salvador came with the case of P. Rutilio Grande. Grande insisted on equality and offered the mass as a symbolic sharing in a land where actual sharing of goods was rare and inequality the norm. "The material world is for all without limits. It's a common table with a large tablecloth like this Eucharist. With a spot for everyone." In El Salvador, he continued, "It is practically illegal to be a true Christian [because] . . . the world around us is radically based on an established disorder, before which the mere proclamation of the Gospel is subversive. . . . I'm very afraid that soon the Bible and the Gospel won't be able to enter our borders. We'll just get the bindings because all the pages are subversive." Grande was murdered "while driving through cane fields on his way to say Mass" (Peterson 1997: 123).

5. In the tradition of evangelical Christianity, believers bear witness to their faith by reaching out to convert others and by assuming external markers of a converted existence. These can range from modesty in dress and avoiding temptation (such as alcohol or pornography) to insistence on separate schools or a broader political agenda. For those inspired by liberation theology, bearing

witness entails commitment and actions in the public sphere. One witnesses to the truth of values of equality and justice by giving up privilege, sharing the conditions of the poor, and working with them to challenge injustice and promote change. Witness of this kind makes sense in the context of liberation theology's characteristic stress on *accompaniment,* which underscores the need for the church and church personnel to accompany people in their daily lives and struggles.

6. In *Leviathan* (chapter 42), Hobbes insisted that martyrs must have seen Christ in order to merit the title (i.e., no contemporary martyrs), but contemporary usage rejects that view. I am grateful to Arlene Saxonhouse for pointing this out to me.

7. See Levine 1993a and 1993b for a discussion of the relation between cultural analysis and presumptions of order and control.

8. This approach can be found in scholars as varied as Dodson and O'Shaughnessy 1992; Drogus 1997a; Drogus and Stewart-Gambino 2005; Ireland 1992; Lehmann 1990, 1996; Mainwaring 1986; Christian Smith 1991; and also in my own work (Levine 1981, 1992).

9. See John Burdick 1993; Cleary and Stewart-Gambino 1992, 1997; Chesnut 1997, 2003; Drogus 1990, 1997a, 1999; Drogus and Stewart-Gambino 2005; Freston 2001, 2008; Froehle 1994; Mariz 1994; Smilde 2007; Steigenga 2001; Stoll 1990, 1993.

10. In Warner's terms, these are nascent and spirit-filled religions (Warner 1988).

11. Robert Orsi stresses how hard it can be for scholars of religion to enter into the logic and appeal of spirit-filled religious movements. By disciplinary training and tradition, they are committed to an ameliorative and benign view of religion and attracted to themes like empowerment, transcendence, movement building, and civil society. For too many academics, he writes, "True religion, then, is epistemologically and ethically singular. It is rational, respectful of persons, non coercive, mature, non anthropomorphic in its higher forms, mystical (as opposed to ritualistic), unmediated, and agreeable to democracy (no hierarchy in gilded robes and fancy hats), monotheistic (no angels, saints, demons, ancestors), emotionally controlled, a reality of mind and spirit, not body and nature. It is concerned with ideal essences not actual things, and especially not about presences in things. Students of mine over the past twenty years in classrooms in New York City, Indiana, and Massachusetts have unfailingly refused to acknowledge as 'religious' the practice of putting holy water into an automobile's transmission (as pilgrims to a Bronx Lourdes shrine commonly do). Whatever this is, is it not 'good religion'? All the complex dynamism of religion is thus stripped away, its boundary-blurring and border-crossing propensities eliminated. Not surprisingly, there is only one methodology and one epistemology for studying this 'religion'—critical, analytical, and 'objective' (as opposed to subjective, existentially engaged, or participatory)" (Orsi 2005: 188).

12. Much social science scholarship in Latin America in the 1970s and 1980s suffered from an additional problem when addressing cultural change,

identities, and ideas. Many of the ideas and movements that concern us here crystallized in Latin America at a time of intense ideological ferment, when Marxist thinking and action seemed to many to provide a clear guide to the future, and categories of class dominated discourse. Carlos De Gregori, Cecilia Blondet, and Nicolás Lynch (1986) comment on the evolution of scholarship in Peru in terms that are relevant here. By the early 1960s, they note, identification with the Indian (*indigenismo*) and concentration on community studies lost appeal and force of conviction as society urbanized and few unstudied communities remain. "Just when a search for new directions and a turn to the city became urgent, a 'cold wave' of Marxism engulfed us all. Structures now took precedence over actors, and attention went to the economic base, not the cultural superstructure. . . . The rich accumulation of anthropological monographs became little more than raw material, with concern for usages, customs, or values painted as superfluous, even frivolous, in light of the urgent need to grasp the scientific (read, economic) laws, essential for the advent and ultimate success of a revolution thought to be imminent. . . . Suffice it to say that life showed us that social actors don't let themselves be confined by laws that reduce them to epiphenomena of structures. Culture elbowed its way in, forcing us in many tangible ways to recognize how far it was from being merely a reflection, a super structural frill" (De Gregori, Blondet, and Lynch 1986: 14–15).

13. Casanova points out that it is not religion in the abstract that is returning, nor is it returning everywhere. "At most, the crisis of secularity can serve as a common conditioning factor that allows certain religious traditions that have not yet been weakened excessively by processes of secularization to respond in certain ways" (Casanova 1994: 227).

14. Data from other cases (like the United States) provide a more nuanced view of the impact of intergenerational change (Putnam and Campbell 2010).

15. See Parker 1996, 2005, 2009; Mallimaci and Villa 2007; Mallimaci 2005, 2009; Blancarte 2009; Loaeza 2009; Romero 2009; and Levine 2009b. Fortunato Mallimaci (2005: 60) writes that "in today's Argentina, people do not believe—be it in politics or be it in religion—more or less than in other periods, but in a different way." See also Parker 2009; Blancarte 2009.

3

Transformations in Catholicism and Protestantism

Christianity is utterly dominant in Latin America and throughout the Americas, making the Western Hemisphere the most Christian of all world regions, as well as the most Catholic, now and in the foreseeable future (Barrett, Kurian, and Johnson 2001; Froehle and Gautier 2003; Jenkins 2002). This means that for present purposes, the most important distinctions among religions within Latin America are those that separate Catholics from Protestants and mark variations within Protestantism itself.[1] Differences between Catholics and Protestants go back, of course, to the Reformation in sixteenth-century Europe, when new churches emerged out of the unity of medieval Christendom, creating multiple identities within the overall community of Christians, beyond the Catholic-Orthodox divide of 1054 A.D. Regardless of denomination, all Protestant churches reject the unifying authority of the Vatican, and most also reject veneration of Mary, which itself increased in Catholicism in reaction to the Reformation. From the beginning, Protestantism underscored the centrality of faith and scripture and stressed the ability of all believers to have equal access to the scripture. The combined stress on faith, free access to the Bible, and individual responsibility made for equality among believers, and for a historic emphasis on literacy (so that all could read the Bible on their own) that remains a powerful attraction of many new churches for converts.

Definitions and Demographics

Definitions become problematic when we move beyond dichotomies like Christian–non-Christian or Catholic-Protestant. Protestant churches differ widely among themselves in how they are organized. Anglicans, for example, approach Catholic hierarchical models with a structure of archbishops, bishops, and the like. Others define leadership differently, and some, like Quakers, dispense with formal leadership entirely, relying instead on the consensus of the community. Many observers draw a further distinction between Protestant churches rooted in the Reformation and those arising out of nineteenth- and early twentieth-century developments in the United States, including Jehovah's Witnesses, Seventh-Day Adventists, Mormons, and the Pentecostal movement generally (Barrett, Kurian, and Johnson 2001; Noll 2009).

Scholars of Protestantism in Latin America commonly stress several lines of distinction. One contrasts historic or mainline denominations with Pentecostal or neo-Pentecostal groups, while another distinguishes nineteenth- and twentieth-century waves of transplanted and missionary Protestants from more recent interdenominational faith missions and Pentecostal or neo-Pentecostal churches. Many of the latter were started by foreign missionaries, but have been distinguished lately by local growth and local leadership. For all the differences among them, Protestants in the region (who often describe themselves as evangelicals, believers, or simply as Christians) share a few common elements: stress on change of life through a conversion experience; entire sanctification (freedom from sin achieved through grace and faith); activism (stress on proselytizing and missionary efforts); and special importance attached to the Bible, although not necessarily belief in its inerrancy (Algranti 2010; Blancarte 2000; Freston 2001, 2008; Oro and Semán 2000; Steigenga 2001; Stoll 1990).

The phenomenon of Pentecostalism, which embraces both Protestant Pentecostal and neo-Pentecostal churches, along with the rapidly growing Catholic Charismatic Renewal movement—requires separate attention. The contemporary Pentecostal revival in Protestantism has its origins in the Azusa Street revival in 1906 in Los Angeles, with denominations like the Assemblies of God playing a leading role[2] (Cox 1995; Noll 2009). This movement revived elements of early church practice that involve direct experience of divine power (such as speaking in tongues or healing). Recent innovations include the introduction of powerfully charismatic leadership models. Many of these new churches also appear to rely more on oral and visual transmission of the message than on the written word. Together these trends may undermine the equalizing effects of literacy and congregational organization often attributed to Protestantism (Algranti 2010; Bastián 1993, 1997; Cox 1995; Chesnut 2003; Gifford 2004; Kramer 2005; Oro and Semán 2000). I discuss these effects more fully in Chapter 5.

All Pentecostals are strongly committed to empowerment through direct experience of the divine presence and sharing in the gifts of the Holy Spirit. The term *pentecostal* itself comes from experiences recorded in the Bible. Shortly after the death of Jesus, the Apostles were gathered in a room.

> When the day of Pentecost had come, they were all together in one place. And suddenly a sound came from heaven like the rush of a mighty wind and it filled all the house where they were sitting. And there appeared to them tongues as of fire, distributed and resting on each one of them. And they were all filled with the Holy Spirit and began to speak in other tongues, and the Spirit gave them utterance . . . [citing the prophet Joel]. And in the last days it shall be, God declares That I will pour out my Spirit upon all flesh, and your sons and your daughters shall prophesy, and your young men shall see visions; and your old men shall dream dreams. Yea and upon my menservants and my maidservants in those days I will pour out my Spirit, and they shall prophesy. (The Acts of the Apostles 2:1–4, 17–18 [Revised Standard Version])

The point for contemporary Pentecostals is that this experience did not just happen once in history; it is available now. Manifestations of divine power include glossolalia, or speaking in tongues; exorcisms of evil spirits; and divine cure of afflictions ranging from illness to alcoholism or domestic stress.[3] To this basic commitment, neo-Pentecostal churches commonly add a belief that divine power will bless believers with material wealth and well-being.[4] Virginia Garrard-Burnett (2007: 222) states that "the distinguishing characteristic of contemporary prosperity theory is the miraculous quality of the blessing; material welfare is not merely a Horatio Alger like byproduct of virtuous living, but it is, *ipso facto,* God's supernatural gift to the faithful, not unlike other gifts of the Holy Spirit such as glossolalia (speaking in tongues) or faith healing."

Most Pentecostal and neo-Pentecostal churches and believers are Protestant, but the rediscovery of charismatic power and Pentecostal practices also extends to the Catholic Church. The Catholic Charismatic Renewal movement, which arose in the late 1960s in the United States, has had a major impact in Latin America, where it has grown sharply.[5] Part of the appeal within Latin American Catholicism arises from a search for effective ways to combat competition from Pentecostal

Protestantism (Chesnut, 2003), but the Catholic Charismatic Renewal's growth and spread cannot be explained simply as the result of a tactical adjustment by the hierarchy; Edward Cleary (2011) documents independent sources for the Catholic charismatic movement in grassroots movements throughout the region. Regardless of the interpretation one chooses, it is important to acknowledge the scale of the phenomenon. Pentecostal and neo-Pentecostal churches represent the leading edge of growth within Latin American Protestantism, and the Catholic Charismatic Renewal is perhaps the single largest social movement in the region (Barrett, Kurian, and Johnson 2001; Cleary 2011; Johnson and Ross 2010; Noll 2009).

Taking all its denominations and variations together, Christianity is the largest religion in the world, followed by Islam. Now, and in the likely future, it is also a religion of the global South, with Latin America and especially Africa providing prime areas of growth.[6] In Latin America, the number of Catholics grew 165 percent between 1950 and 2000 (compared to overall population growth of 174 percent). The corresponding figures for Africa show a growth of 708 percent for Catholics in a population that itself has grown by 313 percent. By the year 2000, Africa and Latin America together accounted for 62 percent of Catholics worldwide, with Europe providing only 27 percent (Froehle 2010a, from Froehle and Gautier 2003). Something similar can be said for Protestantism, as Pentecostal churches have made rapid gains in Latin America, Africa, and Asia (Barrett, Kurian, and Johnson 2001; Freston 2008; Gifford 1998, 2004, 2008; Jenkins 2002; Johnson and Ross 2010; Lumsdaine 2009; Noll 2009; Ranger 2008a, 2008b). Jenkins points to the emergence of a truly global Christianity, dominated by groups and peoples from the southern half of the globe. "By 2025," he writes, "Africans and Latin Americans will make up 60 percent of Catholics, and that number should reach 66 percent by 2050. . . . The twentieth century was clearly the last in which whites dominated the Catholic Church: Europe simply is not The Church. Latin America may be" (Jenkins 2002: 195).

A closer look at the data for Latin America reveals a sustained pattern of growth and increased pluralism to the point that Brazil now has both the largest Catholic population and the largest Pentecostal population (after the United States) of any country in the world.[7] Although the overall trends are clear, considerable care is required in dealing with specific numbers. Many may be "doubly affiliated" (counted as baptized Catholics but now participating in other denominations), conversions can be short-lived, and multiple memberships are not uncommon

(Barrett, Kurian, and Johnson 2001; Cleary 2004a; Froehle 2010a; Froehle and Gautier 2003; Johnson and Ross 2010; Pew Forum on Religion and Public Life 2006). Even with these qualifications, it is clear that in the region as a whole, Catholics have more or less kept pace with population growth while Protestants have grown more rapidly, with much of the impulse coming from the creation and expansion of Pentecostal and neo-Pentecostal churches. Between 1900 and 2010, the total number of Catholics in the region expanded by more than 700 percent, slightly behind overall population, which grew by 864 percent. Over this same period, the number of non-Catholic Christians grew by almost 5,500 percent, while the doubly affiliated expanded by over 17,000 percent.[8] Some of this extraordinary rate of growth is a statistical artifact of beginning from a small base. Examination of the data since 1970 indicates that growth has indeed slowed but also shows that the numbers of non-Catholic Christians continue to outstrip population growth, while Catholics more or less hold their own (Barrett, Kurian, and Johnson 2001). Table 3.1 provides overall numbers, growth rates, and estimates for Catholic growth from two different sources.

If we look beyond the raw numbers to what Bryan Froehle and Mary Gautier (2003) call the "installed capacity" of the churches[9] (the structures and personnel that place the church in contact with the population—dioceses, parishes, pastoral centers, clergy, sisters, and catechists), here as well the Catholic Church shows steady growth, but a tendency to fall behind population growth. One significant element not shown by these numbers is the fact that throughout Latin America, the Catholic Church, which has long depended on imported clergy, has managed to replace foreign- with native-born clergy on a considerable scale. Despite a slight decline in numbers of women religious (sisters) (which, set against population growth, means a substantial drop in capacity to staff institutions that have long depended on them), substantial growth in ordinations of diocesan priests (those who are in most contact with parishioners) suggests that the prospects for growth of clergy in the future are good. The Catholic Church has also dramatically expanded numbers of other personnel, like deacons and catechists, new post–Vatican II categories that began to grow substantially in the 1970s. In combination, these figures augur well for the institution's ability to staff churches and church institutions well into the future (see Table 3.2). In global terms, it is striking how much Latin America lags behind Europe and North America in terms of the institutional capacity of the Catholic Church, despite having an equal or greater Catholic population (Froehle and Gautier 2003).

Table 3.1 Christian Religious Affiliation and Growth Rates, 1900, 1970, and 2010

	1900	1970	Change (%)	2010	Change (%)	Change, 1900–2010 (%)
Population						
(PRB/US/UN)	58,700,000	274,300,000	367	566,000,000	106	864
Catholics						
(WCD/ASE)	56,703,790	239,065,000	322	488,338,000	104	761
Catholics[a]	56,703,790	245,377,290	333	473,190,678	93	735
Non-Catholic						
Christians	1,969,210	27,537,911	1,298	108,722,507	295	5,421
Doubly Affiliated	280,000	11,156,000	3,884	48,968,527	339	17,389
Disaffiliated	121,000	954,043	688	3,281,400	244	2,612
Unaffiliated						
Christians	1,551,890	6,207,608	300	4,385,387	–29	183

Sources: Population figures for 1900 and 1970 are from Brea 2003 (PRB). Figures are calculated for the seventeen countries of Latin America in 1900 and the eighteen countries in 1970 from figures provided by Brea, plus figures for Puerto Rico taken from the United States Census. Population figures for 2010 are from the United Nations, Population Division (UN), and from the United States Census for Puerto Rico (US). See http://esa.un.org/unpd/wpp/unpp/panel_population.htm and http://www.census.gov/popest /puerto_rico/. All figures are rounded.

Note: a. Figures for Catholics are calculated from the research version of the World Christian Database (WCD), October 2011, courtesy of Todd Johnson, director, and Peter Crossing, programmer, Center for the Study of World Christianity, Gordon-Conwell Theological Seminary.

Figures for Catholics for 1970 and 2010 based on the *Annuarium Statisticum Ecclesiae* (ASE) are also given. All other figures are calculated based on figures in the World Christian Database, research version (October 2011). The figure for "Non-Catholic Christians" includes all groupings of Christians given in the WCD not counted as "Roman Catholic." This includes unaffiliated Christians, Anglicans, Independents, Marginals (long used by the WCD and its antecedents, this category encompasses primarily Mormons and Jehovah's Witnesses), Orthodox (such as Greek Orthodox), and Protestants (historic denominations such as Lutherans). Those who are doubly affiliated are presumed to be counted as baptized Catholics but also members of a group of non-Catholic Christians. The disaffiliated are those Christians counted as baptized or otherwise affiliated with a Christian tradition but who have since broken their affiliation to embrace another religion or no religion at all. Unaffiliated Christians are included in the count of non-Catholic Christians but also given separately due to the ambiguity of their affiliation. The group includes generic Christians who may have once been baptized within a Christian tradition, or into Catholic popular religion without benefit of baptism by a priest, and remain identified as Christian but have no specific organizationally tabulated affiliation.

The internal diversity of Protestantism makes it difficult to come up with precisely comparable statistics, but evidence from a series of studies (Algranti 2010; Chesnut 1997, 2003; Kamsteeg 1998; Oro and Semán 2000; Smilde 2007) suggests strong growth in numbers of churches, schools, and related institutions, along with steadily decreasing reliance on funding, staff, and control from North American and

Table 3.2 Installed Capacity of the Catholic Church, 1970 and 2009

	1970	2009	Change (%)
Catholics	239,065,000	488,338,000	104
Baptisms	6,551,185	7,082,826	8
Ecclesiastical territories[a]	581	779	34
Pastoral centers[b]	27,157	109,405	303
Parishes	17,182	33,166	93
Bishops	919	1,266	38
Priests	45,232	69,463	54
Diocesan priests only	23,449	45,835	96
Diocesan priest ordinations	404	1,700	321
Deacons[c]	na	7,241	na
Women religious (sisters)	119,363	119,923	.5
Catechists[c]	na	1,399,907	na
Catholics per pastoral center[d]	8,803	4,464	−49
Catholics per parish	13,914	14,724	6
Catholics per priest	5,285	7,030	33
Catholics per diocesan priest	10,195	10,654	5

Source: Annuarium Statisticum Ecclesiae for indicated years.

Notes: a. An ecclesiastical territory is a diocese or units like a diocese, such as a vicariate apostolic, or a prelature, consisting of parishes organized under a bishop or a prelate serving in a role similar to a diocesan bishop.

b. Pastoral centers include parishes and other regular worship sites such as mission stations, chapels, and so on.

c. Permanent deacons and catechists are new categories in Catholic ministry that developed as a result of the Second Vatican Council (1963–1965) and were not reported in 1970. Numbers at that time, where they did exist, would have been negligible.

d. These figures mask massive variations across countries, between rural and urban areas, wealthy and poor areas, and so on.

European sources. Ani Pedro Oro and Pablo Semán state that a central aspect of "the change effected in the religious field by Pentecostalism is its breach in the hegemony, and more important, the representation of the hegemony, historically attributed to the Catholic Church" (Oro and Semán 2000: 621). For Philip Berryman (1995: 109) all this is a sign that "becoming Protestant no longer takes one beyond the pale of family and social relationships as it once did. We are witnessing something of a coming of age of Latin American Protestantism." The bottom line is that Protestantism has become a substantial presence in many societies, such that pluralism and innovation are now the new normal of the religious field in the region.

Considerable variation between and within countries in Latin America suggests that general statistics and regional averages need to be viewed with some caution. To go beyond overall figures, Tables 3.3, 3.4, and 3.5 provide data for six countries (Argentina, Brazil, Chile, Guatemala, Mexico, and Peru) that together represent much of the variation of the region as a whole. The tables are presented separately for reasons of space. Mexico and Brazil are among the largest Catholic countries in the region (and the world). Guatemala and Chile show some of the highest rates of Protestant growth in the region, while Argentina and Peru have both witnessed expansion and diversification within the Protestant community. The numbers for these countries confirm regional trends with a few twists worth noting. Everywhere, the growth of Catholics lags slightly behind population, except for Chile, where Catholics grew at half the rate of the general population between 1970 and 2009. In all cases, the expansion of non-Catholic Christians and of the "doubly affiliated" far outstrips that of Catholics. The most spectacular rates of growth for these categories are in Guatemala (1,088 percent for non-Catholic Christians and 2,933 percent for doubly affiliated). In Argentina, where the surge of Protestant growth is more recent, the number of non-Catholic Christians still expanded by almost ten times that of Catholics in the same period.

The data from these countries affirm that the Catholic Church has worked effectively to prepare itself for the future, above all by expanding its installed capacity. Numbers of ecclesiastical territories grew steadily between 1970 and 2009, led by a 45 percent increase in Mexico. Most members come into contact with the church in smaller settings like parishes and pastoral centers, where there has been a substantial expansion over these years (pastoral centers increased 469 percent in Brazil, and 152 percent in Argentina). In terms of personnel, the decline in women religious is notable across the board, and although overall numbers of priests continue to lag population growth, figures for seminarians and ordinations to the diocesan priesthood outstrip population growth in most cases, rising by 900 percent in Brazil, 600 percent in Guatemala, and 577 percent in Peru.

Organizations and Innovations

The preceding discussion affirms that Latin America has moved away from religious monopoly toward a situation of pluralism and growing diversity. This is part of a global pattern of change for all Christian

Table 3.3 Church Growth and Installed Capacity in Argentina and Brazil, 1970 and 2009

	1970	2009	Change (%)
		Argentina	
Population (WCD)	23,961,810	40,738,000	70
Catholics	22,431,530	36,311,000	62
Non-Catholic Christians (WCD)	1,104,906	6,066,300	449
Doubly affiliated (WCD)	1,006,436	1,654,786	63
Ecclesiastical territories	55	73	33
Pastoral centers	3,812	9,598	152
Parishes	1,830	2,729	49
Priests	5,439	5,871	8
Diocesan priests only	2,630	3,956	50
Diocesan priest ordinations	26	95	265
Women religious (sisters)	12,823	8,206	−36
Catholics per pastoral center	5,559	3,876	−30
Catholics per parish	11,580	13,632	18
Catholics per priest	3,896	6,337	63
Catholics per diocesan priest	8,057	9,404	17
		Brazil	
Population (WCD)	96,020,772	198,982,000	107
Catholics	81,815,000	163,900,000	100
Non-Catholic Christians (WCD)	12,734,867	55,460,000	335
Doubly affiliated (WCD)	6,347,000	29,145,067	359
Ecclesiastical territories	199	273	37
Pastoral centers	8,396	47,805	469
Parishes	5,408	10,210	89
Priests	12,472	19,999	60
Diocesan priests only	5,021	12,385	147
Diocesan priest ordinations	55	551	902
Women religious (sisters)	36,786	31,594	−14
Catholics per pastoral center	9,745	3,429	−65
Catholics per parish	15,129	16,053	6
Catholics per priest	6,560	8,195	25
Catholics per diocesan priest	16,295	13,234	−19

Source: Annuarium Statisticum Ecclesiae for indicated years, except where the source is specifically noted as WCD, the World Christian Database.

Table 3.4 Church Growth and Installed Capacity in Chile and Guatemala, 1970 and 2009

	1970	2009	Change (%)
	Chile		
Population (WCD)	9,496,003	17,134,000	80
Catholics	8,835,000	12,532,000	42
Non-Catholic Christians (WCD)	1,677,933	5,603,000	234
Doubly affiliated (WCD)	1,126,891	3,245,201	188
Ecclesiastical territories	24	27	13
Pastoral centers	1,690	4,115	143
Parishes	824	947	15
Priests	2,309	2,327	1
Diocesan priests only	981	1,197	22
Diocesan priest ordinations	11	22	100
Women religious (sisters)	5,838	4,529	−22
Catholics per pastoral center	9,746	3,045	−69
Catholics per parish	4,752	13,233	178
Catholics per priest	3,478	5,385	55
Catholics per diocesan priest	8,187	10,470	28
	Guatemala		
Population (WCD)	5,243,415	14,377,000	174
Catholics	4,109,000	11,376,000	177
Non-Catholic Christians (WCD)	381,645	4,532,400	1,088
Doubly affiliated (WCD)	94,870	2,877,781	2,933
Ecclesiastical territories	13	15	15
Pastoral centers	354	804	127
Parishes	302	471	56
Priests	608	1,058	74
Diocesan priests only	185	600	224
Diocesan priest ordinations	3	21	600
Women religious (sisters)	792	2,730	245
Catholics per pastoral center	11,607	14,149	22
Catholics per parish	13,606	24,153	78
Catholics per priest	6,758	10,752	59
Catholics per diocesan priest	22,211	18,960	−15

Source: Annuarium Statisticum Ecclesiae for indicated years, except where the source is specifically noted as WCD, the World Christian Database.

Table 3.5 Church Growth and Installed Capacity in Mexico and Peru, 1970 and 2009

	1970	2009	Change (%)
		Mexico	
Population (WCD)	50,596,201	110,293,000	118
Catholics	46,007,000	98,831,000	115
Non-Catholic Christians (WCD)	2,146,101	10,977,000	411
Doubly affiliated (WCD)	1,424,321	3,351,526	135
Ecclesiastical territories	64	93	45
Pastoral centers	3,455	12,703	268
Parishes	2,888	6,572	128
Priests	8,707	15,985	84
Diocesan priests only	6,282	12,105	93
Diocesan priest ordinations	170	370	118
Women religious (sisters)	22,859	27,913	22
Catholics per pastoral center	13,316	7,780	−42
Catholics per parish	15,930	15,038	-6
Catholics per priest	5,284	6,183	17
Catholics per diocesan priest	7,324	8,164	11
		Peru	
Population (WCD)	13,192,672	28,894,000	119
Catholics	12,839,000	25,635,000	100
Non-Catholic Christians (WCD)	380,913	4,308,500	1,031
Doubly affiliated (WCD)	136,215	2,586,764	1,799
Ecclesiastical territories	41	45	10
Pastoral centers	1,481	6,006	306
Parishes	866	1,533	77
Priests	2,264	3,111	37
Diocesan priests only	859	1,827	113
Diocesan priest ordinations	13	88	577
Women religious (sisters)	4,429	5,884	33
Catholics per pastoral center	8,669	4,268	−51
Catholics per parish	14,826	16,722	13
Catholics per priest	5,671	8,240	45
Catholics per diocesan priest	14,946	14,031	−6

Source: Annuarium Statisticum Ecclesiae for indicated years, except where the source is specifically noted as WCD, the World Christian Database.

churches, whose most salient feature is a transition from monopoly to diversity, Christendom to pluralism, with a corresponding loosening of organizational and institutional ties, and a burst of creative innovation that has made its presence felt in religious life (Froehle and Gautier 2003; Noll 2009). Because Catholicism was a lazy monopoly, with significant organizational and resource gaps, the coming of pluralism can make all religions more vital. Noll writes that

> historically, Eastern Orthodoxy, Catholicism, and the major European Protestant denominations had differed substantially among themselves, but almost all assumed that Christianity required Christendom—which meant taking for granted formal cooperation between church and state, as well as a permanent place for the churches in the formal legal life of a society. It also meant that great weight was given to historical precedent—how things should be done depended as much on previous patterns as upon assessments of current opportunities. . . . The new [American] pattern did not abandon the Christendom model entirely but it nonetheless embodied a much more informal Christianity and pushed consistently for ever more flexible institutions and ever newer innovations in responding to spiritual challenges. (Noll 2009: 112)

The most notable organizational changes that affect the character of the religious field are the emergence (out of Protestantism) of models of church organization that are new to the region, the creation of megachurches (most of them Pentecostal or neo-Pentecostal), the consolidation of national organizations and national and regional federations, and the transformation of transnational ties and connections. One of the advantages of a new beginning is that innovators are not tied down by buildings to maintain, services to keep up, and a preexisting pattern of authority to maintain. The complex organizational structure of the Catholic Church, with its heavy sunk costs in established institutions, makes adaptation to changing conditions slow and difficult.[10] In contrast, from the outset Protestant and particularly Pentecostal and neo-Pentecostal churches have been notably entrepreneurial in Latin America (as they have in Africa) in their use of mass media and how they adapt their structure, message, and music to appeal to particular segments of the population. Those with more resources, including some Pentecostal megachurches, engage in careful market research before deciding where to build new churches. They mark out and hold territories and build from there. Territories may be based on the location of buildings, but they can also designate regular places for preaching (a specific corner or square) and the creation of a broad media presence (Algranti 2010; Chesnut 1997, 2003; Freston 2001; Fonseca 2008; Smilde 1999, 2004b, 2007; Stoll 1990, 1993).

Like the Catholic Church, Protestant and Pentecostal churches have also significantly expanded and strengthened their national and region-wide organizations. Beginning in the late 1960s and with growing force ever since, dependence on foreign (mostly North American and North Atlantic) ties has weakened as new churches have been founded and homegrown leadership has emerged (Algranti 2010; Chesnut 1997, 2003; López 1998, 2004, 2008b). National confederations have been created, often with competing organizations for Pentecostal and main-line Protestant churches. The effort to build regionwide Protestant organizations dates to the late 1970s, with the foundation of the Latin American Council of Churches (CLAI, Consejo Latinoamericano de Iglesias) in 1978. An alternative regional organization, the Latin American Evangelical Fellowship (CONELA, Confraternidad Latinoameri-cana Evangélica), was established around the same time, by evangelical and Pentecostal leaders concerned about CLAI's ideological and finan-cial links with the World Council of Churches and its progressive agenda. The foundation of CLAI was also followed about a decade later by the creation of a Latin American Evangelical Pentecostal Commis-sion (CEPLA, Comisión Evangélica Pentecostal Latinoamericana). All these groups sponsor regional meetings, put out publications, develop a staff that can provide resources and services, and promote interchange and cooperation among members.

For its part, the Catholic Church has also worked hard to keep up with the growth and change (e.g., more urbanization) of the population, creating more points of contact with the faithful—more dioceses, parishes, educational and charitable institutions, and clergy. The efforts of this "installed capacity" have been reinforced by a notable strength-ening of national and regional organizations. National bishops' confer-ences have acquired professional staff; specialized commissions (for example, on land, housing, or education) have assumed important roles in promoting groups and lobbying for particular positions; national fed-erations of religious congregations have greater presence; and region-wide organizations like the Council of Latin American Bishops (CELAM, Consejo Episcopal Latinoamericana) or the Confederation of Latin American Religious Orders (CLAR, Confederación Latinoameri-cana de Religiosos) have assumed important roles in setting agendas, monitoring developments, collecting statistics, providing information, sponsoring conferences, supporting publications, and serving as arenas in which an agenda can be debated and established for the church in the entire region.

Together with demographic changes reviewed earlier, the pattern of organizational innovation suggests that, along with much of what used to be called the Third World, Latin America has moved from being primarily a receiver and consumer of global influences to the status of producer and exporter, with notable influence in ideas and in the export of new churches with Latin American roots to other parts of the world, including Africa and the United States (Garrard-Burnett 2007; González and González 2008; Jenkins 2002, 2006; Noll 2009).

Ideas

In Chapter 2, I pointed to a series of ideas that have been central to the evolution of religious and political discourse over the past half century in Latin America. These ideas are best seen not as successors but rather as competitors in a never-ending struggle to set the agenda and claim the moral authority of religion in public life. The rise and eclipse of issues have roots both in changes within the churches (the constant creation of new ideas, the incorporation of new groups who may bring their experiences into the church, the arrival of new leadership generations with different experiences and orientations) and in the changing engagement of religion with society and politics. Limitations of space preclude a detailed analysis here of all the ideas that are and have been on the table in the churches. Here I want to center attention on two: for Protestants, the emergence of new perspectives on "the church in the world" and what they mean for social and political involvement; for Catholics, the emergence of liberation theology and its relation to progressive Catholicism of the 1960s, and to the view of the world manifested in 2007 at the bishops' meeting in Aparecida.

Growing numbers, diversity, and institutional strength have brought an important group of new ideas and practices front and center in the Protestant community. I have already mentioned the surge of Pentecostalism and charismatic practices and the increased openness to political action as a proper and often necessary expression of faith. The next chapter, on religion and democracy, shows that this also entails new willingness to cooperate across denominational and ideological lines, even with Marxist groups. These changes together make for a new engagement with the world and specifically with politics. Oro and

Semán (2000: 616) write that "by transposing holiness—the distinction between the world and divine affiliation—into a sort of guarantee of protection and success, neo Pentecostals make inroads into various societies." They go on to affirm that "in the counterpoint between the world and the sacred, Pentecostalism intervenes in the religious and cultural fields bringing traditions together. Pentecostalism creates a specific cultural atmosphere with its own values and sensibilities as a consequence of its own ability to elaborate original synthesis attuned to diverse audiences. With its innovative practices and adaptation of modern means of organization and communication, Pentecostalism generates a religious and cultural project that creates its own demands and proves capable of disarticulating existing constituencies deemed as captive" (Oro and Semán 2000: 623).

Harvey Cox states that "Pentecostals preach less about an imminent return of Jesus and more about how to live in a fallen world, and sometimes make it a better place" (Cox 2009: 207). In his study of Pentecostal megachurches in Argentina, Joaquín Algranti affirms that attention to the power of the Spirit in the world (and on finding means to cope with suffering) carries with it a search for new ways that the churches can support and empower attempts to deal with suffering and its causes. He details the varied political strategies and connections that the churches enter into in pursuit of their goals. "This has to do with a specific trait of the neo Pentecostal ethos, which, recovered within a context of crisis, works to strengthen sense of belonging in the face of a society that most often appears as excluding and overbearing" (Algranti 2010: 219). The point to underscore here is the growing presence within all branches of the Protestant community of a broad view of the mission of the church that now grants legitimacy to the idea of social and explicitly political action. Not all these initiatives are well thought out or successful nor are they necessarily heralds of some kind of broad Protestant front in politics. The very pluralism of Protestantism works against this (Freston 2001, 2008; Steigenga 2001). But they do indicate a maturing of the community and of actors within it, and a resulting willingness to take stands, create organizations, and when necessary, lobby and mobilize vigorously to see them to fruition.

Progressive Catholicism and liberation theology raise similar questions about what faith requires and how best to achieve it but look to very different solutions. Liberation theology is often depicted as the inevitable successor and replacement for earlier variants of progressive Catholicism. But it is more accurate to see liberation theology less as a successor or replacement than as a competitor, a profoundly radical effort to understand what religion is all about and to find ways of acting that would be true to that new sense of mission. Elements of a distinctly progressive position emerge and consolidate in Latin American Catholicism in the decade or so after World War II. Central to this overall stance was a simultaneous commitment to reform and modernization of the church and to progress and "development" in society and politics. The emergence of progressive Catholicism was tied closely to efforts by some church leaders to disengage the institution from traditional alliances with state and social elites. The progressive position arose often in close concert with Christian Democratic parties and movements, which themselves had evolved out of earlier national and international Catholic youth movements. Disengagement meant erosion or breaking of traditional alliances with Conservative political parties; development of new positions in areas like agrarian reform, housing, and popular education; and efforts to implement them through public policy and mobilization of social movements.

Progressive Catholicism arose in a time of relative political openness and defined itself in terms of reform and progress, with great faith that civilian democratic politics (parties and elections, and Christian Democratic parties in particular) offered a viable path for achieving change. Liberation theology came on the scene later, in very different and much less hopeful circumstances. The generation of writers who created liberation theology had lost faith in ordinary politics and in the promise of reform. They looked for more thoroughgoing change in society and politics, and not incidentally, in religion itself. The differences between these two positions were put into recognizable packages by contrasting attitudes to the church itself. Progressive Catholics looked to church leaders and church doctrine for guidance; liberationists included the church in their criticisms. They remained within the church and with rare exceptions resisted efforts to marginalize and exclude them, but from the outset made democratization of the church itself a major element in their program.[11] Michael Lowy summarizes the contrast as follows:

> This is precisely where the difference between liberation theology and the European progressive theologies lies . . . the latter consider exclusion (of the poor and of Third World countries) as temporary or accidental. The future belongs to the West and to the economic, social, and political progress it brings. Liberation theology, by contrast, conceives of history from the reverse view point, that of the defeated and excluded, the poor (in the broad sense, including oppressed classes, races and cultures) who are the bearers of universality and redemption. (Lowy 1996: 65)

If we turn from progressive Catholicism and liberation theology to Aparecida, the change in optic can be startling. Like Santo Domingo, Aparecida was focused on defending and strengthening the Catholic faith of the region, which was described as a fundamental component of the identity, originality, and unity of Latin America and the Caribbean and among its greatest riches. The central theme of Aparecida was the identity of the church and faithful as *missionary disciples*, striving to bring the good news of the Gospel joyfully and with hope but also in a way that resonates with the realities of daily life in the region. How these realities are understood reveals a lot about the positions taken by the church and its leaders. In their own ways, both progressive Catholicism and liberation theology are optimistic about the long-term possibilities of change, even as they disagree about what has to be done to get there. Was Aparecida similarly hopeful? Did the bishops see Latin America in optimistic terms, as open to change? Did they see the present as a *Kairos*, a moment of grace in which commitments and solidarities could be reaffirmed? Or is this instead a defensive moment, concerned with preserving, protecting, and reinforcing what exists?[12]

The debates and final documents of Aparecida depict a Latin America filled with threats and perils (Levine 2008). Inroads from a globalizing culture undermine Catholic ideas of a proper moral sphere, deny the church its primary role in ordering that moral sphere, and lead to the dissolution of a worldview united around the Catholic faith and guided by its official leaders.[13] Concern over the decay of traditional gender roles is prominent. These are compounded by the threat of competition by other churches and the peril posed by indifference, apathy, and a tendency of many to see themselves as disengaged from church supervision and discipline. All these dangers are reinforced by accelerated social dissolution manifest in poverty, violence, and drugs. Given the power of globalizing cultural trends, the dilemma for an established institution like the Catholic Church is either to adapt and participate in change, bringing its own enthusiasm and transformative message to the process (a position identified in broad terms with much of the legacy of Vatican II or Medellín) or to resist and rebuild with discipline and common purpose. All in all, Aparecida takes the second position.

The prevalence of fear and a sense of retrenchment at Aparecida stand in sharp contrast to the dogged optimism of both progressive Catholicism and liberation theology. Why was fear so prominent at Aparecida, and what does this suggest for the future role of the Catholic Church in society and politics? The demographic trends discussed earlier confirm the loss of Catholic monopoly and the coming pluralism, but why should these produce such overwhelming fear? Pluralism and competition do not necessarily mean decay and loss; they can also stimulate growth and innovation (Levine 2009b). After an exhaustive review of global statistics for Catholicism, Froehle and Gautier conclude that in most of the world,

> for the foreseeable future, the Church is more likely to be a significant minority than a highly concentrated presence. Available church statistics over the twentieth century suggest that the Church may be the most effective in this situation. In countries where the Church has long existed side by side with evangelical Protestants in an open, pluralist setting, Catholics have developed particularly strong forms of parish life, commitment to practice and participation and a sense of stewardship and relatively high church giving. In other words, the Church has learned from the strengths characteristic of these other traditions. (Froehle and Gautier 2003: 132)

In the same vein, Cleary (2011) affirms how much competition and pluralism spurred the innovations that have made the Catholic Charismatic movement into such a visible presence in the Latin American church.

The fear that is so prominent at Aparecida is not really about changing numbers, but rather about loss of control. This fear is partly compounded by an older tradition that error has no place alongside truth, but more is at issue. The underlying concern is that faith is shallow and is likely to lose in competition with others unless it is buttressed by state support and extensive clerical advice, supervision, and control of the faithful. The current generation of Catholic bishops (most of whom were appointed by the late Pope John Paul II) remains wedded to models in which state support is expected and guaranteed. Froehle and Gautier point out that

> these experiences poorly prepare European Catholicism [and the Catholic Church remains controlled by Europeans even if most of its members are found elsewhere] to understand religious pluralism. A "secular state" in European experience, after all, typically meant an atheist state that has secularized Church property and eliminated the Church's voice in civil society. Conversely, a state that respects religion has often translated as a state that controls religion through restrictive legislation, tax policy, or patronage and financial largesse. Whether a carrot or stick approach, the concept of religion as a fully respected part of civil society outside state influence is not part of the European tradition. . . . In an increasingly globalized and pluralistic world, Catholics may find that these long established European traditions are more the exception than the rule. (Froehle and Gautier 2003: 133)

Catholicism may remain first among equals in Latin America, but in this view of the world, loss of monopoly means loss in general.

Explanations of Change

The preceding discussion paints a portrait of far-reaching and long-lasting transformations in Catholicism and Protestantism, changes marked by elements that Latin America shares with much of the world. How to account for these tectonic shifts? Some have argued that what looks like profound change is little more than relabeling, a reorganization of corporate and hierarchical relations under new names. Jean Pierre Bastián asserts that although Protestant movements in the nineteenth century had close connections with radical political liberalism, the current waves of growth "derive from the culture of popular, corporatist, and authoritarian Catholicism. Whereas nineteenth century Protestant movements represented a religion of the written word, of civil and rational education, the current Protestant movements constitute an oral religion that is unlettered and leveling. Whereas the former were vehicles for practices that inculcated democratic liberal values, the latter are vehicles for caudillo style models of religious and social control" (Bastián 1993: 53). There are difficulties with this analysis. Bastián identifies all of contemporary Latin American Protestantism with the experience of some megachurches where congregational life is weak and strong leadership is very much present. But Protestantism in Latin America is too diverse for all churches to fit comfortably under one label, and there is too much dynamism and creativity for assumptions of continuity to be of much help.

The value of Bastián's analysis is further undermined by a static and essentialist view of culture. If we were to accept his view, only those Protestant churches with continuing strong ties to immigrant communities (like the nineteenth-century movements to which he refers) could bring change to an entrenched culture. Bastián's apparent belief that the persistence of cultural traits is normal means that change from within is highly unlikely. What was perhaps at other times and places a source of dynamic and liberating forms of social engagement now runs up against "the deeply rooted mental constructs of Latin American societies" (Bastián 1993: 36). This view is provocative but reifies culture and treats Latin American cultures as if they are always and necessarily the same when, of course, cultures are made by humans and they necessarily change as circumstances and conditions evolve (Levine

1992, 1993a, 1995a, 2003). Bastián (1993: 45) also appears to be puzzled by the phenomenon of frequent church switching, which he takes as a sign of shallow belief and commitment. But this could just as well be seen as a reflection of the intense mobility and change of contemporary Latin American societies, and is in fact common in other parts of the world, like the United States (Putnam and Campbell 2010).

Another set of explanations attributes religious transformation, including affiliation with new or different churches, to anomie or "loss of culture." Deiros (1991: 155) argues that the transition out of rural society (presumably integrated and harmonious) to the heterogeneous and unfamiliar world of city and factory life produces a cultural and social collapse that leaves migrants open to new churches and their messages.[14] This account of change is highly problematic. The author relies on discredited notions that oppose rural harmony to urban disorganization. But rural communities have never been as harmonious as their mythology depicts them, and migrants are drawn not primarily from the disoriented, but rather from the best qualified and most aspirant of their communities. Contemporary research on migration has also exploded the notion that moves to the city involve isolation and the loss of social integration. Individuals rarely arrive in the city without some prior experience of towns and smaller cities, and most come with some contact or connection that gives them a start: the name of a relative, a church, or a regional association. Research on rural life, migrants, and migration shows that migrants actively work to create new lives for themselves and their families. City life is shot through with family and associational connections, and there is a continuing moral discourse in poor communities: religious innovation is just one of many kinds of innovation at issue. Anomie is an inappropriate description of the process or its outcome (Perlman 1976; De Gregori, Blondet, and Lynch 1986; on this point in Islamic societies, Eickelman and Piscatori 2004).

Theories that attribute transformation in religion to disorientation and a search for solace in the face of troubling changes suffer from static assumptions and an unfortunate, patronizing tone. They assume that churches and their clienteles are passive objects of anonymous social forces. But these are active subjects, and the historical record shows considerable self-moved change at all levels. Churches have been transformed in structure and message, and those coming to religious institutions have changed as well. The patronizing tone is present in the assumption that a turn to religion is sparked above all by the search for solace or escape. This view is based on the same assumptions that for so long dismissed religious belief as epiphenomenal, presumably doomed to privatization and disappearance. The argument is that lacking scientific or rational insight into their problems, ordinary men and women flee crisis by escaping to religion. But if we set the expressed consciousness of converts against what we know about their background and overall social condition, what emerges is not so much escape as mobility through a search for self-fulfillment. Manuel Marzal's account (1988: 386) of the reasons given for conversion to new churches in Lima is suggestive: first is a general sense of change in life, followed (in order) by access to biblical truth, the desire to find Christ, and the experience of healing and health. Chesnut (1997) locates the appeal of Pentecostals in the positive solutions they offer to "pathogens of poverty" such as poor health, alcoholism, domestic discord, and unemployment. These solutions include extensive outreach and follow-up to help new believers reorganize their lives and social relations. In his work on new churches in urban Venezuela, David Smilde (2007) demonstrates that conversion is something of a forward contract between believers and God. Believers offer faith and commitment, while God (through the church) offers reinforcement in new ways of living. On reflection, converts to Pentecostal churches have much in common with members of liberationist groups like base communities. The target population and much of the social process (small intense groups, egalitarian social relations, salience of the Bible) are similar (Levine 1992, 1995a). As Cleary notes for Guatemala, "In effect, Pentecostalism and reform Catholicism offer bridges for the socio economic and political changes taking place in the country. Both offer symbolic systems by which to live a life adapted to changed conditions" (Cleary 1992: 185). The difference lies in the greater cultural and organizational autonomy the new churches provide.

It is common to hear Catholic prelates in the region argue that conversion to Protestant or Pentecostal churches carries with it a "loss of cultural identity." As we have seen, this was a major theme at the regional meetings of Catholic bishops at Santo Domingo in 1992 (with explicit concern about "the invasion of the sects") and was reinforced and extended by worries about negative globalizing influences at Aparecida in 2007. In this view, the identity of Latin America is so closely bound up with being Catholic that conversion to other churches must mean cultural abandonment. To be sure, five hundred years of Catholic presence counts for something, but cultures do not persist automatically. They are put together by real people in particular historical circumstances; they are made and remade all the time by human agents. The notion that conversion means loss of culture rests on a problematic view of culture as something fully formed and passed down intact from the past. But exclusive stress on cultural continuities washes out critical dimensions of conflict and power, ignores variation, and obscures sources of change. As social, economic, and political configurations change, it stands to reason that cultural formations will also evolve. The issue is best understood not as acculturation or loss of culture, but rather as cultural change. The new element in the equation is the extent to which initiatives of change are being promoted by hitherto marginal and powerless groups. Swanson records a telling exchange between Ecuador's late archbishop Leonidas Proaño and a group of indigenous evangelical leaders. The bishop was a well-known advocate of liberation, an ally of indigenous groups, and a champion of their rights. But he regarded conversion as defection and worried openly that converts were abandoning their culture.

> A brother said, well Mr. Bishop Proaño, would you like to see us back in the condition our parents were in before us? Their poor feet scarred and a little hat sewed over old ones? Do you want to see us like that? Why don't you want to see us now as transformed people? Or don't we have the right to dress with dignity? So he said, "Well, yes, but you have changed your culture." So I said to him, "We speak Quichua. Here is my wife, she has not lost her language, the dress that we wear, the bayeta, the anauco." I explained all this to him. "We'll talk more about this later" he said, but we never had another meeting. (Swanson 1994: 94)

Politics and the Transformation of Religion

Transformations of religion are not well understood in isolation from social and political change in general. Politics and connections to the political play a central role in opening (or closing) opportunities and shaping the direction of change. The relation is one of continuous borrowing and mutual influence. This point needs to be stressed in light of some views that argue that religious innovation represents a sharp break in the "sacred canopy" of culture and power. David Martin, for example, draws a sharp distinction between culture and politics and asserts that religious innovation in Latin America originates and draws its power "solely at the level of culture" (Martin 1990: 44). In his view, locating change at the level of culture means breaking old connections with power and making possible the assertion of a different, and presumably more autonomous, pattern of group life. This thesis relies on parallels to Anglo-American experiences with the decay of religious monopolies, and on a view of preexisting Latin American patterns according to which cultural change is impossible without total cracking of the system (Martin 1990: 280). "Once we take into account the coiled up resistance of the social mechanisms in Latin American society to any moral initiatives," he writes, "it is not surprising that Pentecostals erect a dualistic wall between the safe enclosure of faith and the dangerous wilderness of the world" (Martin 1990: 266).

Apart from the dubious notion that Latin American societies resist moral initiatives (which ones? when?), and setting aside ambiguities about cultural change (does everything have to change for anything to be different?), the meaning of culture and power, and problems with historical parallels, for present purposes it suffices to acknowledge that Martin raises a critical issue. If conversion to Pentecostal Protestantism means denial and withdrawal from a historical order of things where culture and power are closely intertwined, can such conversion be understood as the effort to enter a nonpolitical world? The evolution of Pentecostal views about engagement with the world, reviewed earlier in this chapter, undermines the validity of any assertion that conversion entails a nonpolitical or a political stance. It is important to respond to the view that religions that center attention on the "otherworldly" have little to say about "this world," and little impact on day-to-day behavior. This is at best simplistic, at worst a major distortion of the truth. The transformative power of ideas and experiences that at first glance may appear to be "otherworldly" is evident throughout history and across a wide range of societies and religious traditions. As with the Protestants who so occupied Max Weber's attention, the groups before us here are very much in this world, with a spirituality and a pattern of organization and everyday life that engage society and politics in ever evolving ways. Stephen Warner puts the point sharply:

> The special potency of religious institutions comes from answers they give to a group's need for faith in the justice of their cause, and the inevitability of triumph. Such faith depends on the conviction, mis-leadingly called "other-worldliness" of the existence of a religious reality. If one assumes a sacred/secular dichotomy, supernatural beliefs can seem at best irrelevant to this-worldly action, antagonistic at worst. In this view, shared by many social scientists and some libera-tion theologians, the most progressive religions must be the most demythologized; thus, for their own good, oppressed groups must slough off their superstitions. But on the model of the African-American experience, where sacred and secular are inextricable, the

new paradigm expects otherwise. To insist that rebels be iconoclasts is to deprive them of one source of their courage. (Warner 1993: 1069–1070)

A further question concerns collective action vs. individual transformation. Liberationist views may privilege collective action, while their Protestant counterparts stress changing individuals and distinguish public from private in ways that can discourage efforts to form broad transformative political alliances. But this does not make the one any more or less "political" than the other. Anyway, who is to say that only efforts that begin by targeting structures of power can make for change? Why not consider the possibility of change emerging over time as a multiplier of the creation of greater numbers of effective, autonomous groups scattered throughout the social order? Each affects politics not only through actions that challenge the social and political order in direct and explicit ways, but also as a result of broad efforts to transform cultural expectations, create new social spaces, and build up new forms of community (Levine and Stoll 1997). As David Stoll (1990: 317) puts it, liberation theology

> is the salutary contrast we are supposed to draw because it seems to express the interests of the poor so clearly. Yet there are reasons to be wary, among them the capacity of politicized religion for losing touch with the people it claims to represent . . . partisans of liberation theology assume that churches can thrive only by fighting for broad social reform. Yet Pentecostal churches have reached mammoth proportions without supporting such causes. Their success in improving the situation of many members suggests that no relation exists between the perspicacity of their social analysis and their survival value to the poor.

Religious innovation and transformations affect society and politics, bringing new groups and projecting new values into public life. In the same way, social and political change affects religion by creating new skills and expectations in the population, opening or closing opportunities for voice and action. The gradual consolidation of democracy and the lowering of barriers to collective organization have made access to the public sphere easier for all groups, while diffusing new ideas about equality and accountability. The discussion in this and the preceding chapters underscores the extent to which any effort to grasp the character and dynamics of the religious field in Latin America today must begin by acknowledging the multiple, permanent, and continuing ties that bind what ordinary speech separates as "politics," "religion," and "society." We can separate them for analytical purposes and recognize that each has its own history, traditions, and sources of change. But having done that, we must also pay attention to how they come together and influence one another in thought and action.

Notes

1. There are also small Orthodox Christian communities as well as small non-Christian communities, including Jews, Muslims, and Buddhists. Syncretic devotions like the Santa Muerte in Mexico can attract large numbers of followers (Levine 2009a; Chesnut 2011).

2. Mark Noll (2009) insists that this portrait is incomplete and argues that Pentecostal movements around the world are not so much American outposts as groups equally inspired by the Bible. See also Jenkins 2002.

3. The Pew Foundation Ten Country Survey of Pentecostals distinguishes between charismatics, who practice gifts of the Holy Spirit but may not belong to classical Pentecostal denominations (thus including Catholic Charismatics), and Pentecostals, for whom speaking in tongues is "necessary evidence of baptism in the Holy Spirit." Pew uses "Renewalist" as an umbrella term for both (Pew Forum on Religion and Public Life 2006: 11, 12). There are substantial variations across regions, with speaking in tongues, for example, much less frequent in Africa than in Latin America (Gifford 2004, 2008).

4. The term *neo-Pentecostal* is one that scholars apply to work out distinctions among churches—it is not used by believers themselves.

5. A 2006 study found that 62 percent of Catholics in Guatemala and 57 percent of urban Catholics in Brazil identify with Pentecostal and charismatic practices (Pew Forum on Religion and Public Life 2006).

6. The sharpest growth for Catholics, as for all Christians, has been in sub-Saharan Africa, while Europe has declined and the church in North America has more or less held its own (Barrett, Kurian, and Johnson 2001; Froehle 2010a, 2010b; Jenkins 2002; Johnson and Ross 2010).

7. The proportion of the population declaring itself Catholic in the Brazilian census has dropped from 95.2 percent in 1940 to below 70 percent in 2010.

8. The category of non-Catholic Christian includes a wide range of denominations (Orthodox, Anglican, Mormon, Jehovah's Witnesses, and mainline and Pentecostal Protestants). It provides a useful baseline on the relative growth rate of Catholics and of alternatives to Catholicism.

9. I prefer this measure to Frances Hagopian's calculation of the "institutional reach" of the church. Her analysis is directed at the church's capacity to mobilize civil society, which is not at issue here (Hagopian 2009). I do not include measures for charitable or educational institutions, because variation in the growth and maintenance of these organizations depends heavily on public subsidies and is therefore not a reliable guide to the capacity of the institutional church.

10. Cf. Berryman, who states that "a pastor of a parish is a branch manager who can be transferred at the stroke of a bishop's pen. Even if a priest were to

devise new 'product,' its success would depend on its acceptability to the head office, not its appeal to buyers in the local market" (Berryman 1995b: 30).

11. This has led to censure of some leading theologians like Leonardo Boff and Jon Sobrino.

12. The concept of *Kairos* denotes an opportune moment, a historical crisis that is also an opportunity for change, an appointed time in which a document can resonate. In South Africa, the 1985 *Kairos* document identified just such a moment and called for the churches to be present in the struggles that brought an end to apartheid.

13. Like all such meetings, Aparecida was not monochromatic and discussions of threat, danger, and decay do not exhaust the agenda presented there. These concerns are accompanied by recognition of progress in politics (with democracy), education, ecological concerns, and recognition of the dignity and rights of excluded groups, especially indigenous communities and those of African descent. But the predominant note is fear and a resolve to strengthen the institution insofar as possible (Levine 2008; Pelton 2008).

14. "For those who migrated, the conditions of anomie produced the possibility of religious change. Uprooted from families and religious traditions, living in slums and at the mercy of criminals and sometimes governmental predators, the urban poor became a fertile seedbed for evangelical proselytization. The weakening of traditional social controls, the sense of confusion and helplessness, the anonymity of city life, the shock of new social values sometimes accompanying the adaptation to industrial work, the absence of familiar community loyalties, and of the encompassing paternalism still characteristic of rural employment, all these conditions favored the growth of an acute crisis of personal identity for the migrants. Under such conditions, the exchange of old religious values for new ones was (and remains) likely to occur" (Deiros 1991: 155).

4

Democracy, Pluralism, and Religion

Churches and religiously inspired groups played a critical role sheltering democracy and democratic ideals during repressive periods, supporting democratic movements, and brokering and nurturing transitions to democracy in Latin America. This is a central theme of the past fifty years and constitutes a core legacy for the future. In the twenty-first century, this engagement with democracy has been expressed in many forms of active participation in politics: lobbying governments on issues of public policy, mobilizing opinion, organizing religiously linked political parties, and supporting religious candidates. These new realities are rooted in a combination of ideological change, theological reflection, and practical experience. Pluralism is the indispensable foundation, and the multiple experience of religion with pluralism has been magnified by new ideas in the churches that have enhanced the value of democracy as a way of organizing political life.

Religious pluralism and democratic politics are closely related in the recent experience of Latin America. They emerge more or less in the same time period and they arguably reinforce one another. The opening that came with the creation or restoration of democracy was accompanied everywhere by the emergence of a vibrant and competitive civil society with lowered costs of entry. The combination of political opening with a flourishing and less regulated civil society provided opportunities for groups to enter the public scene and create a visible presence. Many religious entrepreneurs took advantage of these possibilities to found new churches and to seek and win new audiences. Democratic politics and civil openness also brought ideas about equality, activism, and participation into the churches, ideas carried forward by new strata of members and a generation of leaders with new social and political skills and a wider range of political orientation than was hitherto common in the churches (Chesnut 1997, 2003; Freston 2001, 2008; Fonseca 2008; López 2008a, 2008b; Catalina Romero 2009; Smilde 2007).

Democratic politics and religious pluralism both begin to flower in Latin America in the 1970s and 1980s, but of course there are precursors. The seeds for the surge of Protestant and Pentecostal growth can be traced back generations in many cases (Chesnut 1997; Steigenga and Cleary 2007; Kamsteeg 1998; Lalive d'Epinay 2009; Parker 1996) but the numbers really began to take off in the 1970s. This is when one began to see a proliferation of new churches, an expanded presence of such churches in public life and in the media, and the multiplication of groups and of new orientations to social and political action that have utterly transformed the religious map of Latin America from what it was fifty years ago. Emergent religious pluralism has reshaped the relation of the churches to democracy.

Several elements are at work here. The churches have generally accommodated to democracy as a good way to organize societies, and to equality and participation as valid social norms. The reconciliation of the churches—particularly the Catholic Church—with democracy is a project that began in the interwar period in Europe and was propelled by the struggle with fascism. World War II and its aftermath turned many in the Catholic Church—once drawn to integralist models—to a new appreciation of the virtues of democracy as a form of government, and of democratic politics and democratizing assumptions of equality and participation as good ways to organize society. These tendencies were reinforced and extended within Catholicism by the influence of Vatican II, Medellín, and Puebla. Although the accommodation to democracy remains an incomplete process, one that has sparked intense conflict within some churches (for example, Argentina; see Mallimaci 2005; Morello 2011a), it is worth underscoring the importance of the broad move to legitimate democracy. This is a social, cultural, ecclesial, and political shift of major proportions.

For its part, the emergence and consolidation of the Protestant community have been accompanied by a reevaluation of democratic politics and of the legitimacy and necessity of political participation by the faithful. Among Protestants in Latin America, politics was long depicted as a realm of violence, corruption, and contamination. Believers were enjoined to be dutiful citizens, and there was a general antileftism (tied to the association of communism with atheism), but active participation in politics was eschewed. Politics was for the impure and energies should be directed to saving souls and "growing the church." With the end of the global cold war, the restoration of democracy, and the advent of open, less regulated civil society, new positions found a hearing, and many Protestant and Pentecostal churches and leaders moved vigorously to enter the political game, complete with religious parties and religiously identified candidacies.

Religious pluralism also supports democracy in less explicitly political ways. By their multiple presence in society—in churches, schools, neighborhood groups, and social movements of all kinds—the churches help to create and nurture a diverse and active civil society. Nascent ideas about democracy within the churches have been reinforced in many cases by the practical experience of defending democracy—providing spaces (often literally safe rooms or buildings in which to meet), shelter, and protection to democratic initiatives during periods of dictatorship and brokering the return to democracy. None of this experience came cheaply, nor did it happen without mistakes or without conflict within churches or between churches and elements in the political order. This chapter examines this experience and sets it in the larger context of the engagement of religion and the churches with pluralism.

General Considerations on Democracy and Religion

The relation of religion with pluralism and democracy has inspired the most varied reflections and interpretations. Tocqueville found the United States of the 1840s to be exceptionally religious: filled with churches and religiously sponsored groups of all kinds. "Religion," he wrote, "which never intervenes in the government of American society, should therefore be considered the first of their political institutions, for although it did not give them the taste for liberty, it singularly facilitates their use thereof. . . . The religious atmosphere of the country was the first thing that struck me on arrival in the United States. The longer I stayed in the country, the more conscious I became of the important political consequences resulting from this novel situation" (Tocqueville 1967: 292, 295). The key element that made religion so different in the United States was its detachment from state power, which was in sharp contrast to the old regime in France, where close mutual support of throne and altar contributed to the power of anticlericalism in the revolution and to ongoing church-state conflicts and continuing powerful anticlerical tendencies enshrined in laws and institutions in modern

France.[1] In contrast, the new world offered a different kind of space for religion in public life, with the possibility of new connections among politics, religion, society, and culture.

I noted earlier how discussions of secularization often carry with them the unstated assumption that the decline of religion will strengthen democratization by restricting religion's role in the public sphere. This view is strongly disputed by Richard Neuhaus (1984) and Stephen Carter (1993, 2000) and put into context by José Casanova (1994, 2001), who insists that the point is not decline, but rather how to understand the continuing role of religion in multiple and secularized societies. Given the history of the United States, where religious pluralism and political democracy have long coexisted and supported one another, it is no surprise to find that much writing on the United States has taken quite a different tack. In general discussions and in work on specific movements, churches, and communities, many scholars (such as Warner 1988, 1993; Wuthnow 1988, 1992, 1999; Ammerman 1994a, 1996; Morris 1984; Harris 1999; and most recently Putnam and Campbell 2010) have pointed to multiple ways in which religious faith, participation, membership, and organization contribute to democracy by providing legitimating values, participating in the creation of a strong and diffuse civil society, and equipping citizens and members with multiple social skills that are put to use in sustaining civil society. The diversity and tolerance associated with religion in the United States particularly impressed Robert Putnam and David Campbell and are the specifically "American grace" that gives their book its title.

Most scholars who look at politics and religion in Latin America recognize that although the region is clearly part of "the West," it is a distinctive subset of Western tradition. What makes Latin America distinct is of course its Catholic heritage, and the characteristic form and content this has given to law, institutions, and public opinion. This is true, but as stated, it is too simplistic to be of much help because it works with a static image of what is a dynamic and often highly conflicted reality. Latin America remains overwhelmingly Christian, and the Catholic Church remains the largest and most prominent Christian tradition, but despite undoubted continuities with the past, no one would identify this *Christianity* and this *Catholicism* with those of half a century ago.[2]

One might argue that for religion to have a viable role in changing society, religion itself has to change, and one direction of such change is the incorporation of democratic ideas and practices. This would require acknowledgement of the autonomous value of social actors and of their participation. We have already seen tension over issues of autonomy and control expressed in the Catholic bishop's documents at Aparecida. There is continued suspicion of such developments among conservative Catholic bishops whose project has centered less on learning to live with pluralism than on marshaling resources for reevangelizing society, reconquering it in the name of the faith. The tension between greater democracy and autonomy on the one hand and control and supervision on the other constitutes a central thread of current debate within the Catholic Church about how to position the church in the public sphere.[3] It may be helpful to frame the issues by putting general discussions of politics and religion aside for a moment and beginning instead with the fact of democracy itself, and the impact that democratic politics can have on religion. In her study of religion and public space in Peru, Catalina Romero (2009) points to the emergence of something like a civil society within the church, manifest in a vigorous set of associations, groups, and forms of cultural expression. Developments like these bring ideas about equality and participation inside the church, invigorating and refreshing religious experience while contributing to the construction of civil society. Experiences of this kind and the groups that carry them all have links to the church, but to the distress of many prelates these links most often do not carry with them the assumptions of control and obedience built into traditional Catholic organizational nets.

Frances Hagopian (2009) has pushed the discussion forward in a recent book that advances several important ideas (along with much valuable empirical data) on the issues. In her view, the Catholic Church in Latin America today is caught between a desire to recapture lost hegemony over cultural norms and the fact that its ability to control organizations, mobilize people, and shape the sources of cultural formation (media, universities, and publishing) is contested and limited. She acknowledges that church leaders fear independent groups, and she recognizes that their reaction has been to close these privileged spaces of association, participation, expression, and opinion as part of a deliberate attempt to retake control of public space. Hagopian laments the results of this strategy. "Without a set of eyes and ears on the ground," she writes, it is "hard for church leaders to understand the anxieties and aspirations of their base; without priests and lay workers, it is hard for ordinary people to gain the support of the hierarchy in the struggles of their daily lives" (Hagopian 2009: 443).

But this is to assume that such groups ever were or now constitute "eyes and ears on the ground." Their very autonomy suggests otherwise. In a plural society, people have multiple ways in which to organize, acquire information, and seek support. The hierarchy (and the church in general) can no longer operate as if it were a privileged funnel for action. It is one among many. This conclusion is reinforced by a close reading of the data provided by contributors to Hagopian's work, including Catalina Romero along with Roberto Blancarte, Cristián Parker, Soledad Loaeza, and Patricia Rodriguez. These authors provide evidence from a range of cases demonstrating how religious identification works within a plural and secularizing society. There is continuing faith and Catholic identity, but they come in ways that erode the hierarchy's claims to direct groups and to stand as sole arbiter of social values. Blancarte (2009: 236) writes that

> a secularized Catholic population now differentiates politics from religion, the public and private spheres, as well as the affairs of church and state. Mexican Catholics defend by a wide margin the lay state (estado laico), the separation of spheres (82%) and reproductive rights (96%). They would like to see a church devoted to the poor and protecting human rights and much less involved in party politics. Above all, Mexican Catholics want a more tolerant institution that is much more sensitive to the needs of worshippers and their rights as citizens and members of the church. (Blancarte 2009: 236)

Hagopian concludes that there is a

> clear correlation between the strategies chosen and the type of impact the church can have. If the church accepts protection for its institutional interests, it will not be able to shape the terms of the public debate. Its actions will be circumscribed by the fear of alienating its staunchest defenders, who may be on the political right. But if it can rely on its own social networks, or voters, then it will have more latitude to cross traditional left-right borders and address issues of its choice in the public arena. It can champion issues of social justice at the same time it can stay vigilant on issues pertaining to public morality. It will have the opportunity, in other words, to formulate a response that opposes both economic and social, but not political liberalism. In order to do so it must look within. It may even need to change. (Hagopian 2009: 459)

The alternatives as Hagopian outlines them are striking but not altogether realistic. The social networks in question have neither the consistency nor the kinds of links to the institution that can make them into resources easily moved around a social or political chessboard. The bishops' capacity to manage groups and members is much weaker than they would like or than they often imagine. Many of the "resources" that prelates commonly list or rely upon turn out on closer inspection to be hollow shells, groups that exist more on paper than in reality. Even where groups as such do survive, members prove much less malleable than the evidence of formal ties and documents might indicate. The effort to ensure loyalty by insisting on separate groups with built-in clerical supervision runs into the problem of control in a world where citizens have too many skills, connections, and possibilities to be treated as sheep led by a shepherd, or to be controlled or moved en bloc in traditional ways. In the contemporary world, loyalty is more likely to be secured through provision of spaces and engagement with group agendas, not by demarcation of boundaries.[4] The alternative to reliance on the state may not be for the Catholic Church to rely on its own resources in this sense but rather simply to enter the public sphere and state its case as well as possible. The effort to re-create control of the old kind, albeit in new garments, is only likely to undermine the possibility of success, however defined.

If we take a long view of the matter, it is clear that religion is something of an empty vessel with respect to politics. Religious groups, symbols and resources, and institutions have been identified with political positions ranging from the revolutionary ideas of liberation theology to the notion of the Anglican church as the British Conservative Party at prayer. Religions have promoted monarchies and democracies, crusades and pacifism. Religious slogans have united communities in political struggles but also divided them. Even the most pacifist religions have at times actively promoted violence in the name of preserving the community. These considerations suggest that it is never wise to reify the situation of religion and politics, that is, to assume that it is once and in all places the same. These are historical configurations, products of discussion, debate, and struggle.

The dynamism of the process, and the close connection of religion and the churches to politics and power, require us to take a different angle of view when addressing the relations of religion to pluralism and to democracy in contemporary Latin America. The institutional churches, and religion as a broad set of identities and norms, contribute to democracy as a result of their participation in the broader pluralization of Latin American societies. This political experience takes place on levels that do not always work well together. At the level of formal, explicit "politics," we find lobbying and occasional efforts to promote religiously linked candidates or confessional parties. Religious parties are not in themselves new in Latin America. Christian Democratic parties were founded across the region after World War II, and there are other experiences like Brazil's Catholic League (1932–1937). New parties or candidates that are explicitly Protestant and often Pentecostal are especially notable in Brazil, Peru, and Central America, where their performance has been at best mixed (Freston 2001, 2008).

Alongside their participation in formal, explicit politics, the churches also contribute possibilities of pluralism through their multiple presence in society (in social movements, schools, and associations of all kinds) and by their legitimation of such plurality. Much of the democratizing impact of religion takes place under the radar of formal politics, through involvement in associations and social movements that provide members with civic skills and the self-confidence to act as participant citizens. This has also been a prime location for the involvement of women, who commonly form the majority in local associations and local churches. It is here that the practical experience of emerging pluralism in society and culture acquires a presence in the routines of everyday life. As Alfred Stepan notes, the emergence and consolidation of democratic institutions and practices that embody these ideas are closely related to, and depend on, "the opportunity for the development of a robust and critical civil society that helps check the state and constantly generates alternatives" (Stepan 2003: 216).

Jean Elshtain argues that "in a thick democracy we can expect the religious convictions of citizens to play a role in how they think and act politically and this is not to be lamented so long as those thus thinking and acting abide by the democratic rules of the game." She continues,

> to be sure, those of us who find entirely acceptable a strong public role for religion in the democratic public sphere must acknowledge that historically religion has at times underwritten intolerance and vindicated injustice. Thankfully, in the dominant religion of the West there was a prophylactic internal to the faith that enabled, indeed required, it to criticize and halt its own worst excesses. Also, over time, we have seen religious orientations once considered antidemocratic—Roman Catholicism for example—become the most enthusiastic defenders of human rights and democracy worldwide. (Elshtain 2009: 16)

Elshtain's comment frames the relation of religion to democracy in Latin America in the context of twin areas of question: the internal dynamic of religions, and the fit of religion (any religion) to democracy as a system of government and a pluralist form of social life. The strength of political democracy in Latin America today is enhanced both by institutional changes and by long-term processes that have strengthened civil society (Levine and Molina 2011). It is this combination that presents both opportunity and challenge for the long-term relation of the churches to democracy. The potential for the churches to make a contribution to democracy, either as political actor or as member and promoter of civil society, rests on prior changes within the churches and on their relation to society and politics. Casanova has pointed out that the "third wave" of democracy was in many respects "a Catholic wave, not just because the countries where it occurred happened to be Catholic, but also because the transformation of Catholicism was itself an important independent factor in producing the wave" (Casanova 2001: 1043). These changes within Catholicism were not limited to ideological transformations but also included active promotion of civil society and models of active participation and citizenship legitimated at Vatican II and after.

To the extent that the churches embrace and support pluralism, their contribution to democracy is enhanced in practice as it is in theory. But where churches remain wedded to integralist visions (in which *the* church provides imperative guidelines to society) or commit themselves in some form to the reconquest of social space in the name of a unitary vision of a properly organized society, this potential contribution is stillborn, or worse, turned into support for authoritarian solutions (Donatello 2008; Mallimaci 2008b; Morello 2011a). Before we can assess the likelihood of any of these solutions, a review of the state of democracy itself would be helpful.

Democracy in Contemporary Latin America

The current period of democratization in Latin America, which got under way as military regimes began to leave power in the mid-1980s, has been more extensive and long-lasting than any in the history of the region (Levine and Molina 2011; Peter Smith 2005). The nations of the region have replaced military governments with civilian regimes (Argentina, Brazil, Chile, and Uruguay), dislodged civilian authoritarian regimes (Mexico and Peru), opened the door to peaceful democratic political processes (Nicaragua, El Salvador, Guatemala, and Peru), and set in motion far-ranging initiatives to promote citizen participation (Bolivia). Even Paraguay, which for so long was dominated by a hegemonic party, has recently elected an opposition candidate as president. These transitions, and the stabilization of democracies across the region, affirm the enduring appeal of democracy, reinforced by new institutions and support from citizens and social movements.

How to understand the origins, workings, and quality of democracy is a question that has occupied scholars of politics since Aristotle. In the context of the current cycle of democracy in Latin America, analysis of the quality of democracy has become something of a growth industry. An abundance of studies exist on issues ranging from the specifics of institutional formation, electoral systems, and political parties; to efforts to identify minimum "requisites for democracy"; to governance and public policy and efforts to set political democracy in a general context of rights and liberties (Munck 2007; Munck and Verkuilen 2002; Tilly 2007). In our book on the quality of democracy in Latin America (Levine and Molina 2011), José Molina and I draw on the work of Robert Dahl, who takes the understanding of democracy beyond a simple listing of social requisites or specifying a requirement of competition (which may or may not be democratic) to something more nuanced and dynamic. In a series of foundational books (Dahl 1971, 2002), Dahl specifies elements that any working definition of democracy must include: free, fair, and frequent elections; untrammeled equal access to voting and to institutions; information that is accessible and sufficient for citizens to make a reasoned judgment; elected officials empowered to govern but also accountable and responsive to their constituents; and an inclusive definition of citizenship. These are not all-or-nothing conditions but continuous processes that may be expanded or contracted in a given political system.

The consolidation of democratic politics and of an open civil society altered the scene for the churches in substantial ways, leading many church leaders to withdraw from costly direct involvements in politics and rebuild ties with states and elites. For Catholics, such initiatives were reinforced in the 1980s and 1990s by consistent Vatican pressures, including the replacement of a whole generation of bishops. Withdrawing from a leading role in confrontations with the state and cutting social movements loose of course do not mean "getting out of politics." The churches, Catholic and Protestant, continue to be involved in politics, often with vigorous lobbying on public issues. At the same time, confessional political parties or explicitly religious candidates have lost much of their appeal and have not done very well at the polls, except arguably in Brazil. Christian Democrats remain strong only in Costa Rica and Chile. Despite widespread expectations about the emergence of evangelical electoral fronts or political parties, these have generally sputtered. They have acquired lasting political clout only in Brazil, where the churches place members across the party spectrum rather than forming a party of their own. As noted earlier, the agenda of concerns has also shifted. The social justice, mobilization, and political agendas of the previous period have been replaced by something we might call "normal politics," in which churches and religious groups lobby governments and elites on behalf of a more conventional agenda: public morality; sexuality and reproductive issues such as birth control, divorce, abortion, and family law (Htun 2003, 2009; Vaggione 2009a, 2009b); and a drive for new or continued public subsidies (Brian Smith 1998).

Plurality, Pluralization, and Pluralism

Before going further into particulars, a brief conceptual clarification is in order. The concept of "plurality" is used here in quantitative terms, to denote the growing number of groups, activists, spokespersons, chapels, churches, denominations, communications media, public spaces, and the like. In contrast, the concept of pluralism is social, cultural, and political, and points broadly to the construction of rules of the game that incorporate these new actors and voices as legitimate participants in an open social process. Plurality is necessary but not sufficient for pluralism to emerge and be consolidated as a legitimate form of social and political practice. Together, the new facts of plurality and pluralism are reshaping the public face of religion in Latin America, as they intersect with the equally new facts of pluralism in politics and civil society. A plurality of churches, social movements identified with religion, and voices claim the moral authority to speak in the name of religion; a pluralism is increasingly evident in civil society and in lower barriers to entry into public spaces. Barriers to organization drop as the rules of the game for a plural religious arena are gradually worked out and put into practice. This is a two-way street. Religious plurality and pluralism transform social and political life, putting more actors, voices, and options into play. At the same time, the consolidation and expansion of democratic politics, the reduction of barriers to organization and access, and the gradual elaboration of practical rules of the game for a plural civil society have a visible impact on the daily life of religion, and change the way religious institutions situate themselves in society and politics.

The emergence and consolidation of plurality and pluralism present the institutional Catholic Church with both a challenge and an opportunity. The challenge is to its traditional role as *the church*—the officially acknowledged wielder of moral and social authority within the boundaries of a defined national territory. The opportunity lies in the chance to acquire new followers, to reach and energize them in new ways, and to exploit new media. At the very least, more open politics means the possibility of greater choice, more options for competing for the allegiance and membership of the potential audience, and less regulation of that effort. Casanova argues that efforts to hang on to the status and privileges of being a monopoly church run counter to the logic of an open and more varied society. Only when religions abandon the status of "the church" can they be fully compatible with a modern society. "The conception of modern public religion that is consistent with liberal freedoms and modern structural and cultural differentiations," he writes, "is one that builds on notions of civil society" (Casanova 1994: 217).

As noted earlier, this position is not yet fully accepted in much of the Catholic Church. Indeed, the general thrust of Vatican policy under John Paul II and now Benedict XVI runs in quite a different direction. The evolution of ideas and projects within the Catholic Church, from Santo Domingo to Aparecida, points to an evolving concept that has the church making an effort to reconquer social space, to reevangelize the region. Hagopian states:

> The Roman Catholic Church in Latin America is not yet ready to live with a smaller market share, accept minority status, or fundamentally reorder the institution to allow more internal pluralism and democracy. Instead, it seems bent on pressing ahead with its ambitious, perhaps utopian post Vatican II project to evangelize culture. . . . The problem with this project is that it assumes two preconditions—religious hegemony or at a minimum a status of first among equals, not pluralism, as well as a willingness on the part of plural democracies to accept the principle of a public sphere organized on a religiously based morality and ethical code—that do not conform to the contemporary reality of Latin American religious and political pluralism. (Hagopian 2009: 457)

This is an old script, but the players and circumstances are very different. One result of this situation is that awareness of social weakness may impel church hierarchies to reinforce connections with existing political, social, and media elites. In this vein, Fortunato Mallimaci points out for Argentina that "in situations of terminal crisis, such as those the country lived through in 2001 and 2002, the church will try to appear . . . as the only institution able to 'carry the nation on its back.' It pursues power by colonizing the state and political parties, given the fact that its faithful barely participate in Sunday services nor do they follow the dogmas or social and moral guidelines the institution lays out for them" (Mallimaci 2008b: 90).

Pluralism of a kind has always been present, whether it be the choice between parish life and religious brotherhoods (*cofradias*) or the competition among Catholic religious orders for schools, resources, and territories. But two factors combine to make the present scene qualitatively different. The first is the reorganization and redirection of institutional Catholic resources (with Vatican sanction) away from support of social movements and innovative religious voices to a *resacralization* of its projected message (Drogus and Stewart-Gambino 2005). Resacralization entails a renewed focus on more conventional religious concerns (morality, sexual purity, and schools) along with a consistent effort to situate these within a framework set by the authoritative teaching of church leaders. Resacralization also speaks to renewed concern in the Catholic hierarchy with maintaining control and loyalty to the institutional church, elements that can hinder action in a fluid environment (Levine 2008).[5]

There is corresponding pressure on groups and individuals to withdraw from what is seen as "undue politicization." With the restoration of democracy throughout the continent, many Catholic leaders believe that such tasks can and should be left to professional political actors such as political parties or trade unions (Drogus and Stewart-Gambino 2005).

The second factor is the presence of vigorous competition for members, resources, and public space (Chesnut 2003; Gill 1998) and of what Timothy Steigenga (2001) terms the "pentecostalization" of religious belief and practice. Elements once limited to Protestant (and specifically Pentecostal) experience—including stress on the direct experience of charismatic power, divine cure of diseases (faith healing), speaking in tongues (glossolalia), certain kinds of music, and patterns of group organization and leadership—have been diffused widely in the Christian community, crossing denominational boundaries (Cleary 2011).

These dimensions of pluralism are reinforced by the reality of loosened ties and reorganized commitments to the institutional church by believers that we have documented. There is nothing new about the gap between the expectations and projections of leaders and what followers will commit to, but in the context of growing competition from other churches, the matter seems now more urgent to Catholic leaders because of the implications for control, as well as the challenge it raises to the status of the Catholic Church as *the church*. Within the Protestant community, pluralism of course remains the norm, and churches and congregations have resisted efforts at regional or even national coordinating bodies that might yield a single authorized voice.

The challenge that pluralism poses for the Catholic Church in particular is complicated by the multiple and overlapping ways in which religions are present in society, politics, and culture. The emergence of real pluralism reflects and reinforces a reconfiguring of these relationships that is open-ended and out of the control of church hierarchies. For purposes of exposition, it helps to break our consideration of the issues into component parts and treat each aspect separately. The most visible expression of plurality and pluralism in religion in Latin America obviously comes from the sheer number of churches, venues, and spokespersons and the visible impact of competition for members, loyalties, and resources. In a very concrete sense, more religion is available in Latin America now than in the past: more churches, more chapels, a greater presence in the mass media, more opportunities for participation, and a greater number of groups of religious origin or inspiration present in social life. All this is evidence of a great capacity for sociocultural change and innovation (Parker 1996).

The emergence of social and cultural pluralism, along with democratic rules of the game in politics, has also raised challenges to the activist collection of groups, ideas, and practices that emerged within Catholicism in the crucible of the 1970s and 1980s. For those inspired by liberation theology, the global and regional collapse of the Left in the 1990s required wrenching reappraisals of democracy as a goal and of the meaning of politics and political activity. Accommodation, compromise, and alliance building are more the norm in plural societies than revolution and the construction of something utterly new. The opening of politics has drawn many group members and leaders into the political game and into public office, depriving groups of some of their most dynamic members. The effects of this shift were reinforced by decisions of many Catholic hierarchies to reduce support for groups and movements, cutting many loose from the resources and legitimation that they had long enjoyed (Drogus and Stewart-Gambino 2005).

Plurality and pluralism have also brought challenges to the growing Protestant community. The continued and accelerating growth detailed in Chapter 3 has brought a shift in the public presence of Protestantism and the elaboration of innovative means of managing its new status in a changed political arena. No longer isolated minorities and weak supplicants for public recognition, Protestant churches have vigorously pressed claims to equal status in the public sphere and a share of the benefits (including subsidies for schools) long allocated to the Catholic Church. They have also actively contested barriers to the ordinary life of their communities, such as laws regulating "noisy churches" (Brian Smith 1998).

In case after case, churches, interchurch alliances, and individual figures have moved to become active in what was once seen as the tainted and corrupting world of politics. Protestant churches have also engaged a broader set of issues and entered into a wide range of social and political alliances that would have been unimaginable a few decades ago. The established historical tendency to fissiparous growth within Protestantism is fully exemplified in contemporary Latin America. Competition among Protestant churches and alternative national and continental confederations—for members, resources, and public voice—is now as notable as Protestant-Catholic competition.

Although precursors can be found in every instance, most observers agree that for Catholicism, the overall process of pluralization and a shift in the way religious activism was expressed in politics got under way in the post–World War II period, with the emergence of reformist currents within the churches, including a loose network of pastoral centers, journals, and locally based initiatives that in different ways represented a search for ways to create a more effective church presence throughout the region. Related and spin-off organizations soon crystallized into Christian Democratic parties, breaking long-standing ties between Catholic groups and conservative politics. The social and political impact of these changes was magnified and extended by the political experiences of the 1970s and 1980s that drove activists into the churches (often the only space remaining open), where they were often met with welcome and shelter. All these movements of change created and legitimized new voices, new agents, and new venues for religious action whose social and political meaning was magnified beyond the original intent of many by political circumstances (Levine 2005, 2006a, 2006b, 2006c; Christian Smith 1991).

The Protestant story began to consolidate into a visible and public presence of pluralism about twenty years later. With roots in a long, slow process of church "planting" and growth, Protestant groups and spokespersons found their way in growing numbers onto public platforms and into politics on a large scale starting in the late 1980s. With the end of the Cold War and the move of prominent early figures like Guatemala's Efraín Ríos Montt off center stage, Protestant groups began to consolidate a substantial, varied public presence—building churches, creating schools, acquiring a media presence, and so forth.

For many years, Protestants and particularly members of the growing Pentecostal community operated on the principle that politics was the realm of contamination and of the impure. The core concern was to build the church and to maintain purity of practices in a community of believers, not to repair the political order. This position recalls the classic stance of North American fundamentalists, whose move to engage the political world was spurred in the 1960s by preoccupations about cultural drift and moral decline that were articulated by figures like Pat Robertson or Jerry Falwell, who created political vehicles by exploiting new mass media and other mobilizational tools, including direct mail. Although these developments have not led to any explicitly Protestant political party in the United States, the association of elements of the religious right with the Republican Party has been extensively documented and continues to the present (Harding 2001; Wilson 2007).

Despite the common move out of self-imposed isolation and into the political world as children of light, the Latin American dynamic differs in tone and direction from its North American counterpart. There has been a revaluation of politics itself: once seen as the realm of corruption and evil, it is now presented as a possible, legitimate, and even necessary field of action for believers. Where once the children of light were enjoined to concentrate above all else on personal salvation and building a community of the elect, they now visualize politics, despite the dangers it holds, as a central part of their identity and responsibility. All this provides an indispensable platform for entering the political arena. The end of the Cold War liberated the churches not only from the obsessive anticommunism of the past, but also from close dependence on foreign (mostly North American) leadership and resources, which now were directed in growing measure to capturing souls in the former socialist bloc. Together these developments facilitated the emergence of a diverse range of interests and positions (Fonseca 2008; Freston 2001, 2008; Steigenga 2001; Stoll 1990).

In his work on Pentecostals in Central America, Steigenga found that politically derived concepts of left and right do not match up well with religious divisions. Commitment to particular ideas and practices (speaking in tongues, experience of divine cures or miracles, belief in a judgmental God) is more important than denominational affiliation in setting the tone and direction of political action. Protestants and Pentecostals also divide on the issues, much like their Catholic counterparts. Steigenga concludes that "the overriding theme that emerges . . . is that Protestantism is highly unlikely to be translated into any sort of coherent and sustained political movement in Latin America. Protestants may well vote for Protestants, but they will likely be divided in terms of their political agenda. Protestants may be good citizens, who respect authority and abide by the laws, but this does not mean that they will embrace authoritarianism or hold ultra conservative views" (Steigenga 2001: 154).

Set in a general political context, pluralization suggests that building and sustaining a new role will require groups to play the old politics more skillfully and more consistently than in the past. This means working to maintain the presence of groups and hold on to members, sustaining grassroots democracy while working on allies and connections, and assuming a realistic bargaining stance in politics. Groups need to bargain for better terms with everyone and enter into alliances only with great care and caution. Allies, connections, resources, and the shield they provide remain of critical importance; they are required precisely because what ordinary people need in politics and what define a system as legitimate in their eyes are predictability, accountability, and a sense, however minimal, of being a legitimate part of something larger. Although none of these can be achieved only at the local level, continued work at the local level is the bedrock on which anything else must be built (Drogus 1990, 1997a).

That this came as a surprise to many observers is a sign of the extent to which a lot of groups representing the grassroots and new religious voices were blinded by faith in their own Gramscian agenda. Many of the groups that appeared and began to consolidate in the conflict-charged circumstances of the 1970s and 1980s in Latin America shared a concept of politics according to which *the people* (defined primarily in terms of social class) constituted a natural majority. In this view of the world, *the people* would ultimately construct a new counterhegemony whose eventual victory would obviate the need for ordinary politics. Once a counterhegemonic understanding could be forged and spread in the population, these people would join together and create a new and different kind of political order. Such hopes have often been disappointed as the return of democracy brought burnout, demobilization, and division to many of these same groups (see Chapter 5).

For their part, newly confident Protestant groups entered the political arena in the 1990s, believing that as children of light they would bring a new ethic and political style, moralizing politics and the political world. But in leading cases like Guatemala, Nicaragua, Brazil, and Peru, initial enthusiasm about the prospects for building a new Jerusalem and a new kind of politics soon yielded to disillusionment and discredit (as in Guatemala or Peru) or to an evangelical pluralism in which utterly new churches (like Brazil's Universal Church of the Reign of God) have emerged as self-confident players of the "old politics" (Fonseca 2008; Burity and Machado 2006). As was the case with an earlier generation of Catholic progressives, the old politics proved tenacious—not merely resisting new movements but also effectively incorporating, dividing, and deactivating them.

Much analysis of pluralism and plurality often works from the point of view of groups and leaders: from what those working in a rational-choice vein would term the "supply side." This is important but incomplete. Ignoring the audience for change is a little like discussions of governability that center attention exclusively on control and order, without addressing issues like voice, representation, and access. In religion, as in politics or social life as a whole, we need to ask how such plurality appears to those on the receiving end. From the point of view of the target audience or audiences, the presence of a plurality of options opens possibilities. To be sure, many new churches are exclusive in membership and make extensive demands on new believers. But the choice to assume these demands and obligations is freely made. In the patterns of ordinary life, what we know is that those who belong to new churches are in fact rarely exclusive in group membership. They belong to groups of all kinds at rates pretty much comparable to those of other religious groups. This opens possibilities for creating and maintaining ties and relationships across groups, keeping the flow of information open, and undergirding the possibilities of common action.

Defending, Promoting, and Practicing Democratic Politics

The transformations outlined in the previous section have had many and varied impacts on politics. The salient institutional presence of the Catholic Church and the relatively high levels of public confidence all churches enjoy in the region provide the underpinnings for an extensive role in political mediation ranging from hostage crises, prison revolts, and housing or land invasions to arrangements for truces, an end to civil war, and political transitions from authoritarian rule to democracy. In 1958, the church was active in the endgame of Venezuela's last military dictator, General Marcos Pérez Jimenez. Church officials were prominent among critics of the regime and played a key role in brokering the transition and legitimating the idea of democracy to many in the

Catholic constituency who remained nervous about the kind of political system that might follow military rule (Levine 1973). In the Dominican Republic, following decades of a close mutually supportive relation with the regime of Rafael Trujillo, the Catholic Church turned to mediation as a means of developing a political and social stance acceptable to all groups in the society. Emilio Betances argues that mediation was a survival strategy for the Catholic hierarchy, undertaken as a means of ensuring a continued role by becoming acceptable to all major players. In his view, this was the only way the church could manage a "reincorporation" and "reinsertion" of the kind that new times require—nonpartisan, socially concerned, but not giving up state support and subsidies.[6]

These concepts are familiar from Vallier (1970) and suggest that beginning in the late 1970s, church leaders in the Dominican Republic took pains to avoid partisan or radical positions of any kind and to offer themselves as brokers or mediators, for example, in arranging terms of participation in the 1974 elections. They maintained, longer than in many other cases, a conservative mix of neo-Christendom orientations (which rely on the notion of the church being official and officially backed) with a powerful antileftism. The defeat of revolution in 1965 (by US occupation) squelched not only the political Left, but also the ecclesial Left, the same groups that elsewhere in the region advanced ideas of liberation, the "popular church," and alliances with the political Left. In what is something of a precursor for what followed in transitions to democracy elsewhere in the region, what emerges in the Dominican Republic after the mid-1970s is a Catholic hierarchy that is conservative, nonpartisan, generally supportive of elections and political democracy, available to broker disputes, and increasingly involved in social outreach.

Once church leaders and groups decide to support democracy they have many instruments to work with, and it is instructive to enumerate them. A classic means of influence is through public statements, pastoral letters, and documents challenging and delegitimating authoritarian rule while promoting democratic ideals and practices. Words do count, and the words and statements of church officials in defense of democracy in Chile, Brazil, Peru, or Central America helped keep these ideals alive in hard times. A second set of tools, very prominent in the the 1970s and early 1980s, is visible in the role churches played in sponsoring, promoting, and sheltering groups, equipping them with resources, political cover, legal assistance, and national as well as transnational connections. In this way, the churches provided spaces where democratic practices could be carried out and information—a scarce commodity in authoritarian regimes—could be acquired and exchanged (Drogus and Stewart-Gambino 2005; Levine 1992; Hagopian 2009; Mainwaring 1986; Doimo 1989; Cáceres 1989). Related to this is the continuing legacy of liberation theology, above all its insistence on *accompaniment*, maintaining a presence among the poor and the vulnerable. This has had particular impact in work with human rights groups and in addressing the effects of violence, both by aiding victims and by simply maintaining a presence in areas of the worst fighting.

The churches also supported democracy in striking ways by withdrawing traditional religious means of regime legitimation—for example, liturgies and masses, like the Te Deums traditionally celebrated to mark important national occasions or the installation of governments. There are innumerable cases. Here I cite only two. In Chile, just after the military coup of September 11, 1973, the new regime requested that Cardinal Silva Henriquez celebrate a Te Deum on the Chilean National Day, September 18. The cardinal had already issued statements of sorrow for the violence and loss of life, along with a request to honor the dead, particularly President Salvador Allende, who was killed the day of the coup. The new military regime wanted the mass to be celebrated in the Military Academy rather than the Metropolitan Cathedral. Cardinal Silva refused, "because it would have symbolized a church that was taking sides with the military, and he strongly suggested that the Cathedral should be the place for the liturgical service. In response, military advisors suggested that there were snipers in the area and that it was not safe for anybody" (Aguilar 2003: 719). After tense negotiations, a place was found (the Church of National Gratitude, built after the end of the War of the Pacific against Peru and Boliva) and the mass was held. But the tone had been set, and Cardinal Silva continued to be a voice in opposition who combined his words and statements with concrete gestures, as the church took a leading role in the defense of human rights, first through Committee of Cooperation for Peace in Chile (COPACHI, Comité de Cooperación para la Paz en Chile) and later through the Vicariate of Solidarity (Drogus and Stewart-Gambino 2005).

In Paraguay, the Catholic Church was one of the main voices in opposition to the long-lasting (1954–1989) dictatorship of General Alfredo Stroessner. Starting in the 1970s, church leaders promoted social movements, including Catholic peasant leagues, and maintained an active human rights group, the CIPAE (Comité de Iglesias Para

Ayudas de Emergencia, Committee of Churches for Emergency Help), which was modeled on Chile's Vicariate of Solidarity.[7] Leaders of the Paraguayan Catholic Church also organized a series of marches and processions protesting official repression, including several Processions in Silence and Marches for Life, which took place toward the end of the regime. Following Pope John Paul II's visit to the country, the government resumed its crackdown, arresting and expelling a Spanish Jesuit who had been invited to speak about liberation theology at the National University. This was justified as part of a campaign against "Marxist infiltration of the Church" and it drew a swift response. "In retaliation, Archbishop Rolón cancelled the traditional Te Deum mass in the Cathedral to celebrate the 8th inauguration of Stroessner as well as the 451st anniversary of Asunción. The unanimity and swiftness with which the Church moved to express its displeasure testified both to its own internal cohesion as well as the solid front it was willing to display to face down Stroessner" (Miguel Carter 1990: 94).

For the Catholic Church, the politics of papal visits provide a uniquely powerful and visible instrument for public action. Papal visits are carefully arranged and highly choreographed events. Where the pope goes, whom he sees, and what he says often resonate strongly in national life. As we have seen, Latin America is very important to the Vatican, and recent popes have made a point of visiting the region. Pope Paul VI, who did not travel that much, was present in Colombia to inaugurate the landmark meetings of Latin American bishops at Medellín in 1968. The travels of his successor, John Paul II, are well known. Of the 104 overseas trips that Pope John Paul II undertook, almost a quarter (25) were to Latin America, where he visited every country at least once. His first trip to the area, just after being elected pope, was to Mexico, where he presided over the bishops' meetings at Puebla. Thirteen years later, he was in Santo Domingo for the next general meeting of the Conference of Latin American Bishops. His other visits included moments of great political significance. In Nicaragua in 1983, facing a hierarchy fearful of the leftism of the Sandinistas and a government that wanted his support in efforts for peace, he spoke out against division between the popular church (which sided with the Sandinistas) and the institutional hierarchy and lectured crowds calling for peace on the need to obey the bishops. In Chile in 1987, as opposition to the regime of Augusto Pinochet was rising, he criticized the regime as a dictatorship and asked the country's bishops to campaign for free elections. As part of his schedule, he met with and embraced Carmen Gloria Quintana Aranciba, a young woman who had suffered severe, almost fatal, burns after being detained by police during an antiregime street demonstration. This and other gestures were important to the opposition, which was then gathering strength.

In his 1988 visit to Paraguay, the pope played a similar role. The government insisted on removing one diocese (Concepción) from the itinerary. The bishop of Concepción was one of the country's most outspoken, and the visit was scheduled to include a meeting for the pope with 3,000 people, including representatives of labor, community groups, and unrecognized parties. The government tried to bar this meeting and "accused the bishops of 'disorienting the people and setting their mission aside,' thereby demonstrating 'a lack of comprehension and tolerance for those who should be models in this respect'" (Miguel Carter 1990: 87). The bishops refused to yield, and the visit was almost canceled but finally went forward after the government reluctantly agreed to allow the meeting, which was rescheduled and held in the capital, Asunción. In Paraguay, as in the previous year in Chile, the pope stressed the need for participation of all sectors in politics and greater respect for human rights. The final and perhaps the most famous visit that Pope John Paul II made was to Cuba in 1998, where he appeared in public with Fidel Castro and effectively put his seal of approval on a long-term process of accommodation between the church and the regime. His successor, Benedict XVI, was present at the Aparecida meetings in 2007, where he played an important role in shaping the debates and the content of the final documents (Levine 2008; Pelton 2008).

I do not want to give the impression that there was a consensus in the region's churches about the validity of the positions taken by the popes in these cases: there was not. These were controversial and often highly contested positions, but with the passing of authoritarian rule, the conclusion of open civil wars, and the return to democracy across the region, the positions taken by churches or church leaders no longer occupied so prominent a place, and the impetus for the churches to promote groups and sponsor mobilizations also began to fade. Once the external threat (the oppressive regime, the war) disappeared from the scene, politics could safely be left to the professional politicians. In Chile, where the Catholic Church had played a highly salient role in opposition to military rule, following the transition to democracy in 1990 Catholic leaders pulled back on two fronts. They reduced their support for social movements and for specifically political initiatives, arguing that these were no longer needed in the context of democratic politics (Drogus and Stewart-Gambino 2005). They also shifted the direction of their lobbying and public declarations away from the social justice issues of the past to concerns about moral order. A review of church documents and letters following the transition to democracy reveals a growing emphasis on moral order, which in practical terms means a concern with sexuality (including opposition to sex education in schools), reproduction and abortion, gender roles, and divorce, which was only legalized in 2005, after a bruising political battle (Haas 1999: 50; Htun 2003). The church's lobbying efforts were all the more effective given the credit their stance against dictatorship gave them in the public eye.

The effort to create an effective and effectively democratic political presence has been a continuing thread in the recent public presence of religion in Latin America. The defense and promotion of democracy took the churches into uncharted and potentially dangerous territory. Danger came not only from opposing armed and fearful regimes who saw any opposition as subversion, or forces like Peru's Shining Path, which was determined to eliminate all competition for popular support. There was also the peril, deeply felt by many church leaders, of losing their way and allowing their public stance to be set by purely political considerations. Because the churches had often stood alone against regimes, many had been attracted into their organizations who otherwise would not have participated in church-defined settings. For some church leaders this presented an opportunity to reach out and evangelize, but from another perspective it brought danger through the presence within the church of elements whose political interests and egalitarian ideals fit only with great difficulty into conventional, hierarchical understandings that undergird church practices.

Another prominent form of participation comes with entry into partisan electoral politics, either by forming religiously linked or religiously identified political parties, backing religiously identified candidates, or deploying religious language or religious symbology as means of persuading citizens and gaining their vote. As noted earlier, there are ample precedents for religiously linked or identified political parties in the region. Conservative parties of the nineteenth century were closely identified with the Catholic Church and advanced its claims in core areas like education or marriage law (Htun 2003, 2009).[8] The emergence and consolidation of Christian Democratic parties in the postwar period represented a very different angle on religiously inspired participation in politics. Christian Democracy was an effort to marry Christian principles (as enunciated in Catholic social teaching) with modern political democracy. A generation of young leaders joined the transnational Catholic movement Pax Romana and later played critical roles in the formation of Christian Democratic parties in their countries across the region, achieving power in Chile, Venezuela, Costa Rica, and Guatemala.[9] Christian Democratic parties have retained strength and visibility only in Chile and Costa Rica. Chilean Christian Democracy provided two of the four democratic presidents elected after the transition from the military rule of Pinochet.[10] The Christian Democratic Party in Costa Rica has elected presidents four times, most recently for the 2002–2006 period.

As they developed a political role for themselves, many Protestant and Pentecostal churches in Latin America began by seeking alliances and connections that would put them on a more equal footing with Catholics. This includes public recognition, a share in official subsidies (e.g., for schools, clinics, ministerial salaries), and better treatment on issues like visas for missionaries, long a sticking point. This effort has not been contingent on the ideology of potential political partners. Evangelicals and Pentecostals have provided early support for regimes as different as Pinochet in Chile and Hugo Chávez in Venezuela, because they responded to the way these leaders recognized and reached out to them. In each case, the outreach by political leaders was undoubtedly impelled by the opposition they were experiencing from Catholic leaders. As he emerged in Venezuelan politics in the 1990s, Hugo Chávez also garnered evangelical backing because of his strong stand against corruption. At the other end of the spectrum, Guatemala's president Efraín Ríos Montt folded his own Protestantism into the aggressive antisubversive war waged by his short-lived regime (Garrard-Burnett 2010; Kamsteeg 1999; Levine and Smilde 2006; Smilde 2004b; Smilde and Pagan 2011).

Attempts by Latin American evangelicals to establish their own political parties and to make specific political alliances have had mixed success. Like Christian Democrats a generation earlier, evangelical leaders expected their very presence to carry with it a cleansing and moralization of politics, but things have rarely worked out as they had anticipated. As they engaged the political world, groups and actors of religious inspiration have proven no more immune to the temptations of the old politics, including corruption and abuse of power, than anyone else. Among evangelicals, explicitly religious parties or candidates have failed to mobilize or guarantee a bloc vote of the faithful in cases ranging from Nicaragua and Chile to Peru and Venezuela (Kamsteeg 1999; Freston 2001; Smilde 2004b; Smilde and Pagan 2011; López 2008a), nor have they attracted masses of voters of any kind. Paul Freston comments that "they arise at election times, seeing the churches as fields where votes could be harvested. They lacked long term objectives, merely alleging the right to represent the evangelical community and the necessity of having Christians in power because of their superior spiritual discernment" (Freston 2008: 26). They also generally lacked much preparation.

The experience of Peru's evangelicals is instructive. A wave of politically inexperienced evangelicals were swept into office in alliance with Alberto Fujimori in 1990, and many remained bound to the regime until its ignominious collapse a decade later. These deputies and political figures were compromised by the corruption of the Fujimori-Montesinos regime (Conaghan 2005). Darío López states that evangelical leaders and a succession of short-lived evangelical parties in Peru "usually emerged without any previous reflection on political theology. In contrast, they were often motivated by a belief that 'the moment had arrived' for evangelicals to have their own representation in public life. One of their objectives was to demand equal treatment for all religious confessions, and they started with the premise that the only ones who could present the demands of the evangelical community were the evangelicals themselves" (López 2008a: 140). The role of such groups in public life should be distinguished from the rich experience of activists and ordinary members of the evangelical churches working at the level of civil society, for example in urban survival movements, community kitchens, neighborhood groups, human rights organizations, and the Rondas Campesinas, or peasant patrols. López argues forcefully that the new civic capacities and social capital created at the base have a greater chance of nurturing and sustaining democracy in the long run than does the cultivation of official favors and partisan political ties.

> Those evangelicals who supported the regime contributed neither to the articulation of alternative spaces for participation in formal politics nor to the creation of a distinct political ethos. Instead, the experience of the past decade, following the only democratic period of Fujimori's Presidency (1990–92) shows that those evangelicals who served in the Congress during the Fujimori years (1990–2000), all closely tied to the regime, reinforced traditional political practices, adopting with ease all the vices of the old political class, most notably corruption and nepotism. . . . The presence of evangelical believers in social movements presents a very different image. As part of these citizen movements, sharing in the dynamic of civil society, and working collectively with the poor in the settlements that encircle our great cities as well as with peasant communities suffering directly from the violence of those years, evangelicals crafted new forms of "doing politics" which in the

long run helped keep democracy from collapsing completely. (López 2004: 124, 125)

More recently in Peru, evangelicals have returned to the option of explicitly political organization. A case in point is the National Restoration Party, organized by Pastor Humberto Lay Sun, founder of the Iglesia Bíblica Emanuel (Emmanuel Bible Church). Pastor Lay ran for president on this ticket in 2006 and received about 4 percent of the vote, but the party has not survived. He ran again in the 2011 elections, prompting a declaration by a coalition of Protestant leaders that called for the churches to remove themselves from partisan politics and keep their churches from being staging grounds for political campaigns. Other cases present a comparable evolution. Following the Sandinista electoral defeat in 1990, a number of evangelical parties and candidacies flourished as part of the development of competitive electoral politics in Nicaragua. There was great enthusiasm in the evangelical community about the prospects of a moralization of politics, but most of these parties were short-lived, based on charismatic leaders, and proved no more immune to corruption than any others (Zub 2008). In Guatemala, the short-lived and bloody regime of the evangelical General Ríos Montt opened the way for explicit participation by Protestant groups and leaders in Guatemalan politics (Garrard-Burnett 2010; Samson 2008). Several years after his ouster from office, another neo-Pentecostal figure, Elías Serrano, was elected president. He was forced to resign in 1993 in the midst of charges of abuse of power and corruption. Since that time, Protestant and Pentecostal initiatives for political participation have shied away from electoral vehicles, broadened ideologically, and worked to build firmer roots in civil society (Samson 2008).

The most successful examples of explicitly political action linked to Protestant churches have come in Brazil. The presence of Protestants in Brazilian political life is not itself new. The first Protestant deputy (a Lutheran from the German immigrant community in the south) was elected in the 1930s. But recent developments have witnessed the emergence of new leadership groups and utterly new leadership styles in the churches. Media skills are notable and careers in religious or other broadcasting are increasingly common stepping-stones to political candidacies. The strong presence of evangelicals on the national political scene became evident during the transition to democracy in elections for the Constituent Assembly of 1986 and has grown steadily in subsequent electoral cycles. A notable element in this growth has been the emergence of the neo-Pentecostal Church of the Universal Reign of

God (IURD, Igreja Universal do Reino de Deus), which has become a dominating presence. The IURD takes advantage of its extensive radio and television networks to reach and mobilize voters, while using its many temples effectively to leverage electoral districts. The IURD also carefully controls the selection of candidates who receive the church's stamp of approval and has developed a strategy that allows it to maintain a presence in parties and movements all across the ideological spectrum. This is partly a hedging of political bets, but also reflects a profound demographic fact. The growth of new churches and religious movements has been so rapid and so extensive in Brazil that it has brought into the churches many groups with widely differing political and social experiences. This has not only created potential sources of new leaders, but also provided the underpinnings for a new ideological diversity (Silveíra Campos 2006; Oro 2006; Fonseca 2008).

The rise of the IURD raises a range of questions about how to understand the long-term implications of religiously linked participation in politics. At one level, the church clearly contributes to the diversification and pluralization of the field by the very fact of creating an alternative presence. Through the 1990s, the IURD moved away from the automatic antileftism that characterized earlier generations of Pentecostals, supporting leftist candidates like Lula da Silva and advancing a new collection of policies framed by ideas about social justice (Fonseca 2008; Silveíra Campos 2006; Oro 2006). The idea of an alliance between an evangelical church and a socialist political leader would have been unthinkable as recently as twenty years ago, but the IURD and other churches in fact cooperated with the government of Lula on many projects and agencies. The 2002 presidential elections found the IURD supporting Lula, while the Assemblies of God, the oldest and traditionally the largest single Brazilian Pentecostal church, supported the government candidate, José Serra. Freston comments that this shows "how exaggerated are all fears of an evangelical political hegemony that would threaten democracy" (Freston 2008: 32).

The ascendance of the IURD in Brazilian society and politics raises other questions about the quality of the democratic participation that the church offers and promotes. Norms of democratic participation are far removed from the practice of these churches, just as they are from similar groups that have expanded spectacularly in Africa or in the United States in recent years (Algranti 2010; Gifford 2004; Harris 1999; Harris-Lacewell 2007; Kramer 2005). If we expand our focus beyond parties and politics to consider the spread of civic skills and the creation of democratic citizenship, there is cause for concern. It is of course possible for groups to contribute to a democratic play of interests in society at large without being democratic in their inner life. But as Frederick Harris (1999: 183) reminds us in his work on African American religion and politics, participatory ideals can find it hard to survive within theocratic structures. Within the IURD, the pastor is treated as a "superhero of the people," an example to be emulated and followed (Kramer 2005: 104). The long-term implications of this pattern remain to be worked out (see Chapters 5 and 8).

Examination of the relation of the churches to democracy in Venezuela offers insights into a different range of possibilities. Venezuelan experience differs from much of the rest of the region for several reasons: the long-term weakness of the Roman Catholic Church, the country's lengthy experience with democracy (which began in 1958), the decay of that democracy, and the accelerated conflict, mobilization, and polarization that have accompanied the rise to prominence and power of Chávez, president since 1998. Venezuela also lags behind much of the region in the timing of Protestant and Pentecostal growth, which got under way as the country's economic and political crises became acute beginning in the late 1980s (Levine 1981; Smilde and Pagan 2011).

As we have seen, despite long-term suspicions of democratic politics, which were sharpened by conflicts during the country's first experiment with mass democracy in the late 1940s, the Catholic Church played a salient role in opposing Venezuela's last military dictator, Marcos Pérez Jiménez, brokering the transition to democracy in 1958, and legitimating democracy to wary elites. The Catholic hierarchy was aided in this role by its close ties to the Christian Democratic Party, whose presence in government provided a guarantee of stability and good treatment. The church benefited substantially from its accommodation to democracy, achieving enhanced legal status and official support for everything from clerical salaries and maintenance of buildings to education and welfare activities.

Beginning in the mid-1980s, Venezuela's democracy entered a long decline, marked by severe economic problems and the hollowing out of core institutions like the political parties, which lost support and public confidence. Social and political decay burst into the open in massive urban riots (1989) and successive failed military coups in 1992, which launched Chávez into public prominence. After spending two years in prison for his participation in the coup, Chávez received a presidential pardon and set out to build a movement. The decay and discredit of the old parties combined with the country's lingering economic crisis to sweep him to victory in 1998 on a platform that excoriated the corruption of the old system and called for moralizing the nation and creating new and more equitable institutions and practices (Levine 1994). The elections of 1998 set in motion tendencies that continue to shape politics, and by extension the relation of religion and the churches to the country's democracy, in important ways. The dramatic weakening of the old political parties made for a drastic simplification of political alternatives into pro- or anti-Chávez, and until the recovery of the political opposition after 2006, created a situation in which religion and churches became prime media for conflict.

Church leaders and groups participated actively in political debates and mobilizations, but they were never unified. All churches turned out to be as affected by the pervasive polarization of the country as any other sector. The country's Catholic bishops distrusted Chávez from the outset and have been steady critics of the regime. They were wary of the president's violent rhetoric, unhappy about the failure of the Constitutional Assembly of 1999 to include a complete ban on abortion in the final text, and distressed about what they saw as a reduced status for the church in the new constitution.[11] These differences gained public salience after the failed coup of April 2002 that removed Chávez from office and installed a conservative interim government that lasted only a few days. The top hierarchy of the Catholic Church was visible in its support of the coup and the new regime, while other Catholic groups, most notably religious orders and organizations involved in grassroots work, opposed the coup and opened their grassroots contacts and (for the Jesuits) their radio networks to the opposition (Smilde and Pagan 2011).

For its part, the Protestant community has been divided between evangelical churches concerned about authoritarian tendencies who tried to maintain distance from politics and a collection of neo-Pentecostal churches supportive of the government. Each has its own national association.[12] In contrast to their brethren elsewhere in the region, when Venezuela's evangelicals turned to politics in the twenty-first century, they did not create religious political parties. This reflects the political options available in the highly polarized political space that Venezuela presents and also rests on the discredit of earlier experiences. In the last decades of the twentieth century, Godofredo Marín, a Protestant pastor, established a political party called the Authentic Renovating Organization (ORA, Organización Renovadora Auténtica), which won seats in Congress in several elections. The party's name is a self-conscious play on words: in Spanish, the acronym ORA also means to "pray," from the verb *orar*. In the wake of the 1998 elections, when Marín allied himself with old-line leaders who were widely seen as corrupt, the party effectively disappeared. Subsequent political engagement by Protestant and Pentecostal churches has instead taken the form of public preaching rallies and marches, and a series of public events where Pentecostal leaders shared platforms with Chávez (Smilde 2004a, 2011a; Smilde and Pagan 2011).

From the beginning of his political career—as leader of a movement, as candidate, and later as president—Chávez has reached out to evangelicals, providing them public recognition. David Smilde comments that "these public mentions of evangelicals and attempts to reach out to them have been wildly popular. They [evangelicals] have interpreted these outreaches as evidence that God is working through Hugo Chávez" (Smilde 2011a: 311). His anticorruption and moralizing message is appealing, and the fact that he regularly employs Christian and biblical references in his speeches convinces many in these churches that God is working through him. These messages appeal because they fit well with the prevailing evangelical understanding that links both personal difficulties and the visible decay of the country (economic decline, inflation conflict, and rampant corruption) to a turning away from God. In these ways, the churches provide believers with concepts that help them make sense of what is happening in their lives and to their country, and reinforce their motivation to act within a supportive setting along with key elements of solidarity and organization (Smilde 2004a, 2004c, 2008, 2011a; Smilde and Pagan 2011).

The Venezuelan case affirms the importance of political context. The long history of democracy and its decline in the 1980s means that democratic politics were the norm rather than a goal to be sought. For many activists, democracy as it existed in the last few decades of the twentieth century constituted the established disorder, which needed to be reformed and replaced with something better. The widespread criticism of democracy for its corruption and inability to address the nation's difficulties means that the Catholic hierarchy's defense of liberal democracy against the political project of President Chávez gets less general support than it might in other cases. At the same time, the relatively recent emergence of the evangelical and particularly the Pentecostal churches means that the public recognition offered by Chávez is all the more valuable.

Throughout this book, I have underscored the transformation and opening up of political orientations and options that have characterized Latin American Protestantism over the past few decades. Venezuelan experience strongly confirms this. Coming to maturity and operating in the context of the tumultuous, conflict-ridden situation of those decades, the experience of religious groups in Venezuela (Catholics and Protestants, pro- and anti-Chávez alike) demonstrates the shallowness of views that makes religion either a necessary ally of any particular political option or simply a new name for older forms of political domination. Catholics and Protestants and their organizations have been divided along similar lines, as polarized as the rest of the country. Although tensions remain, particularly between the Catholic hierarchy and the Chávez government, the political recovery of the opposition in Venezuela and its increasingly credible showing in elections have helped move churches and religion off center stage.

Something similar happened in the region as a whole. The end of dictatorships, the resolution of civil wars, and the return to civilian politics and democracy provided a welcome opportunity for many churches to reduce their political exposure and get out of explicitly political and partisan conflict. It is worth repeating that this does not mean moving out of the public sphere entirely. Whatever the issue or the specific arena, the fact is that with the restoration of "normal politics," other voices, including those of straightforwardly political movements along with a range of social movements and new churches, fill public space. Religious spokesmen no longer command immediate attention; religious discourse no longer occupies center stage. Even if it did, there is no longer a single voice, even within a particular religious tradition. For their part, activists and especially grassroots members face a more elemental challenge: how to hold members and keep organizations alive in the teeth of hard times and when the state is at best indifferent, impervious, unable, or uninterested in providing services.

If we shift the focus of analysis from specifically political initiatives and civil society to the uses of religion in political discourse, campaigning, and persuasion, the results affirm the mixed portrait outlined above. Working with data from a survey in Juiz de Fora, a midsized Brazilian city, Amy Smith shows that the most successful religious messages about politics are the most general. Exhortations to church members to vote conscientiously register with citizens, while candidate-centered or partisan messages have little impact. Amy Smith argues that in this way the churches strengthen the connection of members as citizens to democratic processes, but efforts to enter the partisan arena have little resonance with church members. She also affirms that Protestant and Pentecostal congregations show higher indices of religious practice and are more homogenous than typical Catholic parishes, and for that reason messages may also have more impact (Amy Erica Smith 2010). The evidence from recent presidential campaigns in several countries also confirms the renewed push of Catholic leaders, allied at times with Protestants, to make issues of sexuality, including abortion and single-sex marriage, central to the image and position of campaigns (Vaggione 2009a). In Costa Rica, Laura Chinchilla Miranda pitched her successful 2010 campaign for president on opposition to decriminalization of abortion, to gay marriage, and to efforts to modify the constitution to remove mention of religion (Arguedas Ramírez 2010). The broad push back by the church against efforts to decriminalize abortion has also been visible at the regional and local levels, as for example in Mexico (Malkin 2010).

Conclusion

The experience of religion with democracy and pluralism in Latin America resists efforts to draw a definitive balance. Part of the difficulty arises from the dynamic character of our subject matter. Change is continuous and comes from multiple sources, and the continued energy and creativity of those on the ground will surely produce as yet unanticipated patterns. Drawing a balance is further complicated by contextual variation. The common thread of pluralism and plurality shapes the actors and provides them with resources and orientations, but what they do with these varies greatly depending on the structure of opportunity in any specific time and place.

The opportunity of political expression and engagement comes with the perils of losing religious voice for political ends, or getting sucked into the corruption and manipulation of ordinary politics. Almost a hundred years ago, Max Weber addressed the relation of religion with politics in terms that are relevant here. Weber worried about a kind of politics that linked ultimate ends to what are inevitably fallible human means and methods and underscored the distinction between what he called an *ethic of ultimate ends* (good or evil, building the Kingdom of God on earth) and an *ethic of responsibility*. In his view, politics required an ethic of responsibility because such an ethic forces actors to take account of consequences. In contrast, working in politics with an ethic of ultimate ends endangered not only politics but the ultimate ends as well. He wrote,

> He who seeks the salvation of his soul or of others should not seek it along the avenues of politics, for the quite different tasks of politics

can only be solved by violence. Everything that is striven for through political action operating with violent means and following an ethic of responsibility endangers the salvation of the soul. If however, one chases after the ultimate good in a war of beliefs, following a pure ethic of absolute ends, then the goals may be damaged and discredited for generations, because the responsibility for consequences is lacking. (Weber 1978: 222)

Earlier in the same text, Weber spoke of the Sermon on the Mount and its ethic of peace: "By the Sermon on the Mount, we mean the absolute ethic of the Gospel which is a more serious matter than those who are fond of quoting the commandments today believe. This ethic is no joking matter, and the same holds for this ethic as has been said of causality in science: it is not a cab which one can have stopped at one's pleasure: it is all or nothing" (Weber 1978: 224).

Weber's concerns underscore some of the reasons for the failure of early enthusiastic bids by Protestant churches to enter politics and, as children of light, save it. They suggest that the greatest contribution churches and religious groups can make to strengthening democracy may not be in partisan politics at all, but rather through the creation of civil society. This is a long, slow process that entails the building of community before efforts can be made to reconstruct the larger society (Levine and Stoll 1997; Levine and Romero 2006). Although the ideological commitment to democracy is widely shared among church leadership, it has never been universal. In Argentina, for example, the core of the Catholic hierarchy maintained a strong alliance with the military for more than fifty years, and suspicions of democracy remain even now when the last military regime (1976–1983) is long past. At the conclusion of his careful examination of the Catholic Church and politics in Argentina, José Ghio comments that "even if the church had made advances by 1981, openly declaring its preference for democracy, between 1983 and the visit of Pope John Paul II in 1987, the spirit of a defensive crusade against a government that it perceived as its enemy reinforced traditional anti liberal currents in the hierarchy which perceived democracy as a risk" (Ghio 2007: 166). I examine the Argentine church's difficult relation to liberalism and Peronism and its close involvement with the military in Chapters 6 and 7.

Calculations of political benefits or possible subsidies that may have led church leaders to support dictatorship in the past could easily surface again at moments of crisis. These possibilities are constrained by underlying tendencies to pluralism, which present all the churches with a situation in which—precisely because no one has a monopoly— it is in the interest of all to keep the arena open. At the same time, the consolidation of pluralism in religion, in civil society, and in politics presents all the churches with a context in which such shifts of position are more difficult, and likely have less definitive effect than in the past. The range of groups and voices that now exist escape control and must be recognized as autonomous if they are to be real, rather than paper, organizations. This has not been a welcome conclusion for much of the core leadership of the Catholic Church, which continues to equate loss of control with loss of influence and position, and with the possibility that a predominantly Catholic moral ethos will no longer provide an authoritative model for culture and social life. But control is essential to continuity only if control is built into the very definition of what is being continued, in this case "the church" and the Catholic community conceived in hierarchically dependent terms. This is not the only Catholic model available on which to build. As Catalina Romero has pointed out, "Understanding persons as friends of God is quite different than looking upon them as serfs, in the same way that inviting them to follow God's project is different than ordering them to follow the law" (Romero 2009: 394).

The plurality and pluralism that are now so visible were predicted by very few, and it is a challenge for the churches to absorb, accept, and adapt to so much change in so little time. The erosion of Catholicism's religious and cultural monopoly, the new presence of competition among religions, and the coming of real pluralism impact the public image of religion and have a clear feedback effect on the internal life of the community of faith. The seemingly sudden shift to openness and open competition preoccupies and concerns much of the Catholic hierarchy, but as I have argued here, openness and competition can also be a source of potential energy and commitment in as yet unknown forms. Whatever the social and political interests or commitments of any given religious community, all experience the impact of incentives that draw new kinds of leaders onto the scene, of innovative forms of organization, and of trying out hitherto unknown alliances.

Among the most urgent tasks any agenda for the future must take up will be finding ways to make sense of the multiple consequences of religious pluralism, as much for religion as for politics, and for democratic politics above all. One way to get at possible futures is to think about how churches as institutions reposition themselves to cope with the new realities of plurality and pluralism in religion and politics. Repositioning is partly ideological and thus can be found in the statements and actions of those who speak in the name of religion, "authorized and official" or not. But the matter cannot be limited to official statements.[13] Among the long-term legacies for democracy of changes in the churches are concepts of rights and accountability that have altered the agenda of public discourse and found roots in a newly diverse and enriched civil society that advances these ideas in manifold practical ways. Repositioning is also behavioral and resource based and is particularly evident in the reallocation of church resources away from social movements to more conventional lobbying that I noted earlier. Changes in the public stance taken by Catholic bishops, with backing from the Vatican, threaten to widen the gap between official church policies and many of the activists and groups supported in earlier struggles. Although shifting Vatican policies can undermine the possibilities of grassroots action, it is now too late to put that particular genie back in the bottle.

Notes

1. Tocqueville wrote that "the Americans combine the notions of Christianity and of liberty so intimately in their minds that it is impossible to make them conceive the one without the other" (1990: xxx). He went on to comment, "In France, I had almost always seen the spirit of religion and the spirit of freedom pursuing courses diametrically opposed to one another, but in America I found that they were intimately united, and that they reigned in common over the same country" (Tocqueville 1990: 308).

2. Cf. Paul Freston (2008: 10): "It is the poor part of the Western world, an ambiguous position that is often cited as a reason for the emergence of liberation theology. There is little chance (except in a few areas) of taking refuge in a pre-modern non-Western culture, an anti-Western reaction, or a return to pre-colonial roots."

3. Gustavo Morello (2011a) argues that the struggle over the legitimacy of group autonomy is part of a broad reaction to secularization that affirms individual and group rights. The Right, backed by most of the hierarchy of the Catholic Church, rejected such autonomy as a sign of disorder and moral decay. They allied themselves firmly with the military in an effort to eliminate disorder and (re-)create the kind of unity they believed to be proper.

4. Hagopian acknowledges that "in the best of circumstances, conquering the public sphere via civil society would be a broad pull for a church that has never really gone it alone without state help" (Hagopian 2009: 461).

5. The relevance of this drive for control figures prominently in Andrew Chesnut's (2003) account of the Catholic Charismatic Renewal in Brazil. Edward Cleary (2011) describes the growth of the movement, in Brazil and throughout Latin America, as much more driven by grassroots initiatives.

6. Betances (2007) also shows that the hierarchy's relation of mutual support with Trujillo was highly political, not to say valuable. Over the period

of his rule, he gave the church more than US$26 billion—a huge sum then—and helped them build churches and expand parishes. They gave him support and praise until, under Vatican pressure, a slow distancing began in the early 1960s, and the bishops refused an official request to name Trujillo "Benefactor of the Church" as he was already "Benefactor" of the nation as a whole. If this is not a political relation, one wonders what can qualify.

7. Miguel Carter writes that "from 1968 to 1973 the Paraguayan Church was one of the most vocal and progressive within the Latin American Church. It embraced a number of features of the popular church model, particularly in parts of the rural countryside where a heightened Christian faith led to strong support for grassroots activism" (Carter 1990: 87).

8. One notable case was Colombia, where the Catholic Church, inspired by its opposition to liberalism and the Liberal Party, was an active player in civil wars to the middle of the twentieth century (Levine and Wilde 1977).

9. José Napoleon Duarte, a leader associated with Christian Democracy, was president of El Salvador from 1984 to 1989, but his rule was so intertwined with the endgame of the war that it fits only with difficulty into the democratic model of Christian Democracy.

10. Although the Christian Democratic Party remains a formidable presence in Chile, by now little remains that is distinctively Christian about it, and the currents of Catholic social teaching that were key sources of its ideology and legitimations no longer command the attention or enjoy the prominence they once had (Scully 1992; Brian Smith 1982; Fleet and Smith 1997).

11. The constitution of 1999 expands provisions about the freedom of religion to include not only belonging but practice, eliminating elements of the previous constitution that required the state to monitor practice to ensure its compatibility with morality and good custom. The Catholic Church saw this as opening the way to proselytizing abuses by its competitors (Smilde and Pagan 2011).

12. These are, respectively, the Evangelical Council of Venezuela (Consejo Evangélico de Venezuela) and the Pentecostal Evangelical Council of Venezuela.

13. Hagopian (2009: 304ff.) reviews church documents issued from 2000 to 2007 for seven countries (Argentina, Brazil, Chile, El Salvador, Mexico, Peru, and Venezuela) and finds no consistent common pattern.

5

Social Movements and Civil Society

An extraordinary number and variety of social movements have emerged in Latin America over the past fifty years. These include human rights organizations, insurgent unions, peasant groups, new professional associations, neighborhood associations, women's groups, cooperatives, cultural centers, and educational initiatives, along with religious groups like ecclesial base communities. The churches were present at the creation of many of these groups, providing moral and material support, legal and political protection, spaces (often literally rooms in which to meet, chairs on which to sit), finance, education, training, as well as national and transnational connections. This spurt of creative activity responded to pressures from within the churches and also to the political circumstances and opportunities present in Latin American societies in this period (John Burdick 2004; Miguel Carter 2003, 2012; Drogus and Stewart-Gambino 2005; Feinberg, Waisman, and Zamosc 2006; French 2007; Levine 1992; Levine and Romero 2006).

Social movements are groups organized around the pursuit of specific goals—the very idea of social movement entails mobilization and collective action of some kind. These can range from regional or national public campaigns (for direct elections, protests over the cost of living, land reform, or human rights) to local efforts to get support for a school, a police post, better transportation services, or a community kitchen. The churches have been involved in all of these, but their social presence is not limited to movements and campaigns. The multiplication and diversification of the churches contribute more generally to the creation of civil society as they fill the social landscape with chapels, schools, and groups of all kinds, bringing people together in new ways.

The relation of the churches and of religion more generally to social movements and civil society raises two further issues: the empowerment of members and the construction of social capital. Empowerment points to ways in which groups provide members with both tools for action and a sense of efficacy and possibility. The concept of social capital is related but distinct and directs attention above all to civic skills and dispositions of trust and reciprocity that are in principle transferrable from one area of life to another (Anderson 2010; Fox 2004; Hadenius and Uggla 1991; Harris 1999; Levine and Romero 2006; Levine and Stoll 1997; Mendoza-Botelho 2010; Putnam 1993, 2000). The questions before us are to understand how and how much the involvement of the churches in social movements and civil society has promoted empowerment of members, to assess the extent to which personal empowerment has been joined with political effectiveness and access to power, and to consider how (if at all) the social capital created contributes to democracy.

Until the late 1950s, political activism of religious origin or inspiration in Latin America came in a well-defined set of organizational vehicles. Catholic political parties had been tried and failed (for example, in Brazil) and in the period immediately following World War II, political options for the churches remained dominated by ties to traditional elite networks, with surviving Conservative political parties (as in Chile or Colombia) or through the many Catholic Action movements founded throughout the region during the interwar years. Associations of Catholic workers, students, professionals, peasants, journalists, lawyers, men, women, and so forth were set up across the region, each with "clerical advisers" appointed by the hierarchy who supervised group activities to ensure doctrinal and practical conformity with the bishops' views.

By the mid-1950s, both Catholic Action movements and traditional Catholic political vehicles had lost considerable ground. Catholic Action movements foundered as membership claims to autonomy ran up against the hierarchy's push for control. Such movements remained vital where (as for example in Peru or Brazil) they were able to break out of the straitjacket of clerical control and move into open, autonomous forms of social and political organization. Claims by conservative parties to represent "the church" were also challenged by new Christian Democratic parties, whose political program rested on a new reading of Catholic social teachings. The characteristic Christian Democratic political model combined faith in development and confidence in moderate reform with emphasis on party organization over movement autonomy. The experience of Chile is instructive. With the rise of Christian Democracy, grassroots groups were preempted or channeled through the party. When the military government (1973–1989) banned political parties, groups and movements again took a central role, only to be displaced with the return of democracy (Aguilar 2003; Drogus and Stewart-Gambino 2005; Fleet and Smith 1997; Brian Smith 1982).

Despite the churches' well-deserved reputations for conservatism, the 1950s also brought a range of initiatives that gradually acquired substance, which were aimed at redefining the political and social presence of the churches. Together, these formed the basis of a constituency for change that was legitimized and enhanced by the initiatives taken at the Second Vatican Council, and later at Medellín and Puebla.[1] The biblical concept of "signs of the times" (Matthew 16:3) was revived and given new force by Pope John XXIII, who made it a centerpiece of his convocation to the council. Stress on reading the "signs of the times" encouraged a more open stance to change and a search for effective sociological tools with which to understand change and participate actively in it. Commitment to reading the signs of the times also undercut traditional distinctions of "church" from "world." Reading the signs of the times thus affirms the value of ordinary experience, opening the door to egalitarian perspectives on knowledge and action. If the signs of the times were to be read, who better to read them than the men (and grudgingly, the women) actively engaged in the work of the world?

Alongside the hierarchical, trickle-down models long identified as typically Catholic, democratic views began to find expression and room to grow. Average people were seen to have something to offer apart from faith and passive obedience: elites lost their monopoly on truth and inspiration. The church itself was enjoined to change: as part of the world, it shares in changing circumstances, and must learn from them. Participation, understood as informed and active voluntary involvement, became not only possible but also encouraged. The collapse of hopes for democracy and development (punctuated by coups in Brazil and Chile and Central America's rise to civil war and revolution) further reinforced the critical perspectives emerging around this time in the churches. A prophetic and utopian view emerged. It was prophetic in its commitment to confronting and denouncing injustice and to acting in the pursuit of change. This is what Hebrew prophets like Isaiah, Amos, and Jeremiah did. It was utopian not in the common-language sense of being impractical, but rather in a more basic and original sense in which the word *utopia* (as used for example by Thomas More) referred at the same time to no place and to a good, well-ordered place (Levine 1990a).[2] Constructing utopias makes change possible by imagining worlds beyond the present and spurring efforts to bring them into being.[3]

Together these developments created capacities for voice, action, and cooperation that challenged the traditional Latin American social pyramid with its tiny elite, small middle class, and broad oppressed masses. These new voices sparked hopes for thorough cultural and political democratization, grounded in belief in the emergence of what in other work I have described as a "new popular subject," composed of "confident, articulate, and capable men and women from hitherto silent, unorganized and dispirited populations" (Levine 1993b: 171). This new historical subject consolidates as people acquire skills and orientations that equip them for active democratic citizenship (see also Hirschman 1984).

But what the churches give they can also take away, and in many cases they have done precisely that. With notable exceptions that I examine here, since the settlement of civil wars and the return to democratic politics, institutional churches across the region (both Catholic and Protestant) have gotten out of the business of promoting and sustaining social movements. Facing a diverse and competitive civil society and a more open political arena, many church leaders believed that there was no longer a compelling justification for them to invest resources in promoting social movements and encouraging them to be active in politics. Politics could and should be left to professional politicians, political parties, and public officials. Church resources were now redirected to competition with other churches for members, for public subsidies, and for presence on the public stage.

The vision of change energized from below has also come under attack in recent scholarship that calls into question the viability of this portrait of a transformed set of movements and an energized civil society laying the foundations for a different kind of politics (Oxhorn 1995; Avritzer 2002). Religiously linked groups often turned out to be more traditionally pious and less socially concerned than depicted. Democracy itself brought partisan division into groups, and promising leaders were co-opted into government or political parties (Blondet 1991; Schoenwalder 2002; Ottmann 2002). In case after case, the new politics was easily absorbed into the old, "normal" politics of parties and influences.[4] Questions have also been raised about whether the groups ever were as democratizing or mobilizing as painted, or if this portrait was simply wishful thinking on the part of scholars and activists (Bastián 1993, 1997; John Burdick 1993; Gaskill 1997; Hellman 1992; Ortner 1995). The return to democracy was also accompanied in many cases by severe and extended economic downturn (Peter Smith 2005) that gutted the capacity of poorer citizens to continue their involvement in political mobilization. The struggle for personal and family survival took precedence over collective action. In these circumstances, the pullback by the institutional churches took a heavy toll on groups, which lost resources and often felt abandoned (Gaskill 1997; Ireland 1999; Kurtz 2004; Levine and Stoll 1997; Stewart-Gambino 2005).

Although early expectations that religious change would spark broad cultural change and a new way of doing politics were clearly exaggerated, it does not follow that new movements represented no change. The evidence is anything but uniform: instances of group failure and abandonment by allies can be matched by experiences of continued vitality and sustained commitment. To sort out the record and address the issues in a balanced way, this chapter examines the relation of the churches and religious groups to social movements under several related headings. I ask if the weaknesses and failures experienced by religiously linked movements are the result of internally generated difficulties, or are rather by-products of failure or betrayal on the part of allies in churches and politics. I also ask how and in what ways participation makes for empowerment and contributes in some measure to the formation of social capital. It is common to hear group members talk about how "empowered" they feel, but decades of activism have often left members only marginally (if at all) better off than when they began. The paradoxical combination of activism with disempowerment raises questions about what empowerment means in the first place, and why there should be a gap between empowerment and power (Levine and Romero 2006; Levine and Stoll 1997).

How and in what way do religiously inspired and sponsored social movements contribute to the formation of social capital? The concept of social capital combines dispositions to trust, reciprocity, and collective action with acquired civic and social skills that turn these dispositions into grounds for enduring action. The process is often viewed as cumulative and self-reinforcing, with successful instances leading to imitation.[5] Churches bring a promise of legitimation along with material and organizational resources, but they also commonly insist on control in ways that can stifle group life. There are ironies here: the greater the involvement of institutional churches with movements—the greater their investment of resources, training, and control—the weaker and less survivable movements often turn out to be. Distance may make for movements that can survive better on their own (Drogus and Stewart-Gambino 2005; Froehle 1994; Levine 1992; Levine and Romero 2006).

Are Weaknesses Internally Generated or the Result of External Factors?

The weaknesses and vulnerabilities of religiously linked or sponsored social movements have both internal and external sources. Internal sources include limitations on mobilization and activism posed by gender identities, scarcity of resources, and difficulties arising from a working image of politics that exaggerated the possibilities of popular mobilization and failed to prepare for the compromise and accommodation that are characteristic of democratic politics. The cumulative weight of changes in Vatican policies over the past few decades—appointment of conservative bishops, reassignment of sympathetic clergy, withdrawal of the institutional church from "undue politicization" (and hence from support for confrontational politics and movements), and drastic cuts in the flow of human and material resources to grassroots groups—has had a devastating effect on many groups (Della Cava 1992, 1993; Drogus and Stewart-Gambino 2005; Haas 1999). The loss of ideological support and material and organizational resources crippled many movements and made it harder for them to attract and hold on to members. Many religious activists identify these changes, along with the effects of competition from other groups (including other churches), as prime sources of the problems they have experienced (Stewart-Gambino 2005). Although these factors are important, they are not sufficient by themselves to account for the problems groups have experienced. As Philip Berryman reminds us, "Not all the difficulties of the progressive wing of the Catholic Church can be attributed to the Vatican" (Berryman 1996: 15; see also Cousineau 2003).

Many religiously linked social movements in Latin America emerged as extensions of the ecclesial base communities (CEBs, *comunidades eclesiales de base*) that started up all across the region beginning in the 1970s. A common working definition takes off from the meaning of the three words that give the groups their name: striving for *community* (small and homogeneous), stress on the *ecclesial* (links to the church), and a sense in which the group constitutes a *base* (either the faithful at the base of the church's hierarchy or the poor at the base of a class and power pyramid). Base communities were intended to supplement and sometimes replace parish life, providing opportunities for religious education and participation in the absence of clergy, who are often scarce on the ground. The term *ecclesial* should be distinguished from *ecclesiastical*. The root word for church in Greek, *ekklesia*, means community, and from the beginning the emphasis in CEBs was on building community through participation. *Ecclesiastical* refers more to the church's formal structures of authority.

There is much dispute over precisely what counts as a base community. Very different kinds of organizations, from devotional prayer circles to neighborhood committees, are commonly often lumped together under this heading. Whatever else they may be, at a minimum base communities are small groups of ten to thirty people, homogeneous in social composition. Whatever else they may do, at a minimum they gather regularly (once every week or two) to read and comment on the Bible, to discuss common concerns, and occasionally to act together toward some concrete end. Reading and commenting on the Bible in a community setting soon became the common foundation of group activities. Stress on participation and equal access to sacred knowledge, through the Bible, reinforces ideas of egalitarianism and action in common as the outgrowth of a transformed religious faith (Fields 1985; Hewitt 1991; Levine 1992). Whatever their form and orientation, the communities do not spring unbidden and full-blown "from the people." They are not autonomous or isolated from the institutional church. They are born linked to the churches, specifically to initiatives by bishops, religious orders, priests, nuns, or lay agents commissioned by the church. These ties are maintained through a routine of courses, visits by clergy and especially sisters, and the distribution of mimeographed circulars, instructional material, and cassettes. Meetings follow a common pattern. The group gathers weekly or biweekly in a church facility, community center, or on a rotating basis in the homes of members. Meetings open with reading from the Bible, followed by commentary and discussion aimed at connecting the scripture passage to personal and community issues. They commonly close with a prayer. Although the Bible is central to group life, base communities should not be confused with fundamentalists. Members do not view the Bible as an inerrant text, a source of formulas to be applied in some mechanical fashion, but rather as a set of values, ideals, and role models. Discussion is active and open, with members jumping in to point out how what is spoken of in the Bible is happening to people like themselves.

The newness of base communities rests on the model of governance they embodied. Breaking with traditional Catholic trickle-down models, in which the bishops know more than the priest, the priest knows more than the sisters, the sisters know more than the laity, and so on down to the bottom, CEBs and similar groups with different names underscored equal access to knowledge (through the Bible) and equal participation in managing group affairs. The links between base communities and social or political action have been varied, but all begin with a decision to address some pressing local need. Health communities, cooperatives, schools, and local efforts to supplement subsistence (for example, through the organization of community kitchens) are prominent. These short-term connections are amplified by the way participation in base communities legitimizes activism and autonomous organization. By diffusing skills of organization and providing spaces for self-governance and self-expression, base communities contribute to a general democratization of culture while providing an environment in which new sources of leadership can emerge.

Members look for fellowship, moral support, and specific improvements like access to water, education, credit, and health services, and goals are distinctly modest, nonpolitical, and nonrevolutionary. Typical activities include sewing, visiting the sick, and "social action," which usually means collecting money, clothing, or food for those in extreme need. There are also attempts to found cooperatives, which are commonly limited to very small-scale savings and loan operations, or at most to collective marketing or shared purchase arrangements. No matter what the social or political agenda may be, from child care to sewing circles, from cooperatives to strikes or land invasions, in all instances there is great stress on prayer and Bible study. The appeal of Bible study is also evidence of the powerful attraction of literacy to newly mobile communities. In Latin America, as among the Puritans of sixteenth-century England, equality of access to sacred knowledge laid the foundation for a claim to equality in general (Dodson and O'Shaughnessy 1992; Levine 1992; Zaret 1985).

From the beginning, base communities developed in ways that responded to a perceived need for participatory experiences in the church that could provide meaning, structure, and support in a difficult and changing world. All this was appealing and would have had some impact in any event. Where the communities developed strong links with political activism, as in El Salvador, Nicaragua, Chile, Brazil, and Peru, repression and authoritarian rule decisively magnified and extended their impact. By restricting political spaces and shutting down organizations like unions or political parties, fearful governments drove activists into the churches: there was often nowhere else to go. The communities supplied a generative base for activism, applying new ideals and drawing hitherto unorganized communities into group-like cooperatives, neighborhood associations, and rural or urban unions. The result was something really new: prophetic ideals and activist drives embedded in movements that were small in scale, decentralized in structure, but still connected with and energized by the institutional churches.

The groups also had substantial and specific appeal to women, for whom they offered opportunities for self-improvement, sociability, and work for the community, all with an imprint of religious legitimacy. Much writing on CEBs stresses their social and political consequences, but it is important not to lose sight of the opportunities for sociability outside the home. Sociability and the chance for cooperative and collaborative effort provide a basis for group coherence, but as we shall see, they can also limit the extent of commitment as women often filter messages of social justice through a lens that stresses caring and cooperation over confrontation (Gilligan 1982; Drogus 1997a). These general considerations on gender are relevant because many of the social movements sponsored by the Catholic Church in the 1970s and 1980s relied on women for the bulk of their members, activists, and resources, and women continue to carry much of the day-to-day presence of religion in civil society. This is not because women are necessarily more pious or spiritual than men, but rather because religion provides a culturally approved place for women to participate in groups outside the home and beyond the reach and control of male family members (Drogus 1997a; Drogus and Stewart-Gambino 2005; Harris 1999). In periods of authoritarian rule, women were also more available than men and were actively recruited by churches and the groups they sponsored and promoted.

Despite their patriarchal image, Protestant and Pentecostal churches also have a well-documented appeal to women in Latin America. Much of this appeal rests on the promise to control male drunkenness and promiscuity, enhance stable family life, and provide access to education, literacy, sociability, and (in the Pentecostal churches) gifts of the Holy Spirit in equal measure with men (Smilde and Steigenga 1999). Women are often the first in the family to convert, bringing male partners and family members along. Carol Ann Drogus suggests that Protestant groups appeal to women precisely because they enhance life in the private sphere, promoting equality and providing solutions to immediate pressing problems such as alcoholism and domestic abuse. In contrast, Catholic groups, particularly those inspired by liberation theology, emphasize collective action in the public sphere, a goal that may seem remote to someone trapped in an abusive relationship (Drogus 1997b; see also John Burdick 1993).

Participation offers women opportunities for voice and citizenship that were hitherto closed (López 2008b), but the evidence suggests that this participation is often shaped and mediated by cultural constructs of proper feminine roles. Drogus finds that "gender may be at least partially accountable for the CEBs' apparent inability to generate enthusiasm for what women regard as 'dirty' competitive male dominated politics. . . . At the same time, however, gender seems to have provided the glue necessary to hold a social movement of divergent political beliefs together" (Drogus 1997a: 141). To avoid unwanted connotations of struggle and conflict, participation is framed in terms of motherhood and community. The emphasis is on face-to-face contact, caring, and helping of others, rather than on more general and potentially confrontational mobilizations in pursuit of social justice (Drogus 1997a: 108–109). The result is that although groups commit many women to participation and activism, members are often not willing to go as far as leaders believe, or as group slogans may suggest. When messages are filtered in this way, it is impossible to understand the scope of activism by paying attention only to what leaders say and do or what formal documents indicate. We need also to look at how members receive, interpret, and act on these general declarations. The difficulty women experience lies not in participation itself, but rather in the cost it carries with family, the resistance and pressure they experience from male relations, and the ability and desire of participants to extend their actions in time and across social levels. The potentially self-limiting quality of participation undermines possibilities for the consolidation of civil society. To be sure, the record is not all the same. Many women have moved into broader spheres of participation, using motherhood and charity to justify activism (Bayard de Volo 2001; Drogus 1997a; Fonseca 2008).

If we ask how civil society acquires consistency and enduring social presence, how it "thickens," one answer lies in the ability of individual groups to move out of locally confined endeavors and make connections to larger institutional networks. Social movements make for empowerment by "scaling up," that is, entering into broader networks that provide support, resources, and information (Fox 1996, 2004). But the self-limiting quality of much of women's participation undercuts this potential line of growth. For Drogus, "the specifically gendered basis of the movements might also reinforce a tendency toward cyclical decline. The mobilization of women around issues related to motherhood and social and family reproduction tends to generate a pattern whereby women mobilize but later withdraw from politics" (Drogus 1999: 41). Women also commonly encounter a glass ceiling in the churches, with positions of influence and authority reserved for men. The result is considerable burnout and dropout, and in any event, a high personal cost for activism and leadership—a cost that is also paid by nuns, who run into many similar problems in what, after all, remains a strongly patriarchal as well as hierarchical institution (Gillfeather 1979).

The experience of women in Lima, Peru, in the 1970s and 1980s is illustrative. Many women from grassroots religious communities in Lima were drawn into broader activism through the Glass of Milk movement, which was established in 1983 by the newly elected leftist government of the municipality of greater Lima. The goal was to improve the diet of the most vulnerable of the poor by delivering a protein supplement—a glass of milk a day—to all children under the age of six, as well as to nursing mothers and pregnant women. At the neighborhood level, management of the program (receiving powdered milk, preparing it, and arranging for distribution) was in the hands of local committees of women and mothers' clubs. By 1986, more than 100,000 women participated through 7,500 committees delivering milk to a million recipients daily. The program drew strength from existing survival organizations, including popular kitchens (*comedores populares*) also managed by women, which were central to nets of local organization (Blondet 1991; Blondet and Trivelli 2004; Levine and Stoll 1997; Schoenwalder 2002).

These movements were part of a wave of grassroots organizations that got under way in Peru in the 1970s. The progressive military regime of General Juan Velasco Alvarado (1968–1976) encouraged a range of grassroots initiatives that inspired emulation and ultimately proved difficult for the military to control. Movements also got invaluable backing and ecclesiastical "cover" from top leaders of the Catholic Church, like Monsignor Juan Landázuri Ricketts, cardinal archbishop of Lima, and Monsignor Luis Bambarén, auxiliary bishop of Lima, who took a key early role in promoting organization in poor neighborhoods. National-level church institutions like CEAS (Comisión Episcopal de Acción Social, Episcopal Commission for Social Action) also worked to spur popular organization and legitimize activism and mobilization. The Catholic Church's prominent role in the struggle against poverty, and later in the promotion and defense of human rights, opened new areas for common action with other organizations in civil society, as well as with international agencies sharing the same goals. Facing a reality of high inflation and economic crisis, in 1988 the church created a space for bringing together different actors in an emergency social program, including international cooperation agencies, business entrepreneurs, and grassroots leadership. Later, in response to the violence that wracked the country in the 1980s and 1990s, the church supported human rights organizations and put its newly gained religious legitimacy behind the efforts of their pastoral agents (clergy, nuns, and laity) to care for the relatives of people missing and tortured and those innocent in prison.

> In many parts of the country, clergy and Catholic lay workers developed new, more egalitarian ways to work with the poor through parishes and the expanding network of Christian base communities. These Catholic activists, along with CEAS, whose Human Rights Department was founded in 1976, played a very important role in the development of human rights work in many different areas of the country. CEAS became one of the most important human rights organizations and played an important role in the creation and institutionalization of the Coordinadora Nacional de Derechos Humanos [the National Coordinating Group for Human Rights]. (Drzewieniecki 2001: 4)

Trusted by residents and perceived by outsiders as able to "deliver" groups and blocs of voters, religious activists easily slipped into brokerage roles, trading influence over residents for urgently needed goods, services, and contacts (Fleet and Smith 1997: 203–205). In the short term, these mediating roles empowered groups and helped them get going. But over the long haul, and in particular as resources became more scarce, reliance on mediators and outside resources turned into a debilitating dependence, and the distance among sponsoring institutions, activists, and rank-and-file members grew (Pásara 1989; Pásara et al. 1991; Blondet 1991). Susan Stokes writes:

> Church workers faced a series of tensions and pressures that led them, against their will, to compromise their role as community and shift to a role of patrons or brokers. One such pressure was competition from other religious groups, mainly Protestant evangelicals who proselytized actively. There was also competition from secular leaders and parties, which Catholic workers saw as competing for the time and energy of the most activist residents. Nuns and priests also felt pressure from more conservative Catholic orders and from conservatives within the Catholic hierarchy . . . finally, as the economic crisis deepened, some of the church's most active followers began to withdraw from community affairs and spend more time trying to increase their income. Whenever numbers fell at community dining hall meetings, catechism classes, or open air masses, church workers had to find new

ways to bring their followers back. This last pressure in particular led church workers in Independencia [the neighborhood Stokes studied] to compromise their self-stated mission of "creating consciousness among the poor" and focus instead on producing immediate benefits that would attract souls to the clubs and classes. (Stokes 1995: 57)

The early promise of the movement was also undermined by political shifts: a new and less sympathetic local government, persistent efforts by political parties to colonize and control the groups, and the growing violence of the 1980s, which led the Shining Path guerrillas to attack any organized effort not under their control. The experience of Villa El Salvador, now a self-governing municipality within Greater Lima, is relevant here. Villa El Salvador began as a resettlement project for squatter settlement invaders elsewhere in Lima. Over the years, residents of Villa El Salvador created a dense and interlocking network of economic, social, cultural, and political institutions founded on basic notions of popular participation and self-governance. Cecilia Blondet's study of women's organizations in Villa El Salvador documents the emergence of women's organizations, the internal conflicts they experienced, and the gradual consolidation of a model of organization that was egalitarian, democratic, and participatory.

Political commitments, and the absence of viable alternatives, led a contingent of young women from the parties of the left to propose the construction of feminine organizations distinct from time honored traditions of clientelism and charity. The Church also conceived nontraditional forms of organization, and feminists themselves accepted the notion that gender identity had to arise, in the first place, out of a social and political identity that historically had been denied. On this diverse base, a project of feminine organization emerged that was grounded in universal rules and procedures. . . . [It was a] process of great breadth and significance, valuable not only because it was a popular and feminine initiative, but also because it led to new, democratic ways of "doing politics." The very youth of the movement kept it in a permanent tension between authority and the search for consensus on forms of leadership, and between dependence and autonomy in relations with external institutions and with the State. (Blondet 1991: 179)

From the beginning, groups in Villa El Salvador (like others in Lima) had close ties with political parties, above all, on the left, and with a number of nongovernmental organizations (NGOs) that provided critical material support. As the country's political and economic crisis intensified, these relations grew in importance, and groups became ever more dependent on these contacts. Setbacks and defeats soon followed.

Local initiatives soon ran up against two "seemingly invincible giants: The first is the personalist and patrimonial state, which far from encouraging links with society attacks any expression of social democratization. The second is a generalized crisis that has eroded the bases of what little institutional life exists" (Blondet 1991: 179). Already weakened by economic crisis and pressure to attend to urgent family needs, these women and many of their groups were further buffeted by political divisions originating in the national politics of the Left that divided the movements in the late 1980s. Blondet states that "as party leaders fought a cold chess game to gain control of base groups, rank and file members suddenly found themselves divided and set against one another. They saw the unity of their organizations destroyed, and in personal terms felt the anguish on seeing a promising project collapse before their eyes" (Blondet 1991: 176).[6]

Some have argued that the apparent success of these groups was an illusion to begin with. Luis Pásara asserts that the efforts of what he calls "Peru's leftist angels" were contaminated from the outset by a "radical Catholic style" (compounded of utopianism, clericalism, elitism, intellectualization, and verticality) that undercuts the validity of any claim to empowerment of the poor (Pásara 1989: 291–301). In his view, progressive Catholicism was simply another manipulation of the poor, and he approvingly cites one critic who accused liberation theology of "'taking for popular whatever sociology says about the people'" (Pásara 1989: 298–299). Pásara also underscores the ambiguous role played by NGOs in organizing and financing groups and mediating their access to international resources and advice. He states that NGOs commonly advance their own agenda, presenting it as the "voice of the people." Kristin Norget (2004) makes a similar point for southern Mexico, where the Catholic priests who serve as leaders and intermediaries for indigenous communities are not themselves from the community and may be adopting ethnic identity politics because it promotes their broader liberationist agenda. These tensions among pastoral agents, NGOs, and the communities they "represent" help explain why many groups develop only shallow roots in the community and have a hard time surviving any loss of aid, let alone sudden shifts in the interests of their outside supports (Pásara et al. 1991; Norget 2004; Steigenga and Lazo de la Vega 2012; for a general discussion of NGOs, see Brian Smith 1990).[7]

Michael Fleet and Brian Smith address the issues from a different angle. Working with data from Chile and Peru, they focus on the relation of religion (churches, groups, and activists) to the transition to democracy and to democracy's possible consolidation in the two countries. Although they acknowledge the scope and depth of popular mobilization in Peru, Fleet and Smith insist that the very radicalism of the effort, and its pervasive stress on participation and confrontation, undercut the ability of the groups (and religious institutions and their leaders who supported them) to contribute to building and maintaining democracy. Peruvian groups were too independent, and the bishops too divided, for the church to assume the kind of coordinating, consensus-building, and controlling role that their Chilean counterparts would later take on (Fleet and Smith 1997: 215).

Fleet and Smith see Christian Democracy as a model for organizing the connections of religion and religious groups with democracy in the most fruitful manner, a prime vehicle for channeling religious energies into politics. They locate the core of the difficulty with Peru in the fact that the Peruvian church never developed a secular counterpart like the Christian Democratic Party in Chile (Fleet and Smith 1997: 89–91, 107). Their summary judgment on Peru is telling. "Under Archbishop Landázuri," they write, "social Christianity became the dominant tendency in both the episcopacy and Catholic Action circles during the late 1950s but by then the political space in which a Chilean style Christian Democratic party might have operated successfully had been filled by forces not particularly attractive to progressive Catholic voters" (Fleet and Smith 1997: 108). The dominant style of popular mobilization in Peru, rooted in local, territorially based groups and stressing the need to meet immediate popular demands for housing and services, worked against the possibility of building broad political coalitions. Peru's bishops were divided and "left politics to the politicians even as they pulled in contradictory and antagonistic directions. Locally, Catholics were active in a variety of neighborhood based organizations housed in parish facilities and encouraged by area priests and nuns. But they were more concerned with the provision or distribution of material services (meals, medical supplies, access to water, land titles etc.) *than with political matters as such*" (Fleet and Smith 1997: 219, emphasis added).

I underscore "than with political matters as such" to point up the terms in which Fleet and Smith define the political problem. Their explanation stresses how the absence of moderation, compromise, and coalition building can undermine the ability of organizations to consolidate and endure. There is of course nothing wrong with compromise and coalition building, but it is a curious view of politics that distinguishes the satisfaction of needs from *politics as such*. What is politics all about if not the satisfaction of needs? Few can be expected to organize and sustain action in favor of political pacts and agreements in the absence of attention to the needs of daily life. The inescapable fact is that from the mid-1980s on, the steady worsening of conditions of life for most people in Peru, added to the loss of allies and support from the outside, did serious damage to the popular movement, eroding its base and weakening the capacity of its organizations to act.

It is in any case not clear why one would assume that a Christian Democratic outcome was feasible or even desirable in the Peruvian context. It is true that Christian Democracy never got off the ground in Peru, and options for reform in the kind of liberal democratic political framework favored by Fleet and Smith were rarely available, but the heart of the problem for popular movements in Peru, and in particular for those linked with religion and the churches, was neither excessive concern with local, material needs nor the absence of Christian Democratic political mediation. The core of the problem was a misreading by activists of who the base was and what it wanted, the fickleness and unreliability of allies, and the devastating impact of a decade of violence and civil war compounded by economic disaster (Klaiber 1992; Levine and Stoll 1997; Levine and Romero 2006).

Some of these issues are common to Latin America as a whole, but others, like the violence of the civil war, are specific to Peru itself. The bottom line is that by the early 1990s the popular movement in Peru was in disarray. Political parties and, indeed, the very project of "democracy" itself were not in much better shape. The Left went through a series of ruinous divisions, whereas the rise of Alberto Fujimori to power subverted and destroyed institutions while shrinking the state and reducing traditionally important parties like the American Revolutionary Popular Alliance (APRA) and Popular Action to marginal status (Conaghan 2005). Lacking reliable allies and ever more dependent on external institutions for support, popular movements receded. Stokes (1995) suggests that the participatory model group action that characterized the "popular project" in Peru, where activism was seen as both necessary and good in itself, is best understood not as a cultural transformation but as an alternative that people were willing to use as long as it delivered results. Repeated failure and high costs made group members open to a return to more traditional means of gaining benefits. Given the failure of collective mobilizations, many returned to old strategies of clientelism and exchanging votes for benefits. Radicals had once put their faith in democracy as a means of changing the class state "into a citizen's state, one that saw to the needs of those at the bottom as well as those at the top. They certainly associated democracy with a state constituted through electoral mechanisms. But even then, they saw democracy as contingent on the untiring pressure that social movements from below could bring to bear." By the early 1990s, however, a different way of thinking about politics and democracy was evident, "one that was simpler and more ominous. This version, entertained even by some of the distinctly more politicized residents, might be thought of as the 'historical' view of democracy. It went something like this: democracy returned to Peru in 1980 and has produced three Presidents, hyper inflation, unemployment, *Sendero Luminoso,* cholera, blackouts, chaos, loss of national self-esteem, an internal war with twenty-five thousand dead" (Stokes 1995: 135).

Negotiating access to institutions (religious or political or cultural) on a regular and regularly autonomous basis has been problematic for religiously linked grassroots groups throughout Latin America. In the Peruvian case, urban popular groups did not become the driving force behind the democratization of local government as many had expected, and the transfer of real power to the movements "halted almost before it began" (Schoenwalder 2002: 149). It proved difficult to institutionalize new participatory structures and integrate them into city government in a workable way (Schoenwalder 2002: 99–102). For some scholars, the problem is more general. As noted earlier, Jean Pierre Bastián (1993, 1997) argues that new groups, and new Protestant and Pentecostal churches in particular, are simply folded into and end up reinforcing existing patterns of hierarchical domination and control. In the same vein, Newton Gaskill states that "in Latin America, the organizational structure of the churches which have been most successful at attracting converts seems also to encourage leaders to engage in the sorts of patron-client relations that frustrate more substantively democratic politics" (Gaskill 1997: 88). In his deeply pessimistic account of the decline of liberation spirituality in Brazil, Goetz Frank Ottmann (2002) argues that core liberationist concepts such as people, struggle, and liberating journey (*povo, lutta,* and *caminhada*) have been gutted of relevance in new political and social contexts. Militants and activists raised in earlier movements were marginalized and co-opted.

> Once charged by academic observers with the task of transforming Brazilian society morally and socially and democratizing the Catholic Church from the bottom up, the popular church has been emptied of its militancy in the institutional politics of both church and state. . . . Nudged out of the church, Catholic activists intent on pursuing an overt political mobilization of the grass roots are increasingly forced to anchor their projects in the secular realm. Yet this realm too has

> been changed dramatically since 1985. Before 1985, grass roots based
> social movements, deeply suspicious of any dealings with the state,
> sought to construct alternative centers of governance. After 1985,
> activists formed part of state focused political parties, pressure groups
> or NGOs integrated in global communication networks. If this reality
> of a new Brazilian democratic politics is correct, the space available
> for radical liberationist activists with a commitment to grass roots
> mobilization has diminished in the secular realm as well as in the
> church . . . an era of liberationist militancy seems to have drawn to a
> close. (Ottmann 2002: 162–163)

Not least among the challenges facing popular social movements in the new era has been the need to rethink the meaning and value of democracy. In the activist vocabulary of the 1980s, words like *democracy* referred more to popular mobilization and equality than to the classic issues of liberal democracy, such as arrangements for elections, legislatures, accountability, and legitimizing the rule of law. But with transitions to democracy across the region, these are precisely the issues that now occupied the center of political attention. The move from military to civil rule was managed everywhere by conventional politicians working through negotiations, reaching pacts and agreements that for the most part left popular activists and most of the groups of interest here marginal to the process and marginalized by its results. The organizations and activists who in many cases had sparked opposition to the military and taken great risks to keep up the pressure now found themselves on the sidelines.

David Lehmann argues that the survival capacity of many grassroots initiatives has been further undermined by an ideology of *basismo* that was common in many inspired by liberation theology. As the name suggests, *basismo* placed exclusive confidence in the base, "the people." This is a long-standing characteristic of populist movements: what groups do and how they see themselves should be guided by the wisdom of the people. Participation is seen as more than a means to a given end: in some measure participation is the end, a good in itself.[8] Such faith in "the people" brings with it a pervasive distrust of structured organization and wariness about connections with other levels. These are perceived as vehicles for co-optation, sellout, and manipulation by self-interested elites (Lehmann 1996). The commitment to participation as good in itself has deep roots in the theory and practice of liberation theology, with notable support from sources as varied as the educational theories of Paulo Freire to the image of democracy advanced by Alexis de Tocqueville. The vision is appealing but there are evident problems.

Under the best of circumstances, resources are in short supply, and social movements need allies, connections, and concrete help if they are to consolidate and endure, delivering benefits to their members not only in terms of sociability, but also through the delivery of concrete goods, services, and connections.[9] The preceding discussion brings me to the issues of empowerment and social capital.

Empowerment, Disempowerment, and the Ambiguities of Social Capital

Empowerment is a multidimensional, people-friendly concept that points to a kind of social and political process and a pattern of structure and organization that can provide citizens with a sense of efficacy and a set of skills that help them act together effectively. The idea of empowerment thus promises both psychological fulfillment and tangible success in organizational and material terms. This is a lot for any social process to deliver, and it is not surprising that many movements have not been able to fill the bill. Even the briefest review of recent scholarship on social movements in Latin America reveals a slow recovery from a hangover brought on by exaggerated expectations, laced with a heavy dose of idealization of the new movements. The autonomy of movements (vis-à-vis institutions such as political parties, state institutions, or church) was overdone, and a romantic image of the "small is beautiful" kind made many observers anticipate that a totally new kind of politics would arise from the seedbed of these new movements (Eckstein 2001; Hellman 1992; Levine and Romero 2006).

The results have been limited. One problem for religiously linked groups is that hierarchical structures can disempower groups even when the stated intention is to equip them with resources and skills for independent action. The most densely structured and provisioned groups may well be less apt venues for the creation of civic capacities and social capital than those with less exclusive and exhaustive internal ties. Mark Granovetter's notion of the "strength of weak ties" is relevant here. He stresses that when ties within a group are demanding and exclusive, the group is effectively shut off from others, and there are significant problems of survival. In contrast, weaker internal ties facilitate alliances between groups, and the group keeps itself open to the flow of information (Granovetter 1973). In this vein, Drogus and Hannah Stewart-Gambino (2005) find that grassroots groups and the women activists associated with them survived the general lowering of church support better in Brazil than in Chile. Both churches devoted substantial efforts to the creation and support of grassroots movements, many of which played a key role in struggles for democracy. But the distinctive style of each hierarchy's involvement shaped how withdrawal took place, with what effect, how it appeared to group members, and what was left behind. In Chile, heavy investment of resources was accompanied by more control and direction from the top, making groups more dependent. In Brazil, the operative model of the "progressive church" made for more autonomy but fewer resources. As the institutional church backed away from its commitments and support, Chilean groups were highly vulnerable, and members were left feeling frustrated and abandoned (Stewart-Gambino 2005). Brazilian clergy favored autonomy and decentralization for the groups, and hoped that organizations beyond the local level would play only a coordinating role. In the end, Brazilian women appear more open to the construction of new alliances and connections but have fewer tools with which to operate in an admittedly difficult environment (Drogus and Stewart-Gambino 2005). The contrast is instructive and fits well with the conclusion that Bryan Froehle draws from his work on Venezuela. "The more outside resources are present, the weaker the resulting GRO [grassroots organization] and the less likely it is to organize other GROs or to seek out additional members" (Froehle 1994: 153–154). This result ties into my own work on the democratizing potential of religious change, which suggests that less central control may be related to more cultural democratization (and a more open and participatory model of social life), with the downside of fewer resources (Levine 1992).

Despite the obstacles and difficulties noted here, movements do persist and achieve substantial gains, and brief consideration of some successful experiences may yield useful insights. Jan Hoffman French (2007) and Madeleine Cousineau (1995) suggest that pessimism about the fate of movements can be overdone and attribute the problem to excessive focus on one kind of movement (CEBs) and on urban developments, without sufficient attention to what is going on in the countryside. French's study of the careers of two priests and their link with peasant and indigenous movements in the northeast of Brazil shows what can happen when efforts to mobilize the poor are undertaken in a way that combines organizational resources with development of local leadership and a sustained effort to craft a sense of identity. She writes, "With the development of its support for indigenous people and *quilombo* communities,[10] in addition to its traditional focus on nonidentitarian peasant communities, pastoral agents have helped structure alternatives to CEBs that have permitted the Church to span its shift from opposition to a military government in the 1970s to partnership with a democratic government in the twenty-first century" (French 2007: 409). These efforts, like others in rural Brazil, were underwritten by a substantial commitment from the Brazilian church, above all through its various commissions (the Pastoral Land Commission, the Commission on Indigenous Affairs, and the Pastoral Commission on Justice and Peace), which continue to invest resources in training, informing local leaders of rights, and facilitating their work through the legal and political system.

Among the efforts that have enjoyed notable success is work with peasant communities that helped spark and sustain what is now one of Brazil's largest social movements, the movement of landless (MST). The MST has a core of leaders who emerged out of contacts and work with church agents, but who operate independently and maintain the autonomy of their organization. The combination of independent leadership with the continuing power of liberationist ideas and symbolic references (the use of biblical imagery, often from the Book of Exodus; collective reference to the cross erected in the camps and to processions and regular celebrations of the mass as focal points for community gatherings; and music and singing in common as ways to reinforce solidarity) reinforces group identity while promoting something like empowerment that is both personal and collective (John Burdick 2004; Miguel Carter 2012). The origins of the MST lie in an alliance between pastoral agents and church leaders inspired by a new sense of mission with peasants in desperate need of land. The history of this alliance (which began with peasant land invasion at a place called Natalino's Crossing) reads very much like the history of the civil rights movement in the United States. In both cases, clergy and religiously inspired activists provided connections, networks, and a sense of legitimacy that enabled groups to resist powerful state pressure (including political intimidation and armed force) and eventually construct a movement that endured and has in fact continued to deliver goods to its members—for Brazil, in the form of land; for the United States, in the form of a wide range of rights (Miguel Carter 2003, 2010, 2012; Harris 1999; Morris 1984). The overall conclusion that French draws is worth citing at some length:

> With the rise of "new historical subjects," pastoral agents who adhere to liberationist doctrine and practice have become sensitive to the relationship between poverty and discrimination. From the side of the subjects, we can also see the consolidation of faith through ethnic identification, leading to the conclusion that the assumption of ethnic

identities is not simply pragmatic, but is considered by many of the Indians and quilombolas as the fulfillment of a religious commitment. In fact, what is often missing from analyses of new ethnoracial identification in Latin America is the role of the liberationist Church in the story of identity reconfiguration and empowerment. (French 2007: 440)

I consider questions of identity and ethnic movements later in this chapter. The point I want to underscore here concerns what it takes to turn the personal energies and sense of efficacy that empowerment provides into an enduring capacity for collective action. There is a long tradition in the Latin American churches of serving as "a voice for the voiceless." This is an important and honorable role. Over the years, those acting as a voice for the voiceless have rescued countless victims, helped families, and supported communities in the search for a better life. But serving as a voice for the voiceless retains presumptions of distance and authority that fit easily into directive roles that have been traditional for the clergy. For those raised in a hierarchical and paternalistic tradition, serving as a voice for the voiceless can be a lot easier than standing aside to let the voiceless speak for themselves, hearing what they say, and trusting them to act. As groups are created, they need and use this support and these connections, but if the effort is to endure, church agents also need to know how to stand aside and let the voiceless speak for themselves.[11]

The difficulties of empowerment noted here suggest that as applied to social movements, the concept is not so much mistaken as incomplete. Many men and women have indeed acquired new skills and self-images and imparted these to others in their communities. Difficulties arise more with links to organization and the reliable construction of representation, whose absence undermines the consolidation of gains and the recognition of groups as legitimate actors and claimants of rights and goods. On the basis of his work in Jardim Oratorio, a neighborhood in São Paulo, Brazil, Rowan Ireland concludes that many of those with whom he worked are competent but frustrated.

> The story of Jardim Oratorio suggests how accounts of the limitations and decline of base communities might be reconciled with claims that the new Catholic popular subjects and the civil associations generated from grassroots Catholic life are still to be found. Jardim Oratorio somewhat belies the notion that the base communities are dysfunctional and declining, as well as the assertion that popular Catholicism has been transformed to the point that it nurtures a new popular subject and generates civil associations . . . the comisao [local commission]

emerges as a civil association . . . and at least some of its executive members and other activists are essentially competent if increasingly frustrated popular subjects. (Ireland 1999: 122)

The general debate about social movements is relevant to issues of empowerment and power. Social movements have often been conceptualized in terms either of resource mobilization or moral economy. Those focusing on resource mobilization highlight the ability of groups to create organizations, nurture leaders, and accumulate resources. Moral economy views acknowledge the importance of resources but also insist that people must be convinced that there is a compelling issue and that activism is itself legitimate. Resource mobilization and moral economy approaches are both important but insufficient by themselves to understand the fragility of activism, the gap between empowerment and power, and the possibilities of disempowerment. For most people most of the time, action is costly, often dangerous, and runs counter to received social norms. From this perspective, the central issue is not so much the creation or maintenance of organizations (more important to organizers than to people who want benefits) than the perception of chinks in the armor of domination and the short-term availability of allies. In this light, the empowerment that leads to collective action may be not so much a sign of irreversible cultural transformation as an alternative that people use as long as it works (Piven and Cloward 1977, 1998).

Alberto Melucci offers a different perspective. In his view, formal organization is less important than the creation of what he calls "submerged networks," dispositions and skills that persist and can be called up at moments when opportunities open up. There is both strength and weakness here, or to be more precise, the strength at issue is different from what earlier models lead us to anticipate. The capacity for mobilization and the kind of social power generated in the groups reviewed here do not fit neatly into existing categories or channels. Submerged networks provide a generative base for action of any kind, and actors "are mobilized for a definite period of time and only for certain issues of concern to them; they take part simultaneously in several activities which they see as compatible; and following their period of mobilization, they are drawn into other channels, towards the market or other institutions" (Melucci 1998: 78). The concept of submerged networks is helpful if we think about recent experience as a cycle of protest, a period of "heightened conflict and contestation across the social system" marked by the "rapid diffusion of collective action from more mobilized to less mobilized sectors; a quickened pace of innovation in the forms of contention; new or transformed collective action frames; a combination of organized and unorganized participation; and sequences of intensified interaction between challengers and authorities which can end in reform, repression, and sometimes revolution" (Tarrow 1994: 153).

Precisely because cycles of protest are cycles and not linear trajectories, they necessarily both rise and fall. Activism is costly and difficult to sustain, opponents call on new resources, and it is common to find movements that once seemed filled with boundless energy and confidence in open horizons falling into division and decay. The key question may be less whether cycles rise and fall—they do so by definition—than what if anything is left behind. As Jonathan Fox puts it, "From the point of view of social capital accumulation, the key issue is how much societal political residue—whether organized or informal—is left after each window of opportunity closes, and how it can be sustained until the next one opens. Even though societal actors often fail to win their immediate demands, if they manage to conserve some degree of autonomy in the troughs between cycles of mobilization, they retain a crucial resource to display at the next political opportunity" (Fox 1996: 1092).

Sidney Tarrow points to three long-term and indirect effects of a cycle of protest, even in decline: the collective protest on the political socialization of those who participate, the effect of the struggles on political institutions and practices, and contribution of protest cycles to changes in political culture (Tarrow 1994: 177). Conceived in these terms, the legacy of 1980s activism linked in some way to the churches is substantial. Through their participation in groups, the men and women who gained opportunities for voice, and came to see themselves as citizens with rights equal to those of others, were in that measure set on the road to see individual and collective action as normal and possible. A generation of participants and activists was called into being, personal lives were transformed, and many experienced empowerment as "an awakening or a revelation, and they claim that the new experience of speaking and acting publicly changed their personal lives and opened up new possibilities for them" (Drogus and Stewart-Gambino 2005: 103). Personal trajectories were altered and new ideas about trust, rights, equality, activism, and accountability emerged and began to find organized expression. Darío López writes that in Pentecostal churches in Peru members encounter an alternate society in which they are valued and in which they can claim citizenship. Women, in particular, "recover speech and discover that they are capable of doing things distinct from the traditional role assigned to them in society" (López 2008b: 10, 128).

All this is impressive, but much depends on whether persistent difficulties of connection and representation on a larger scale will undermine the ability of these legacies to endure. Do the capacities and orientations that have been created in these years constitute social capital of a fundamentally new sort? Like empowerment, social capital is a fragile resource: slow to create, difficult to maintain, and easy to dissipate. Like empowerment, social capital is also a by-product. Efforts to create this resource by fiat or government action are likely to fail as they lack the real social basis required for solidarities to be meaningful (Anderson 2010; James Coleman 1990; John Coleman 2003; Mendoza-Botelho 2010; Putnam 1993, 2000; Smidt 2003). In the recent experience of Latin America, religion and the churches contribute to the formation of social capital to the extent that groups establish bases for social trust and reciprocity in forms of freely given cooperation with the potential to reach beyond explicitly religious activities to undergird cooperative activity in other walks of life. The trajectory followed by many grassroots religious movements, from prayer group to cooperative, community organization, and political action (without stopping prayer), illustrates the point (John Burdick 2004; Miguel Carter 2012; Kincaid 1987; Levine 1992).

The gradual construction and reinforcement of relationships of trust among individuals and groups establish an indispensable foundation for broader kinds of civic engagement, giving substance to the very notion of a "civil society" (founded on organized citizen initiative and independent of the state), a concept that was little more than a catchphrase through most of Latin American history. This view of civil society, and of how ethos and habits spill over from one arena to another, echoes Tocqueville's arguments about the relation between associational life and democracy. It also recalls Max Weber's argument for the link between congregational and self-governed forms of religion with an individual's sense of social responsibility, and the capacity for participating in collective governance (Ireland 1999; Levine 1992, 1993b; Warner 1993).

Recent scholarship offers important insights into the origins and dynamics of social capital. Throughout his work, Robert Putnam has argued that once established, horizontal networks of civic engagement are more durable and self-sustaining than vertical absolutist traditions. The self-reinforcing and cumulative nature of social capital allows us to speak of circles that are virtuous rather than vicious, that is, a series of actions that lead to growing levels of trust and cooperation, expanding networks of civic engagement, and societies where "stability" is created from below, not imposed from above (Putnam 1993, 2000). The concept of social capital underscores the mutually reinforcing effect of cultural and social creations and points our attention to how the moral bases of community are worked out in practice, by embedding them in the structures and routines of daily life. "Trust itself," Putnam states, "is an emergent property of the social system as much as a personal attribute. Individuals are able to be trusting (and not merely gullible) because of the social norms and networks within which their actions are embedded" (Putnam 1993: 177).

Useful distinctions have been drawn among different kinds of social capital: bonding, bridging, and stretching (Anderson 2010; Fox 2004; Mendoza-Botelho 2010). As the terms suggest, the key element at play here is the extent to which the skills, dispositions, and capabilities created and nurtured within groups contribute to building enduring relations within and among them, and between groups and other elements in society. Internal bonding is obviously central to group coherence and survival, but as noted earlier, if the bonds are too exclusive, the group will be isolated. The ability to bridge social levels has much to do with access to information and lowering of transaction costs for groups. The greater their relative autonomy, the more likely these results will be. The difficulty groups experience in creating and sustaining lateral connections undermines their capacity to create social capital in the first place. As I have suggested, the capacity of grassroots groups to operate autonomously turned out to be a lot weaker than many observers had anticipated in the first rush of enthusiasm. The problem is not limited to technical matters of organization. The truth is that liberationist groups never enjoyed majority support. At best an activist minority among popular groups, they proved highly vulnerable to competition from other, more appealing alternatives such as sports, television, politics, and lately new Pentecostal and neo-Pentecostal churches (Stoll 1990, 1993; Stoll and Garrard-Burnett 1993; Berryman 1995a; Hallum 1996).

In any event, not all religion is the same. Competing tendencies and alternative spaces may also coexist within a religion, making for very different projects and styles of interaction. John Coleman (2003) argues that a critical distinction explaining variation in religiosity and the generation of social capital is the differentiation between horizontal and vertical relations of authority: the greater the autonomy and self-governance of the community, the more likely it is to generate the kinds of trust and reciprocity that can form the networks we think of as constituting social capital. The ambiguities of social capital are closely tied to the gap between empowerment and power noted earlier. Coleman also points out that the social capital generated locally can remain dormant or contained. "It is important to remember," he writes, "that some religious units either pay scant attention to social capital or do not know how to turn it into politically or civically relevant social movements, service, or volunteerism. As a result, much of the social capital of some congregations remains frozen within the local unit, or it becomes isolated into separate pockets of friendship cliques within the congregation, failing to spill out into the larger society" (John Coleman 2003: 38). Don Browning et al. argue further that reliance on metaphors like *social capital* can be misleading when applied to religion. "It is dangerous to think of churches in terms of social capital. Churches are carriers of stories that reveal God's will and grace. Salvation, not the increase of social capital, is the primary purpose of churches and their narratives. . . . Christians do not live the Christian life to produce social capital, but it appears that increased social capital is a long term secondary consequence of Christian life" (Browning et al. 1997: 268).

Social capital may be a long-term secondary consequence of interaction and the construction of networks, but a great deal depends on the way in which the groups, relationships, and networks that generate it are linked to larger institutions, and what in fact local religious life is like. To the extent that leaders stress a return to control and top-down coordination, and the content of group life returns to the purely devotional, the participatory quality of membership—so central to the democratizing effect of involvement—may be undermined. Coleman writes, "Those forms of religiosity that are mainly individualistic in nature and unrelated to or anchored by real or ongoing groups do not seem to generate much social capital" (John Coleman 2003: 37). A return to this kind of religiosity can feel like betrayal or abandonment to activists, but the institutional churches may be quite satisfied with the results. Stewart-Gambino (2005) reports that in Chile, for example, vocations in the priesthood are up and group membership has expanded as a new generation has replaced the activists of the 1980s. The new members are less interested in social activism, more attuned to devotional matters, and more focused on improving the physical infrastructure of the parishes, repairing and painting buildings, planting trees and flowers, and so on. "So the problem that my respondents see is not that the parishes remain empty. It is, rather, that their Church has abandoned them because it prefers a hierarchical structure where there is obedience, and where women return to their role as followers of the Church's spiritual instruction" (Stewart-Gambino 2005: 133).[12]

Social capital need not be explicitly political, and for the most part it is not. For many group members, the concept would be remote, and its connection to overtly political projects far-fetched. For ordinary people, social capital means concrete resources (tools, a house, shares in a cooperative, a car), not the group per se or its "project." This makes theoretical as well as practical sense, for the core of any workable concept of social capital is to identify a process that constructs new orientations and capabilities out of everyday life routines and struggles.

Social capital is ultimately founded on relationships that nurture trust and reciprocity (Smidt 2003). The networks that emerge from these relationships are strengthened by repeated use, building on small victories, accumulating social resources, and reaching from family, neighborhood, or business to larger structures and institutional arenas. Seen in this light, it is clear that time is needed, perhaps generations, for the process to have any chance of taking hold. Success is unlikely when efforts are made to leap directly from small-scale actions to "politics" on a grand scale. One longtime observer of church-related peasant groups in Venezuela argues that insisting on beginning with an explicitly political project can be self-defeating. "A political project is something immense. It means nothing less than the pretension to arrive at power, take power and project a new type of organization for Venezuelan society. Very logical for those who work at conceptual levels. But for those working at the practical level, it's like asking a peasant who is making a slingshot to kill birds if he has thought about building an atomic bomb" (Micheo 1983). To be sure, building power in civil society is itself an immense project, and time alone will not do the job. Success requires sustained effort, with attention not only to building networks but also to the whole process of building and maintaining linkages among levels. Analysis needs to devote attention as much to conceptualizing power and networks on this level as well as on the level of national politics and big institutions.

Strengths and Weaknesses of Churches as Sponsors of Social Movements

The theoretical problem is to discern what there is about the way in which empowerment and social capital have been sought and connections built by religiously linked social movements that may have self-limiting or perhaps self-destructive qualities. In his work on religion in the United States, Stephen Warner writes that "it is to be expected that the empowerment functions of religion are latent. At an individual level, those who seek well being in religion tend not to find it; those who gain well being from religion are not those who seek it" (1993: 1070). The logic of Warner's apparent paradox rests on an argument that locates the capacity to create and use new skills and dispositions in the long-term construction of community and the creation and nurturing of trust, not just in creating or joining organizations, and much less in simply "getting the goods." Moving too quickly to activism can short-circuit the process. Another problem is that groups that campaign for democracy can of course remain authoritarian within, and leaders find it difficult to let new generations come to the fore. Failures of leadership replacement are notorious in groups linked to the Catholic Church (as many have been), where dependence on clergy makes for enormous vulnerability if and when more conservative clergy arrive on the scene. Finally, with the opening of new political spaces (through transitions to democracy or reforms within democratic systems) groups lose leaders as activists find less costly and perhaps more rewarding outlets for their energies.

It is important to remember that although the empowering capacities and social capital in the sense used here are clearly new, the religious networks at issue are never created out of thin air. They arise within enduring social, cultural, and political structures, including the churches. Such continuities provide a valued sense of legitimacy, of belonging to something bigger than self, family, or community. They also open doors to resources and to connections otherwise unavailable to small and weak groups. But in the same measure, they are a source of constraint and weakness, subordinating group interests and agendas to those advanced by larger institutions. Just as the churches have long had to beg from the rich to give to the poor in charity, in the same way contemporary efforts to "empower the poor" and give them voice depend on support and resources from big structures of power and privilege, and remain vulnerable to erosion or removal of these elements.

A Note on Religion, Ethnicity, and Social Movements

For centuries, indigenous populations and other subordinate minorities (for example, populations of African origin) were seen by the churches as unlettered pagans, to be shepherded, instructed, guided, and controlled. Such views undergirded traditional missionary work, both

Catholic and Protestant (Bonilla 1972; Stoll 1982; Garrard-Burnett 1998; Cleary and Steigenga 2004a). Indigenous peoples account for about 10 percent of the total population of Latin America, with heaviest concentrations in the Andes, Mesoamerica (Mexico and Central America), and the great basins of the Orinoco and Amazon rivers. Even where they constitute a majority of the population (for example, Guatemala, Ecuador, Bolivia, and Peru), until recently indigenous peoples were marginalized minorities who did not enjoy full citizenship and had little status in law (Yashar 2005; Van Cott 2000, 2008; Stoll 1982). But beginning in the late 1960s and with growing force thereafter, broad currents of thought and action within the churches advanced a revaluation of indigenous experience and its religious value, and a shift of position from instruction of the pagans to discerning where God may be at work in other cultures. This position was knit together by "a theology of inculturation that promoted notions of the dignity of all persons, the worth of native cultures, a political role for all in society, and justification for presenting one's interest in the political arena" (Cleary 2009: 83). The working out of this theology in practice has involved promotion of local languages for worship and instruction, training of clergy in these languages, recovery of memory and tradition, development of new schools and research centers in indigenous languages, active promotion of local leaders and recruitment of indigenous clergy, sponsoring of social movements, articulation of political grievances, and a commitment to stand with and support communities in their struggles. The results are visible across the region (Steigenga and Lazo de la Vega 2012).[13]

These initiatives draw on ideas about *accompaniment*, according to which the church must accompany the poor in their struggles, not lead or direct them. To this end, church resources have been dedicated to support these efforts in countries like Guatemala, Ecuador, and Bolivia, with striking results in terms of the promotion of new leaders and political movements in Ecuador and Bolivia (Brysk 2004; Cleary 2004a, 2009; Cleary and Steigenga 2004a). Extended and politically powerful collective action by indigenous movements in these two countries was facilitated by religious networks, including the use of church radio stations and citizen media (Cleary 2004b: 54–55). Even in Peru, where so many groups were caught between the violence of Shining Path on the one hand and the Peruvian state and military on the other, successful resistance by indigenous communities to both was legitimized and supported by church networks, Catholic and Protestant (Cleary 2004b; De Gregori 1985, 1989; Ranly 2003; Cecilia Tovar 2006a).

These patterns of outreach, and the new kinds of social and political involvement they generate, are not limited to areas of majority indigenous populations such as Mesoamerica or the Andes. Comparable efforts are visible in Chiapas, where the Zapatista movement gained strength from local Catholic networks; in the Orinoco and Amazon basins; and in much of rural Brazil where the Catholic Church, through its Pastoral Land Commission and its Council on Indigenous Affairs, has devoted important resources to promoting land claims by indigenous communities (French 2007; Kirk Johnson 2005). The relation of the churches to other ethnic minorities, and in particular to populations of African descent, has been less prominent, but here as well there are signs of movement, including the renovation of a *pastoral negro* (black pastoral strategy) in parts of Brazil, with elements such as the incorporation of traditional images and music into worship, revaluation of images of blackness in Brazilian culture, efforts to recruit and promote more black clergy, and as with indigenous communities, attempts to accompany black communities in the pursuit of social and political interests (John Burdick 2004; French 2007).

Conclusion

The involvement of churches and religious groups in the promotion of social movements and the development of civil society presents a mixed record. Creative innovation and heroic commitment to mobilization are often accompanied by affirmation of routine and by an insistence on control that stifle autonomy and hinder the emergence of new leaders. The lamentable if unsurprising persistence of patriarchal attitudes has a particular impact on women, constraining their participation and limiting the scope of connections they are able to make and sustain. The limitations of religiously inspired social movements and the difficulties they have experienced in consolidating and enduring suggest that expectations may have been too high to begin with. Many of these hopes depended on a fragile combination of democratic internal life with supportive allies in church and politics. Where this alliance persists, as in Brazilian peasant organizations studied by Miguel Carter (2003, 2012) or French (2007), democratizing tendencies have a chance to consolidate, eliciting new groups of local leaders able to continue the effort on their own. But the more common situation finds groups persisting but fragmented and weak.[14] The image of the competent but frustrated citizen (Ireland 1999) or the activist who feels abandoned by the churches (Stewart-Gambino 2005) is telling.

The fragility of these initiatives has many sources. Repression and open warfare took an important toll, particularly in Central America and Peru. Political division and co-optation, and the general difficulty that groups experience in making and holding reliable connections to institutions, are also pervasive themes. Three additional factors must be addressed: gender, resources, and lack of relative autonomy. The salience of gender issues underscores the situation of women, who face multiple pressures that constrain participation and commonly run into a glass ceiling in male-dominated institutions. This is of course not particular to Latin America, but it is notable there. Scarcity of resources (for potential members and for groups) constrains activism by privileging the daily struggle for subsistence and throwing multiple obstacles in the way of collective action of any kind. These two factors are discussed in some detail above; the question of effective autonomy warrants further comment here.

Much of the expectation about the possible effects of religiously linked or sponsored social movements rested on the hope that groups would in some sense replicate the experience of congregational life, which encourages self-government and participation of members on a relatively equal basis. In her study of congregations in the United States, Ammerman speaks of congregations as "spaces of sociability." Congregations and other voluntary organizations "generate the basic social capital of association, along with the civic capital of communication and organizational skills. They do this especially well for those least advantaged in other sectors of the society, acting as subaltern counter publics. . . . They provide not only human resources for the work of sustaining modern social life, but material resources as well—meeting space and vehicular transportation, bulletin boards and public address systems, copying machines and paper" (Ammerman 1996: 366). To understand what is happening in a community, she points out, "it may be more useful to observe the stock of skills and connections it comprises than to inventory the organizations themselves. This 'social capital' is the essential stuff of our lives together, the network of skill and trust that makes civic life possible. Social capital is the raw material out of which new organizational species can be created, the residue left when old organizations die" (Ammerman 1996: 347).

All this is by now familiar, but the problem in Latin America is that the groups in question rarely arise out of congregations in this classic form. They are either linked to large hierarchical organizations like the

Catholic Church or embedded in Protestant and neo-Pentecostal churches that enhance the power of leaders, treat the pastor as super-hero, and leave little room for self-managed participation (Bastián 1993, 1997; Kramer 2005; Gaskill 1997; Gifford 2004; Harris 1999; Harris-Lacewell 2007). Where democratic or democratizing models do emerge, as in the early experience of CEBs, they often run into powerful coun-terpressures (Levine 1992; Drogus and Stewart-Gambino 2005; Romero 2009). Finally, the combined effects of economic and political crisis have divided groups and made for an understandable focus on localized, short-term survival strategies. Peruvian sociologist Teresa Tovar cor-rectly insists that

> we need to get away from searching for a historical subject [in the classical Marxist sense], something privileged and sacralized by virtue of its position in the social structure and from whose vantage point one can make sense of society and history as a whole. Instead, we need to see a plurality of subjects, whose identities are created through their own interactions and forms of understanding, and whose positions are therefore changeable. (Teresa Tovar 1991: 31)

The key point here is not to reify groups or communities, to identify them once and forever with a single organizational form or program. We need to see them in all their complexity and contradiction, made up of individuals trying to chart a course in difficult and changing seas.

The record of religion's involvement with social movements, and its uneven contribution to civil society in Latin America, underscores the importance of grounding new ideas in supportive social structures. The religious legitimation of ideas about equality and activism that found expression in early waves of organization turned out to be a nec-essary but not sufficient condition for these social movements to mature, consolidate, and even survive at all. Those advancing new ideas also need to win and hold allies, gain access to church and political institutions on a regular basis, and learn to navigate the potentially treacherous waters of newly open politics and civil society. That so far they seem to have done so with more success among indigenous move-ments in Bolivia, Ecuador, or the northeast of Brazil suggests the importance of bonds of identity—beyond a social agenda—to hold the groups together.

Elsewhere I have argued that the future of empowerment may well be disempowerment, that the obstacles to sustained collective action are too great, and the fickleness and frailty of available alliances too likely to short-circuit group efforts (Levine and Romero 2006). The evidence of disempowerment is before us in the demise or fragmentation of many of the groups founded with such high hopes in the 1970s or 1980s. But although the record is full of reverses, not all is disempowerment. New kinds of groups appear all the time, slipping out of the control of hierarchies and formal institutions (Catalina Romero 2009). The capacities created by grassroots action can and do spill over to other areas. The ability of the churches to provide legitimation and resources, while at the same time taking a step back and actually letting the voiceless speak for themselves, is central to the future capacity of religions to infuse civil society with different voices and a new presence.

Notes

1. Many of the region's bishops had in fact only met for the first time at council sessions, and their exchanges reinforced a sense of common identity and shared problems.

2. "Since in his correspondence More calls his island Nusquama, meaning 'nowhere' it seems probable that he began by calling his book by the Latin title, and later shifted to the Greek, liking the double meaning of 'Utopia' and the way this strange coinage would mask the imaginary quality of the book from those lesser souls who knew only Latin" (Marius 1985: 154).

3. Karl Mannheim contrasts utopias with ideologies. Ideologies, in his view, are ways of thinking and systems of ideas best understood as expressions of group interest, and thus of necessity bound up with existing structures of domination. Utopian thinking, in contrast, reaches beyond the present: "never a diagnosis of the situation, it can be used only as a direction of action" (Mannheim 1961: 40).

4. The only case of a successful political party with roots in these movements is Brazil's PT (Partido dos Trabalhadores) (Keck 1995). The experience of power and government has turned the PT into a more conventional political party, with distrust of allies like the landless movement, which continue to press an agenda of protest mobilizations with the PT in office (Miguel Carter 2010).

5. "The growth of civil society is thus a process marked by the furnishing of successful examples; under such conditions, the number of organizations is likely to grow geometrically. . . . Once collective action proves successful in one field, its practice is likely to spread. Organizing and administrative skills become more widely held, and the level of trust and sense of community—so crucial to a viable civil society—increase" (Hadenius and Uggla 1991: 1624). See also Hirschman 1984; Putnam 1993.

6. Not surprisingly, leaders in Villa El Salvador were also a prime target for Shining Path. Some, like María Elena Moyano, were brutally assassi-

nated, while others like Michel Azcueta narrowly escaped death (Riofrio 1981, Part II, "Estudio de Casos. Villa El Salvador: Tiempos de Lucha y Organizacion").

7. The problem is not unique to Catholic clergy or NGOs. Protestant groups have also been accused of pursuing their own agenda when working with indigenous groups. A case in point is the Summer Institute of Linguistics (SIL), which has been broadly criticized for its activities in Ecuador and Colombia (Brysk 2004; Steigenga and Lazo de la Vega 2012; Stoll 1982).

8. Stokes (1995: 120) argues that the belief that participation in activist movements was itself good deeply influenced tactics, making members and leaders think that such participation was also necessarily effective.

9. Groups can be betrayed as much by clerical organizers as by political allies. One promising case in Venezuela, in which Catholic grassroots groups in Maracaibo had organized a bus line and were engaged in extensive efforts to promote community mental health, came undone because the priest working with the group was siphoning money from group accounts (money provided by the regional government) to promote his own political agenda in collaboration with a local political party (Levine and Levine 1994).

10. *Quilombo* communities are formed from the descendants of escaped slaves.

11. Theologian Jon Sobrino argues this is precisely what characterized Archbishop Oscar Romero's work in El Salvador, where he strove to put resources in the hands of the poor (Sobrino 2003).

12. Robin Nagle (1997) reports in similar terms on a split in the Morro da Conceiçâo, a neighborhood in Recife in the Brazilian northeast, between those backing a liberationist priest, Reginaldo, and those supporting the bishop who replaced him and called in police to reclaim the church building from his supporters. For those supporting Reginaldo, his version of Christianity provided an understanding of faith that was grounded in reality. For those against him, "this very grounding served to evacuate Jesus from the church. Women and men whose lives provided little relief from the daily indignities of relentless poverty found that Reginaldo had removed their one sure solace and replaced it with reminders of the very problems from which they needed relief. Reginaldo did not bolster their faith; he betrayed it" (Nagle 1997: 76).

13. "Adventist schools around Lake Titicaca [had a role in] producing graduates who would go on to fill local and national leadership roles. In Ecuador, Mexico, Bolivia, and Chile, Catholic seminaries trained indigenous and nonindigenous priests who would later go on to become community leaders and key organizers in indigenous social movements. In Guatemala, the individuals trained under Catholic Action came to represent a new generation of leadership in indigenous communities. Some Protestant pastors (particularly Mayan Presbyterians) have also emerged as local and national indigenous leaders of the Mayan movement. Religious leaders also played a key role in the National Reconciliation Commission and 1996 peace agreements in Guatemala" (Steigenga 2004: 241).

14. On the basis of his study of neo-Pentecostal churches in Guatemala City, Kevin O'Neill (2010) argues that the churches provide members with their sense of citizenship but that this citizenship is ultimately privatizing. But he pays little attention to the ordinary activities of citizenship (talking about politics, voting, lobbying, participating in groups) or to structural factors of the kind discussed here that weaken their connection with politics.

6

Religion and Violence

Latin American history over the past half century is marked by the powerful mutual impact of violence and religious change. Violence—intense, widespread, and often targeted directly at religious actors—is central to this relation, creating victims and engendering an identification with the victims in important sectors of the churches. In addition to the brute facts of violence, it is important to take into account religious reactions to violence, including a search for how to defend persons and communities and to explain the violence in ways that make sense in a larger context of faith and commitment. Is violence the result of sin, the inevitable preliminary to the coming end of the world? Or is violence better understood as a social and historical phenomenon, a product of injustice and oppression, something that can and should be resisted? Two further issues require attention: (1) recourse to religiously inspired and justified violence, which flared briefly in the 1960s and 1970s, and (2) a long-term commitment to nonviolence and to accompaniment of victims of violence, sharing the risks they face and often sharing their fate as well.

Reading through the many reports on violence and human rights prepared in the past decades in different countries of the region, a few common themes appear.[1] There is the brutalizing intent of official violence, the systematic effort not merely to frighten and silence individuals and groups but also to undermine family and community bonds and to remove any degree of certainty from ordinary lives. There is a common effort not only to attack political opponents, but also to threaten, frighten, and attack religious groups and churches that harbor potential sources of independent thinking, action, or care for victims. From the point of view of the targets and victims of violence, common factors include physical and long-term psychological and social trauma and the dilemmas posed by what are often truncated processes of achieving accountability. The physical and psychological scars of violence remain with survivors, particularly those who have no means of finding, identifying, or publicly remembering the dead (Becker et al. 1990; Robben 2008).

General Considerations on Violence

The effort to map and to understand the relation between religion and violence has generated a rich and varied literature, which aligns closely with the alternative theoretical positions outlined in Chapter 2. Some have tried to explain the stances taken by institutional churches when confronted with state violence and repression as part of an effort to retain influence or to seek influence in new sources of support (Bruneau 1982; Gill 1998). Others have stressed how the complexity of church institutions shapes their response (Ghio 2007; Fleet and Smith 1997; Serbin 2000), while a different track underscores the importance of new theologies and of an evolving sense of self and of mission in the church (Aguilar 2003; Berryman 1995a; Donatello 2008; French 2007; Levine 1990a, 1992; Mainwaring 1986; Mallimaci, Cucchetti, and Donatello 2006; Donatello 2008). Those working in a rational choice vein argue that the positions assumed by churches reflect not new ideas but rather the degree to which the long-dominant church (the Catholic Church) faced visible competition. Anthony Gill (1998) argues that the greater the competition, the more church leaders turn to social justice issues (including those raised by violence) in the search for a new clientele; less competition makes for more conservative positions. Another group has centered attention on how the churches' situation as targets of violence and victims of terror turned many in the churches (Catholic and Protestant alike) to the defense and protection of human rights (Levine 2006a, 2006b, 2009a; López 1998; Morello 2011a).

Each of these perspectives is important, but none is sufficient by itself to grasp the phenomenon of religion and violence, because the relation and mutual impact of these two elements reach beyond the institutional churches and beyond "politics" as ordinarily understood. We must also account for the impact of nonpolitical kinds of violence, and for ideas and actions that emerge and play out beyond the boundaries of formal institutions. Both violence and religion come in many forms, and as a first step, it is useful to differentiate among the kinds of violence and the transformations of religion most salient in the recent history of the region.

We can distinguish kinds of violence by their level as well as their source and intention.[2] At the most general level, there is a group of *civil wars*, in Central America, Peru, and Colombia (which is the longest-lasting case, but the one that is least suited to conventional categories). There have also been important phenomena of *state repression*, on a scale and with numbers of victims not seen before. State repression in this period has been associated with systematic attacks on churches, claiming numerous victims among bishops, clergy, sisters, catechists, and laypeople. There are precedents in the civil wars of the nineteenth century, but the change of scale is noteworthy. Such attacks have been salient in the civil wars of El Salvador, Guatemala, and Peru, and also in countries where the repressive apparatus of the state held sway for many years, such as Chile, Brazil, and Argentina.

Alongside the violence associated with state repression, resistance, or internal warfare, there is a pervasive violence of daily life. In the discourse of Latin American Catholicism since the conference of the region's bishops at Medellín (1968), it has been common to incorporate this under the rubrics of *institutionalized violence* and *structural sin*, underscoring the impact of factors like unemployment, economic inequality, poor health, low life expectancy, and social injustice on the quality of individual, family, and community life. These concepts have been very influential but often fail to recognize other components of this violence, including alcoholism, drugs, crime, local or family vendettas, and the domestic violence and physical abuse inflicted on women and children, which are commonly linked to these elements. The violence of daily life in the cities also includes a growing toll of abuse and killings inflicted by security forces, mostly on young men[3] (Arnson 2011; Brinks 2008, 2010). Personal and community experiences of such violence and a resulting sense of crisis have sparked a search for a different way of living that has led many into Pentecostal and neo-Pentecostal churches, which offer the possibility of exit from a difficult and dangerous life, and entry into a new and supportive community of faith (Chesnut 1997; Steigenga and Cleary 2007; Smilde 2007).

Important distinctions can also be made among kinds and levels of religion. As we have seen, the available supply of religion—in churches, chapels, radio and television programming, campaigns, associations, publications, schools, and more—has increased and diversified as never before, placing a wide range of possibilities for participation in front of ordinary people. Beginning in the mid-1980s, as political democracy returned throughout the region, a more open and less regulated civil society emerged, and barriers to access to the public sphere dropped. New churches appeared and entered this space to compete for members and resources and to demand equality of conditions (including public recognition and legitimacy) along with the Catholic Church. The combination of new forms of violence with an evolving religious reality did much to shape the character and political meaning of religious change.

Violence and the Transformation of Religion

Much of the explicit impact that violence has had on churches and religious life can be found in two areas: the victimization of churches and religious personnel in the process of violence, and the reaction of the institutional churches (and affiliated and sponsored social movements and individuals) to this violence. In the midst of repression and open civil war, churches have often defended victims, in the process becoming targets of attack themselves. Religious personnel and church institutions (like radio stations or educational organizations) have been prime targets of violence in El Salvador, Guatemala, Chile, Brazil, Paraguay, and Peru. This direct experience of terror led many in the churches to see themselves as victims, to identify with victims, and to ally themselves with victims in defense of the right to life and the right to be free from abuse and torture (Noone 1995). As targets and victims of violence, religious institutions, groups, and individuals caught up in the violence tried to make sense of what was happening and at the same time to bear witness to the violence, searching for responses that would defend and preserve the lives of loved ones and of the community as a whole. In Brazil, Chile, Peru, and El Salvador, church leaders and church-sponsored organizations became prime protagonists of movements for human rights. This was often undertaken through ecumenical coalitions.

The positions assumed by some Catholic leaders and groups in these cases have not been universally shared in the region's Catholicism. The most visible and best-documented counterexample is Argentina, where, as we shall see, the top leadership of the Catholic Church provided moral and sometimes material support to military rule.

Some church figures were also complicit in the worst excesses of the last period of military rule, from 1976 to 1983, including torture.[4] Since the return of democracy, Argentine Catholic leaders have also opposed efforts to "recover historical memory" (including efforts to promote Truth Commissions, to name and prosecute offenders, and to name and honor victims), which are notable in other cases. This case and others are discussed in more detail in the next chapter.[5]

The multiple impacts of these different dimensions of violence are magnified in cases of massive state repression, torture, and abuse. The capacity of sustained violence to convert persons into objects (along with the psychological trauma experienced by both victims and perpetrators of violence) is a salient feature of the experience of numerous Latin American countries in the past fifty years. Victims are abducted, often tortured, lose their lives, or at the very least suffer severe physical and psychological damage. Family members disappear, and the bodies are never located, never given a formal burial. The philosopher and theologian Simone Weil discusses violence in terms that are relevant here. In her commentary on *The Iliad*, she argues that the real hero of Homer's poem of invasion and conquest is violence itself, a violence that is described in graphic terms. Weil affirms that violence has a rhythm and dynamic of its own; once unleashed, it is difficult to contain. "Force," she writes, "is as pitiless to the man who possesses it, or thinks he does, as it is to its victims; the second it crushes, the first it intoxicates. The truth is, no one possesses it" (Weil 1986: 171). Weil's text bears on the mutual impact of religion and violence in Latin America because it underscores the power that violence has to corrupt both persons and institutions and indicates how great the challenge is for those who oppose it, how hard it is to reverse the tide, to recover memory and legitimacy, and to claim a measure of accountability. The long-term psychosocial consequences of violence include a legacy of fear, nightmares, suicides, alienation, numerous impoverished widows and orphans, and the erosion of community as a result of forced migration and the prohibition of public rituals of mourning.[6] The perpetrators of the violence themselves commonly experience nervous and emotional problems and unsettling fear of retribution (Archdiocese of São Paulo 1998; Comisión de la Verdad y Reconciliación, Peru, 2004; Becker et al. 1990; Hedges 2002; Robben 2008; Staub and Pearlman 2001).

As part of this volatile mix of violence and religious transformations, important changes took place in the ideological repertoire of the churches, both Catholic and Protestant. Issues of justice, rights, participation, and liberation were articulated in church documents, and there was a sustained effort to give these issues a prime place on the agenda of church institutions and affiliated groups and movements. As we have seen, beginning with the documents of Medellín (1968) and Puebla (1979), articulated further in the theology of liberation, and carried to the public sphere in numerous pastoral letters and in the programs and commitments of groups and social movements, elements in the Catholic Church broke long-standing alliances with political and social power, and put themselves on the side of those seeking change (Gutiérrez 2004; Levine 1988, 1990a; Christian Smith 1991). They articulated a view in which suffering is not the result of sin or a sign of the coming of the millennium but is rather to be understood as the result of an unjust social order and a repressive government. Believers identify these as structures of social sin, and this legitimizes resistance and enjoins work-ing actively with others in defense of life. From this position, elements in the churches put themselves on the side of social and political change and resisted authoritarian rule.

To put oneself on the side of change in this period in Latin Amer-ica has had varied meanings: forming and supporting reformist groups and Christian Democratic parties; backing social movements of slum dwellers or landless peasants; opposing dictatorship and promoting and defending human rights; providing legal, moral, and material support for new trade union movements; and sometimes allying with insurgent movements, as was the case in Nicaragua, El Salvador, and with some groups in Argentina. The ideas articulated at Medellín, Puebla, and in liberation theology took practical form in the legitimation of stances like these, which were framed in terms of the need for people of faith to accompany the poor and the vulnerable, showing by their presence that these victims were not alone. As noted, the concept of accompaniment is central in liberation theology, and calls on church people and church institutions to build and maintain a permanent presence among the poor and vulnerable, sharing their lives and often being subject to the same risks. Justified in this way, church sponsorship and protection of social movements became critical in times and places where open organization was restricted or dangerous. Church leaders took on this role as part of their new sense of what the church's mission should be, in reaction to official attacks, and often in response to desperate appeals from below (Drogus and Stewart-Gambino 2005; Levine 2006b, 2009a; Oxhorn 1995).

The attribution of suffering to oppression, the injunction to collec-tive action in the pursuit of change, and the concern for rights that are central to liberation theology (Berryman 1987, 1995a; Levine 1990a;

Peterson 1997; Christian Smith 1991) do not exhaust religious responses to massive and sustained violence. The extreme character of violence and civil war in Central America, Peru, and Colombia brought a different kind of impact on religious life. The experience of Guatemala, a leading case of Protestant growth in the region, is apposite here. In Guatemala, small, independent (and heavily Pentecostal) churches grew in spectacular fashion following the devastating earthquake of 1976 and intense and widespread violence of the subsequent decade. In this context, the idea that suffering is somehow deserved as punishment for sin, that these are the end times and violence represents a purifying trial required for transition to the new millennium, resonated strongly (Chesnut 1997; Stoll 1993; Garrard-Burnett 1998). Virginia Garrard-Burnett writes that under the brief but bloody rule of Guatemala's Protestant president, General Efraín Ríos Montt,

> the howling forces of modernization, violence and community disintegration that drove people into Protestant churches accelerated dramatically. Where political and economic change had weakened the power of local sources of authority as the century progressed, Ríos Montt sometimes eliminated them entirely. Where the Catholic Church's spiritual hegemony ebbed through the twentieth century and fragmented into competing bits, Ríos Montt's very public membership [in The Church of the Word, a North American Pentecostal import] served notice that new types of religious membership were there to fill the void. (Garrard-Burnett 1998: 161)

Garrard-Burnett carries the argument further in her revealing account of the ideology of terror that Ríos Montt constructed and implemented during his short period of rule. She situates his own conversion to Pentecostal Protestantism in the context of a broader wave that had attracted many Guatemalans who were seeking "some kind of spiritual refuge in a disintegrating political and social milieu" (Garrard-Burnett 2010: 56). The violence and destruction all around them were signs of "Guatemala's *kairos* [opportune moment or place] to bear witness to the Great Tribulation but to rise, faithful and triumphant, with the Lord on the day of his final coming. This was not a rationale for violence so much as an exposition on suffering" (Garrard-Burnett 2010: 135). Ríos Montt was able to put these elements together in a way that situated counterinsurgency in the context of a larger and religiously legitimate struggle.

> His dark genius lay in his ability to manipulate violence, images, and language in such a way as to reinvent them to serve the interests of the

state, his New Guatemala. As a military matter, Rios Montt's scorched earth campaign accomplished its two objectives: to defeat the guerrillas in the field and to seize from them their claims to moral authority (the promise of a Marxist utopia). The military accomplished this first task through the outright physical destruction of the guerrillas and their base of support, but the second—the reinvention of Guatemalans' moral universe—remained Rios Montt's task alone. . . . His was a moral discourse of a sort that built for him both political and cultural legitimacy. His use of evangelical language and the Sunday sermons are the most obvious evidence of this but the discourse in fact ran much deeper, touching on themes of Guatemalans' deeply rooted insecurities about race, nationalism, status and identity. (Garrard-Burnett 2010: 175)

The extreme quality of violence in a case like Guatemala should not lead us to see the waves of conversion to new churches as no more than an escapist response to dislocation. In a context experienced as one of crisis (generalized or personal, stemming from war, disease, domestic strife, forced migration, alcoholism, or injury), those who convert do so not only to escape, but also to reach forward in ways that link personal transformation to a religious narrative that motivates and legitimizes while at the same time providing a network of support. Personal and family experiences lead many to a contract with God—offering faith, belief, and loyalty, in return for which God is expected to provide shelter, protection, and a promise of health and prosperity (Chesnut 1997; Smilde 2007; Garrard-Burnett 1998; Steigenga and Cleary 2007).[7] The specific appeal of neo-Pentecostal churches, which stress the direct experience of divine power through the cure of illnesses and the acquisition of material goods, rests further on a sense of healing through atonement, "empowerment on earth through proper faith in God. Closely related is the belief that material prosperity is the entitlement of the faithful: money, good health, and security are all tangible evidence of God's benediction" (Garrard-Burnett 1998: 164).

Violence in the Name of Faith

Over the past half century, Latin America has seen relatively little of the deliberate use or justification of violence in the name of faith that has been prominent elsewhere, for example, in Islamist movements or in the volatile fusion of Buddhism and Sinhala nationalism advanced by Buddhist monks in Sri Lanka, which I discuss, along with other cases, in

Chapter 8. There have also been no armed millenarian movements comparable to the Canudos rebellion in nineteenth-century Brazil (Della Cava 1968; Jerryson 2010; Kepel 2002, 2003; Schober 2007; Tambiah 1992). Some calls for violence in the name of authentic faith were heard in the 1960s and 1970s, with variable impact. These include Camilo Torres, the Colombian priest who died as a guerrilla fighter in early 1966; the clergy collected in the Movement of Priests for the Third World (MSTM) in Argentina, active in the 1960s and 1970s and present at the creation of the Montonero guerrilla movement; and the notable alliance of the Sandinista Revolution with elements in the churches. At the other end of the spectrum, faith was invoked to justify repressive violence during military rule in Argentina.

Camilo Torres remains for many the most significant example of a guerrilla priest in the recent experience of Latin America. Born into a prominent family, he joined the priesthood and was sent for advanced studies in sociology to the University of Louvain, in Belgium, which was then (as now) an important center of reformist Catholic thinking. He returned to Colombia in 1958, and following a meteoric career as priest, educator, and public figure, became convinced that only organized political action (and, ultimately, revolutionary struggle) could break the stalemate in which Colombia found itself and make it possible to resolve the country's problems. He sought release from his status as a priest in order to devote himself full-time to the struggle and in short order founded and promoted a broad political movement (the United Front of the Colombian People), joined a newly formed guerrilla front, and was killed in combat on February 15, 1966, in his first engagement.

Since that time, Camilo Torres has acquired iconic status in the Latin American Left, becoming, as his biographer put it, a kind of Che Guevara for Catholics (Broderick 2002: 21). His decision to take up arms and his death in combat posed the stark challenge for people of faith to abandon accommodation and an easy complicity with power and make an active choice for revolution, even at the cost of violence. Torres is of particular interest here because he came before critical markers of change like Vatican II, Medellín, Puebla, and the emergence of liberation theology. He was aware of the currents of change then bubbling up around the continent and participated in many critical encounters with others of similar mind, but his commitments and actions came before many of these were consolidated. Elsewhere I have written extensively on Camilo Torres (Levine and Wilde 1977; Levine 2011).

The brief account that follows centers attention on the relation among his conception of faith, the decision to take up arms as a necessary expression of that faith, and the impact he had in Latin America.

Torres returned to Colombia in 1958 to find a country whose political and social situation had been frozen in place by agreements between the Liberal and Conservative parties (known as the National Front) intended to bring to an end the massive civil violence known in Colombia simply as La Violencia.[8] These agreements privileged power sharing between the established parties, economic growth, and some limited reform. The Catholic hierarchy avoided taking sides between Liberals and Conservatives, and denied legitimacy to any challenge to the National Front. For Torres, this was hypocritical. In his view, church leaders had not withdrawn from politics but had simply replaced the politics of partisan choice with the politics of the established (dis)order. He grew frustrated with elite persuasion, reformist methods, and the assumption that his work should remain within the boundaries of ecclesiastical structures and rules of procedure.

Central to the ideals of faith that moved Torres (and which he urged on others) was love of neighbor expressed in actions to improve the lives of one's neighbors. If we ask who are one's neighbors, the answer is the majority of the people. In a Message to Christians (Mensaje a los Cristianos, August 26, 1965) he wrote that

> the core of Catholicism is love of neighbor. He who loves his neighbor fulfills the law (Paul to the Romans, XIII, 8). For this love to be true, it must be effective. If social programs, alms giving, creating a few free schools and or scattered housing programs and everything we call "charity" do not manage to feed the hungry, clothe the naked, or teach the majority of those without learning, then we need to search for effective means that will improve the welfare of the majority. The privileged minorities who hold power will not do the job because it would mean the sacrifice of their privileges. . . . Therefore it is necessary to take power away from the privileged minorities and give to the poor majorities. If this happens rapidly, this is the essence of a revolution.[9] (Torres 1965a: 114–115)

It was not enough to study and understand the situation. The essential point was to take the side of the weak against the strong and enter politics in pursuit of justice. Action was imperative and since the established power structure was upheld by force, violent action was necessary and legitimate. Thus,

> if one wants to really be a Christian, in more than words, then it is essential to participate fully in change. A passive faith is not enough to get close to God: charity is indispensable, and charity means concrete-

ly to live in light of sentiments of human fraternity. This sentiment is manifested today in revolutionary movements, in the need to unite all poor and oppressed countries in a struggle to eliminate exploitation, and in all this, our position is clearly on this side, not on the side of the oppressors. (Torres 1965b: 76)

Torres was acutely aware of the many ways in which an unjust social order inflicts violence on its citizens. The term *institutionalized violence* had not yet been coined, but Torres's usage comes close. He contrasted pervasive violence of this kind with the counterviolence of revolution, which he justified (with appeals to St. Thomas Aquinas) as resistance to tyranny. Comparable distinctions among kinds of violence were drawn not long after in the documents of Medellín and filled out (in the context of revolutionary war) a decade later in the pastoral letters of Archbishop Oscar Romero of El Salvador. Romero distinguished types of violence according to their origin, intention, and legitimacy: structural or institutional violence, arbitrary violence exercised by the state, the violence of the extreme Right, terrorist violence, insurrectional violence, and a violence of legitimate self-defense. Romero was sensitive to the dangers of violence getting out of hand, in spirals of destruction that are difficult to contain. In contrast, Torres never engaged the practical business of violence (the violence that coerces, bombs, shoots, maims, kills, and destroys), nor did he consider how violence can lead to self-sustaining spirals of death and devastation (Levine 2011).

The choice for violence, the decision to take up arms as part of a revolutionary movement, warrants closer examination. Torres had no romantic illusions about violence as a creative force. He is far removed from figures like Georges Sorel (1999) who saw violence not just as an instrument of change, but more broadly as a creative means of breaking through the bonds of convention to utterly new ways of understanding and organizing society. The decision to pursue the revolution by violent means appears in Torres's writings and speeches as a practical choice, a possible and preferable alternative given the blinders of the ruling class, the only option remaining to anyone sincerely interested in change. "I am convinced," he wrote, "that it is necessary to exhaust all peaceful means and that the last word on the path to be chosen does not really rest with the popular classes, since they are the majority, and therefore have the right to power. We need instead to ask the oligarchy how they will surrender their power. If they do so by peaceful means, we will take it in an equally peaceful manner, but if they refuse to give up power, or defend it with violence, then we will take it violently. I am convinced that the people has ample justification for violence" (cited in Brienza 2007: 80).[10]

For Torres, revolution was the necessary means to fulfilling the effective charity that Christian love requires. "It is a sociological absurdity to think that a group would act against its own interests. This is why the taking of power by the majority must be promoted, as a way to realize the structural reforms—economic, social, and political—in favor of these same majorities. This is called revolution, and if it is required to realize love for neighbor, then Christians have to be revolutionaries" (Torres 1965c: 249). The most direct statement of the logic and need for revolution appears in his letter to the Cardinal Archbishop of Bogotá requesting laicization, in a declaration to the Bogotá press that same day (which uses the same words), and in "Crossroads of the Church in Latin America" (Encrucijadas de la Iglesia en América Latina) (Torres 1965c, 1965d, 1965e). Torres argues for revolution as an imperative derived from the Christian commitment to love of neighbor and describes his own commitments in this way.

> I became a Christian because I believed that there I found the purest way to serve my neighbor. I was chosen by Christ to be a priest forever, moved by the desire to commit myself full time to the love of my fellow men. As a sociologist, I hoped to make that love a reality through science and technology, but my analysis of Colombian reality has made me realize the need for a revolution to feed the hungry, give drink to the thirsty, clothe the naked, and achieve a better life for the majority of our people. I believe that revolutionary struggle is a Christian and priestly struggle. Only in this way, in the concrete circumstances of our country, can we realize the love that all men should have for their neighbors.
>
> Since I began my priestly ministry, I have tried in every way to get lay people, Catholics and non-Catholics, to commit themselves to the revolutionary struggle. In the absence of a massive response by the people to these actions, I have resolved to commit myself, in this way realizing part of my work of bringing men to mutual love through the love of God. I consider this activity essential to my Christian and priestly life as a Colombian. (Torres 1965d: 2, 228)

Torres's declaration to the press ends with these words: "I believe that my commitment with my fellow men to realize the love of neighbor imposes this sacrifice on me. I sacrifice one of the rights that I love most deeply—to be able to celebrate the rites of the Church as a priest—in order to create the conditions that make this ritual more authentic. I will run all the risks that this choice requires of me" (Torres 1965e: 107–108). Torres went on to argue that the eucharistic celebration could only be valid in a just society. "When my neighbor has nothing against me, when the revolution has been completed, I will offer mass again if God permits me. I believe that in this way I fulfill the command of Christ: if you bring your offering to the altar and there you remember that your brother has something against you, leave your offer at the altar and go reconcile yourself first with your brother. Come and present your offering later" (Torres 1965a: 76; the biblical citation is from Matthew 5:23–24).

For Camilo Torres, working within the system (for example, in elections, which he rejected) was to be complicit with the injustices that the system kept in place.[11] What was broken could only be repaired by the organization of countervailing power, specifically by revolutionary struggle. He knew that many found it difficult to accept the idea of a priest taking such positions, but he insisted that authentic faith requires active commitment to better the lives of others. His understanding of the mission of Christianity drove his consistent efforts to link Christians with the theory and practice of revolution. Properly understood, the Christian mission was to announce the good news, and the authentically faithful disciple of Christ was one who puts his life on the line to create a society where that message can be heard and lived. The logic was inescapable. One cannot be truly faithful to that message and ignore the core of its meaning: true love and true charity require action to change the conditions that make charity necessary and hinder social life.[12]

Torres's rapid move to radical action and revolutionary violence makes particular sense in the context of Colombia, but his ideas and commitments make sense as part of the general ferment and change that were under way in Latin American Catholicism in these years. His public life in Colombia overlapped with the Second Vatican Council (1962–1965), which brought so many changes to Catholicism. He was aware of the currents of debate and of the conclusions of the council, but by the time they crystallized he had already concluded that being true to the Gospel required commitments that would reach far beyond the boundaries of the institutional church. He did not live to witness the conferences of Medellín (1968) or Puebla (1979) with their condemnations of institutionalized violence and structural sin and their commitment to a preferential option for the poor. He also did not live to see the crystallization of many of these ideas in what came to be known as liberation theology. But it is unlikely that these would have altered his commitment to change through armed struggle.

Torres had perhaps more resonance in death, as a symbol of martyrdom and commitment, than he had in life. His biographer suggests:

> In Camilo as martyr they [Catholic activists] found an attractive symbol with clearly Christian characteristics. Christian churches were experiencing an awakening of social consciousness. Camilo did not invent the new church: in reality it was the surprising leadership of Pope John XXIII that brought it to life in the few years of his reign. But Camilo formed part of it, and ended up as one of its stellar figures, if not one of its saints. (Broderick 2002: 22)

Notable emulators include Catholic components of the Sandinista coalition in Nicaragua, a significant portion of the base of the guerrilla movement in El Salvador, elements of Argentina's Movement of Priests for Third World and of the Montonero guerrilla movement,[13] a section of Colombian guerrilla movement that at one time formed a Union Camilista of the National Liberation Army (ELN, Ejército Nacional de Liberación),[14] and numerous individual cases like that of Nestor Paz in Bolivia.[15]

Despite scattered emulations, the truth is that apart from the Sandinistas in Nicaragua, movements and individuals inspired by or following the example of Camilo Torres achieved only limited political success. Their impact in setting the agenda for discussion, debate, and action in religion and politics did not last long. They did not constitute the central defining dimension of religion and politics or of church-state conflict, nor were they core actors in most cases. Liberation theology, which in practice emphasizes long-term consciousness raising, popular education, and social movements, has arguably had a broader and more lasting impact.

Reactions to Violence: Peru and Argentina

Reactions to violence by churches and religious groups have ranged from resistance, accompaniment, and promotion of human rights to denial and complicity with repression. Here I want to consider the decisive role played by a core group of ideas that set the direction taken by these responses. How much and in what way the leadership of particular churches followed the ideas and practices derived from Medellín, and constructed a social presence modeled on these ideas, were central to how they framed and justified their reaction to violence. A closer look at the cases of Peru and Argentina underscores the different possibilities. Each country experienced intense and sustained violence with direct and deep impacts on the churches.

In Peru, the civil war unleashed in 1980 by Shining Path claimed over 75,000 dead and created hundreds of thousands of widows, orphans, and internal refugees over the next twenty years (Comisión de la Verdad y Reconciliación, Peru, 2004). Terrible as these figures are, they do not account fully for the enduring psychological and social trauma afflicting the population. As the civil war intensified, churches, religious activists, and communities were caught between Shining Path and the military and often suffered equally from both. The leadership and central institutions of the Peruvian Catholic Church openly supported human rights, promoted peace, and defended victims. In contrast, the bulk of the violence in Argentina came from state repression, as the last military regime (1976–1983) launched an all-out attack on groups and individuals that it perceived as linked in any way to the opposition. This campaign claimed upward of 30,000 dead and disappeared. For at least a decade before the military took power in 1976, there had been growing turmoil, mass mobilizations, conflict, and violence, and it is not an exaggeration to say that Argentina was in a prerevolutionary situation. This explains the fact that well before 1976, the military was laying the groundwork for the violence it unleashed once it was in control of the state, with an extensive program of surveillance of civil society along with harassments and arrests of opposition figures. At the same time, parastate and paramilitary groups like the Argentine Anti-Communist Alliance conducted a widespread campaign of kidnapping, torture, and killing, which included the murder of some of the most notable clergy and bishops associated with liberationist currents. As state security services ramped up their campaign against what they labeled "subversion," they reserved particular fury for leftists of all kinds, for Jews,[16] and for liberationist Catholics, who were regarded as traitors to the true faith. For their part, groups on the left initiated their own campaign of violence in the early 1970s, a campaign that drew on the alliance between leftist Catholics and Peronist youth noted earlier. One result of this alliance was the Montonero movement, which was joined in insurrectionary struggle by a Trotskyist Revolutionary Army of the People (ERP, Ejército Revolucionario del Pueblo).[17]

In the decade before the eruption of the war in Peru, the country's Catholic Church had undergone extensive changes in ideology, theology, organization, and institutional practices that in combination set the way it responded to the violence. The influence of the ideas articulated at Medellín was reinforced by the presence on the ground of numerous activists and groups inspired by liberation theology, whose early and prominent spokesman was the Peruvian theologian Gustavo Gutiérrez. Pedro Hughes argues that the influence of Medellín helped create "a church that was poor, missionary and self sacrificing (*pascual*), free of ties to temporal power and fully committed to liberation" (Hughes 2006: 639). He acknowledges that the church was not prepared for the scale of the violence (hardly anyone was) but points to numerous ways in which a response was made concrete. The church was active at national, regional, and local levels, striving in all cases to maintain a presence of active nonviolence, defense of life, and promotion of peace. Committees for the Defense of Life were established in Huacho, Sicuani, and Puno, and Vicariates of Solidarity or similar organizations were set up throughout the Andean South, where they worked to strengthen civil society while denouncing abuses, following cases, and helping victims (Cecilia Tovar 2006b: 27, 30).

Several issues in combination drove these new commitments: a definition of the poor that was concretely focused on the materially poor— the innocent, the vulnerable, the dispensable (Cecilia Tovar 2006a: 640); the conviction that God's presence in history is an affirmation of life and provides a basis for the defense of life and the denunciation of its destruction; a commitment to *accompaniment* that is central to liberation theology; and the emergence of an institutional option for the poor, which committed the church and its organizations to stances and actions that defended the poor and vulnerable and promoted peace building in specific ways. Taking stances like these put the church and its agents squarely in the path of competing powers, and in the gun sights of the military and of Shining Path.

A concrete sign of the new positions was that church personnel remained active in areas of intense violence (like Ayacucho) when others judged the situation too risky and left the scene. This continued presence reflects liberationist ideals of accompaniment and provided evidence and assurance that people were not alone. Where church-sponsored networks were maintained, as in the Andean South, Shining Path made relatively little headway.[18] The churches also created and sustained institutions that promoted civil society under very difficult conditions: groups were sponsored, legal defense was provided where possible, and information was diffused through public meetings, distribution of flyers, and church-supported radio networks (Cleary 2004b). Public activities like marches, demonstrations, funerals, and memorials to the dead were also kept going, often under very hostile circumstances, in an effort to break the violence-imposed silence and give public witness of the persistence of groups. Commitment to peace and to peace building found further expression in the creation and promotion of human rights committees and of a National Coordinating Group on Human Rights (Coordinadora Nacional de Derechos Humanos). In all these ways, the churches inserted themselves in a daily reality of suffering and struggle, making themselves and their people likely victims of continuing violence and future reprisals from all sides.

The incorporation of a commitment to rights as an integral part of the discourse and the agenda of the churches was not limited to Catholicism. Numerous individual Protestant churches, along with national and regional organizations and lay groups, joined ecumenical coalitions in defense of human rights, while at the same time organizing to defend their own churches and membership. These new positions were often spurred by the direct experience of violence. Protestant and Pentecostal churches grew massively during the 1980s and 1990s, a period that coincides with the rising arc of violence related to the Shining Path insurrection. Like Catholics, they soon found themselves trapped between the insurrectional violence of Shining Path (which targeted any group that tried to mobilize the population) and the repressive actions of the army, police, and special forces. As the toll of victims among the Protestant churches grew, the National Council of Evangelicals of Peru (CONEP, Concilio Nacional de Evangélicos del Perú) began to create organizations and to take public positions in defense of human rights (López 1998). Evangelical churches took up the struggle in active ways, joining human rights coalitions and in numerous cases arming themselves to fight back in self-defense. Darío López writes that "when Shining Path tried to control the personal and collective lives of the peasants, including their religious practices, it came up against a rival power that told it they could not 'serve two masters.' This rival power provided the strength needed both to resist Shining Path indoctrination and violence and to organize and fight against them" (López 2008a: 153).

With the capture of Abimael Guzmán (the founder and leader of Shining Path) in 1992, and the group's subsequent defeat, concerns with violence, rights, and the defense of civil society became less prominent in the public positions of all the churches. In the Protestant community, the end of the war brought growing pressure to return to a more traditional emphasis on preaching the word of God, "growing the church," and staying out of politics (López 1998). For the Catholic Church, this shift is associated with broad changes impelled by Vatican policy in these years, which have dramatically reduced the prominence of commitment to rights and open support of organizations working in these areas. The decision (1992) to close Chile's Vicariate of Solidarity, which had been a central source of support and leadership in this area, marked an important milestone.[19] Across the region, Catholic hierarchies moved away from confrontational stances, directing their resources to more conventional moral issues and to responding effectively to Protestant competition. These trends made their presence felt in Peru through a series of appointments of new bishops that turned one of the continent's most progressive hierarchies into one of its most conservative.[20] The rising power of this group is epitomized by the career of Bishop Juan Luis Cipriani (later archbishop and now cardinal). Throughout his career, Monsignor Cipriani has shown little tolerance for issues of human rights and has dismantled the institutional structures of the option for the poor wherever he has been in control. He rejected the validity of Peru's Commission on Truth and Reconciliation and famously disputed its conclusions on the very day that the report was given to the president (Klaiber 1992; MacLean 2006b).

The experience of Argentina is very different from that of Peru. The impact of Medellín was felt here as well and inspired numerous bishops, clergy, and activists to reject institutionalized violence, promote justice, and work for social change. These positions inspired the Argentine bishops' Declaration of San Miguel (1969), which provided legitimation to the newly formed Movement of Priests for the Third World and related groups of clergy, seminary students, and activists.[21] But the core leadership of the Argentine Catholic Church never embraced these positions, nor did they promote individuals or groups who did. Instead, a long-standing alliance with the military was reinforced, as church leaders offered ideological support, material cooperation, and in some cases direct complicity in the torture that was so common in that period.[22] The Argentine church also had an unusually large military vicariate (including up to 10 percent of clergy), which in word and action supported a view of the country's violence as a noble and justifiable crusade against communism (Ruderer 2010). The terror directed by the military at clergy and lay activists sympathetic to the Left or even simply just working in poor areas had a particular fury at its core. To the military and security services, those involved were not just political opponents. They were heretics whose actions undermined the proper and natural alliance between forces of order epitomized by the Catholic Church and the military. They had to be punished and cut out from the body of the nation. "That is to say," Donatello writes, "that they were not marked only as false Catholics, but as false Catholics and false Argentines. . . . this aspect of repression reveals a theological-political character based in a concept that accorded religious power to the military, including the power to determine who could and could not form part of 'Catholic Argentina.' This was possible because many religious authorities backed it up"[23] (Donatello 2008: 177–178).

Divisions within Catholicism thus became entangled and identified with public issues about legitimizing political power. Gustavo Morello states that "this may explain why the ecclesial was one of the most violence prone sectors in the social and political crisis in Argentina in the 60s and 70s" (Morello 2011a: 1). Further confirmation of this view comes from the files that security services in Argentina kept on leftist priests, which were justified not only in terms of national security but also in the name of Catholic doctrine.[24] This operation began well before the last military dictatorship got under way. In 1971, a secret document compiled by the State Security Service Secretariat for State Information (SIDE, Secretaría de Informaciones del Estado) was leaked to the press as part of what Michael Burdick describes as a rising media campaign to discredit the MSTM. The threat posed by the MSTM "was not necessarily ecclesial but temporal; that is, if the *tercermundistas* ["third worldists," a reference to the MSTM] succeeded in gaining power, then the country would fall to 'totalitarian socialism'" (Michael Burdick 1995: 176). Surveillance continued through the decade. Reports compiled by the Naval Operations Command of the General Belgrano Naval Base cited "well founded reasons to believe that among these priests there are communist activists [who have] deliberately infiltrated since the seminary and who have known how to convince the well intentioned but naïve" (Catoggio 2008b: 183). One report describes MSTM priests in these terms:

> They are not teachers of the Catholic religion; they do not profess the faith of the Church, given that they knowingly reject Christian philosophy and theology, replacing them with sociology, psychology, and economics, disciplines in which, according to experts, they also fail to achieve an acceptable level of knowledge. Holy Scripture is gutted of its authentic interpretation in tradition and Church teachings, and is reduced to an exposition which has no place for concepts of the immortal soul, original sin, grace and supernatural life. In extreme cases even the Trinity and the very existence of a transcendent God are silenced. (Catoggio 2008b: 185)

Liberationist groups and their sympathizers were outnumbered and defeated within the Argentine church by a majority position that rejected the implications of Medellín and the idea of a commitment to link faith directly to actions for justice, even without violence. Instead, top church leaders reaffirmed their alliance with the military, considered as two forces that together defined order and stood for the nation, above politics and social divisions (Mallimaci 2005, 2009; Devoto 2002; Donatello 2008; Ghio 2007). Horacio Verbitsky (2005, 2006, 2007, 2008, 2009) demonstrates that the alliance between the Argentine Catholic hierarchy and the military included more than general statements of support: the hierarchy also provided land where torture centers could be mounted, identified individuals and groups for arrest, and refused to defend church figures kidnapped and tortured by the military and security forces. Some clergy were also actively complicit in torture and in the distribution for adoption of babies born to political prisoners in captivity who were allowed to have the children but then killed.[25]

Morello (2011a) records a case in the city of Córdoba that is illustrative of the tendencies. Córdoba, the second largest city in Argentina and a major industrial center, was an early focus of MSTM recruiting and organization and a center for trade union mobilization. The city also had an important military presence, with a commander, General Luciano Benjamin Menéndez (now convicted of human rights crimes), who was particularly aggressive in the fight against what he viewed as "subversion." Religious dissidents and religiously inspired activists were prominent among the potential and actual sources of subversion feared by the local garrison and other security forces. For its part, the Catholic Church in Córdoba had ample expression of both liberationist and conservative tendencies. In 1975, the Congregation of La Salette (Missionaries of Our Lady of La Salette) got approval to establish an alternative form of seminary education. Unlike traditional seminaries, this would not be an isolated physical space, but would instead occupy an ordinary house in a neighborhood. The seminarians (five students and one teacher, the Reverend James Weeks, an American) would have regular contact with the community, conduct Bible study, operate a health clinic, and take jobs in the community. Experiments of this kind were not uncommon in Latin America in these years, but in the highly charged political circumstances of Córdoba (and Argentina) they appeared deeply subversive of the proper order of things. In an interview with the superior of the congregation, General Menéndez stated that he did not understand "how there could be a seminary with only one priest and five seminarians. A seminary had to be like the army: a big building and this was just an ordinary house in a poor neighborhood" (Morello 2011a: 270).

The new seminary soon drew the attention of the army and its intelligence services, and on August 3, 1976, the Reverend Weeks and the five seminarians were arrested on charges of subversion. They were taken to a detention center and subject to interrogation and torture by officers well versed in Catholic doctrine, who appeared to specialize in cases of radical Catholics. The squad that carried out the arrests took pains to trash the chapel and to confiscate potentially subversive materials, including Bolivian folk songs. It is likely that the only reason the group survived at all was that one of those present, Sister Joan McCarthy, was for some reason not arrested. She went to the US embassy and began a chain of contacts that led to Representative Robert Drinan, a Jesuit member of the US Congress, who immediately began efforts to rescue them, and in the process to throw light on the abuses of military rule in Argentina.

The arrest, imprisonment, and ultimate freeing of the prisoners stretched over several months, and during this time the top hierarchy of the Argentine church, both in Córdoba and nationally, did and said nothing in public. They acted to block aid to the prisoners, including provision of Bibles and religious services. Morello states that "[Bishop] Tortolo, President of the Argentine Conference of Bishops,[26] denied a specific request from the provincial of the congregation to provide sacramental assistance [communion and confession] to the prisoners. He refused to arrange for them to receive sacraments and to have access to the Bible." Morello comments, "We are facing a special kind of religiosity, in which the church did not consider itself attacked by the kidnapping of these victims (all seminary students, aspirants to the priesthood) because they were not considered to be true Catholics. Their lack of merit to receive communion or confession symbolizes the fact that the prisoners were not considered authentic believers and as such, they could be cast out of the community" (Morello 2011a: 346–347).[27]

The cases of Camilo Torres, Peru, and Argentina illustrate very distinct ways in which religious leaders and activists have understood, engaged in, and reacted to violence. Camilo Torres and those he inspired took up arms not because of some personal predilection for violence, but rather because they saw revolutionary violence as the only realistic path to effect the kinds of changes required to create a society in which loving one's neighbor could be more than a hypocritical statement. The varying reactions of church leaders and activists to civil war and repression in Peru and Argentina show a different dynamic. The core leadership of the Peruvian Catholic Church (like their counterparts in El Salvador or Chile) drew on Medellín and liberation theology to construct a reaction to violence that accompanied victims while promoting rights and mediating in pursuit of peace. In contrast, the divisions in

Argentine Catholicism were violent because the church was split by the same divisions as the country at large. As in the country, so in the church: those on the left were defeated and pushed to the sidelines, when not kidnapped, tortured, and killed if they could not somehow make it into exile. The kidnapping and torture of the seminarians in Córdoba show how deep the division was and how far violence, this time in the defense of religion allied to the established order, would go.

Active Nonviolence as a Strategy and a Commitment

The weight of violence and the salience of responses to violence in shaping the public presence of the churches make it easy to miss a continuing and important thread of active nonviolence in the presence of churches and church-related groups in Latin America. Although nonviolent strategies and tactics in Latin America never acquired the scale of Gandhi's India or the US civil rights movement, they have played a role that deserves attention. Gene Sharp specifies 198 methods of nonviolent action, including communication and public pressure, social and economic noncooperation (strikes and boycotts), and political noncooperation, such as withholding of allegiance and denial of public support along with "literature and speeches advocating resistance" (Sharp 1973: 127). A review of Latin American experience with religiously inspired or linked nonviolent resistance turns up a wide-ranging and not much studied recourse to protest methods of this kind. Among the most notable have been public speeches and documents, group or mass petitions, prayer and worship, marches, and religious processions and pilgrimages (numbers 6, 20, 38, and 40–41, respectively, in Sharp's list).

Argentina's Mothers of the Plaza de Mayo are a particularly well-known example. This is a group of mothers and grandmothers who march regularly around the Plaza de Mayo, in the heart of Buenos Aires, in silent witness to their children or relatives who have been kidnapped and "disappeared" by the military regime. The marches began in 1977 and continue to the present, with added concern about identifying children born to political prisoners who were then executed after giving birth. These children were given in adoption to friends of the regime. Protests and legal action strive to reunite children with their biological families.[28] The movement has evolved and now maintains an independent university, bookstore, library, and cultural center. Marching was itself risky (particularly in the early years), and more than a few of the mothers were kidnapped and disappeared.

The efforts of the Mothers of the Plaza de Mayo arose in response to the crisis of their families and of the country, but this group and others like it are part of a broader transnational effort. The mothers got important help at the time from the Service for Peace and Justice in Latin America (SERPAJ-AL, Servicio de Paz y Justicia–América Latina), a group that was established in various centers across Latin America in the early 1970s as part of a transnational Quaker outreach (Pagnucco and McCarthy 1992). Working through the international Fellowship of Reconciliation (FOR) and in coordination with civil rights movements like the Congress of Racial Equality (CORE), a broad effort was mounted to bring nonviolent techniques of social organization to Latin America. FOR is a classic example of religiously linked movement halfway houses, which "may serve as repositories of information about past movements, strategy and tactics, inspiration, and leadership. They are distinctive in that many of them survive short term fluctuations of social movement cycles and finally, that many of them receive critical support from established religious groups" (Zald and McCarthy 1987b: 74).[29]

SERPAJ-AL was established at a continent-wide meeting in Medellín, Colombia, in 1974. From the beginning, it operated as a transnational clearinghouse for ideas, leadership training, and the diffusion of organizational models. The Argentine branch was founded soon after by a group led by Adolfo Pérez Esquivel that had been looking for ways to inform people about nonviolence and to oppose the mounting violence in Argentina. They began publishing a newsletter entitled *Peace and Justice Latin American Non Violent Action (Paz y Justicia Acción No Violenta Latinoamericana)* that addressed a broad range of issues, including but not limited to human rights. Rising violence in the country and the growing likelihood of a military coup led to a strengthened focus on human rights. In 1975, Pérez Esquivel proposed that the Argentine Catholic Church strengthen its Peace and Justice Commission and work on human rights. This overture was rejected, and "consequently in February 1976 Pérez Esquivel helped start an Ecumenical Human Rights movement. The emergence of this group was viewed with suspicion by the military and by top leaders in the Argentine Catholic Church" (Pagnucco and McCarthy 1992: 142). Pérez Esquivel also helped in setting up the Mothers of the Plaza de Mayo, providing training, orientation, publicity, and transnational contacts. The efforts of SERPAJ-AL and the actions of groups like the Mothers of the Plaza de Mayo were kept at arm's length by the hierarchy of the Argentine Catholic Church. In the view of church leaders, victims were lamentable but unavoidable in the context of what was understood to be a legitimate and necessary struggle to save Argentina from Communist terror and maintain public order and Christian civilization. Human rights were discounted as an issue. Not surprisingly, the award of the Nobel Peace Prize to Pérez Esquivel in 1980 was greeted "critically by the military regime and ignored or downplayed by the Argentine media. The Argentine Catholic Information Agency simply stated that SERPAJ was not associated with the church's Peace and Justice Commission" (Pagnucco and McCarthy 1992: 143).

The Argentine case is deservedly well-known, but there are many others in which nonviolent actions framed the public presence of religious groups in situations of violence. I already noted efforts in Peru to accompany the poor and vulnerable and to maintain a presence in areas of the greatest violence. These acquired particular focus during the heights of violence that accompanied the civil war between Shining Path and the state throughout the 1980s. The Confederation of Religious Orders of Peru (CONFER, Confederación de Religiosos del Perú), which grouped members of various congregations in Peru, collaborated on a training program for priests and sisters that included measures for self-protection (e.g., houses with thick walls to shield them from bullets and answering knocks on the door from the second floor), understanding the tactics of the insurgents and the military, working with psychologists on fear, and developing a spirituality of nonviolence and even of martyrdom based on the image of Jesus. The theory and practice of nonviolence were explored in detail, with much interest in the examples set by Gandhi and Martin Luther King Jr. (Ranly 2003: 124). "The fundamental decision was to remain in the area. This is not an easy or superficial decision. A concrete, active, personal presence is basic. The reality of threats and violence means that there was not much chance for large scale projects. Almost any kind of human promotion effort was prohibited and made impossible. So the question arises: what to do when nothing can be done?" (Ranley 2003: 130).

One notable answer came in response to the armed stoppages (*paros armados*) regularly decreed in the highlands by Shining Path, when all activity was to cease. "During the armed stoppages decreed by Shining Path, it has to be crystal clear that the priests and sisters are with their people. In a total armed stoppage: with no traffic, no stores open, no classes for students, no mobility to go to work, in many places people come out of their houses and play in the streets. The religious should go into the streets also greeting them and perhaps playing sports.

We are with the people" (Ranly 2003: 118). Maintaining an active presence was dangerous. There are numerous cases of priests and sisters threatened and executed by Shining Path (as were villagers) for their "collaboration with imperialism," or for diverting people from revolutionary struggle by working in development projects, teaching the Bible, giving candy or "Yankee food," or spreading "Yankee ideas" by providing schoolbooks to children.[30] The decision to maintain a presence in the emergency zones of highland Peru was sustained throughout the worst periods of violence.[31] For such a commitment to be present in the midst of violence was not universal in Latin America: at the height of Guatemala's civil war in the 1980s, the Catholic Church withdrew from areas of most intense conflict (Stoll 1993).

Strategies of nonviolent accompaniment have also been employed by transnational groups like Witness for Peace, which has brought North American and other activists to conflict zones in Nicaragua, Colombia, southern Mexico, and elsewhere. Other instances of nonviolent action are less dramatic. Daniel Zirker (1999) documents a range of nonviolent actions in Brazil following the 1980 expulsion (by the military government) of an Italian priest (P. Vito Miracapillo) accused of political activities. Many clergy in Latin America are of foreign origin, and expulsions of this kind have been common in democratic as well as authoritarian regimes. The Brazilian case is noteworthy because the expulsion of Padre Miracapillo fit within a larger pattern of actions in which Brazilian clergy and bishops, inspired by liberation theology, challenged the status quo, particularly in the north and northeast of the country where conflicts over land brought political clashes that included violence against clerics siding with the landless—a pattern that continues to the present day (French 2007; Miguel Carter 2012). The principal nonviolent technique, public declarations by clergy and bishops questioning the independence of Brazil and the rights of citizens under dictatorship, "led to at least four results: limiting violence from the government, unifying the church in response, increasing support for the church, and a broader pattern of mass based non-violent resistance to the anti-democratic policies of the dictatorship was initiated and later became crucial in such events as the *dirietas ja* movement calling for direct elections as part of the transition to democracy in 1984, and even the impeachment of President Fernando Collor de Melo in 1996" (Zirker 1999: 274). The strategies tested out here were extended in subsequent years in Brazil to work with peasant and insurgent union groups; mediation among landless, strikers, and the military; organization of marches, rallies, and other forms of solidarity; and material and ideological support for protesters subject to official violence.

Conclusion

The brutalizing violence of the past fifty years contributed in many countries to the creation of movements for greater accountability and control over police and military, and a sustained effort to recover the historical memory of the violence and its victims and perpetrators (Peter Smith 2005; Perruzzotti and Smulovitz 2006; Wilde 2011, 2012). Commenting on the report of Peru's Truth and Reconciliation Commission, Gustavo Gutiérrrez explicitly rejects the argument that the commission was stirring up memories that are best left forgotten, reopening old wounds in ways that are useless and may be dangerous for the country. Those who hold this view, he states, "lack the respect due to the dead. They forget that for those who directly suffered harm and loss from the violence, for those who do not know if their loved ones are dead or where their bodies may be, all that happened is not in another time, for them it is a lacerating present" (Gutiérrez 2004: 566). The urge to recover historical memory is often countered by desires for a return to "normality" and to keep details of past violence as something of a public secret (Stoll 1993). The end of civil wars and the return to civilian democratic politics were taken by many in the churches as an opportunity to cut costs, withdraw from exposed public positions, mute public confrontations, leave the defense of rights and the promotion of movements, and return to traditional themes of public morality, control of sexuality, and competition for public subsidies. These are, of course, no less political, but the quality of action, the relation of the churches to social movements, and the kinds of movements and actions promoted are different.

That the religious panorama of Latin America is so different now from what it was fifty years ago owes much to the intersection of violence, religious innovation, demographic transformations, and evolving patterns of legitimation. The influence that flows from the mutual impact of violence and religious change is visible at the level of discourse and legitimation, in laws and institutions, and in the actions of citizen groups and social movements in a more open and less regulated civil society. Victor Turner (1974) argues that in moments of crisis people find themselves in a *liminal* condition, where neither existing norms nor the pattern of laws and institutions seem to fit the situation or provide convincing guidelines for action and evaluation. In such times, there is an open cultural space and an available audience for the construction of new norms, and of a practical culture that ends up organizing and valuing life in different terms. Do the changes reviewed here constitute a liminal moment? Do the processes we have examined represent a historical turning point, a real moment of change, or simply another turn in the cycle of peace and internal war, democracy and authoritarianism, that is so familiar in Latin American history?

It is too early to be confident about the specifics of the practical culture of politics that may emerge from the changes detailed here, but a few elements are clear. One of the results of violence has been a heightened awareness of rights and an effort to strengthen rights and give accountability a central place in agendas of public discussion. There is also a broad and as yet incomplete effort under way in many churches to articulate a position with respect to current patterns of violence (crime, drugs, gangs, vendettas, and domestic abuse) that would have the coherence and moral force of the critiques of institutionalized violence of the 1970s and 1980s. These initiatives provide a normative base and a set of practical tools with which the churches and the faithful can begin a creative response to the violence of the future, whatever forms it may take.

Notes

1. See Argentine National Commission on the Disappeared 1986; Berryman 1995a; Archdiocese of Lima 1990; Comisión de la Verdad y Reconciliación 2004; Falla 2001; Garrard-Burnett 1998; Peterson 1997; REMHI 1999; Stoll 1993; Maclean 2006a.

2. In his last two pastoral letters, Archbishop Oscar Romero of El Salvador drew a distinction among structural or institutional violence, arbitrary violence exercised by the state, the violence of the extreme Right, terrorist violence, insurrectional violence, and a violence of legitimate self-defense. He underscored the peril of spirals of violence that easily become impossible to control and concluded that the most rational and efficient thing governments could do would be to use force not to defend the structural violence of an unjust order, but rather to guarantee a democratic state based on a just economic order (Romero 1985).

3. Cynthia Arnson (2011) reports that Latin America has the highest level of youth violence in the world: more than double that of Africa and thirty-six times the rate of developed countries. Victims are disproportionately male, and the effects of violence reach far beyond the total of fatalities: for every fatality there are twenty to forty victims of nonfatal violence.

4. As in the case of Father Cristián von Wernich, convicted of crimes against human rights and sentenced to life imprisonment in late 2007 (Brienza 2003; Ferguson 2007).

5. See also Argentine National Commission on the Disappeared 1986; Bonnin 2010; Catoggio 2011; Devoto 2002; Feitlowitz 1988; Ghio 2007; Mallimaci 2005, 2008b; Mallimaci, Cucchetti, and Donatello 2006; Morello 2011a; Mignone 1988; Verbitsky 2005, 2006, 2007, 2008, 2009.

6. The widespread practice of kidnapping and disappearance during the last military regime in Argentina limited possibilities for public mourning and contributed to public and scholarly concern in subsequent years with the reconstruction of memory (Mallimaci 2008b). The ban on public mourning in Guatemala undermined much of traditional community life (REMHI 1999; Wilson 1991). In Peru, both the army and Shining Path (like the Romans in antiquity) forbade access to the bodies of the dead along with public burial and rituals of mourning. The trauma for families and communities was exacerbated by the lack of certainty that death had in fact occurred (given the absence of a body) and the psychological weight of not knowing enough or, alternatively, of having seen too much (Comisión de la Verdad y Reconciliación, Peru, 2004, ch. 7, "Las Secuelas del Conflicto"). Such bans are not limited to Latin America. In Zimbabwe, "the crimes committed to entrench Mr. Mugabe's rule date back to the 1980s, when thousands of civilians from Zimbabwe's Ndebele minority in Matabeleland were killed by the notorious North Korean trained Fifth Army brigade. According to historians, among the Ndebele, the tears of the living must be shed to release the souls of the dead. But the Fifth Brigade insisted that there be no mourning for those they killed, and in some cases shot family members because they wept, according to 'Breaking the Silence,' a 1997 investigation based on the testimonies of more than 1,000 witnesses" (Dugger 2009).

7. The long-term impact of a culture of contract and the durability of conversions and of life changes associated with them are rich areas for study. See Zaret 1985 for a discussion of contractarian views in the English Reformation.

8. The violence claimed over 200,000 lives in the decade following 1948 (Guzmán 1968; Oquist 1978).

9. Unless otherwise indicated, all translations from Camilo Torres are by the author.

10. Monsignor Romero drew this distinction clearly in his last two pastoral letters, *The Church and Popular Organizations* (August 6, 1978) and *The Church's Mission amid the National Crisis* (August 6, 1979) (Oscar Romero 1985).

11. From an interview with French journalist Jean Pierre Sergent, in *Semana al Día*, Bogotá, August 1965. The idea of just wars and justified tyrannicide is not new in Catholicism. *Populorum Progressio* no. 31 (March 1967) says: "Everyone knows, however, that revolutionary uprisings—except where there is manifest, longstanding tyranny which would do great damage to fundamental personal rights and dangerous harm to the common good of the country—engender new injustices, introduce new inequities and bring new disasters.

The evil situation that exists, and it surely is evil, may not be dealt with in such a way that an even worse situation results."

12. This recalls Dietrich Bonhoeffer's (1959) insistence on avoiding complicity and being satisfied with the cheap grace of easy accommodations. A common trajectory begins with sympathy for victims of injustice, moves swiftly to concern for human rights, and ultimately results in active resistance to institutions that maintain and enforce the injustices that violate rights and create victims. Parallels to South Africa are detailed by Borer 1998, Johnston 1994, and Walshe 1983, 1991.

13. He was a role model for the MSTM and was cited regularly by a group of militants who founded the journal *Christianity and Revolution* (*Cristianismo y Revolución*), which appeared from 1966 to 1971. One article by Juan Garcia Elorrio on the role of Christians in the revolution states that Camilo died in "the only effective way of realizing love for all. . . . This revolution, although at times violent because of the hardness of human hearts, is really the only way to rescue Hope and Love for Humanity" (cited in Morello 2007: 11).

14. "Camilo Torres: Priest and Guerrilla Fighter," www.greenleft.org.au /1996/219/15042.

15. Paz (1978) cites Torres several times in the letter he left behind announcing his decision to join the Bolivian guerrillas. Paz died of starvation after seventy days in the campaign.

16. The anti-Semitism of the Argentine military is well-known and well documented, and Jews were a disproportionate share of the victims (Timmerman 2002; Feitlowitz 1988). Major instances of anti-Semitic violence after the military left power include, spectacularly, the 1994 bombing of the AMIA (Asociación Mutual Israelita Argentina, Argentine Jewish Mutual Aid Association) in Buenos Aires, which killed eighty-five people and injured hundreds. No one has ever been arrested or prosecuted for this crime. Argentina has the largest Jewish community in the Americas outside the United States, but anti-Semitism is not unknown elsewhere in Latin America. Luis Roniger (2009) reviews debates about official anti-Semitism in Venezuela. On the specific surveillance and persecution of liberationist Catholics, see Michael Burdick 1995; Catoggio 2008b, 2010; and Morello 2011a.

17. The ERP was shattered by state security forces within months of the 1976 coup.

18. The report of the Commission on Truth and Reconciliation states that "in general, wherever the church had renovated itself on the lines of the second Vatican Council and the Episcopal Conferences of Medellín and Puebla, there was much more resistance to the appeals of subversive groups, because [the churches] developed a social presence that linked them to the population and responded to their needs with a discourse of change and a demand for justice while rejecting violence. In contrast, where the church had not taken into account the changes pushed by the Council, subversion encountered much more fertile ground in which to root itself" (Comisión de la Verdad y Reconciliación, Peru, 2004, Volume III: 415–416).

19. The multifaceted work of the vicariate included protection of human rights, support of victims' relatives, promotion of organizations and social movements, and serving as a source for food, education, medical help, and shelter. The testimonies and documents collected by its legal section were transferred to the archdiocese in a new organization called the Foundation of Archives of the Vicariate of Solidarity (Fundación de Archivos de la Vicaría de la Solidaridad), and have continued to serve as an important resource for human rights lawyers.

20. Many of the new bishops were members of the highly conservative Opus Dei (as of 2011, two archbishops, including one cardinal, and eleven bishops). Once in office, they went about dismantling many of the pastoral structures so visible in earlier decades. According to the Comisión de la Verdad y Reconciliación, "The majority of bishops, priests and sisters and many lay people constituted a moral force and a source of hope. Nonetheless, we note that in some places ecclesiastical authorities maintained a deplorable silence about the violations of human rights committed by security forces" (Comisión de la Verdad y Reconciliación, Peru, 2004, volume III: 379, cited in Tovar 2006: 28).

21. In this document, the bishops condemned capitalism and called for national social change. In both language and mentality, the document was in sharp contrast to the bishops' earlier pronouncements. "It is our duty," the bishops wrote, "to work for the total liberation of man and to illuminate the process of changing unjust and oppressive structures." Burdick notes that the San Miguel declaration was an anomaly for the Argentine episcopacy—its language, style, and orientations did not reflect the attitudes of many senior bishops. Just as there was a conservative backlash in the Council of Latin American Bishops (CELAM) after Medellín, so too a backlash occurred within the Argentine Episcopal Conference (Michael Burdick 1995: 144).

22. The situation is more complex than the notion of a simple alliance might suggest. Progressives were also an integral part of the church and cultivated relations with the military—the Montoneros had their own chaplains. Growing violence eliminated this possibility, as security services and the military assumed the role of deciding what was and was not authentically Catholic (Donatello 2008).

23. Donatello (2008) cites a document from the conference of Argentine bishops in 1976, a month and a half after the military coup, that legitimized military violence in these terms: "It must be remembered that it would be easy to make mistakes out of good will and a search for the common good if we were to pretend that the security services could operate with chemical purity as in times of peace when in fact blood is being shed every day, when disorder—whose depths we know all too well—reigns, without accepting the drastic measures that the situation requires. [The choice is either to accept] or not to accept the sacrifice for the common good of that measure of liberty that the current circumstances require, or on the other hand seek with pretended reasons of faith to implement Marxist solutions" (communiqué issued by the Argentine Episcopal Conference, May 15, 1976).

24. A well-known progressive translation of the Bible, the *Biblia Lati-noamericana,* was specifically condemned by the military government (Catoggio 2006).

25. The most well-known case is that of Christian von Wernich, a priest convicted in October 2007 of multiple counts of murder and violations of human rights (including active involvement in torture), all carried out, in the words of the judge, "under the mark of genocide" (Brienza 2003; Ferguson 2007). Von Wernich had been protected by the Argentine hierarchy and transferred under another name to a parish in Chile, where he was discovered and brought back for trial. Von Wernich has never acknowledged doing any wrong, and after the trial the Argentine bishops' conference limited itself to a general statement claiming that his acts were individual and urging all Argentines to "put away hate and rancor" and take the path of reconciliation. "Priest convicted in Argentine Dirty War Tribunal" (www.truthout.org/article/priest -convicted-argentine-dirty-war-tribunal) and "Argentina Dirty War Priest Gets Life" (CBS news report, www.cbsnews.com/stories/2007/10/10/world/main335 1642 .shtml).

26. Before becoming president of the conference of bishops, Monsignor Tortolo had been chief military vicar. His long involvement with the military vicariate, and the importance the vicariate had in the Argentine church, underscore the significance of his role as head of the bishops' conference. On the military vicariate in Argentina and Chile, see Ruderer 2010.

27. Morello records a subsequent meeting of some in the group with the Papal Nuncio, Pio Laghi. The meeting was to facilitate passports and visas, as the group (now released from prison) urgently needed to leave the country. The Nuncio recommended that they speak with Bishop Tortolo, who was the person in charge, and one in the group responded by recounting his own meeting with Tortolo where he tried to show him the scars from his torture. Tortolo's response is worth recording: "'Don't speak of this any more. The military are men of God, Christians who love the Church.' I felt the pain of the abuses I had suffered running through my veins and I stood up, took down my trousers and said: 'Look. This is what they did to me. This is what they did to me.' He said, 'what kind of shit is this?'" (Morello 2011: 280).

28. Alexei Barrionuevo (2011) recounts a case in which one young woman discovered that the man she had always called "Father" was in fact the military officer responsible for the killing of her parents.

29. Efforts by FOR to spread the ideas of nonviolence in Latin America go as far back as 1919, but as late as the early 1950s "even those few groups in Latin America committed to non violence did not advocate direct action. FOR groups in Latin America tended to have a more passive, non confrontational view of non violence" (Pagnucco and McCarthy 1992: 134). Beginning in the mid-1960s, FOR made a concerted push to create networks of groups and clergy committed to nonviolence. "For example, in March 1970, [Brady] Tyson, a dynamic Methodist minister who had been a missionary in Brazil, an associate of Dr. Martin Luther King Jr., an SCLC [Southern Christian Leadership Council] executive board member, and an FOR member introduced the Rev.

Ralph Abernathy who succeeded King as Head of the SCLC to Dom Helder Camara in Recife, Brazil. Together Camara and Abernathy issued the Declaration of Recife, calling for a worldwide movement of nonviolent protest against the unjust structures that maintain poverty, racism, and war" (Pagnucco and McCarthy 1992: 134).

30. Sister Irene McCormack was executed by a Shining Path column on May 21, 1991, in the town of Huasahuasi, over the protests of local residents who pointed out that she was Australian, not American (Henderson 2003).

31. Ernesto Ranly (2003: 82–83) points out that the commitment was initially organized through a Commission for Missions but soon evolved into a Commission for Support of Emergency Zones.

7

Rights and
Reconciliation

Struggles over rights, and efforts to promote peace and reconciliation
in the wake of dictatorship and violence, are prominent in the recent
experience of Latin America. From the late 1960s through the mid- and
late 1980s, the Latin American churches, sometimes alone, but often
through ecumenical committees of cooperation, became prime agencies
for the articulation, promotion, and defense of rights.[1] This commonly
began as a defense of classic human rights in the face of dictatorship
and official abuse and therefore focused on the right to physical
integrity of the person, to be free from arbitrary arrest, detention, torture, and death. The effort soon expanded to embrace a long list of
rights, including the rights to health, education, land, vote, and organize, along with the rights of indigenous communities, of children, and of
women. In the same way, the category of those recognized as victims of
abuse also broadened from direct objects of state action to those
affected by the multiple violence of the time—the poor, the vulnerable,
and the marginalized. The rationale for action itself grew from an initial
defense of the churches' own agents—bishops, priests, sisters, and lay
leaders—to a view that accorded rights to human beings qua human, as
children of God.

At the outset of this book, I asked why the churches took up ideas
about rights: Why at this time and why in these specific ways? What
effect did these new ideas have on society, on politics, and on the
churches themselves? We already have part of the answer. Concepts
about rights (in law and in theology) gained immediacy in much of
Latin America in the face of the political crises of violence, dictator-

ship, and open warfare that afflicted so many countries. These ideas acquired further resonance within religion through the involvement of church leaders and institutions—tentative at first—with victims and as part of the impact of becoming targets and victims themselves. These answers are important, but there are prior questions that call for our attention. There is nothing inevitable about claims of rights, much less about their recognition in law and in the operation of institutions. For much of human history, most people have been given to understand that they have no rights, an understanding confirmed by their day-to-day experience with power and privilege. One question, then, concerns the creation of a vocabulary of rights, both in general and specifically within the churches.

For the words in this vocabulary to acquire a meaningful social presence, to become embedded in laws and institutional practices, a few things have to happen. Concepts of rights need to be created and given legitimacy in the churches and other institutions. In addition, some-one—perhaps the same person who articulates the concept—must spread the message, packaging it in an accessible form and bringing it to an audience. Those who hear the message also need to have a sense that what the words articulate is not only good but also possible. This requires trust in the agents who bring the message and also benefits from a sense that one is not alone. The experience of group solidarity is critical in turning individual claims of rights into something with ordered social meaning.

An example may help to drive the point home. In its work with landless peasants in Brazil, and with the landless movement, the Pas-toral Land Commission of Brazil's Catholic Church has worked long and hard to inform peasants of their rights. When the earliest peasant delegations went to discuss land claims with government officials, they were asked to demonstrate that they had rights. At a loss for words, they left crestfallen. Given this experience, teams from the Pastoral Land Commission developed booklets and flyers detailing precisely how rights to land were specified in legislation. These pamphlets were widely diffused and were the subject of much discussion in peasant meetings. They gave legal specification to the broader belief that God made the land for all, not just for a few landowners. This conviction, enhanced by group solidarity, reinforced the capacity of peasants to make and sustain claims in the future. The Pastoral Land Commission strengthens this capacity by deploying teams of lawyers and extensive networks of pastoral agents dedicated to work with land claimants from the outset of their struggles (Miguel Carter 2012; French 2007; Patricia

Rodríguez 2009). The process recalls Harris's description of how religious faith and membership work on politics in the African American community of the United States. The churches, he notes, provide micro and macro resources: micro resources include a sense of legitimacy and personal efficacy, which gain effectiveness through the tangible macro resources that collective organization can provide—a place to meet and material support for action (Harris 1999, 2003). Examples could be multiplied indefinitely: the point is that the experience of rights is multidimensional, putting the creation of new words and symbols together with agents who can package these and deliver them to people and social innovations that provide a framework for sustained collective action.

The issue of rights is not itself new. There is much precedent, internationally and in Latin America, in laws, constitutions, international treaties and declarations, and theological debate and reflection (Cleary 2007a). Ideas about human rights are in any case not unique to the churches, although there is significant precedent for Latin America in the example of Bartolomé de las Casas, the sixteenth-century Spanish Dominican friar who was an early defender of the humanity of the Indians and of their rights to equal treatment as children of God (Gutiérrez 1993). What is really new in the past half century in Latin America is not so much the idea of rights as *the practice of rights*, a practice advanced and sustained by networks of groups in civil society, networks often initiated and supported by critical backing from the churches (Brysk 2004; Cleary 2007a; Levine 2006a, 2006c; Sikkink 1993; Wilde 2011). Edward Cleary writes that the major change of interest to observers of Latin America "is active response from the grass roots, the middle levels of society. Latin America, to the surprise of many, became a movement society, one in which movements concerned about various issues appeared, many of them focused on human rights" (Cleary 2007a: ix). The defense of rights brings the leaders of institutions like the churches into working relations with middle levels of society, inspiring lawyers, NGOs, and a range of civil society groups, including the churches, to new commitments and forms of practice that advance rights.[2] Among these are a wealth of human rights committees and movements, many with links to the churches. Iain Maclean affirms that

> the national churches became the recorders of crimes of the military in addition to preserving the memory of oppression and providing martyrs in the liberation struggles. The churches also became the source of legal and other aid for those targeted by regimes and so, in Brazil and elsewhere, served as the voice of the voiceless. In these and similar

ways, they became in some way unwillingly, the mid wife to new structures of civil society so critical to the empowerment of citizens of democratizing nations. (Maclean 2006b: 34)

Direct experience of violence and repression, mediated by concepts derived from the theology of liberation, led many in the churches to identify with victims of violence in general. The new positions and outreach from the churches gave concrete meaning to the "preferential option for the poor" and allowed victims to see the churches as potential allies and sources of help (Drogus and Stewart-Gambino 2005; Lernoux 1982, 1994; Levine 1992, 2006a, 2006c; Peterson 1997). This convergence of interests opened the churches to new ideas about rights, and turned its leaders and institutions into promoters of human rights in key cases like Brazil, Chile, El Salvador, Peru, and later, Guatemala. With support from transnational organizations and networks, the churches provided critical resources in support of human rights and in aid of victims of repression, helping individuals and families find shelter and work, offering legal assistance, and collaborating in the difficult task of finding the disappeared, or at least trying to discover if they were still alive. The reason for this commitment was not only self-defense but also a belief that rights were inherent to all, as children of God, and that the promotion and defense of rights were an essential element of the Christian message[3] (Brysk 2000, 2004; Byrnes 2011; Drogus and Stewart-Gambino 2005; Brian Smith 1982; López 1998; Wechsler 1990).

The defense of classic human rights (to be free from arbitrary arrest, abuse, and torture, and to reject the impunity of political leaders, military, and police) was accompanied by efforts to promote and make effective rights to collective organization (by the landless, by slum dwellers, by indigenous communities, and in a more halting way, by women), rights to health and education, and in general to assert the right and to enhance the capacity of the poor and powerless to participate in political and social life (Berryman 1984, 1995a; John Burdick 2004; Miguel Carter 2012; French 2007; Levine 2006a, 2006c). The concept of social sin articulated at Medellín also shaped ideas about reconciliation and recovery from violence, with notable involvement by churches, religious groups, and religious figures in truth commissions, most notably in Peru, Chile, and Guatemala, and in publicizing human rights in Brazil.

A practical vocabulary of rights was created, a vocabulary that identifies rights and points to instances in which these rights arise and can be exercised. Churches that assumed this role made important contributions to the evolution of a new culture of politics in Latin America, not least by giving rights a prominent place on the agenda of states and institutions and adding legitimacy to demands for accountability from officials and political leaders. I use the term *practical* for the vocabulary of rights and for the culture of politics to underscore the significance of elements of association and practice in the emergence of new norms and how they become embedded in the expectations and everyday life of communities and the practices of institutions.

Where does the basic concept of rights come from? How and why does it acquire an audience that embraces these ideas and advances them in civil society, in the judiciary, in politics, and in international forums? It is often said that words are cheap, but words have real consequences: people can be killed for the words they use. Words also focus attention, channel energies, and inspire those who use them to see and evaluate reality in specific ways, and to seek allies, connections, and means with which to work on the world as they see and judge it to be.

A Practical Vocabulary of Rights

New concerns in the churches about rights drew strength in Latin America, as elsewhere in the Catholic world, from the innovations of the Second Vatican Council, which enhanced the role and status of ordinary experience as a source of values. If individuals have inherent rights and their actions can illuminate religious understanding, then these experiences also are a potential source of illumination about rights. The changes in discourse outlined above are most notable and have been most commented on in the case of liberation theology, which had the effect in many cases of leading key figures in the hierarchy, clergy, and lay population to identify with victims of poverty and oppression and to reread their own religious mission as requiring action to change the circumstances that created abuse. Central to this development is insistence on the figure of an autonomous subject, with capabilities, rights (including a right to legitimate voice and participation in the public sphere), and legitimate claims as a result of being human, a child of God.

Liberation theology lays out not only a justification but also a plan for action. Three concepts lie at the heart of liberation theology and together provide a foundation for thinking about rights in a new way: (1) emphasis on God as the God of life; (2) insistence on the unity of sacred and human history; and (3) stress on seeing poverty as a social and historical condition, one that is deeply contrary to God's desires. These three elements are knit together by a concern with poverty that is also a commitment to side with the poor—to take a "preferential option for the poor," articulated at the 1979 meeting of the region's Catholic bishops in Puebla. God gives abundant life and values the life of all beings. The life in question involves more than mere survival over a determined number of years. The life envisioned by the God of life requires adequate health, fulfilling education, family, nutrition, and so forth. Throughout his work, the theologian Gustavo Gutiérrez refers to poverty as "early death"—a condition that leads to limited, truncated, and often painful lives. In the final analysis, he writes, the decision to side with the poor is a decision

> for the God of life, for the "friend of life," as it says in the book of Wisdom (11, 25). In these expressions we find a way of speaking about faith and hope that animate a Christian commitment. Our daily experience of violence and unjust death will not permit us to engage in evasions or abstract reflections on the resurrection of Jesus without which our faith would be in vain, as Paul says. The repercussions on the weak give us a criterion for judging the justice in place in any society. (Gutiérrez 1996: 57)

In the final analysis, "poverty means death. The lack of food and housing, the impossibility of providing adequate health and education, exploitation and permanent unemployment, lack of respect for human dignity and unjust limitations on personal liberty in expression, in politics, and in religious life, daily suffering" (Gutiérrez 2004: 563).

To insist that there is only one history—that human and sacred history are joined—means, in a concrete sense, that one does not wait for salvation or to begin building the kingdom of God after death. The kingdom of God begins here and now, and being true to God's plan also must begin in this life. "The Kingdom of God is not coming with signs to be observed, nor will they say, 'Lo, here it is' . . . For behold, the kingdom of God is in the midst of you" (Luke 17:20–21). Gutiérrez makes an explicit connection among commitment to the God of life, commitment to the poor, and concern for human rights.

> As I stated earlier, in the final analysis, poverty means death: the physical death of many as well as cultural death from the disregard in which many others live. A few decades ago, our perception of this situation led to preoccupation with the theme of life as a gift from the God of our faith. The assassination of Christians, victims of their testimony to the Gospel, made this concern all the more urgent. Reflection on

> this experience of persecution and martyrdom has given strength and breadth to a theology of life that helps us see that the option for the poor is, at root, an option for life. (Gutiérrez 1996: 56)

A vision of God as the God of life and insistence that there is only one history acquire practical focus through the analysis and understanding of poverty not as a natural condition, but rather as the product of specific social and historical circumstances. All social orders are created by human beings acting under particular historical circumstances. No divine approval attaches to any social or political order, much less one that creates and sustains massive and dehumanizing poverty. Because poverty is a historical product, constructed and maintained over time by relations of power, poverty can be challenged and changed using the same methods of organization, collective action, and the exercise of power. This outlook on poverty drives the recourse to social science noted in earlier chapters, which has been such a central (and misunderstood) component of liberation theology. Social science does not replace theological reflection but rather complements it. The evolution of social scientific understanding of poverty in Latin America provided liberation theology with both an explanation of reality and an action program. The explanation locates the roots of poverty in exploitation and class division; the action program is popular organization. Gutiérrez underscores how important structural analysis has been to liberation theology and acknowledges the political problems this has entailed:

> Structural analysis has been an element of the theology of liberation. This has not been without costs, because although it is true that the privileged of this world easily accept hearing about the existence of massive poverty (there is no way to hide it in our times) problems begin when one points to the causes of this poverty. Searching for causes inevitably leads to the topic of social injustice and this is when one finds resistance. Above all if to structural analysis one adds a concrete historical perspective, one that points up personal responsibilities. But the greatest resistance and fear appear when the poor take stock of their own situation and organize. (Gutiérrez 2004: 566)

Gutiérrez is aware of the continuing evolution of the social sciences and points to the corresponding evolution of analytical tools for theological reflection: early reliance on dependency theory has yielded to a broader, more interdisciplinary and culturally nuanced set of references.[4] The conceptualization of poverty that undergirds liberation theology is simultaneously material and concrete, spiritual and a matter of commitment. Gutiérrez states the matter clearly in a text entitled *Where*

Will the Poor Sleep? (Donde Dormirán los Pobres?) that explores the new context of poverty in the world economy.

> We live in a continent that is both Christian and overwhelmingly poor. The presence of this massive and inhumane poverty drove us to reflect on the biblical meaning of poverty. Towards the middle of the 1960s, three understandings of the term "poverty" were formulated among theologians: a) real (often called "material") poverty, as a scandalous state, not desired by God; b) spiritual poverty, in the sense of a child-like spirituality one of whose expressions is indifference to the goods of this world; and c) poverty as commitment, solidarity with the poor and protest against poverty. (Gutiérrez 1996: 7–8)

The power of this formulation lies in how it combines an understanding of poverty and injustice with a commitment to action, rooting both in a biblical vision of the God of life. From this perspective, a phrase like "the right to life," so central in many recent North American debates, extends well beyond issues of conception, contraception, and abortion on which these debates have centered. The perspective advanced in liberation theology shares in a concept often referred to as a "consistent ethic of life," which folds consideration of reproductive issues and abortion into a broad set of positions on health, poverty, capital punishment, war, and care of the terminally ill.[5] The kind of action enjoined is also very specific: there is great stress on solidarity and accompaniment (sharing the lives and conditions of the poor) and working with them to empower change. This position was summed up by the late Archbishop Oscar Romero of San Salvador in a speech delivered just a month before he was shot to death while celebrating mass. Romero called for *recognizing* the poor—seeing them as they really are—and acknowledging their centrality to a proper understanding of the church's mission.

> Our Salvadoran world is no abstraction. It is not another example of what is understood by "world" in developed countries such as yours. It is a world made up mostly of men and women who are poor and oppressed. And we say of that world of the poor that it is the key to understanding the Christian faith, to understanding the activity of the church and the political dimension of that faith and that ecclesial activity. It is the poor who tell us what the world is, and what the church's service to the world should be. It is the poor who tell us what the polis is, what the city is and what it means for the church really to live in that world. . . . The church's option for the poor explains the political dimension of the faith in its fundamentals and in its basic outline. Because the church has opted for the truly poor, and not for the fictiously poor, because it has opted for those who are really oppressed

and repressed, the church lives in a political world, and it fulfills itself as church also through politics. It cannot be otherwise if the church, like Jesus, is to turn itself toward the poor. (Oscar Romero 1985: 179, 182–183)

Romero underscored the sinfulness of inequality. He wrote,

I insist once again on the existence in our country of structures of sin. They are sin because they produce the fruits of sin: the deaths of Salvadorans—the swift death brought by repression or the long, drawn out, but no less real, death from structural oppression. . . . No matter how tragic it may appear, the church through its entrance into the real socio-political world has learned how to recognize, and how to deepen its understanding of, the essence of sin. The fundamental essence of sin, in our world, is revealed in the death of Salvadorans. (Oscar Romero 1985: 183–184)

This stated preference for the materially poor is often criticized as too exclusive, partial, or excessively politicized (Sigmund 1990; Levine 1988, 1990a, 1995b), but those working in a liberationist perspective insist, to the contrary, that their stance is deeply biblical, an essential element of any authentic faith. Gutiérrez puts the matter boldly:

The root motive for commitment with the poor and the oppressed does not come from the social analysis we use, nor from our human compassion, or even from direct experience we may have of poverty. All of these are valid reasons that doubtless play an important role, but for Christians this commitment is based fundamentally in the God of our faith. It is a theocentric and prophetic choice rooted in God's freely given love and demanded by it. In other words, the poor are preferred not because they are morally or religiously better than others, but because God is God, He for whom "the last shall be first." This assertion clashes with our narrow understanding of justice, but it is precisely this preference for the poor that reminds us that God's ways are not our own. (Gutiérrez 2004: 571)

Solidarity with the poor and oppressed requires commitments of a kind that place individuals and groups directly at the center of conflicts. Accompanying the poor and oppressed entails the risk of sharing their fate, and in earlier chapters we have seen some of the consequences. Gutiérrez underscores the deep biblical roots of this commitment to action. He insists that the poor and oppressed are themselves key protagonists of the process.

In numerous and varied ways the Bible teaches us that putting God's will into practice is the most important requirement of faith. The theology of liberation takes on this traditional referent of Christian revelation moved by the witness of those who have committed themselves ever more deeply to the process of liberation from the various servitudes from which the poor suffer.

This commitment draws from the experience of the oppressed themselves as they began turning themselves into agents of their own destiny.

> In effect, in the 1950s and 1960s, we witnessed the first steps in consciousness and organizing by popular sectors in defense of the right to life, in struggle to defend their own dignity, for social justice, and in a commitment to liberation. Here one could see the outlines of a kind of popular protagonist (an actor) which would consolidate in the coming years and which, with advances and retreats, remains a presence in our lives. Many Christians from these sectors have been present in this process . . . their experience has nurtured theological reflection. It is therefore false to argue that theological reflection (la inteligencia de la fe, the intelligence of faith) arose from middle classes, only later extending to the experience of the poor themselves. The truth is that their own commitments, their efforts to organize and their living experience of the faith have been present from the very beginning. To ignore this is to misunderstand what happened in these times or to misrepresent it explicitly: the facts themselves belie such an interpretation. (Gutiérrez 2004: 574)

Gutiérrez acknowledges that many have questioned whether the church may be losing its religious identity through such deep involvement in politics. Others, he notes, have gone further. "From positions of power they have openly violated the human rights defended in church documents and struck blows against those Christians who gave voice to their solidarity with the poor and oppressed." Echoing Archbishop Romero, he continues, "a correct insertion into the world of the poor does not distort the mission of the church. The truth is that this is where the church finds her fullest identity as a sign of the Kingdom of God to which we are all called and in which the poor and insignificant have a privileged place. The church does not lose its identity in solidarity with the poor, it strengthens it" (Gutiérrez 2004: 592).

The conceptualization of poverty in liberation theology provides a ground for an expanding concept of rights, and for a moral vocabulary that legitimizes organization and action in defense of these rights. The demand for solidarity with the poor and the oppressed means active efforts to defend them. It goes beyond the economics of poverty to address broader issues of inequality and injustice. It goes beyond acting *for* the poor to accompanying them and putting institutions and resources at their disposal. From this starting point, the transition to support of movements by landless peasants, urban squatter settlement dwellers, political prisoners, the unemployed, and similar groups is straightforward. In Peru or El Salvador, grassroots ecumenical coalitions worked to defend rights, while in Brazil and Chile, the Catholic Church, with support from others and access to important transnational networks, put resources at the service of the defense of human rights and of the victims of repression (Brysk 2000, 2004; López 1998; Sikkink 1993, 1996; Wechsler 1990). In these and other cases, the defense of classic human rights was accompanied by promotion of organizing efforts and of the right to participation by those without resources.

Religious Change and Networks of Human Rights

The transformation of religious language paralleled the evolution of organizations addressing rights. Throughout Latin America in the 1970s and 1980s, there was a noteworthy expansion in the number of human rights organizations, in their national and local presence, and in the scale and effectiveness of their international connections (Sikkink 1996). Support from the churches, both within nations and localities and at a transnational level, was critical in the initiation, financing, and sustaining of these groups. In the 1990s, these same institutions and groups played an important role in the preparation, staffing, and activities of truth and reconciliation commissions and in negotiations leading to truces and stand-downs from armed conflict (Sikkink and Walling 2006; Wechsler 1990). Kathryn Sikkink distinguishes three moments in the development of human rights organizations and networks in Latin America: creation (1973–1981), consolidation (1982–1990), and refocusing and retrenchment (1991 onward). In the first period, "human rights" was put on the agenda of national and transnational institutions for the first time. North American and particularly European church groups played a prime role in setting up and financing groups in Latin America. Important institutions were created, including, specifically for the Americas, America's Watch, the Inter American Commission on Human Rights, the Washington Office on Latin America (formed by a coalition of church groups), and in Latin America, SERPAJ-AL, the Service for Peace and Justice, which as noted earlier was an outgrowth of organizing efforts by the Quaker-based Fellowship for Reconciliation (Keck and Sikkink 1998; Sikkink 1996; Pagnucco and McCarthy 1992).

In the first period, most national and transnational groups centered their attention on massive violations of rights by military dictatorships and therefore focused on rights of the person and freedom from execution, torture, and arbitrary imprisonment. As groups became more established and transnational networks consolidated, "they now began to address the human rights issues in transitional regimes, increasingly stressing the role of democracy, political rights, and justice for victims of past human rights abuses. The groups began to stress the 'quality' and 'content' of democracy rather than the mere existence of elections; this allowed them to incorporate many of their basic human rights concerns within the debate about democracy" (Sikkink 1996: 155). Sikkink dates reorientation and retrenchment from 1991 onward, a point in time that roughly coincides with transitions to democracy in major countries and the end of massive civil conflict and internal war in much of the region.[6] Although human rights groups remained active, their agenda changed, moving beyond torture to impunity, rights violations, electoral rights, and rights of vulnerable groups such as women, children, homosexuals, and indigenous peoples. Some of the groups founded in earlier periods, such as the Mothers of the Plaza de Mayo in Argentina, who began in 1977 with strong support from SERPAJ, continue to the present day with a broader agenda (Brysk 2000; Keck and Sikkink 1998; Perruzzotti and Smulovitz 2006; Van Cott 2000, 2007, 2008; Yashar 2005).

There is another element to the story that requires highlighting. In Latin America, as in cases like South Africa, groups of religious inspiration (occasionally but not always joined by leaders of the institutional churches) played a key role in brokering an end to dictatorship, in negotiating the conclusion to civil wars, and in the preparation and legitimation of truth and reconciliation commissions. Those opposed to such a role often argue that such efforts simply stir up the past, and some—like the Argentine Catholic bishops—call for a "balanced" history, one that legitimizes the role of military and police institutions in combating subversion (Mallimaci 2005). But on the whole, religious language and organizations have been deployed in support of these efforts. In a commentary on the Report of the Peruvian Commission on Truth and Reconciliation, Gutiérrez notes that ignoring the past means refusing to face a present that has deep roots in that very past, thus making a repetition all the more likely. He insists that pardon (a totally free act taken from a perspective of faith) be distinguished clearly from a just sanction for crimes committed. Citing the biblical injunction (Matthew 5:4) "blessed are those who weep, those who feel compassion, those who feel as their own the sufferings of others," he continues:

> There is a gesture that the prophet Isaiah presents us with in beautiful and moving terms: "The Lord will wipe away the tears from all faces and remove the condemnation of the people from the earth. Blessed, happy are those who act in this way. In the words of Luke, we can say, "Woe to them who present themselves before the God of justice and mercy with dry eyes. Because they did not know how to share their time, their concern and their feelings with those whose dignity as human beings, as daughters and sons of God was trampled upon, those who have suffered forgotten and in silence.
>
> The Bible calls this "consolation." But let us be precise. This consolation has the sense not only of welcoming and listening, but also, and above all, of liberating from all that creates an inhuman situation. . . . Will we let this opportunity pass? The opportunity for reconciliation. We cannot allow truth to remain hidden under ground, in one of these unmarked graves that hold so many dead. (Gutiérrez 2004: 464–465)

It is fair to ask what impact words, in this case the transformation of a language of rights, can have in the long run. Do not actions count more than words? The preceding discussion underscores how closely related words are to actions. The transformations in religion in Latin America outlined here and the creation of a new moral vocabulary of rights have had tangible consequences and long-lasting impact in the region. Human rights is now firmly on the agenda of all major institutions. Networks of local groups of all kinds (including those dedicated to human rights) now exist, often with extensive transnational connections. This is not to say that abuses no longer exist. But there is now an organized and vocal constituency that monitors and denounces such abuse (Sikkink 1993, 1996; Brysk 2000; Cleary 2007a; Friedmann and Hochstetler 2002; Perruzzotti and Smulovitz 2006). The link of religious change to expanded understandings of rights that is expressed in language is also manifest in collective social action through a broad network of social movements—a civil society—that in most cases simply did not exist twenty years ago. Despite the many difficulties such movements have encountered, and the often exaggerated expectations and hopes placed in them, their presence does change the social and political landscape, providing new venues for action and sources of new leadership that are only now beginning to make themselves felt.

Mediation and Peacemaking, Reconciliation, and Recovery of Memory

The relation of religion and the churches to the violence that Latin America experienced over the past half century is not limited to explanation, and not even to short-term reactions of defense of victims and the promotion of rights (Cleary 2007a, 2009). Churches and religious groups have also played a salient role in efforts to mediate an end to conflicts and in efforts to address the legacy of violence, the marks it leaves on the lives of individuals, families, and communities.[7] Inscribed on the bodies and minds of victims, this legacy makes its presence felt in family life and social relations. It acquires a place on the political agenda through efforts to ensure accountability and to recognize and honor victims, families, and communities affected by the experience of violence.

Churches and religious people have taken part in mediations intended to bring an end to civil wars (most notably in Central America) and have also been active in promoting movements for peace. They were also central in the creation and maintenance of archives that preserve the memory of violence and maintain the claims of victims and families. The most famous of these archives is connected with the Vicaría de la Solidaridad in Chile, but groups in El Salvador, Guatemala, and Peru have undertaken comparable compilations of evidence (Cleary 2007a, 2009; Maclean 2006a). In a logical extension of this effort, churches have promoted and participated in the elaboration of reports and in truth commissions that have attempted to bring out the facts and identify perpetrators and victims in cases ranging from Chile, Peru, Brazil, and Guatemala (where the churches had a critical role) to El Salvador, where despite the early heroic role of martyred Archbishop Oscar Romero, the church's participation in mediations, peace settlements, and truth commissions in the 1990s was decidedly more limited. Given what we know about the position of the Argentine Catholic hierarchy, it will be no surprise to note that the institutional Catholic Church of that country had no role in the commission that elaborated a report on the violence of the last military regime and has kept a clear distance from human rights groups in general.

The activities of the churches in promoting peace and mediating an end to open civil war are of particular interest here. The negotiations surrounding the end to the long and bloody civil wars in El Salvador and Guatemala are cases in point. In El Salvador, the war between the guerrillas of the Farabundo Martí National Liberation Front (FMLN,

Frente Farabundo Martí Para la Liberación Nacional) and the military lasted over a dozen years and claimed 75,000 known victims. The murder of Archbishop Oscar Romero and the four US missionary women in 1980 and the murder of the six Jesuits and their housekeepers nine years later provide bookends to the conflict and highlight the salience of religious victims. In the aftermath of the murder of Archbishop Romero, his successor, Monsignor Arturo Rivera y Damas, engaged in a long effort at mediation and the promotion of peace between successive governments and the leadership of the guerrilla movement. These efforts (reinforced by UN mediation) led to a series of meetings (in Mexico, Costa Rica, and Geneva) culminating in a UN-brokered peace agreement. These and other efforts were further aided within the country by the National Commission for the Consolidation of Peace, which incorporated representatives of the FMLN, all political parties, Archbishop Rivera y Damas, and Lutheran bishop Medardo Gómez.[8] The ecumenical quality of this committee carried forward earlier interchurch cooperation in Tutela Legal (Legal Protection), an ecumenical church-sponsored organization prominent in the promotion of human rights and the defense of victims.[9]

Church leaders in Guatemala played an even more extensive role. Following the death of conservative Cardinal Casariego, his successor, Bishop Penados de Barrio, initiated a series of efforts to promote contacts and advance peace. Following on the Oslo accords of June 1994, the United Nations created a Commission on Historical Clarification (CEH, Comisión de Esclarecimiento Histórico) that issued a report in February 1999 that documented the cost of more than thirty years of war: hundreds of thousands of deaths, disappearances, massacres, and the legacy of a scorched-earth anti-insurgency campaign that devastated the countryside. Iain Maclean notes that "the commission received much help from the Roman Catholic Church, which turned over its 'Recovery of Historical Memory Project' (REMHI) archives from its Human Rights Office, the results of an inquiry begun years before the official commission had been established" (Maclean 2006a: 18). The REMHI report differed from the official commission by naming those responsible for murder and genocide and rejecting military and government calls for amnesty. The bishop in charge of compiling and preparing the report, Monsignor Juan Gerardi, was murdered the day after the report was issued (Goldman 2007; Maclean 2006b: 19).

As the Guatemalan example suggests, another way in which churches contributed to recovery from violence has been through their involvement with truth commissions. The recent history of Latin America is, of course, rich in material for truth commissions, and the involvement of the churches has ranged from active promotion (as in Guatemala) to cooperation and staffing (Peru and Chile), and in many cases to the compilation and provision of archives detailing the course of violence and naming perpetrators and victims. As civil wars were brought to an end and military rule ceded to civilian democratic politics, truth commissions were installed in Argentina, Chile, and Peru, and also El Salvador and Guatemala, where the initiative was part of a peace accord brokered through the United Nations. Argentina's truth commission, formally named the National Commission on the Disappearance of Persons (CONADEP, Comisión Nacional Sobre la Desaparición de Personas), was one of the first and most influential. Established after the return to democracy in 1983, this commission was set up and operated with no cooperation from the Catholic Church, which as noted viewed the effort with suspicion and rejected the results. Since that time, more than two dozen such commissions have been established around the world, with Latin America and Africa between them accounting for almost three quarters of the total (Sikkink and Booth Walling 2006). Many but not all of these commissions have issued detailed reports that accumulated evidence and published the names of victims and perpetrators (Hayner 2002).

Although a formal truth commission has never been legally established in Brazil, where the military granted itself an all-encompassing amnesty in 1979 that still holds sway,[10] a coalition of churches nonetheless played a significant role in publicizing human rights through the project that led to the publication of the volume *Brasil: Nunca Mais* in 1985, translated into English as *Torture in Brazil* (Archdiocese of São Paulo 1998). In collaboration with the Lutheran Church and with strong support from the World Council of Churches, the Archdiocese of São Paulo coordinated an effort to document human rights abuses by transcribing, one by one, military records of interrogations and trials. Data were painstakingly gathered, microfilmed, collated, and smuggled out of the country to Switzerland, where the World Council of Churches helped arrange for publication. The appearance of *Brasil: Nunca Mais* caused a sensation in Brazil, where it was a number-one best seller for two years and remained on the best-seller list for ninety-one weeks more (Guider 2006: 124; Wechsler 1990). In the words of one observer, *Brasil Nunca Mais* "gave the faceless faces, and the nameless names. Denial was impossible, the revelations were uncontestable, and the response of silence on the part of the government was to be expected"

(Guider 2006: 124).[11] These efforts by the churches were amplified in Brazil, as elsewhere, by a noteworthy expansion of civil society groups focused on rights. Cleary states that 60 percent of Brazilian NGOs with involvement in human rights are church related (Cleary 2007a: 144; see also Friedmann and Hochstetler 2002).

These highly public efforts were paralleled by years of secret dialogue between a Bipartite Commission, composed of bishops and high military officers, that met regularly during the worst years of repression from 1969 to 1974 in talks that Kenneth Serbin notes "were systematic and encompassed religion, ideology, the moral order, socioeconomic and political development, and human rights." This combination of public opposition and private dialogue[12] sets Brazilian experience off from that of Chile, where church sponsorship of the Vicariate of Solidarity "intertwined religious, humanitarian, and political motives to provide one of the most incisive examples of moral opposition to authoritarian rule in Latin America" (Serbin 2000: 222), and from that of Argentina where, as we have seen, conservative bishops openly supported the armed forces' assault on the opposition.

The involvement of churches and religious groups with rights predates the formal establishment of truth commissions and explains their deep involvement in the commissions subsequently formed in countries like Chile, Peru, and Guatemala. Immediately after the 1973 coup that brought General Augusto Pinochet to power in Chile, two ecumenical committees were formed: the Committee of Cooperation for Peace in Chile (COPACHI, Comité de Cooperación para la Paz en Chile) and the Protestant Foundation of Social Support of the Churches (FASIC, Fundación de Ayuda Social de las Iglesias Cristianas). These groups defended prisoners and offered material and ideological support to opposition groups (Aguilar 2003, 2006; Maclean 2006b). Conflict with the government forced closure of COPACHI after a few years, but the effort was almost immediately reincorporated under the broader mandate of the Vicariate of Solidarity, which attended to human rights as part of a general effort to provide legal help, job services, and support to a wide range of orga-nizations and social movements in the country (Drogus and Stewart- Gambino 2005). Later in the 1970s, a Chilean Committee for Human Rights was formed, which brought together grassroots groups linked to the opposition. Throughout this period, these groups played a key role (coordinated through the Vicariate of Solidarity) in compiling detailed documentation on state violence, preparing dossiers about victims and cases, pursuing cases in the courts, and keeping them in the public eye.

In Peru, where the churches were caught between the violence of the state and military, on one hand, and Shining Path, on the other, the Catholic Church and a coalition of evangelical groups took up the cause of human rights, defending victims in court, supporting peace organizations, and maintaining a presence on the ground in the emergency zones that defined the areas of greatest violence, where martial law was in force. These included much of the Andean highlands and the region around Ayacucho, where Shining Path got its start and long had its stronghold. During this period the leadership of the Peruvian Catholic Church (with Monsignor Landázuri Ricketts as cardinal archbishop of Lima) already had in place a pastoral strategy and understanding of the situation that evolved naturally into a commitment to the defense of rights. Through the Episcopal Commission for Social Action (CEAS, Comisión Episcopal de Acción Social) the Catholic Church pursued the issues on a national scale and put resources behind them. As noted in Chapter 6, the activities of the churches ranged from self-defense, with ties to peasant organizations and support of indigenous groups, to maintenance of networks of groups, particularly in the Andean South, that kept Shining Path at bay.

The degree and nature of involvement of specific churches with truth commissions vary considerably from case to case. Following the transition to democracy in Chile in 1990, one of the first acts of the new government was to appoint a group known as the Rettig Commission. In outlook and staffing, this commission is a clear outgrowth of earlier efforts like COPACHI and the Vicariate of Solidarity. The continuing power and presence of General Pinochet and the armed forces in what was still a recent shift in power meant that the mandate of the Rettig Commission was drawn narrowly to focus only on cases of death or unresolved disappearances. This explicitly excluded many cases of torture, kidnapping, and abuse from the commission's scope of inquiry. This constraint notwithstanding, the Rettig Commission did valuable work bringing human rights issues into the open and putting both the issues and possible solutions on the public agenda (Aguilar 2003, 2006; Cleary 2007a; Hayner 2002; Maclean 2006b). The political caution of earlier years faded with the 1998 arrest of General Pinochet in Britain for human rights violations and his subsequent return to Chile and trial there. President Ricardo Lagos (2000–2006) responded by appointing a new commission specifically charged with investigating torture, the Chilean National Commission of Political Prisoners and Torture, led by Bishop Sergio Valech. The Valech Commission report affirmed that large numbers of Chileans had in fact been subject to torture and began to frame programs for reparations and treatment, including psychological counseling for victims and families. These initiatives were continued in the subsequent government of Michelle Bachelet, which advanced the investigations while actively promoting real and symbolic reparations, for example through direct monetary grants to victims and their families (to the third generation), educational and health benefits, construction of museums and public parks in memory of those who lost their lives, dedication of monuments to victims, and educational programs and campaigns to encourage respect for rights and promote reconciliation (Hayner 2002).[13]

In Peru, after the resignation and self-exile of Alberto Fujimori (in the wake of the fraudulent elections of 2000),[14] the interim government of President Valentin Paniagua appointed a National Commission on Truth and Reconciliation (CVR, Comisión de la Verdad y la Reconciliación).[15] The CVR was prepared by an interinstitutional working group composed of government ministries, NGOs, representatives from Catholic and Protestant churches, and statistical experts. The charge of the commission was to investigate assassinations, kidnappings, forced disappearances, torture and other instances of bodily harm, violation of collective and communal rights of indigenous communities, and other cases of violation of rights of persons. The final report sets these issues in the context of the social and political evolution of Peru, and pays particular attention to the aftermath of the violence—the economic, social, and psychological legacy in widows, orphans, forced migration, and shattered or abandoned communities. The focus of the CVR was framed by the fact that, in contrast to many other cases, atrocities in Peru came not as a direct result of military rule, but rather, as we have seen, in the context of a lengthy civil war. The violence of the civil war continued after the capture of Abimael Guzmán in 1992 and the dispersal of Shining Path, as the government of Alberto Fujimori used the continuing fight against terrorism as an excuse to buttress its rule (Comisión Episcopal de Acción Social 1990; Conagahan 2005; Klaiber 1992).

The CVR took several steps that were innovations for Latin America. Like the Truth and Reconciliation Commission in South Africa, the CVR organized public hearings all over the country. Such hearings gave victims and survivors a chance to have their stories told and listened to in a country that had become accustomed to the Fujimori regime's practice of holding secret antiterrorism trials presided over by judges with hidden faces (*jueces sin rostros*). The commission also had within it a special unit that worked to bring cases to the judicial system and other units that focused on the social and psychological aftermath of the war.

The commission presented its report to President Alejandro Toledo in August 2003. The bottom line was a finding of almost 70,000 dead, several hundred thousand widows and orphans, many more with long-term psychosocial scars, and a devastated countryside.

The preceding is a bare-bones account of some of the most notable features of truth commissions established in Latin America since the 1980s and of the role that churches and religious personnel played in them. Although it is important to establish these relations, we need to go further and consider the model of truth commissions in the light of core religious ideas. Among these is the belief, central to Christian theory and practice, that the healing brought by reconciliation depends on confession, remorse, restitution, and forgiveness. Guider writes that

> the foundational conviction guiding such commissions is the belief that coming to terms with horrific memories of the past is essential for restoring the dignity of victims and preventing violations of rights in the future. In practice, it means bringing to light the truth and creating the conditions for reconciliation including the seeking of reparations in the form of compensation and justice, sometimes retributive, sometimes restorative. Ideally, commissions contribute to re-democratization through processes of truth-telling that open the way to confession and remorse, restitution and forgiveness, healing and reconciliation, deterrence and an unwavering commitment to "never again." In reality, they provide a formal forum for accounts of torture and terror to be told and recorded, for victims and their loved ones to confront abusers, and for those accused of violations to acknowledge responsibility for their offenses. For posterity, the findings of commissions hold citizens of their respective nations as well as other nations accountable for remembering atrocities that many would sooner forget, deny, or minimize. (Guider 2006: 112–113)

Concepts of rights provide the moral and legal underpinnings of all truth commissions. Victims and their families have inalienable rights as citizens and as children of God. Where these rights have been abused or taken away, they must be restored and some kind of restitution or reparation made. Among the rights that victims and families have is the right to information (to know what happened and where the bodies are buried), the right to reparations of some kind, and the right to be free of future fear. The dead cannot be brought back, but at least they can be named and recognized, if at all possible their bodies located and given a decent burial, and their survivors helped in some way. Apart from affirming rights, a central role of truth commissions is also to identify and locate both perpetrators (for possible legal action) and victims.

Various concepts of justice and truth are at work here. There is *forensic* and *retributive justice,* aimed at creating accurate and impartial information about what happened and ultimately imposing sanctions on perpetrators. The workings of truth commissions also encompass what South African archbishop Desmond Tutu famously called *restorative justice*, a justice that can bring healing to individuals and communities (Helmick and Petersen 2001). Such healing is supposed to come through the cathartic process of acquiring information and (at least in the South African case) of bringing perpetrators and victims together in a setting intended to lead to forgiveness. The end result is to allow both individuals and communities to erase the public secret of violence and move ahead in a hopefully more unified community. The concept of restorative justice is closely linked with ideas about forgiveness and reconciliation, concepts that are prominent in the Chilean and Peruvian commissions.[16] Distinctions among forensic, retributive, and restorative justice are matched by distinctions among kinds of truth addressed by truth commissions. The establishment of *forensic truth* with factual information about victims (including locating bodies) and perpetrators is accompanied by the creation of possibilities for *narrative truth* by giving victims a platform to tell their stories and preserving those stories as part of the historical record. There is also a *restorative truth,* which works toward healing and reconciliation by promoting dialogue among all the parties who are forced to confront one another.

Forgiveness and reconciliation are core Christian concepts, central to its doctrine and at the heart of much of its sacramental practice, including atonement, confession, and absolution. As religious rites and social practices, forgiveness and reconciliation are directed at healing what is broken in individuals and moving away from evil and into a more wholesome situation. The religious understanding visible in the discourse and practice of these truth commissions goes further to encompass more ideas about social sin and social healing.

Just as an individual can be absolved of sin and in some way healed, there are comparable ways in which a society can be healed. If we acknowledge social sin and social brokenness, we must also think about forms of action that transcend the individual and heal what is broken in societies (Pfeil 2006). A first step is to be specific about the meaning of social sin. The concepts of institutionalized violence and structural sin derived from Medellín provide a place to begin by looking to the social sciences for ways to identify and measure the meaning of these concepts in the everyday lives of citizens. The Peruvian commission began this process by documenting precisely who the victims were. They were the poor, the marginal, and the ethnically subordinate of Peru. A full 70 percent lived in rural areas, 85 percent lived in the country's six poorest departments, 68 percent had less than a high school education, 40 percent of the dead and disappeared came from Ayacucho, and 31 percent were peasants whose first language was Quechua (as compared to only 16 percent of the population). The next step is to think about the attribution of responsibilities. Under the circumstances of dictatorship, and of the Fujimori regime in particular, Margaret Pfeil writes that "it becomes difficult to assign individual responsibility, yet citizens did participate in upholding judicial, political and military structures that obscured the truth and prevented the pursuit of justice on the part of those most directly affected by the institutionalized violence that gripped the nation" (Pfeil 2006: 181).

In her work on the Peruvian Commission on Truth and Reconciliation, Pfeil places concepts of forgiveness and reconciliation in conversation with theology and with ideas about sin and healing. The understanding of personal sin "cannot account for wrongly ordered patterns of human behavior that eventually become institutionalized. Individuals may be held accountable for sinful acts that contribute to an unethical social structure, but in some cases they may succumb to a kind of moral blindness, participating in a given social institution or system without realizing that their actions, both of commission and omission, contribute to structures of sin" (Pfeil 2006: 172). Considerations of this kind do not exempt actors from responsibility for what they have set in motion. That is a legal question, but the moral force of law is enhanced by the language that identifies social sin with needless and early death and names this as a manifestation of evil. "Its invocation," Pfeil states, "reflects a profound desire to name moral truth precisely in situations where the most vulnerable members of society have been stripped of their names and identities and have even been 'disappeared,' enveloped by a variety of violence far beyond the intentions and capabilities of any one person or group" (Pfeil 2006: 173).

As important as it is to name and identify injustice, more is at issue here. Using the language of structural sin also signals an epistemological choice to view the harm caused from the standpoint of those on the margins of power. Pfeil cites the case of El Salvador's Archbishop Romero, cited earlier in this chapter on sin as the death of Salvadorans, and notes that once he adopted this perspective, "the central moral and pastoral task shifted from identifying concrete sinful acts to comprehending the ethical significance of institutionalized violence that led inexorably to the death of human beings. The language of social sin allowed him to blame and denounce not only particular offences against life but also the social structures that resulted from and prepared the ground for the sins revealed in the crucified bodies of his people" (Pfeil 2006: 175). The experience of Chile's Cardinal Raul Silva Henríquez is comparable. When appointed bishop of Valparaiso, he stated that "I accepted to be a Bishop in order to announce the Kingdom of God to the poor" (Aguilar 2003: 717). This commitment to identify with the weak and powerless was a consistent thread in his leadership of the church. As cardinal of Santiago, he distanced himself from the military regime from the very beginning and provided legitimacy and essential resources (space to meet, funds, and staff) to human rights groups and others through a range of vehicles, the most famous being the Vicariate of Solidarity. Mario Aguilar writes, "In his memoirs, Silva Henríquez suggested that from that moment on (the moment of the coup) it was clear to him that the Church would have to be on the side of the victims, without asking their color or political ideology. The only way to do that was to protect people's human rights. . . . His role was energized by the renewal within the church that inspired him and showed him the kinds of tools he needed to create" (Aguilar 2003: 721).

If the realities of violence in cases like Peru or Chile are understood as social sin, what might constitute social means of atoning for that sin, of healing what has been broken by violence? The measures recommended by the CVR in Peru included plans for social reform, social and psychological help for victims, and reparations, but reparations and prosecution of responsible individuals have had only partial and halting implementation. Reparations went farther in Chile where the Rettig Commission recommended the creation of a single reparations pension fund, a special program by the ministry of health dealing with the emotional trauma and mental health issues created by the violations, and the creation of some mechanism to encourage victims to resume educations interrupted by the violations.[17] More broadly, reparations have been a weak point for truth commissions, with sporadic and limited results that barely address the larger structural context of injustice. Chile and Argentina have also made great strides in efforts to rescue the historical memory of violence, which include the creation of memorials and sites of memory (Borer 1998; Hayner 2002; Maclean 2006b; Perruzzotti and Smulovitz 2006; Wilde 2011, 2012).

Prosecutions of top military and political leaders have gone furthest in Argentina, where the Truth Commission had no legal powers and only distant and tense relations with the institutional churches. Here, the effort to identify, prosecute, and convict the perpetrators of massive human rights crimes was carried forward by coalitions based in civil society and by the judicial system with consistent opposition from the hierarchy of the Catholic Church. The Argentine experience also sparked a lengthy and intense debate in the country about historical memory. Who and what should be remembered? If there is to be reconciliation of some kind, who is to be reconciled with whom, and to what version of history? What should be remembered about individuals—perpetrators, victims, and those connected to victims? Who has social ownership of memory, whose job is it to maintain memory, and in what way? The Catholic hierarchy, the military, and many on the political right have called for a balanced memory, which means to see the violence as the result of an internal war in which there were lamentable excesses on both sides. Calls by the Catholic hierarchy for reconciliation began even before the fall of the military as the bishops urged all Argentines basically to forgive and forget (Michael Burdick 1995). An alternative position, which finally won out as the twenty-first century began, understands the violence primarily as the intentional result of a situation in which an armed state attacked society, with the goal of rooting out enemies (and their associates and often their entire families) and eliminating any possible role for them in the future. This version of memory has on its side the overwhelming number of victims of state terror and has been upheld in numerous trials that since 2000 have put leaders of the military regime (along with members of the clergy) on trial for crimes against humanity. From this point of view, the idea of reconciliation and pardon built into some truth commissions is ill founded. In taking on such a role, the commissions arrogate to themselves a right to pardon and to effect reconciliation in what should properly be also a legal judicial process. Individuals may well forgive, but in the name of what does one forgive serious crimes like kidnapping, torture, rape, and murder on a large scale?

Throughout the region, it has been tempting for governments to treat human rights as a problem that has been addressed in the past and simply to move on (Perruzzotti and Smulovitz 2006). This temptation is also present for the churches, and in any case, as we have seen, ideas about social sin and social reconciliation are not universally accepted. Religious conservatives—like the bulk of the Argentine Catholic hierarchy or the leadership grouped around Cardinal Juan Luis Cipriani in Peru—reject the very idea of truth commissions (along with their specific findings) as unwarranted judgments on what was a legitimate war against subversion. Throughout the region, instances of heroism and determined support of rights have been matched by a pattern of response linked more to institutional defense than to principle. Concluding his review of nations, churches, and reconciliation, Maclean comments that

> the Latin American national churches, largely immobile after the imposition of military or authoritarian rule, were spurred to criticism only when the regime turned upon its clergy, and religious, or prominent laity. Thus, given its prior tactical support of such regimes, the Church somewhat reluctantly found itself in opposition to the ruling powers. However, paradoxically, when regime transition came about, in many places this precise reluctance led to the national Church becoming a trusted broker between opposing forces. This is precisely what happened, with varying degrees of involvement in Argentina, Chile, El Salvador, and Guatemala, although in Argentina, Brazil, and Chile the Churches were accused of either supporting a repressive regime or of not doing enough to remove such a regime. (Maclean 2006b: 33)

Following Maclean, I offer here an interim assessment of the Latin American experience of violence, rights, and reconciliation in terms of four issues: impunity/amnesty, truth, justice, and reparations. Maclean asks what progress has been made on each and reflects on the extent to which ideas about reconciliation make sense and have had any impact. Impunity is the most problematic. Although the number of prosecutions has grown slowly, the amnesties that military and security forces granted to themselves remain in force in many key cases (Brazil, El Salvador, Peru, and Chile, with limited amnesty in Guatemala and a general amnesty in Argentina that was overturned after 2000). Maclean comments that "the rapid granting of amnesty meant that truth was hindered and without truth, justice was denied the victims and their families. The fact that the truth cannot be ascertained meant that the 'official version' was all that remained and the victims suffered yet again in that their stories were discounted" (Maclean 2006b: 26).

The issue of truth is more complex than a simple appeal to "tell the truth" might suggest. Problems begin with decisions about what may and must be done to redress the damage inflicted by kidnappings, disappearances, torture and abuse, or cases like the allocation of children born to prisoners (who were later killed) to families allied with the military. Justice and reparations are among the thorniest issues. Both have often been compromised by the practical goal of inducing the military to cede power. Only in cases of military collapse (Argentina) or conquest by a foreign power (Germany in World War II) has a full-scale retributive justice system been possible. Where the military either retired in good order (Brazil and Chile) or won or managed a stalemate in a civil war (Peru, El Salvador, and Guatemala), the options for justice of this kind are much more limited. It is here that the moral imperative of justice gains prominence, apart from the actions of any given tribunal. This moral imperative can be provided by churches in concert with civil society groups.

As we think about the involvement of different churches on truth commissions and the evolution of religiously linked concepts of rights, social sin, and reconciliation, it is helpful to reflect on the meaning of testimony and witness. As I pointed out in Chapter 2, testimony and witness are concepts that have both a legal and a religious sense. In legal terms, a witness who gives true testimony states as fully as possible what he or she has seen. Truth telling is the core of this kind of testimony and witness. In a religious sense, testimony and witness refer to the way one lives. A person gives testimony and bears witness to the truth of values by living in a way that reflects these values and affirms their worth. Concepts of testimony and witness acquired new and refreshed meaning through the active involvement of churches and religious movements and individuals in the protection of rights and the promotion of peace and reconciliation.

The churches find their witness by entering society, by being what German theologian Dietrich Bonhoeffer (executed by the Nazis shortly before the end of World War II) referred to as a church for others. Being the "church for others" (as Jesus was the man for others) requires the churches not merely to sympathize with victims but to go beyond sympathy to active commitments to change the social conditions that make for victims in the first place. Bonhoeffer insisted that being a person of faith is "less about cautiously avoiding sin than about courageously and actively doing God's will" (cited in Metaxas 2010: 486). Not to act is to be complicit with the existing situation. Bonhoeffer also insisted on the need to go beyond what he famously called "cheap grace" and "cheap reconciliation." Cheap grace is the grace we award ourselves, and cheap reconciliation is reconciliation without acknowledgment of wrongdoing and without forgiveness (Bonhoeffer 1959; Bethge 2000). Each is prey to an easy complicity with evil. The process must go beyond a stance of "forgive and forget" or simple amnesties (particularly the kind of amnesties that outgoing regimes often award to themselves) to include public acknowledgment of wrongdoing, provisions for healing of victims, memorials, efforts to recover the historical memory of victims, location of bodies and their return to families, reparations if possible, and efforts at structural reforms to remove economic and other sources of injustice.

The use of a language of social sin and a vocabulary of rights affirming that people have rights as a result of their status as children of God signals a choice to view the damage caused by social sin—the lives lost, the families broken, the individuals uprooted and traumatized—from the standpoint of those who have suffered. Identifying and sympathizing with victims are necessary at first, but if commitment stops there, the churches are little more than ambulances collecting the victims of the social and political systems. It is essential to move from sympathy and identification with victims, to challenging and delegitimizing regimes and social systems that create victims, and to taking active steps to replace them with something better.

Conclusion

Writing in 1949, Theodor Adorno famously commented that after Auschwitz, writing poetry was barbaric.[18] In a similar way, Gustavo Gutiérrez has asked how it is possible to do theology during Ayacucho, which was ground zero for Shining Path and for official repression in Peru. He asked, "How can we talk about the God of life when life is being massively and cruelly wiped out in the death corner [of Ayacucho]? How can we announce the love of God in the midst of such deep disdain for human life? How can we proclaim the Resurrection of the Lord where death, in particular the death of children, of women, of the poor and indigenous, reigns supreme?" (Gutiérrez 1986: 223).

What indeed is it possible to say in the aftermath of the kinds of violence we have examined? Nothing can remove the stain of this violence, and nothing can fully ease the pain or cleanse the wounds of survivors. But there are things that can be said, and in their best moments, the Latin American churches have created solutions and promoted and enabled their implementation. For Camilo Torres and those he inspired, in situations like these, authentic faith requires immediate and effective action, and taking up arms appears as a logical means to an effective solution. But as I have suggested, violence has its own dynamic and carries its own dangers of spiraling out of control. This is part of the reason why the counterviolence of revolutionary struggle has had limited appeal in Latin America. The more common solution has been to name and identify the causes of violence, to promote and empower rights, to provide legitimacy and material support for mobilizations in support of those rights, and to advance peacemaking and, where possible, reconciliation.

These are not easy tasks, but the effort to work at them has altered the landscape of Latin American public life in profound ways and placed new issues permanently on the political agenda. Accompanying the victims and finding, naming, and honoring the dead (for example, through public memorials) are important first steps. Making restitution, even haltingly, is another. Articulating a concept of human rights and locating it at the heart of religious discourse helped to place the issue of rights on the social and political agenda of the region. The churches were present at the creation of important parts of the human rights movement and contributed to the broad range of social movements and the vigorous civil societies that we find today throughout the region. These enduring contributions have been accompanied by continuing efforts to bring the issue of *rights* (including but not limited to classic human and civil rights) to center stage of both politics and religion, with important legal and institutional consequences. Linked to rights is *accountability*, the idea that churches as well as governments and individuals can be called to account before the law for acts of violence or complicity in such acts. A related notion of active citizenship and participation in an open civil society is also critical and draws strength from many of the changes worked out in religious life, which promoted the idea of participation and activism as legitimate and necessary while in many cases providing the resources and support to make it possible. Together these contributions provide legitimation and terms of reference for a practical culture of politics that was not present, much less imagined, fifty years ago.

Notes

1. There was support for rights in all the churches, but which church leaders took up this cause varied widely. The Chilean and Brazilian Catholic hierarchies confronted authoritarian states and supported human rights. In contrast, the Argentine Catholic hierarchy reinforced its alliance with the military and was complicit in abuses.

2. General demands for accountability do not translate into support for accountability by the leaders of the church. Defense of human and civil rights in general has not meant defense of claims to a right to diversity or, for example, to gay marriage.

3. This position is articulated very clearly in the Pastoral Guidelines issued by the Chilean Catholic hierarchy in 1985. The bishops rooted the defense of human rights in bedrock religious values and made it clear that Christians should be committed "to struggle for the promotion and defense of human rights. This is not the case only because they are laid out in the Universal Declaration of the United Nations. Our commitment is prior. . . . It is out of our faith in Jesus that we defend human rights, and if we want them to be respected in their totality, it is because Jesus Christ has come to liberate all corners of human existence" (cited in Cleary 1989: 84).

4. This has led to the incorporation of new and valuable perspectives from the human sciences (psychology, ethnology, anthropology) that help address an intricate and dynamic situation. "Incorporate means more than just add on; it means meshing with. Attention to cultural factors helps us penetrate into mentalities and attitudes and in this way to explain important aspects of reality. Economic aspects no longer look the same once we give adequate weight to culture, and vice versa" (Gutiérrez 2004: 567).

5. This position is often associated with the late Cardinal Archbishop Joseph Bernardin of Chicago, who also used the term " a seamless garment" to denote a broad agenda of life. Cf. Boyer 2005 on Vatican politics and its influence in the United States.

6. As we have seen, these developments drew many militants into "ordinary politics" and coincided with accumulating changes in the Catholic Church under the papacy of the late John Paul II that led to a withdrawal from activism and the closing of such well-known institutions as Chile's Vicaría of Solidaridad. Similar issues have arisen in Peru, along with controversies concerning the role of Opus Dei, and the human rights positions taken by Cardinal Juan Luis Cipriani (Rohter 2005).

7. Many communities continue in Peru to struggle with legacies of anger and frustration that produce violence, not of an explicitly political kind but rather between individuals and within families, worsening the conditions of daily life. "Perhaps as a way of distancing themselves from the enormous impotence and rage left behind by the violence they have personally experienced, some people have resorted to destructive tendencies of their own, directed at those around them who they perceive as weakest [beating women and children, for example]. Violence has come into their daily life and remained there" (Comisión de la Verdad y Reconciliación, Peru, 2004: 370–371). The report continues, "Along with the family, other areas of social life have felt the impact of the growth of violent conduct. The effort to frighten and the use of terror as methods of protest, and as ways of imposing ideas and evoking submissive responses, seems to have become common sense to many Peruvians. Violence of different levels has become a resource at hand to deal with conflicts and to compensate for feelings of impotence, as much within the family or school as in the neighborhood and community. The fact that all political actors have recourse to the same methods and actions conveys the message that violence 'is there to be used by all.' Insufficient condemnation of this violence has led to a

terrorist and violent style being reproduced in social life. The use of threats becomes commonplace, while control, vigilance, lack of confidence and extremes of suspicion pervade the social fabric" (Comisión de la Verdad y Reconciliación 2004: 371).

8. Although small in numbers, the Lutheran Church in El Salvador (and in much of Central America and Brazil) played a major role in advancing an agenda of human rights and social justice in collaboration with progressive Catholic groups. The Lutherans in these countries were able to use their transnational connections to ward off the worst of the repression, but in some cases, like El Salvador, Lutheran leaders were briefly forced into exile in late 1989.

9. Tutela Legal grew out of Socorro Jurídico, Cristiano (literally Christian Legal Relief), which was begun in 1975 by a group of Catholic lawyers and was made an official institution of the Archdiocese of San Salvador by Archbishop Oscar Romero in 1977.

10. The Brazilian supreme court upheld the validity of the amnesty law in 2010, and by 2012, a truth commission had finally been established in Brazil. Only two countries have overturned such amnesty laws: Argentina and most recently Uruguay.

11. Along with his work in promoting and coordinating the effort that led to the publication of *Brasil: Nunca Mais,* Cardinal Arns opened the Cathedral of São Paulo to memorial services for notable victims of the regime, including clergy, activists, and, famously, the Jewish journalist Vladimir Herzog. In all these ways, the church with his leadership helped to construct and advance a vision of reality, based on documented truth, that would never have been written if it had been left to the official powers of the military state. "The pastor of a nation divided, Dom Paulo made the Cathedral of São Paulo and its surrounding *praca* an ecumenical and inter religious sanctuary of truth, remembrance, solidarity, hope, and freedom" (Guider 2006: 124).

12. Serbin (2000: 233) comments that "the Bipartite exemplified elite conciliation and the highly personalistic nature of Brazilian politics. The participants—bishops, generals, intellectuals—represented the upper strata of society. They were all men, light skinned, and from middle aged to old. Most of them lived privileged lives because of family background or professional success. Many were devout Catholics. Women, Protestants, peasants, workers, victims of the repression, and their families, and politicians had no access to the Bipartite. In so far as it was an 'elite settlement' the Bipartite excluded the people from its deliberations."

13. As of March 2010, there were 330 active cases with 200 convictions recorded.

14. Fujimori is currently in prison in Peru.

15. The chair of the commission was Salomon Lerner Febres, rector of the Pontifical Catholic University of Peru.

16. For its part, the setup and focus of the South African commission were strongly influenced by Chilean experience, as by the broader influence of liber-

ation theology on the churches, visible in the contextual theology developed in South Africa (Borer 1998; Walshe 1991).

17. The commission recommended the creation of a single pension fund providing payments to all victims and recommended that the monthly payment be greater than the average income of a Chilean family, an amount sufficient to rebuild the lives of many of the victims.

18. There is controversy about precisely where this quotation comes from. Originally written in an essay on "cultural criticism and society" published in 1949, it is reproduced in the volume *Prisms* (Adorno 1967). See www.marcuse .org/herbert/people/adorno/Adornopoetry/AuschwitzQuote.htm.

8

Comparative Perspectives

Latin America's experience of politics, religion, and society is distinct but not unique. What has happened in the region is of course shaped by the specific histories, cultural understandings, and conflicts of individual countries. But Latin America also has much in common with the rest of the world and is affected by similar global forces, including demographic changes, growing literacy and access to media, and a continuing struggle to shape and control religion's place in politics and society. If we consider the issues in terms of the relations among ideas, organized social life, institutions, and conflicts, the distinctiveness of Latin America opens itself up to fruitful comparison with other regions and religious or political traditions. The goal of all comparative study is to seek the general in the particular and to illuminate the particular with general principles. Comparing cases helps us identify sources of commonality and variation and makes it possible to link the particular with the general in some reliable way. To be comparable is, of course, not to be identical. Comparing Christian Latin America with, for example, Buddhist Sri Lanka, Hindu India, Muslim Indonesia, or indeed with other predominantly Christian areas does not make them the same, but is intended, instead, to sort why and how a common experience (say, of violence or reconciliation linked to religion) evolves in the particular ways that it does.

All too often, religions are treated as undifferentiated wholes, with assumptions made about uniformity of thought and action from very limited sources. But a closer look shows that all religious traditions have multiple voices, with continuing struggle to control what the public message should be, and what leaders and groups should strive for. This suggests that as a first step, comparative analysis needs to be clear about precisely what is being compared, and on what grounds. How, for example, should we go about comparing the experience of religions organized as differently as Catholicism, Pentecostal Protestantism, Islam, and Buddhism? Do we work with doctrinal texts, with analysis of leadership and what leaders do or say? Can we compare whole traditions, or might it be more fruitful to compare similar units or bodies of experience across religions: the preaching of priests or imams; the organization of brotherhoods, orders of monks, or religious congregations; the evolution of theologies or of religious iconography; or the promotion of social movements? Do we need to move beyond formal religious institutions and examine the relations among politics, religion, and society from the angle of society, centering attention on the social sources of new ideas, the origins and activities of religiously linked or inspired groups, and how they shape resulting outcomes?

Some comparative scholars strive to identify global trends, or uniformities, while others search for causes of variation, asking why what is ostensibly "the same" religion (Islam, Catholicism, Buddhism, or Protestantism) has such varied expression in different cases, and sometimes within nations and churches. Much contemporary work on religion and politics that has global reach has been driven by a limited group of concerns and ideas. Following on the shock of the Iranian revolution and the rise of an aggressive religious right in the United States, a substantial body of scholarship emerged dedicated to searching for common factors in a supposed "religious resurgence" with links to themes of fundamentalism (Appleby 2006; Marty and Appleby 1992, 1995; Kepel 1994). Religious resurgence is also a central theme for much scholarship concerned with religion and violence. There is also renewed interest in secularization and challenges to secularization (Bruce 2010; Casanova 1994; Toft, Philpott, and Shah 2011; Inglehart and Norris 2004; Jurgensmeyer 2001; Kepel 1994; Lawrence 1986). Scholarship directed at the comparative analysis of global patterns in recent years has also addressed the role played by religious individuals and institutions in peacemaking and reconciliation (Appleby 2000; Toft, Philpott, and Shah 2011; Maclean 2006a; Philpott 2006; Johnston and Sampson 1994). Interest in the global relation of religion to democracy is less prominent in this literature, although some recent work has set these concerns in the general context of tracking the patterns and understanding the consequences for politics and social life of what is described as a global religious resurgence (Toft, Philpott, and Shah 2011; Jenkins 2002, 2006) or as an element in the worldwide spread of Pentecostal Protestantism (Freston 2001, 2008; Ranger 2008a; Lumsdaine 2009). Concern with the relation of religion to social movements is more scattered, with important work on the United States and Latin America and occasional studies of other regions and traditions (e.g., Eickelman and Piscatori 2004; Hefner 2000).

A global perspective has the advantage of highlighting the general questions at issue but runs the risk of using variables that are so broadly defined that they lose meaning, or of relying on analysis of cases that is often so superficial as to undermine the validity of any generalization. The purpose of the comparison undertaken in this chapter is not to establish global patterns, but rather to see how what has happened in Latin America, and the way we explain those changes, fit with and are illuminated by other contemporary experiences. Even scaled down in this way, the task remains daunting. There are so many cases and so much has been written on these issues in recent years that it is not easy to know how to proceed. Any selection of cases is open to the charge of cherry picking, choosing cases that best illustrate one's own point of view. For this reason, it is important that any choice of cases have a theoretically grounded rationale and form part of an explanation of events.

Consideration of what cases to choose, and what counts as cases in the first place, cannot be separated from a self-conscious theory about the relations among politics, religion, and society. In epistemological terms, without a theory there are no cases, no way to select items for study out of the immense variety of human experience. The theory that underlies the analysis in this book rests on a combination of ideas with social and institutional transformations that help these ideas make sense to people.[1] It is important to understand what goes on within institutions, but analysis also has to reach beyond formal institutional boundaries to examine how messages are crafted and delivered, how groups are formed, how leaders emerge, and how leadership is exercised. We also need to understand in detail how continuing ties between the religious and the political are negotiated. Scott Appleby reminds us that to get at these particulars "there is no substitute for continual on site analysis, field work of a highly specialized or particular sort that is best conducted by experts in the religious traditions in question" (Appleby 2000: 56). In this chapter, I draw on such sources for a wide range of experiences (the United States, Northern Ireland, Eastern Europe, South

Africa, Ghana, India, Southeast Asia, and a group of Islamic cases). I use these cases, along with some of the general works cited earlier, to examine change and variation on the four dimensions that anchor my analysis of Latin America: (1) democracy, pluralism, and religion; (2) social movements, civil society, and religion; (3) religion and violence; and (4) rights and reconciliation.

Democracy, Pluralism, and Religion

There can be no question that religion in many times and places has opposed democracy and acted to restrict pluralism. Jean Elshtain comments that even those "who find entirely acceptable a strong public role for religion in the democratic public sphere must acknowledge that historically religion has at times underwritten intolerance and vindicated injustice" (Elshtain 2009: 14). In the same vein, José Casanova states that over the last century and a half, the Catholic Church has "fought capitalism, the modern secular state, the democratic revolution, socialism, and the sexual revolution. In brief, it has been the paradigmatic form of anti-modern public religion" (Casanova 1994: 7). But there is another side to the story. Religious institutions and individuals have also protected and promoted democracy, and by their presence in civil society have provided elements of pluralism that undergird democracy. The shift by Latin American churches from unease and opposition to accommodation and open support of democracy and pluralism was powered by the conjunction of ideological change with the evolving impact of religious and social pluralism. Ideas affirming democracy and equality as ideals arose in the churches and were also pushed along by the emergence of new movements and leaders from below. These developments are not well understood in terms of a "resurgence of religion" for the simple reason that religion never left the public arena in Latin America. What changed is not the presence or active role of religion, but rather who acts, with what goals, and in which specific ways.

Monica Duffy Toft, Daniel Philpott, and Timothy Samuel Shah assert that between 1972 and 2000,

> religious actors played a democratizing role in 48 of the 72 countries that witnessed substantial democratization in this period. . . . the bottom line is clear. In most of the cases where democracy was on the march between 1972 and 2009, freedom had a friend in religion. Furthermore, in most of the cases where religion was freedom's ally, it

was a principal combatant. It did not merely cheer from the sidelines but fought on the front lines. (Toft, Philpott, and Shah 2011: 93–98)

To be a friend of democracy can mean several things: to legitimate democracy publicly, affirming its ideals and institutions; to provide active support and empowering tools for aspiring democrats; to broker the creation of supportive alliances and connections; and to promote a vigorous civil society. How does this position arise and what sustains it?

The viability of any democracy depends on more than formal institutions. Thriving democracies are also continuously enriched by vigorous and plural civil societies, which provide citizens with experience of civic skills and generate a wealth of options to be sorted out in the political arena. The relation of religious pluralism to democratic politics rests on the combination of new theologies, the presence of multiple religious communities on the ground, and how they make possible a wealth of interactions across community and denominational lines. Ever since Tocqueville's *Democracy in America,* the United States has been a case in point for this relation. Contemporary work on religion, society, and politics in the United States affirms the continuing impact of religious pluralism on social and political life. Stephen Warner makes the point that religious pluralism and political freedom reinforce one another in the history of the United States. The master function of religion in the United States, he argues, has been to provide social spaces for cultural pluralism (Warner 1993: 1058–1064). Congregational forms of organization, rooted in ideas of local autonomy and self-governance, have spread from their Protestant roots to characterize other religious traditions as they establish themselves in the United States (Warner 1993: 1067).

The continuing impact of religious plurality and pluralism on democratic politics in the United States has been reaffirmed recently by Robert Putnam and David Campbell (2010), who find here the roots of both tolerance and traditions of civic participation. In the face of concerns about weakening levels of participation and declining civic capacity in the United States, Robert Wuthnow cites evidence that religious participation may enhance civic skills, promote voluntarism, build civil society, and encourage political participation.

> Religion may have a salutary effect on civil society by encouraging its members to worship, to spend time with their families, and to learn the moral lessons embedded in religious traditions. But the impact of religion on society is likely to diminish if that is the only role it plays.

> What interested Tocqueville about voluntary organizations was not just
> their ability to provide friendships or to teach people civic skills. More
> important was their ability to forge connections across large segments
> of the population, spanning communities and regions and drawing
> together people from different ethnic backgrounds and occupations.
> (Wuthnow 1999: 362)

Much contemporary writing on religion and politics in the United
States focuses on partisanship, with attention to changes in the political
loyalties, alignments, and positions of different religious groups (Wilson 2007). If we look under the surface of the partisan divides commonly associated with religion, several long-term trends emerge that
shape how religion is linked with democracy in the United States.
Growing numbers of people marry outside the denomination in which
they were raised, contributing to the diversity and tolerance associated
with religion in the United States that particularly impresses Putnam
and Campbell (2010) and is the specifically "American grace" that
gives their book its title. Generational change, along with growing
urbanization, education, media access, and physical mobility, has weakened what once were secure partisan identities and residential blocs
associated with religion. Catholics are no longer a reliable and monolithic voting bloc, the positions taken by evangelicals and mainline
Protestants have diverged notably, and the increasingly salient relation
of religion with political polarization has produced a backlash, with a
small but growing group rejecting polarization (and religious affiliation
of any kind) for a position that is decidedly secularist (Bolce and De
Maio 2007; Mockabee 2007; Putnam and Campbell 2010). Religion
remains associated with volunteerism and the building up of civil society, but there are notable differences among religious communities, with
mainline Protestants being the most committed, followed by Catholics,
Jews, and evangelical Protestants. African American churches continue
to provide members with important political resources (Harris 1999;
Harris-Lacewell 2007).

A few elements are particularly noteworthy in the emerging global
relation of religion to democracy. I noted earlier the idea of a "Catholic
wave" of support for progressive political change, democracy, and
greater autonomy of laypeople and lay organizations within the church
that is part of the broad impact of the Second Vatican Council
(Casanova 2001; Philpott 2004; Toft, Philpott, and Shah 2011: 111ff.).
The Catholic wave has special resonance in global politics, if only
because Catholicism is so widespread and, despite considerable diversity on the ground, has unifying institutional structures[2] (Ferrari 2006;

Hanson 1987). The Catholic wave has been matched by the explosive growth and spread of evangelical and Pentecostal Christianity, but the impact is more diverse and localized. In his study of evangelicals and politics in Africa, Asia, and Latin America, Paul Freston finds few common patterns apart from a shared localism, "which is its weakness and its strength" (Freston 2001: 286). "Being a decentralized faith," he writes, "the globalization of evangelicalism may produce a splintering of political perspectives unable to communicate with one another. Since it has no Rome or Mecca, evangelicalism has difficulty finding a broader view, and its politics tend to be caught up in ethnic, national, or local ecclesiastical questions" (Freston 2001: 286).

The experience of religion with democracy in Africa highlights the shifting positions of the churches over time and underscores differences among Catholic, mainline or historic Protestant, Pentecostal, and African-initiated churches (Comaroff 1985; Fields 1985; Gifford 1995, 1998; Ranger 1986, 2008). Terence Ranger distinguishes three waves of democracy in Africa with a different role for the churches in each. The anticolonial struggle that finally won independence and majority rule in the 1960s (with the exception of South Africa) was followed in the 1980s by growing challenges to military regimes and one-party rule, and in the 1990s by struggles against corruption and for greater accountability and transparency (Ranger 2008a, 2008b). At first, many churches were cautious and wary of demands for independence. They had significant ties to colonial rule and feared the coming of nationalist regimes. But in the second and third phases, the mainline or historic churches have been the foremost challengers of authoritarian and corrupt rule.

> Under the surface of quietism or collaboration with the one party regimes, the historic churches had been gathering strength, multiplying their adherents, recruiting their clergy, and setting up their structures. They offered the only alternative network to those of the dominant party. Despite their complicity with the first generation of nationalist leaders, the churches still retained enough moral authority to act as arbiters and judges. (Gifford 1995: 13)

The role of Pentecostal churches is more ambiguous. As in Latin America, such churches offer members shelter, psychological security, and solidarity in free social space. But in African Pentecostal churches, it is common to find overwhelming stress on the charismatic gifts of the pastor, which undermine any contribution to norms of equality or civic skills that the churches might otherwise make. In his richly detailed account of Pentecostalism in Ghana, Paul Gifford questions the capacity (and the intent) of the new churches to contribute to civil society and politics in an independent way. Like some of Latin America's neo-Pentecostal megachurches, they reinforce a prevailing "big man" view of politics. "I observe in Ghana," he writes, "an enormous increase in the status of leaders. What may have begun as egalitarian spiritual brotherhoods may be very different now. Just watch the evolution of titles: from pastor to general overseer to bishop, archbishop, or even megabishop, from prophet to megaprophet" (Gifford 2008: 227). Most of the churches that Gifford studied in Ghana do little to promote the kinds of civic engagement or entrepreneurial skills classically associated with Protestantism. Moreover, "where the inculcation of democratic virtues is concerned, one must bear in mind that many of these churches are not really communities or fellowships at all. Some are, and many others began in that way, but just as many are now composed of clients of a particular 'man of God'"[3] (Gifford 2004: 185).

The case of South Africa has very particular qualities. During the long dominance of apartheid and the extended struggle to win majority rule, churches played an important role on both sides of the conflict. The apartheid state found roots, justification, and collective rituals of reinforcement in the Dutch Reformed Church, which T. Dunbar Moodie describes as a civil religion for the Afrikaners, one that reinforced their sense of themselves as a chosen people (Moodie 1974; Johnston 1994). The transformation of non-Afrikaner, white Christian churches took them from passive accommodation with power and sympathy for its victims to a position that denied legitimacy to the system and encouraged and advanced overt resistance to state power. Distinctions between religion and politics were rejected as signs of accommodation to an illegitimate state of affairs. These changes played out over decades as political struggles grew in intensity, reaching a crux in the mid- to late 1980s. This process has been well documented (Borer 1998; Johnston 1994; Walshe 1983, 1991) and only a brief account is necessary here.

Several points warrant separate mention. New theological understandings were created challenging the legitimacy of apartheid and questioning the churches' accommodation with established power and privilege. Theologians and activists in South Africa developed a "contextual theology" similar to Latin American liberation theology and influenced by it. The core idea was that theology needed to move away from a focus on abstract principles to root theological reflection in understanding and being part of real social contexts. An authentic interpretation of the Gospels, and of what faith required, had to be grounded in the experience of the vast majority of the population—the poor, the weak, the vulnerable, the nonwhite. The dominant fact in the social context of South Africa was racial inequality sanctioned by apartheid, which was viewed as a heresy, and "if apartheid is a heresy theologically, its practice must be opposed politically" (Borer 1998: 54).

These new positions were advanced and put into organizational practice by a new generation of leaders in the churches. Desmond Tutu, Alan Boesak, and Frank Chikane assumed leadership positions and reinforced the public identification of the churches with the majority of the population. They found allies among dissenters from Afrikaner orthodoxy, like Beyers Naude, whose Christian Institute provided a critical voice and space for the promotion of change (Borer 1998; Walshe 1991). With new leadership in place, the South African Council of Churches took on a vigorous public role, calling meetings, issuing documents, and campaigning for active resistance to the regime. Transnational religious organizations like the World Council of Churches with its antiracism campaigns and its legitimation of liberation movements in southern Africa played a part not only as cheerleader, but also as a critical source of funds and other resources. Finally, the evolution of the political situation, the consolidation of opposition, and the erosion of national and international support for the regime created a context in which activism looked possible and became effective despite the strength of the state. Thus

> politicization was the result of two sources: a changing political context and new religious ideas which interacted in a dialectical fashion. Theological ideas which were brewing below the surface in earlier periods became explosive in response to the worsening political context. Theological innovation in the 1980s was both a reaction to and a cause of the spiraling church-state conflict. What happened in the struggle affected the process of theologizing about that struggle, which in turn affected church action in the struggle itself. (Borer 1998: 126)

The churches did not bring down the apartheid regime all by themselves. The struggles that ultimately made for such dramatic change in South Africa had a much wider scope. But at critical moments, churches and religious people and ideas were friends of a democracy yet to be born. This effort put them at the center of the conflict: denying legitimacy to the "established disorder" of the state, encouraging resistance, and engaging actively in political struggle. To choose one example from many, the religious tenor of the conflict was made evident in a famous exchange between Archbishop Tutu and South African president P. W. Botha. Following a parliamentary inquiry into "undue" political involvement by the churches, the president accused Tutu of promoting the agenda of the African National Congress (ANC) and the South African Communist Party, not the Kingdom of God. He stated that the South African Council of Churches was serving as a Communist front and expressed alarm that clergy "who claim to be messengers of God are in reality messengers of enmity and hatred while parading in the cloth, and hiding behind the structures of the Church . . . they are engaged in the deformation of religion through the proclamation of false so-called 'liberation theology.'" In response, Archbishop Tutu reminded President Botha that the Bible and the church predated Marxism and the ANC by centuries. He concluded with these words: "We are law abiding. Good laws make human society possible. When laws are unjust, then Christian tradition teaches that they do not oblige obedience . . . I work for God's Kingdom. For whose Kingdom do you work?" (cited in Borer 1998: 72–73).

Following the end of apartheid and the transition to majority rule, South African churches continued to play a central role for a while, most notably in the organization and legitimation of the Truth and Reconciliation Commission. Church organizations and leaders like Archbishop Tutu were important to the process of reconciliation, but once South African politics settled into the "new normal" of majority rule, it was difficult for the churches to find a role. Ranger states that many once-radical churchmen now find themselves part of the establishment and need to decide if they are not simply against tyranny, but also for democracy and accountability (Ranger 2008b: 16).[4]

Catholic and Protestant churches played a notable role in the democratization of two Asian countries where they either form a majority or are a very significant minority. Elements in the Philippine Catholic Church were central to the People's Power Revolution of 1986, and both Catholics and Protestants participated actively in subsequent People's Power movements in 2001. In both cases, change in core religious ideas preceded and encouraged the churches' turn to active political engagement. The Philippine Catholic Church was deeply affected by Vatican II and by influences from Latin America, including liberation theology and calls for the churches to exercise a preferential option for the poor. As in Latin America, these gave legitimacy to a more integral vision of the proper mission of the church and made more active engagement with progressive social change seem possible and necessary. Wooster writes,

> But for this monumental change over the two preceding decades, the Philippine Catholic Church would very likely not have engaged in

activist political action on the scale that it did, nor would it as readily have claimed for itself the legitimacy to act as a major force for social change. Although individual bishops, priests and nuns would likely have engaged in some level of political activity, the Church as an institution would almost certainly have remained aloof from, if not critical of, the rebellion. (Wooster 1994: 164–165)

These new ideas led the Philippine hierarchy, under the direction of Cardinal Jaime Sin, to challenge the fraudulent elections of 1986, declare the government of Ferdinand Marcos illegitimate, and put its considerable resources (including mass media and organizational networks) into the campaign against the regime. The role of the hierarchy was dramatically enhanced by broad popular participation in which priests and nuns took a central role on the front lines of confrontation. Evangelical groups played little part in the first People's Power movement, but by 2001, a combination of growth, organizational consolidation, and an ideological transformation with roots in the Lausanne Covenant (1974) helped move evangelicals from pure church building to engagement with the whole society. In the process, many Philippine evangelical churches shed a long tradition of pietistic theology and unquestioning obedience to established authority to encourage and empower opposition to authoritarian rule to the point of participating in street demonstrations (Lim 2009).

South Korea is unusual in Asia because of the close association of Protestantism with Korean nationalism, which consolidated during the long (1905–1945) Japanese occupation of the country. Moved by the same trends noted for the Philippines, Protestant groups joined the democratization movements of the late 1980s. The decision to embrace the democratic movement followed on "a theological self examination by evangelical churches that led to more concern about socio political responsibilities . . . the Lausanne Covenant of 1974 and the follow up Grand Rapids Report emphasized social justice as part of the biblical mandate. These world wide evangelical voices began to influence Korean churches and key evangelical leaders . . . especially in the mid 1980s" (Hong 2008: 190). The churches' support for antigovernment movements in Korea echoes what happened in Latin America and South Africa: "Criticism of the government was illegal . . . so church organizations, being legal entities, and therefore very difficult for the regime to assail, were important for the democratic movement. Some churches were frequent sites for meetings, prayers, and demonstrations, as police hesitated to break up even anti-government activities taking place on sanctified ground" (Hong 2008: 189).

The convergence of new ideas and leadership generations in a pluralizing context undermines the old order as it creates new experiences and possibilities for innovative forms of action. This pattern is not limited to Christian churches. In his illuminating study of Indonesia, Robert Hefner argues that the evolution of what he calls "civil Islam," defined as the creation of independent forms of civil association and political power with Islamic content, played a central role in the transition to democracy in Indonesia after the fall of Suharto in 1998. Civil Islam denies "the wisdom of a monolithic Islamic state, instead reaffirming democracy, voluntarism, and a balance of countervailing power in state and society" (Hefner 2000: 12–13). These movements resisted efforts by the Suharto regime to give themselves a veneer of religious legitimacy and provided leaders, legitimacy, and organizational networks that were vital to the subsequent transition to democracy.

Social Movements, Civil Society, and Religion

Religious institutions have played a salient role in promoting and empowering social movements around the world. The evolution of the civil rights movement in the United States, and the ongoing role of the African American churches in politics, are a prime case in point. The civil rights movement drew much of its leadership, discourse, moral legitimation, and early organizational networks from the African American churches (Branch 1988, 1998, 2008; Morris 1984). Martin Luther King Jr. and his collaborators were an insurgent generation and struggled for some time to gain acceptance within their own churches (Branch 1988). Trained as preachers, they became leaders of social movements. Aldon Morris suggests that much of their ability to move and convince came from the charisma embedded in their role as church leaders and preachers.

> At the heart of the SCLC (Southern Christian Leadership Conference)'s organizational structure was a charismatic center. As in the black church that spawned it, institutionalized charisma was an important resource of the SCLC. It cannot be overemphasized that the SCLC's power grew out of a dynamic combination of organizational strength and charisma. Without the church base, it is unlikely that Martin Luther King Jr. would have become so prominent an organizer and such a potent symbol of an effective mass movement. Being at the center of a church base allowed King to use his charisma as a mobilizing force. (Morris 1984: 91)

Familiar Gospel passages and references were woven into the daily discourse of the movement, giving ordinary acts a clear religious significance and legitimation. In his famous *Letter from a Birmingham Jail*, King responds to the charge that he is an "outside agitator" using religion in "unduly political" ways by grounding himself in the example of the Hebrew prophets and St. Paul. "I am at Birmingham," he wrote, "because injustice is here."

> Just as the prophets of the eighth century BC left their villages and carried their "thus saith the Lord" far beyond the boundaries of their home towns, and just as the Apostle Paul left his village of Tarsus and carried the gospel of Jesus Christ to the far corners of the Greco Roman world, so am I compelled to carry the gospel of freedom beyond my home town. Like Paul, I must constantly respond to the Macedonian call for aid. (King 1986: 290)

King affirmed the need to resist unjust laws, citing St. Augustine to the effect that "an unjust law is no law at all." He justified the need for action here and now and called on the churches to lead society rather than accommodate or follow, to be headlights, not taillights. He rejected the charge of extremism, once again citing Jesus and the Prophets:

> Though I was initially disappointed at being categorized as an extremist, as I continued to think about the matter I gradually gained a measure of satisfaction from the label. Was not Jesus an extremist for love? "Love your enemies, bless them that curse you, do good to them that hate you, and pray for them which despitefully use you and persecute you." Was not Amos an extremist for justice? "Let justice roll down like waters and righteousness like an ever flowing stream." Was not Paul an extremist for the Christian gospel? "I bear in my body the marks of the Lord Jesus." Was not Martin Luther an extremist? "Here I stand, I cannot do otherwise, so help me God." . . . So the question is not whether we will be extremist but what kind of extremists we will be. Will we be extremists for hate or for love? Will we be extremists for the preservation of injustice or for the extension of justice? (King 1986: 297–298)

Along with religious language and imagery, the African American churches created and reinforced a network of "movement half way houses" that shaped tactics, trained leaders, and helped organize and manage campaigns (Morris 1984: 139–173; see also Branch 1988). The churches continue to play an important role, providing members with a combination of micro resources (legitimation and a sense of solidarity and efficacy) and macro resources (places to meet, an organizational infrastructure, contacts) that make such participation both attractive and effective. Harris argues that the African American churches promote an "oppositional civic culture" that encourages active participation, within the frame of existing institutions, to contest prevailing patterns of power and domination. Personal empowerment, community action, and political involvement go together in the experience of church life (Harris 1999; Lincoln and Mamiya 1990). But as in Latin America, the growing presence and reach of neo-Pentecostal megachurches in the African American community raise questions about the continuing power of this tradition (Harris-Lacewell 2007).

The potential of churches to facilitate the creation of social movements and sustain them with ideological and material resources comes out very strongly in the experience of the people's peace movement in East Germany. In the year or so before the fall of the Berlin Wall and the end of the Communist regime, a series of prayer services and vigils for peace began in a few Protestant churches in the city of Leipzig (Bartee 2000; Steele 1994). The services spread quickly, drawing large numbers of people who regularly spilled out from the churches into silent candle-lit processions calling for peace and human rights. Vigils and marches continued despite threats and intimidations from the regime's pervasive political police, the Stasi. The churches provided indispensable elements to the growing movement: a relatively safe place to meet, privileged access to communications (including telephones), and a built-in network of connections across the country. They also offered a powerful vision of an alternative culture, one not under the control of the state, but free to evolve with the protection of the churches, which as Steele puts it, "would have been enough to both mobilize the crowd and incline it to conform with the behavior implied in the themes of peace, justice, and the integrity of creation" (Steele 1994: 141).

As the movement grew, it drew in many small groups with interests ranging from ecology, peace, and antinuclear agitation to resistance to military education in the schools and rights to emigrate, along with other human rights including freedom of speech, the right to enjoy an untrammeled private life, the right to an unbiased judicial system and to free and fair elections (Bartee 2000: 76–101). The movement soon reached the national level of the churches and impelled church leaders, who for years had accommodated with the state, to assume a key role in negotiations that eventually led to the demise of the regime. Clearly, we cannot attribute the fall of communism in East Germany solely to these efforts. As was the case in South Africa, the process was much wider in scope. But as they expanded and became a regular part of the political scene, the protests and vigils jump-started what Germans call Die

Wende, or "the turnaround." Movements brokered and protected by the churches exposed the regime's weaknesses and hastened its end. This experience fits well with others in Eastern Europe (support for Solidarity in Poland, for human rights in Czechoslovakia) and of course with the record of Latin America and South Africa noted here.

The example of civil Islam in Indonesia is relevant in this context. As they evolved, took on consistent form, and developed connections among themselves, varied networks of Islamic associations (devotional, educational, cultural, and political in orientation) helped create new forms of political power and open new arenas for political discussion well before the transition to democracy that came with the fall of Suharto and his "New Order" in 1998. They nurtured democracy by providing "traditions and organization that teach ordinary citizens the habits of the democratic heart. Embedded as democracy in local life worlds, its culture and organization will vary across societies too" (Hefner 2000: 5). The emergence of these organizations is part of a larger participatory revolution in the Islamic world, grounded in growing literacy, media access, and social as well as physical mobility. Dale Eickelman and James Piscatori point out that the emergence of a literate and media-savvy population changes the nature of the religious message and the ways in which it is carried. "In earlier generations, the exposure of students of Islamic ideas would have been through the Qu'ran and religious treatises. Increasingly, however, it is the pamphlet, the popular sermon (*khutba*), the telephone, and the electronic mail news service that distribute information and ideas to all parts of the Muslim world" (Eickelman and Piscatori 2004: 125). Religious knowledge and control of religious symbols thus pass out of the hands of a traditional elite and become the common coin of a new generation of activists and organizers (cf. Fields 1985 on colonial Central Africa). Rather than privilege one local group over another in Indonesia,

> the secularizing policies of the Dutch unwittingly eroded the moral authority of imperial Islam. In so doing, European colonialism encouraged the emergence of a society-based popular Islam. It was this tradition, not the aristocratic Islam of the courts, that underlay new versions of Muslim politics in the twentieth century. . . . Although conservative scholars were unhappy with the new cacophony the net result was not a narrowing of the Muslim political voice but its enrichment. . . . In matters of civic association, Muslims showed themselves second to no one. None of their rivals could match the breadth and vitality of their associations. Even under the New Order, Muslims were better able than others to resist state controls and nurture alternative ideas of the public good. (Hefner 2000: 217)

Not all movements that call on Islamic legitimacy fit the category of civil Islam as outlined by Hefner. Starting in the late 1970s, self-defined Islamist movements arose to challenge secular and leftist organizations, above all among university students and the new urban poor. In short order they swept them from the field. They also found a home in unofficial mosques whose rapid expansion in cities and towns drew strength from an eager clientele (Kepel 1994, 2002, 2003; Gaffney 1994). The ensuing *Islamization of dissent* (for example, in Morocco, Algeria, Egypt, and among Muslim migrant communities in Europe) finds echoes in the ability of North American fundamentalists, Polish Catholics, Israeli militants of the Gush Emmunim, and Palestinian members of Hamas to reshape the agenda of religion and politics. Despite obvious differences among themselves, these movements all strive for religious vocabulary of social criticism that can spark and sustain activism. The moral authority and legitimacy of religion are taken as a starting point for social criticism (Kepel 1994).

The process does not always begin with religion. In numerous cases, social movements with political ties and aspirations use religious symbols and language to recruit and mobilize supporters. But as a practical matter, it is rarely easy to disentangle the political from the religious. The cases of Muslim Hezbollah (the Party of God) and the Hindu Nationalist RSS (Rashtriya Swayamsevak Sangh, Patriotic Organization) in India illustrate the point well. Hezbollah has had a mixed religious and political thrust from the beginning. The movement recruits on religious and political grounds and reinforces membership with religious metaphors, symbols, and rituals. The movement's Mahdi Scouts are a case in point. The scouts manage camps in Lebanon that serve as the vanguard of the party's youth movement. Images of jihad, martyrdom, and sacrifice for the cause are reinforced in camp rituals, watched over by iconic images including portraits of Iran's late Ayatollah Ruholla Khomeini (Worth 2008). In a similar way, Thomas Blom Hansen's study of the RSS in India affirms how the movement employs religious imagery, from images of Ram to chariots and a campaign to carry bricks across the nation to the town of Ayodhya to rebuild a temple to Ram supposedly displaced by the Babri Masjid Mosque in Ayodhya. These mobilizations played a prominent role in the interreligious violence around Ayodhya in the late 1980s (Hansen 1999: 148–153).

The particular force of these movements does not lie in direct confrontation with the state, at least not at first. That comes later, if at all. Rather, movements begin by building and diffusing a coherent set of ideas and practices about how best to organize social life and give it proper moral and juridical form. This requires reworking basic elements of life in common, including relations between the sexes, education, property, and core moral norms. Society takes the lead here, as a complex honeycomb of groups is put in place whose life in common anchors large-scale transformations of politics and culture in the more accessible realities of day-to-day living.

Religion and Violence

Well-known recent public commentary attributes a wide range of social and political ills to religion, including intolerance, cultural rigidity, and the promotion of communal conflicts (Dawkins 2008; Hitchens 2007). A considerable body of contemporary work goes further to ask how religious organizations and religious beliefs provide motivations, legitimations, and a psychological footing for violence.[5] (Jurgensmeyer 2001; Lawrence 1986). Mark Jurgensmeyer puts the question starkly, asking "why does religion seem to need violence and violence need religion?" (2001: 7). His answer is partly psychological, with religiously inspired violence as an outlet for sexual frustration. He also argues that religious ideas and patterns of activism enhance and intensify violence by linking ordinary events to cosmic struggles and providing spaces and routines in which the enactment of violence acquires the sanction of accepted ritual.

This work is provocative but its comparative utility is hindered by several factors. The concepts of terror and terrorism come loaded with value judgments. One person's terror can be another's struggle for liberation or defense of the integrity of a threatened culture or nation. The analytical tools deployed are commonly subordinate to a political and policy agenda concerned with "terrorism" as a problem to be confronted, primarily by states. This makes for a rereading of history around issues of religion and terrorism with questionable results. Thus, Toft, Philpott, and Shah state that "before the nineteenth century, religion motivated virtually all terrorist activity," a tendency that in their view yielded to the impact of secularization but returned in force after 1968 when "religious terrorism has risen and become global" (Toft, Philpott, and Shah 2011: 127). They go on to assert that a third of the world's civil wars since 1940 have been religious in character (Toft, Philpott, and Shah 2011: 153, 155). The explanation they offer rests on reference to the role of religious ideas and institutions that edges on the tautological. Thus, "religious terrorism is likely when a religious actor with an integrationist political theology is deeply dissatisfied with the political status quo, as when a partially integrated political system has not integrated far enough or fast enough to satisfy the religious actor's aspiration, or when a political system flouts the actor's sense of religious correctness." They affirm that "religious ideas that are conducive to terrorism will result in violence" (Toft, Philpott, and Shah 2011: 123). As stated, this is true by definition, and not very helpful. The authors do make an effort to move beyond truisms, noting that political groups may compete for control of religion, and that "religious terrorist organizations recruit members by appealing to religious sentiments but in reality may have nonreligious goals as their focus" (Toft, Philpott, and Shah 2011: 129). But although this is certainly possible, acknowledging the fact does not do much to advance the discussion. In practice, it is not so easy to disentangle what is religious and what is political in any given situation.

We need to dig deeper and work at sorting out how and why the ideas that move people and give focus to public discourse are generated and diffused and why they find an audience, and why in these particular times and places. As a first step, we need to stop seeing religions as undifferentiated wholes, uniform and unchanging. Appleby points out that "the argument that is tradition occurs at every level of religious life. Nothing could be further from the truth, therefore, than the notion that religious are timeless entities, existing above the fray of the temporal, immune to the vicissitudes of history" (Appleby 2000: 40). Change is continuous, and part of the answer to questions about religion and violence lies in a process of change that turns established religious roles and broad understandings of religious doctrine and tradition from passive contemplation to activism, and sets aside doctrinal proscriptions on violence in favor of active engagement. Many religious traditions advance a core ethic of nonviolence and view religious specialists like priests, monks, and nuns as exemplars of compassion and nonviolence. At the same time, suffering and perhaps martyrdom in the name of faith may also be venerated and emulated in passion plays and other ritual reenactments of the kind common in Shi'ite Islam where the martyrdom of the Imam Hussein, killed in the sixth century, is remembered every year (Ajami 1986; Arjomand 1995). The transition from passive acceptance, ritualized emulation (for example, through passion plays), and accommodation to mobilization, resistance, and the possibility of political activism begins with a transformation of religious ideas and stories, and the emergence of a new generation of religious specialists to articulate and diffuse them. Whether or not this leads to a justification of violence or to an equally militant nonviolent activism depends not on religion alone, but on the particulars of leadership, on the creation of a new audience, and on the opportunities available in a given social and political setting.

Beyond Latin America, prime instances in recent experience of such a turn to violence include the association of violence with national or transnational Islamist movements, the role played by Buddhist monks in conflicts in South and Southeast Asia, and the deadly mix of religious and communal violence in Northern Ireland. Priests and pastors were actively involved in promoting violence in Northern Ireland (Bruce 2009), and Buddhist monks have been prominent in violence and warfare in Southeast Asia.[6] They have served as soldiers in Thailand, and as military chaplains and ideologues of violence in Sri Lanka, and Buddhist spaces like monasteries have been effectively militarized in conflict zones (Cady and Simon 2007; Fink 2009; Jerryson 2010; Jurgensmeyer 2001; Kent 2010; Schober 2007; Tambiah 1992; see also Rutagambwa 2006 on the role of the Catholic Church in the violence in Rwanda).

The contrast between Buddhist ideal and reality is so stark that Tambiah found it necessary "to pose the question of how the 'sons of Buddha'—ideally dedicated to nonviolence and required by disciplinary rules to abstain from killing and to be nowhere near marching armies and traffic in arms—have taken on the more compelling identity of 'sons of the soil' which entails militant and violent politics" (Tambiah 1992: 95–96). This citation from a leading scholar of Buddhism and society is representative of a position that expresses surprise and shock that a religion so rooted in compassion and a commitment to nonviolence should see its agents encouraging and legitimating violence and sometimes taking up arms themselves. But if we go beyond doctrine, we find that now as in the past, "lived Buddhist traditions demonstrate a different attitude" (Jerryson 2010: 182). Core Buddhist institutions like the Sangha (orders of monks) have had a close historical association with kingship, and Buddhist states have engaged mounted armies and engaged in warfare, much like other states (Tambiah 1976).

What stands out in recent cases where Buddhist figures have been closely involved in violence is not a denial or transformation of basic doctrine, but rather an argument that invokes violence as necessary for the preservation of a way of life, an identity in which religion, ethnicity, language, and nationality are bound together. "In Sri Lanka, orders of Buddhist monks became standard bearers of religious nationalism. Monks saw themselves as moral guardians of the Sri Lankan nation and defenders of the Dharma, both threatened by ethnic and religious others.

It was their responsibility to pave the way for politicians to safeguard a Sri Lanka where Buddhism would prosper" (Schober 2007: 62). Perceived threats to this identity came from a Tamil (and Hindu) minority that was seen to have been unduly privileged by colonial powers in ways that undermined the core Buddhist identity of the nation. Because of the extremes of violence reached in the country's twenty-five-year civil war, the case of Sri Lanka is exemplary, but it is not unique. Hansen's analysis of religious and communal violence in India reaches a similar conclusion. Hansen locates the rise and tactics of the RSS, its push to advance Hindu nationalism (Hindutva), and repeated waves of religiously linked mobilization and violence beginning with the India-Pakistan partition in the late 1940s as part of a broad effort to define and preserve a communal identity that is perceived to be threatened (Hansen 1999; Appleby 2000: 109–111).[7]

In a similar way, Steve Bruce's account of the career of Ian Paisley in Northern Ireland shows how perceived threats to Protestant identity and successful appeals to local and communal interests empowered both Paisley's church and the political party he founded, the Democratic Unionist Party (DUP). Bruce states that "Protestantism is not just the religion of individuals; it is also part of the shared identity of 'the Ulster Protestant people'" (Bruce 2009: 208). Religion provided a language for the conflict, a clarity of purpose to militants, and undergirded party cohesion. At the same time, the trajectory of Paisley and his party underscores the point that even where religion plays a salient role in politics, religion is not all there is to the story. The trajectory of Paisley's own career is instructive. He founded a church and a political party based on the church, for many years was an icon of intransigence, and ended up as first minister of a coalition government in which his second in command was a leader of the longtime enemy, the Catholic Irish Republican Army. When Bruce asked one party leader what made an agreement that seemed inconceivable in 1974 possible in 2004, this was the answer: "Thirty years!" Bruce comments that the

> party was realistic enough to appreciate that, while some elements of the Agreement could be renegotiated, much of it was what military strategists call "realities on the ground." Power would have to be shared; the equality agenda was in place: the nationalist mandate would have to be accepted; the Irish Republic could not be ignored. But the DUP had the philosophical resources for this realism. After all, it had never taken the view of many Islamic fundamentalists that only those with the right religion should have a vote or be able to stand for office. (Bruce 2009: 131–132)

Connections among religion, threatened communal identities, and violence are often reinforced by an element that is not much present in Latin America—the activities of diaspora groups who raise funds and contribute energies and volunteers to support the cause of their home community. This was certainly true in Northern Ireland, played a role in the violence surrounding Sikh demands for an independent homeland (Khalistan), and provided key support to Lebanon's Shi'ites as they developed political organizations and moved to armed struggle in the country's civil war (Ajami 1986; Ayres 2007; Jurgensmeyer 2001).

No comparative analysis of religion and violence would be complete without attention to the immense literature on jihadist (often misnamed "fundamentalist") Islamic movements. The general tenor of this work is well-known: a stress on Islamic revival in the face of the failure of other alternatives, simultaneous protest against corrupt states and the Islamic institutions they subsidize and control, focus on a lost Golden Age of Islamic rule, scriptural literalism, charismatic male leadership, recruitment of new generations of leaders and followers created by new-found mobility and access to literacy and mass media, and an emphasis on what is seen as the political failure of existing states and parties (Appleby 2006; Arjomand 1995; Kepel 1994, 2002, 2003; Eickelman and Piscatori 2004; Marty and Appleby 1992; Riesebrot 1998; Roy 2004). In addressing this literature, it is important to remember that Islam is a worldwide religion. Its social and political expressions vary greatly according to the culture and the context in which believers and institutions find themselves. A necessary first step in making sense of the experience of Islamist movements and violence is therefore to avoid reifying Islam, as if it were everywhere and always the same. Hefner's comment is apt:

> Religious violence is not the result of an unchanging Islam, every-where fated to extremism. Muslim practice is as varied as that in the West. . . . The struggle for the hearts and minds of Southeast Asian Muslims is the result then, not of a uniform "Islam" but of highly varied interactions between a divided Muslim community, on the one hand, and state and society structures beset with their own problems of coordination, corruption, and sectarianism on the other. (Hefner 2007: 34)

The resort to violence by Islamist and jihadist movements in recent years ranges from the horrific civil war among the Islamic Salvation Front (FIS, Front Islamique du Salut), the Armed Islamic Group (GIA, Groupe Islamique Armée), and the Algerian state to the actions of local groups like those who assassinated Egypt's Anwar Sadat in 1981, the growth and spread of militarized political parties like Hezbollah in Lebanon and Hamas in the West Bank of Palestine, transnational groups with an Islamic claim to legitimacy like Al-Qaida or Islamic Jihad, and regional or national variants such as the Moro Liberation Front in the Philippines and Pakistan's Lashkar e Taiba. These cases have in common a sense of blocked opportunity (by a corrupt state or by British, US, or Israeli power) and a search for energizing legitimacy in a purification of religious practice and expression. In this sense, they can be understood as religious revitalization movements, which assert a new basis for community in a return to religious roots (Gaffney 1994; Kepel 2002, 2003; Roy 2004).

The preceding analysis resting on links to threatened ethnic and national identities makes violence seem particularly intractable, but although conflict and contestation may be inevitable, violence is not. The choice for violence is contingent on events and opportunities and is regularly contested within religious traditions. Violence justified by appeals to religion or to religiously linked identity is shadowed everywhere by ideals and practices of nonviolence and by religiously inspired and promoted efforts at mediation, peace-building, and reconciliation. Evidence for this in Latin America includes groups like SERPAJ and the efforts of Witness for Peace. Elsewhere in the world, militants for peace include Engaged Buddhists in Vietnam, Cambodia, and Thailand; the long-term pacifism and mediation efforts of Quakers and the Mennonite Central Committee; and religiously inspired NGOs like the Catholic Community of Sant'Egidio and the Moral Rearmanent Association (Appleby 2000). In all these cases, the original inspiration lies in a religiously rooted devotion to peace and nonviolence. A practical path to peace is found through the cultivation of friendships across community barriers and the provision of neutral spaces (often literally buildings and meeting places) in which contending parties can come together on a regular basis. The Community of Sant'Egidio, founded by a group of Catholic laypeople in the late 1960s, has worked effectively to create spaces for conflict resolution in the civil war in Mozambique and in other cases. Working out of the pacifist and Anabaptist traditions of the Protestant Reformation, the Mennonite Central Committee and the Quakers have also promoted mediation and peace-building efforts across the world (Appleby 2000; Toft, Philpott, and Shah 2011; Johnston and Sampson 1994; Sampson 1994; Kraybill 1994).

Most of the time the choice for nonviolence rests on a combination of tactics and ethics. If the contest is reduced to one of brute force and firepower, those with more weapons inevitably prevail. As a tactic, non-violence avoids such one-sided confrontations and nurtures solidarity through the affirmation of nonviolent ideals in ways that expose the corrupt nature of state power while mobilizing national and transnational allies. This was the case with Mohandas Gandhi in India, with the US civil rights movement, and with the people's peace movement in East Germany where the churches consistently promoted nonviolence (Steele 1994: 139–140). As the peace movement in East Germany grew and spread, and prayer vigils spilled over into regular and massive candlelit marches, organizers were careful to insist on and maintain a stance of nonviolent protest. The commitment to nonviolence was both tactical and ethical and was effective in sustaining the peaceful nature of protest and reducing the likelihood of official violence. "The strategic nature of the church's commitment to nonviolence," Steele writes, "could be seen in the willingness to apply it in such a way as to minimize the threat even to one's enemy. It was nonpragmatic and nontactical: it was a baseline commitment to do all one could to avoid violence of any kind to anyone. Strategic nonviolence is inherently corrosive to violence based systems like the former DDR" (Steele 1994: 141).

The impact of this position became particularly visible at a critical moment when the Stasi and military forces were poised for violent intervention and talk of a "Chinese solution" (echoing the 1989 repression at Tiananmen Square in Beijing) was in the air. As they left the churches, the watchword of marchers was *frieden schaffen ohne waffen,* "wage peace without weapons" (Bartee 2000: 6). In a prayer meeting that followed a wave of police arrests, one pastor spoke about the use of force. He affirmed that

> "Christ's statement that 'all power is given to me' can apply to Christians as they act responsibly and, against such 'all power' the Stasi apparatus, the militia units, and dog teams are mere paper tigers." His outspoken words called for inner strength and for avoidance of physical violence: "one injured policeman will inevitably lead to escalation." At the conclusion of this rousing sermon the crowd poured out into the uncertainty of the evening singing We Shall Overcome. (Bartee 2000: 20)

Rights and Reconciliation

Forgiveness and reconciliation are core Christian concepts, and ideas about rights also find support in Christian tradition, not least in the Reformation insistence on the autonomy of conscience and of the churches before the state. The desire for rights, and the commitment to achieve and consolidate them, go beyond any single religious or political tradition. Appleby (2000: 207, 255) points to debates within Christianity and Islam that have contributed to the rediscovery and retrieval of ideas about rights. Despite the common accusation that concern with rights, particularly human and civil rights, is an ethnocentric expression of Western culture, ideas about rights emerge and find support in the most varied traditions. One way to understand the assertion of rights is to see it as an outgrowth of the consolidation of social pluralism. There is a double dynamic at work here: the costs of imposing monolithic order rise when multiple organized interests compete for space in a society; at the same time the experience of multiple independent organization stimulates a commitment to rights and to the consolidation of autonomies in theory and practice. Hefner's analysis of the role played by civil Islam in the construction of democracy in Indonesia illustrates the possibilities very well. "Civil Muslims," he writes, "renounce the mythology of an Islamic state. Rather than relegating Islam to the realm of the private, however, they insist that there is a middle path between liberalism's privatization and conservative Islam's bully state. The path passes by way of a public religion that makes itself heard through independent associations, spirited public dialogue, and the demonstrated decency of others" (Hefner 2000: 218).

Latin America's experience with religion, rights, and reconciliation is rich, but not unique. Many of the postviolence truth commissions formed since the 1970s have been deeply influenced by religious figures and by ideas derived from religious discourse about social sin and reconciliation (Appleby 2000: 41–48, 262; Byrnes 2011; Hayner 2002; Pfeil 2006; Sikkink and Booth Walling 2006). The case of South Africa is instructive. The same ideas that inspired a new and more activist vision of rights and resistance in South Africa played a decisive role in shaping the country's experience of reconciliation. Reconciliation and forgiveness were critical if the country's different groups were to find ways to live together without massive bloodshed. Much attention was given to developing ideas of justice beyond retribution, punishment, or the simple accumulation of forensic evidence. These efforts had their fullest expression in South Africa's Truth and Reconciliation Commission, which put forgiveness, reconciliation, and norms of community (*ubuntu*) at its heart (Posel and Simpson 2002). As articulated by Archbishop Tutu, the concept of *ubuntu* suggests that we are only fully human in community and makes the effort to build community central to the postapartheid social and political process. The commission pursued reconciliation by making an explicit link among public apology, forgiveness, and amnesty: amnesty was only available to those who first made a full public confession and apology. The result was to add a goal of *restorative justice*, restoring and creating community, to more conventional concepts of retributive justice and punishment for crimes. The commission also provided a forum for victims and hitherto voiceless persons to share their stories and make them part of the public narrative of the nation. This initiative echoed elements of the Chilean truth commission and was emulated not long after in Peru's Commission on Truth and Reconciliation.

"Exceptional" Cases and Common Themes

There are no truly unique or exceptional cases. We are all human and as humans we operate in worlds of meaning and emotion, power, conflict, calculation, and cooperation. These shared elements run through our experience of religion and of politics, but how they are put together, and with what effect, vary according to time, place, and the specifics of culture, politics, and opportunity. Many concrete links join these varied experiences. Actors in the most varied contexts are aware of, influenced by, and borrow regularly from one another. The example and teachings of Gandhi and Martin Luther King Jr. have had a direct impact on nonviolent approaches throughout the world. Latin American liberation theology was an inspiration in South Africa and East Germany, and protesters across the world sing "We Shall Overcome." Migration and widening access to mass media strengthen Muslim communities throughout Europe. Transnational religious organizations, including religious orders and religiously inspired or church-promoted NGOs, provide global links of action and perspectives (Byrnes 2001, 2011; Brian Smith 1990). The spread of Pentecostal Protestantism has brought its characteristic appeal and pattern of organization to societies around the world (Jenkins 2006; Noll 2009).

Although it is possible to identify long-term trends that heighten the likelihood of democratization in politics, society, and religion—including pluralism itself—the results are never predetermined. A given outcome may appear in retrospect to have been inevitable, but at the time it may well have seemed to those involved that they were incurring great risks with no clear prospects of victory, much less of short-term payoffs. This suggests the inadequacy of analysts like Anthony Gill

(1998) who explain the political choices of the Catholic Church in Latin America (or of comparable groups elsewhere) in terms of short-term calculation of benefits, a simple reaction to competition—more competition, more advanced positions. Religious leaders, activists, and movements have varied greatly in their responses to competition or political conflict. In cases like South Africa, East Germany, the US South, and Indonesia, some doubled down on risky bets while others continued policies of passive accommodation. What makes a difference in these cases is the power of legitimating ideas as they find social expression in a pluralism that continues to bubble up and empower resistance despite efforts to tighten repression and control.

Toft, Philpott, and Shah argue that the role assumed by religious leaders, institutions, and movements in politics depends on a combination of theology and institutional independence. In their view, the rise of "politically assertive religion" depends on the existence of "qualitatively different political theologies that legitimate if not demand intense political engagement" (Toft, Philpott, and Shah 2011: 81). When such ideas are reinforced by institutional independence and autonomous resources, the stage is set for "politically assertive religion." This position is suggestive, but at best it is incomplete, at worst an unreliable guide to making sense of the world. The notion that religion is more assertive politically now than in the past conflates assertiveness with oppositional politics, and ignores what may with justice be called a politics of the established order, which characterizes the position of many faiths and religious groups. Lobbying for educational subsidies or against divorce, abortion, or same-sex marriage is just as political as advocating for human rights in the teeth of repression. The choice is not between involvement and noninvolvement. With the exception of isolated hermits, we are all involved in and affected by what goes on in society and politics. The point is to understand how religion is involved, with what goals, by what means, with which leaders and followers, and with what results.

The theologies and religiously legitimated understandings discussed in this chapter do not just happen, nor do they acquire social and political impact only through the activities of formal religious institutions. Religious institutions (churches, Islamic universities, orders of Buddhist monks, national or transnational church councils, and religiously linked NGOs) are certainly important. They control significant resources and provide critical means of moving people, ideas, and information across national boundaries. But complete analysis requires us to extend our inquiry beyond formal institutions to understand how they engage with civil society and how that engagement can reshape the final outcome. The world can look quite different when seen and experienced "from below," and alternative calculations of benefits, costs, and opportunities are in order. Leaving the independent influence of social pluralism and civil society out of the equation is a little like evaluating a play without paying attention to the audience. If the audience does not like the play, the run will be short, despite what critics and leaders of cultural groups may say.

Reflection on the experiences discussed in this chapter affirms that the potential contribution of religions to democracy, the extent to which institutions and believers actually promote democracy, depends on a prior assertion of the value of democracy as a political system and as a way of living within any given religious tradition. We have already seen this for the "Catholic wave." In East Germany, where the Lutheran churches had a history of accommodation to state power, the two kingdoms tradition (which sharply distinguished civil from spiritual power and had long served as a warrant for subordination of the churches to state power) was transformed from a reason for accommodation to a charter for independent criticism (Steele 1994). Comparable arguments can be made for the evolution of religion's engagement with social movements, violence, and rights and reconciliation. In each case, the emergence of a new position for religion (where it occurs) is the result of the articulation of new ideas and the way they acquire social presence in the multiplicity of groups and influences bubbling up from a plural society. The outcome is not necessarily happy and rarely short-term. A multiplicity of groups is no guarantee of their orientation, although as we have seen, sheer plurality can encourage calculation of the benefits of accommodation.

Violence, rights, and reconciliation present particularly thorny problems for understanding. For better or worse, violence is a part of ordinary life, and in particular circumstances the option to engage in violence can be and often is taken up by religions whose stated doctrine is pacifist. What makes a difference here is not so much ideas about violence or nonviolence per se, but how these are combined with concepts of identity. Something similar holds for the case of rights and reconciliation. The discovery or rediscovery of a charter for rights within religious traditions gives legitimacy to the effort to name and defend these rights. The specifics of reconciliation, and the particular forms that justice may take, depend more on contextual factors (including available political alliances) than on religion itself, although the power of core ideas about forgiveness can give efforts at reconciliation a head start.

Whatever the case, new legitimating ideas never arise in a vacuum. They represent a rereading of texts and theologies in new circumstances by a new generation with new experiences. It is rare that new ideas emerge and gain a hearing without substantial struggle, a struggle that they do not always win. But the creation and circulation of ideas never stop, and they benefit from the growing ease of global communication, and from lowered barriers to organization that come with a more open and plural civil society.

It is important to acknowledge the power of pluralism and the ability to build and hold connections across social levels in determining how religious change engages with society and politics. In a review of cases in which religious groups and individuals worked successfully to promote peace in cases of great conflict and distrust, Appleby points out that "top down structural processes are unlikely to succeed without parallel and coordinated alternative institutions designed to build the social infrastructure of peace" (Appleby 2000: 170). These provide openings to neutral spaces where it is possible to begin the difficult task of building mutual trust and even friendships that can bridge community divides.

The experiences here provide us with elements for reflection about religion's role in the politics and social life of nations and cultures far removed from the southern half of the Western Hemisphere. Along with Latin America, they affirm the continuing power of religions to create new ideas and craft and implement new forms of social action. Religions have a unique consolidating power, a capacity to place everyday events in contexts of ultimate significance and to reinforce religious ideas with material resources and nets of repeated human interaction. This creative power to shape public discourse, to put ideas on the table, and to nurture and sustain movements does not depend on institutional resources alone, although as we have seen it can push the process along in important ways. The continuing vigorous engagement of religion with society and politics around the world affirms what religion can bring to the table and also shows some of its potential limitations. Throughout this book, I have insisted that conventional notions of secularization, which condemn religion to decline and predict irrelevance in public life, are not an adequate guide to understanding. They leave religious believers and institutions in a passive and reactive role. But these are active and creative subjects, participants in a changing world. What Hefner says of civil Islam has general relevance.

> In the end, Muslims are part of our shared world, and Muslim politics are part of our shared but plural modernity. Contrary to earlier forecasts, religion in our age has not everywhere declined, nor been domi-

ciled within a sphere of interiority. Modernity has witnessed powerful religious revivals. Not a reaction against, but a creative response to the modern world. The most successful of these religious reformations have thrived by drawing themselves down into mass society and away from exclusive elites. (Hefner 2000: 218–219)

The core elements common to our cases include ongoing debate and change about core ideas within religion, a turn of religious discourse and institutions away from automatic accommodation of state power or the exchange of legitimacy for support to critical engagement and the emergence of a new generation of leaders and followers who put the package together in the construction of groups, networks, alliances, and the articulation of new positions.[8] Whether or not this process moves further to delegitimize existing authority, activate opposition, and perhaps to empower violent encounters in the name of faith depends less on religion itself than on context and circumstances. A central problem for all religious groups that travel this path is to know what comes next. What to do after the conflict is resolved, how to act after the transition? This is in part a practical question. As we have seen, many religious actors are not well equipped for long-term political engagement: they lack the experience to combine the innocence of doves with the wisdom of serpents, as Jesus memorably advised (Matthew 10:16). A further question is what impact a long-term political role can have on the churches themselves and on the quality of religious leadership and experience. Will religion suffer from a long-term, activist engagement with politics? I consider these questions further in the next and final chapter.

Notes

1. This convergence creates the possibilities for what Max Weber called *elective affinities* between ideas and the life experience of groups. Elsewhere I have cautioned that work with the concept of elective affinities has to go beyond simply identifying a fit of ideas with the circumstances of people's lives (Levine 1992: 16, 323). That is too passive. We must also search for the sources and pathways of change and incorporate dimensions of power, conflict, and change within religion as between religion and politics.

2. Traditions of subordinate association with state power and identification with national aspirations mean that the Eastern Orthodox churches present a different panorama (Stepan 2003; Toft, Philpott, and Shah 2011).

3. In some churches, the prophet is unchallengeable, and those who do contest his authority run up against the authority of God, which the prophet uniquely channels to his church. Contesting authority is dangerous. Gifford

cites the founder of one important group of churches, Winner's Chapel, to the effect that "you become a victim of whatever you criticize in the prophet. If you pick on his prosperity, you die in poverty. If you pick on his success, you become a public and established failure" (cited in Gifford 2004: 186, fn. 74).

4. Archbishop Tutu himself has commented that "now that apartheid is being dismantled, we are finding that it is not quite so simple to define what we are for. . . . We no longer meet regularly as church leaders because the tyranny is over. . . . We knew what we were against and we opposed that fairly effectively. It is not nearly so easy to say what we are for, and we appear to be dithering, not quite knowing where we want to go or how to get there" (Tutu 1995: 96).

5. Such commentary extends to comment and analysis on anti-Muslim extremists like Anders Behring Breivik, the Norwegian who admitted to bombings and shootings in Oslo and a nearby summer camp (committed on July 22, 2011). Behring Breivik saw himself as a crusader against a rising tide of multiculturalism and Islam in Europe. He drew inspiration from a range of anti-Islamic websites in the United States and similarly motivated groups and parties in Europe (Shane 2011).

6. In these and other cases, they have also been involved in efforts at mediation, peacemaking, and reconciliation. I discuss some experiences below.

7. The violence associated with Gush Emmunim and Jewish communities settling in what they regard as the Land of Israel, considered theirs by biblical right, is comparable. See, among others, Appleby 2000: 100–101; Kepel 1994: ch. 4.

8. Political action may not be the goal at the outset, but can come as a result of other changes. In his work on Christians in the Central American revolutions, Philip Berryman (1984: 108) points out that the goal of religious agents working with local communities was "certainly not to turn them from religiosity to activism, but to deepen the traditional religious vision and to transform it from an attitude of passivity (accepting the way things are as the 'will of God') to one of active struggle for change."

9

Looking Toward
Latin America's Future

In the south of Spain, near the small port of Palos de la Frontera, the Franciscan monastery of La Rábida contains a museum dedicated to Christopher Columbus.[1] Columbus and his son lived with the monks for two years while making repeated appeals for an audience with the king and queen, as part of his search for royal sponsorship for his voyages. The audience was granted after the reconquest of the Iberian Peninsula from the Moors was complete with the surrender of Granada to the Catholic kings in 1492. It was in Granada that Ferdinand and Isabella met Columbus and authorized and financed his voyage as an extension of their military power and their religious zeal. The following excerpt from the documents that accompanied Columbus on his first voyage, preserved at La Rábida, conveys the fusion of faith and power that was present from the beginning.

Mandamos estas tres carabellas armadas	We send these three armed caravels
Por mares océanos	On the ocean seas to advance
Por causa de algunos negocios concernientes	Certain interests relating to
A la diffusion de la palabra divina	The spread of the divine word
Y aumento de la fe ortodoxa	And increase of orthodox faith
Y también en provecho y utilidad nuestros	And also for our benefit and profit
Yo el Rey	I the King
Yo la Reina	I the Queen

This close alliance of religion and of the institutional church with power persisted throughout Latin America for more than 400 years. But in the mid-twentieth century, something interesting and for the most part unexpected happened. Once the exclusive province of the Catholic Church, Latin America began to experience religious pluralism as the expansion of Protestant and Pentecostal churches irrevocably altered the landscape. Once the reliable ally of domination, religion became a source and inspiration for freedom. Converging with profound social transformations and political conflicts, these changes opened new ways for religion to make its presence felt in the public sphere. The social and political alliances of the churches were reconfigured, social movements were created, and innovative connections with politics at all levels were set in motion.

Reprise

The core of the argument of this book is that the transformations in the relations among politics, religion, and society that have been so prominent in Latin America arose and gained strength and meaning from the convergence of new ideas with new social groups and political contexts in which these ideas make particular sense. The argument proceeds on three levels. The level of particular cases directs attention to the experience of specific churches, movements, countries, or instances of conflict or cooperation. There is also a regional level, in which apart from the details of any given case, it makes sense to address Latin America as a recognizable subset of the world community, with shared traditions and connections that bind churches and groups and governments in different nations to one another. Finally, a transnational or global level serves as a source of influences, resources, contacts, and connections. In this complex and multilayered reality, religion remains a constant factor in society and politics—as a source of ideas, a generator of groups and initiatives, and a target for others seeking to use the moral authority of religion to whatever purposes they advance. What changes is not the presence of religion in society and politics, but rather who speaks, about what, with which allies, to what ends, and with what success, however success may be defined.

The emergence of new ideas within the churches has sources of its own (recapturing older traditions, ongoing debates) but it is also critically empowered by transformations in society and politics that create new groups, equip them with skills and capabilities, and make it possible for them to enter the public scene. If we ask what groups like this may do once they are activated and present in public life, the only answer is that nothing is foreordained: much depends on context and opportunity. The importance of context and opportunity should not be taken to mean that conditions must in some sense be "favorable." Sometimes the most unfavorable contexts can spur determined criticism, action, and resistance. Outcomes are a matter of debate and struggle, and struggles within religions are closely linked with conflicts in the society as a whole. For this reason, it is essential to avoid reifying religion, as if it were once and everywhere the same. To understand the origins and the dynamics of these contests, they must be situated in the context of particular societies and political systems where opportunities are presented, made, and sometimes lost.

One question that is often asked concerns the relation between religious change and globalization. Is there some sense in which religious transformation and what some scholars like to refer to as "ferment" are more noticeable now than in earlier eras, and can this be attributed to globalization? The recent experience of globalization has clear impacts on religion's role in society and politics, as a by-product of greater mobility, literacy, and access to mass media. But of course, the mutual impact of globalization and religious change did not begin yesterday. Missionary orders, brotherhoods, and pilgrims have been active in spreading different faiths for millennia. Crusades, states, and armies have also played a role. What is different now is not the fact of globalization, but rather the speed and density of communication.

This suggests that scholars who focus on a "resurgence" of religion, which is seen to underpin a growing public presence, may have the question backward. Latin America does not fit the resurgence model very well, but neither does much of the world. What we see is neither a resurgence of religion nor more or less involvement of religion in politics. Instead, what we see is a *different kind of involvement*, advanced by different persons with different goals. One of the difficulties with arguments about a "resurgence" of religion in politics is that those who advance it commonly identify political activism by religious institutions, movements, or actors with activism and opposition to established power. This is misleading because it ignores the ongoing involvement of religious ideas and institutions with the everyday operations of society and politics, a relation that often entails an exchange of legitimation for resources. What is different now is that this kind of exchange is no longer the only game in town, and the "official" spokespersons of religion (bishops, orders of monks, Islamic university faculties, imams) are no longer the only voices claiming to speak in the name of religion.

Putting the issues of "religious ferment" and globalization together brings us up against the heavy hand of conventional secularization theory and the legacy of expectations that it left in generations of scholars and commentators. I discussed secularization in some detail earlier and will not repeat those arguments here, but I do want to offer a more personal note. I have always believed that I was lucky. Since I am not a sociologist (much less a sociologist of religion) by training, I have never had to learn and unlearn the assumptions that made secularization appear to be inevitable, progressive, desirable, and universal. These assumptions never struck me as very compelling. I came to the study of religion through my interest in the social presence of ideas, and as a political scientist, through my enduring concern with power. From that perspective, the interesting questions have less to do with the separation of religion from other spheres of life than with the creative syntheses continuously being invented and put into play around the world. These are further enhanced by changes that place religion outside the state, so that it no longer exercises power directly but instead competes to wield influence in society.

The preceding discussion suggests the importance of paying close attention to the continuing mutual impact of religion, politics, and society. This is a useful corrective to long-standing traditions in the social sciences that relegated religion to the status of an interesting curiosity, doomed to decline and ultimate disappearance. But as we rediscover the enduring creativity of religions and their capacity to shape society and politics, it is also important to avoid making religion assume too great a role in explanation. Religious actors clearly play a role (sometimes a critical role) in society and politics, but they are never alone in the field. Whatever the outcome, the results have less to do with churches as stand-alone actors than with available allies, conditions of organization, and leadership, not to mention the opposition they may encounter.

How Changes in Society and Politics Have Affected Religion

Pluralism, plurality, and growing engagement with civil society and democracy are central dimensions of the impact that changes in society and politics have had on religion. To the extent that the churches in Latin America have disengaged from state power (if not from all forms of power and privilege) they gain the potential to be more open to democratizing ideas and forms of organization. Pluralism and democracy bring both challenge and opportunity to religion and to the churches as institutions. The challenge of adapting to a world without religious monopoly comes along with the opportunity to recruit and hold new members and to craft an effective place in a transformed public sphere. It is precisely the detachment of religion from state power and the associated deregulation of civil society that have energized religious pluralism and sparked new generations of voluntary organizations with visible impacts on society and politics, not only in Latin America, but more generally. I also want to underscore opportunity of another kind that pluralism and democracy can bring to the churches.

Detaching from state power and accommodating to a role as one of many voices opens the possibility of a less closed and defensive stance for religion. Catalina Romero identifies a central challenge facing Catholicism in Latin America as rethinking its role in a secularizing and plural society and finally accepting the fact of pluralism, which requires it not only to assume the status of actor (among many) in civil society, but also to acknowledge and accommodate to the emergence of a nascent civil society with the church itself. This presents the church with "an opportunity to recover its capacity to feel the joys and the pains of the people, [and to move] beyond the rationalist argumentation in which its own defensive attitude to modernity trapped it for so long" (Catalina Romero 2010: 232). It has not been easy for the Catholic Church to give up assumptions of a dominant status and a right to shape society and culture. These assumptions continue to shape Vatican policies and positions, which are carried forward by many church leaders. But it is important to recognize that these positions carry costs and, in any case, are challenged not only by other churches and cultural forces, but also by resistance within the institutional church itself.

One aspect of Latin American experience that presses itself upon our attention is the distinctive impact that different kinds of political regimes can have on religion. Reflecting on the conflict-filled experience of Argentina, Juan Pablo Martín points out that over the centuries, Christian traditions have dealt with politics in a dazzling array of forms and combinations.

> Christian history has long experience of these phenomena, and its secret has consisted not so much in founding or overcoming empires, or in maintaining some kind of sacred geopolitical versions of national values, although it has done all these things. It has, rather, consisted in an ability to construct social realities that are identified not with the church itself, not with a future City of God, nor with any existing state or empire, but which work instead within societies, moved by social ideas that interact effectively with Christian texts and sociological realities. (Martín 2010: 266–267)

Whatever the political choices may be, whatever the pressures or temptations of political action, the decision to engage in direct, often partisan politics can be costly for churches, for the groups they promote and sponsor, and for religious practice itself. Politics can bring division, split religiously linked social movements, and siphon off leaders and resources. Joining political struggle with theological conflict, as in Argentina during the last military regime, or in the Guatemalan civil war, can be particularly deadly. Even in less extreme cases, political commitments may damage religion by tying faith and belonging to political affiliation or dependence on state power.[2]

How Changes in Religion Have Affected Society and Politics

Religious transformations affect politics and society in multiple ways and at multiple levels. The impact of new ideas and the presence of agents and activists inspired by these ideas present us with one side of a coin whose obverse is provided by the ongoing presence of institutions that command loyalties and have the capacity to provide or withhold resources and connections. These multiple impacts resist being reduced to a single formula. In social and political terms, religion is an open space, and religious support has been mobilized and legitimacy provided to widely varying models of the good life and contrasting political and social agendas, which are often sharply contested within churches and religious organizations. Within this overall panorama, a few elements stand out in the evolution of religion's place in the society and politics of contemporary Latin America. Three warrant separate mention here: the expanding and increasingly diverse social and institutional presence of religion, the impact of new ideas about rights and politics, and the surge of Pentecostal movements and the diffusion of Pentecostal practices across religious denominations.

Religion's growing institutional presence, manifest in a dazzling array of churches, chapels, associations, social movements, schools, and media outlets, provides a varied set of platforms for implementation of what it means to be religious in contemporary society. This is a much more diverse, and much less easily controlled, phenomenon than in the past, and all that variation provides underpinnings for a broader social and political pluralism. The impact of new ideas about rights speaks to the ways in which religious discourse can legitimize or delegitimize regimes, policies, and social structures. The specific ways in which these ideas are framed point to alternative forms in which the social energies and resources stemming from religion can be put to use. The particular positions taken have a major impact on how churches and religious groups behave in situations of violence and how they deal with the aftermath of violence, including issues of rights and reconciliation. R. Scott Appleby (2000: 276) states that

> theologies of redemption have dramatic social consequences. Does the Christian minister pour energies and resources into facilitating reconciliation between peoples, or does he "save souls" by preaching acceptance of the atoning death of Christ on the cross? Both options are plausible within a Christian worldview, but they bespeak different interpretations of the divine will and different orientations to the world . . . [and] different pastoral goals and methods of dealing with conflict.[3]

The rediscovery of the power of the spirit and the surge of Pentecostal movements remind us of religion's enduring capacity to surprise, and they underscore the difficulty that institutions have in containing what people see as the expression of divine power. Harvey Cox argues that in its 2,000-year history, Christianity has passed from an Age of Faith (direct faith in Jesus) to an Age of Belief, with established, official creeds and catechisms "that replaced faith in Jesus with a series of tenets about him," to what he terms the Age of the Spirit, marked by rediscovery of the direct presence of divine power in the world (Cox 2009: 2). Because the spirit is inherently difficult to control ("it blows where it will," John 3:8), "the Spirit's inherent resistance to ecclesial fetters still vexes the prelates. But it also inspires Christians in what used to be called the 'third world' but is now termed the 'global south' by those living there, to discern the presence of God in other religions" (Cox 2009: 9). The dramatic expansion of Pentecostal forms of Christianity and their rediscovery within the Catholic Church impact society and politics without necessarily leading to the formation of specific social movements or political parties. These impacts fly under the radar of much political analysis. They rest on the promise of equality of all (all races, all genders, all nationalities) in the presence of the Spirit. They also emerge in the vigorous efforts to create voluntary associations that can energize civil society (Steigenga 2001: 147–154). To the extent that powerful leadership turns Pentecostal churches into something more like dynasties than democracies, this promise may not be fulfilled, but as Cox points out, it is always there in potential, difficult to predict or control.

Knowing About the Future

Throughout this book I have framed the issues in terms of the continuous mutual impact of changes in religion, society, and politics. Although change in each of these areas has autonomous sources and dynamics, they are not well considered in isolation from one another. There is constant interchange, borrowing, and mutual influence. Given our understanding of the sources and dynamics of change, of the patterns of transformation and the factors that give them sustained social power, how should we go about studying religion, society, and politics? What do we need to know to have reliable knowledge of likely and possible futures? How can we best find out what we need to know?

Political context, and the opportunities and challenges that politics presents, provide an essential medium through which religions make themselves felt in society. For this reason, if for no other, we need to pay close attention to society and politics, but two pitfalls must be avoided if analysis is to lead to reliable and accurate understanding. The first appears when scholars allow concerns about short-term crises or immediate political outcomes to dictate their research agenda. Whatever short-term outcomes may be, they are embedded in long-term processes that give shape and content to groups, issues, and conflicts as they arise and are worked out. A crisis-driven approach misses the full range of possibilities and runs the risk of ignoring the fact that short-term losers may well turn out to be long-term victors. The second is related and arises when scholars subordinate their research agenda to the concerns of states and policymakers. The dangers of this connection are evident in the recent work by Monica Duffy Toft, Daniel Philpott, and Timothy Samuel Shah, whose last chapter ("Rules for Surviving God's Century") is pitched to convincing policymakers of the need to take religion seriously and accept its institutional independence, lest they inadvertently enhance the likelihood of what these authors consider to be "pathological forms of religious politics" (Toft, Philpott, and Shah 2011: 220).

Toft, Philpott, and Shah specify ten rules:

1. Acknowledge that religious actors are here to stay;
2. Do not assume that the activism of religious actors can or should be restricted to a "private sphere";
3. Learn to live with the fact that the issue is not whether, but when and how, religious actors will enter public life and shape political outcomes;
4. Do not exaggerate the power of religious actors in public life, thereby replacing secularization with sacralization;
5. . . . but expect religious actors to play a larger and more pervasive role than conventional wisdom anticipates;

6. Accept that the more governments try to repress or exclude religion from public life, the more such efforts will be self-defeating;
7. Acknowledge that the more governments permit religious actors to be autonomous social actors in a system of consensual independence, the more religion will serve as a "force multiplier" for important social and political goods, including democratization, peacemaking, and reconciliation;
8. Take the religious beliefs and political theologies of religious actors seriously because they interact with political structure and context to explain much of the political behavior of religious actors;
9. Accept that if government fails to respect the institutional independence of religious actors, especially through systematic repression, the more these governments will encourage pathological forms of religious politics including religion-based terrorism and religion-related civil wars; and
10. Appreciate that there is strategic value in pursuing religious freedom in the conduct of foreign policy. (Toft, Philpott, and Shah 2011: 208–223)

Most of these rules are commonsense extrapolations from a review of contemporary events, and they can provide a helpful lens for sifting through the tangle of overblown news reporting, but as a group they provide little guidance to understanding the sources of change in religion that may lead to new and possibly what these authors label "pathological forms" of religious politics. The very definition of "pathological," like its opposite (religion as a "force multiplier" for desirable social and political goods), is subordinate to the optic of policymakers. These definitions are problematic for several reasons. That some outcomes are more desirable than others is taken for granted, and these are the outcomes favored by policymakers, particularly makers of US foreign policy, who constitute the authors' target audience. Toft, Philpott, and Shah also work with an undifferentiated view of "religion," which is treated as something of a black box, a source of great and potentially deadly energy, something like a volcanic force or a collection of rushing waters. If channeled and domesticated, the outcome will be good, a force multiplier. But if outlets are blocked or ignored, the danger of explosion or of a dam bursting is increased. This hydraulic metaphor, and the penumbra of threat and danger that surrounds it, reflect a perspective that has become common in much US scholarship, which sees religion as a source of peril. This has replaced the view that dominated in the 1950s, according to which religion was a prime source of common, unifying, and mostly benevolent values (Wuthnow 1988).

The problem with this view is that religions are not well understood in monolithic terms: close examination reveals considerable conflict and diversity. Moreover, subordinating analysis to the needs and agendas of policymakers risks turning short-term concerns into axioms, and reifying current configurations. Generalizations and "rules" of the kind advanced by Toft, Philpott, and Shah urgently need to be historicized. This is a fancy way of saying that they need to be placed in context. It is also essential to acknowledge that what concerns us is not wholly new: it has happened before. This does not mean that there is nothing new under the sun. The current scene does indeed present many new elements and configurations, but like their historical predecessors, the patterns and conflicts that we now see are also subject to change and unlikely to persist in these particular forms into the future.

An alternative strategy for knowing about the future of religion, society, and politics is to examine the kinds of arrangements put together in different societies to frame the relations of religion and politics. Alfred Stepan's (2003) work on the "twin tolerations" identifies different solutions that have been created that allow both religion and democratic politics to thrive, with provision for autonomous spaces, multiple linkages, and mutual accommodation.[4] At the margins, solutions of this kind bar both theocracy and an extreme laicism that subjects the public expression of religion to extremely limiting controls. This is an important and fruitful approach, but it has the disadvantage of taking states and religions more or less as given. In this book, I have focused less on the institutionalization of different kinds of accommodation than on prior shifts in ideas, organizational routines, and actors that may predispose religions to support and engage in democracy. This allows us to see how these accommodations (if they are at all possible) arise, how they find anchors and support in religion and in politics, and why they may or may not succeed or fail. The mixed record of religion with democracy, and its much better record as democracy itself has strengthened in Latin America, suggest that this is an ongoing effort.

A third possibility, which dominated much academic discourse in the 1990s and early 2000s, searched for keys to the future through the lens of "fundamentalism." The resurgence of fundamentalist groups in the United States and the shock of the Iranian Revolution sparked a search by scholars and policymakers for common threads that would help them interpret the world in ways that made a place for vigorous, conservatizing religious change. But the categories derived from the study of fundamentalism (among others, a focus on scriptural inerrancy, patriarchal leadership, antimodernism and longing to return to a lost golden age of idealized tradition) turned out to be less helpful than many had hoped (Appleby 2006; Marty and Appleby 1992). The central axis of growth of new religious movements in the global south has in any case not been fundamentalism, but rather the spirit-filled evangelical, Pentecostal, and neo-Pentecostal movements whose structures, routines, and social projections differ considerably from those commonly ascribed to fundamentalism. Concepts of fundamentalism have been particularly poor guides to understanding change in Latin America. Nancy Tatom Ammerman points out that "beliefs and practices rightly called 'fundamentalism' in the United States are more properly called 'innovation' south of the Rio Grande" (Ammerman 1994a: 14). "Unlike their North American counterparts," she writes, "they find that the evangelical part of their new identity is not part of the culture and must be transformed to make it really 'native.' In Latin America, evangelicals are hoping to forge newly redeemed national identities, not newly restored ones" (Ammerman 1994b: 153).

The perspective taken here differs substantially from those just outlined. Based on my understanding of Latin America, but situating Latin American experience in a broad theoretical and comparative context, I argue that the most reliable way to arrive at valid knowledge of the present and likely futures of religion, society, and politics is to direct attention to the conditions under which new ideas emerge, find agents and an audience, and have an impact in society, changing perspectives and behaviors as they evolve. This is a more complex matter than is allowed for by categories of fundamentalism or "pathologies of religious politics." Understanding this process requires us to attend simultaneously to ideas and their audience, and to ask why they find a hearing and move individuals and groups to action at any given moment. This approach sensitizes us to how religions can serve as something like a generative base for concepts that can later shape behavior in other areas of life, a subversive memory that persists with organizations and patterns of behavior that can sustain action over time, even in the face of considerable danger, until better times appear.[5]

The Likely Future of the Future

The period covered by this book brought a series of changes that have made Latin America a very different place from what it was only fifty years ago. Social transformations like accelerated urbanization, literacy, and media access have been accompanied by dramatic political changes and by a pattern of intense, continuing shifts in the religious field, all wrapped up in a process of considerable conflict and violence. If we think about these years as a period of transition from one dominant pattern of relations among religion, society, and politics to another, what can we say about the shape and content of likely futures? What comes next?

Although it is always risky to extrapolate from current trends into the future, some elements of continued transformation seem well established. In the twenty-first century, Christianity will remain dominant in Latin America, but the Christianity in question will clearly be very different from the past. It will be plural. New leaders, new organizations, and new forms of communication will continue to bring the message to changed publics. Competition among churches and denominations will intensify, in an ever broadening range of arenas and media. There will be continued diffusion of intense, spirit-filled forms of religious practice, growing independence of Latin American Protestant churches from northern sponsors, and an increasing projection beyond Latin America by these same churches as they carry their message elsewhere in the global south, and also to the north. Although Catholicism will likely remain the single biggest church, there will be no successful reconstruction of Catholic monopoly, and no major new confessional political parties of any affiliation. The political connections of the churches will be a lot less predictable than earlier scholarship had assumed.

The truth is that the days of spectacular, eye-catching political initiatives by religious actors or commitments of religious inspiration are over, at least for now. The association of intense religious change with a return to democracy and an open, less regulated civil society suggests a pullback from confrontational politics and renewed concern with conventional issues, including education, sexuality, and public morals. There will also be continued, intense competition for access to public platforms and to state subsidies that provide the churches with valued resources and much-sought-after markers of legitimacy. In any case, the ideas that grabbed headlines and stirred concerns in Washington about "red bishops" or "guerrilla priests" were never an accurate portrayal of a reality that was conflicted and divided, and certainly less radical than this portrait allowed for. The surge of prophetic initiatives in the 1970s and 1980s made sense in the context of the times, but times have changed, and the kind of religiously inspired political action that is now likely to emerge and take hold has much more modest dimensions. Those that survive from earlier periods, like Brazil's MST, have managed to create and sustain a coalition among religious activists, lay intellectuals, and an energized mass base that has acquired an identity of its own.

Toward the end of World War II, in response to a suggestion that the opinion of the Vatican be considered in arrangements for postwar Europe, Stalin is reported to have asked scornfully how many divisions the pope had. The analysis of this book makes clear that although popes and other religious leaders may not have massive armies at their command, they can wield extensive resources—material, ideological, and organizational. What makes Latin America and much of the global south so different now from as recently as fifty years ago is how much more plural and less easily controllable these resources are. If the dominance of Christianity per se in the region is not in question, what remains to be worked out is just how the churches and their followers will fill the less regulated and more democratic public spaces that Latin America is likely to present in the future. Religion and the churches are present in the private life and public spaces of Latin America now in very different ways from the past. There is more religion available in more forms. There is also a notable popularization of language and a diffusion of arenas for religious experience, evident not only in classic evangelical "campaigns and crusades" but also in the effective use of mass media, radio and television, and the adaptation of popular music, visible in the appeal of Christian rock and evangelical salsa (Luis Vázquez 2011). Because our subject matter is so dynamic, it is difficult to draw anything like a definitive balance. This is a moving target. There may well be an end to history at some point, but based on the road traveled thus far, it is not easy to discern what shape this final form may take. The most likely result is that whatever form the future takes will come as a surprise to many.

Does the pattern of religious change outlined here contribute in some measurable way to "modernization" or "development," however these notoriously imprecise terms may be defined? The question has no clear or unequivocal answer. This is not to say that Latin American societies, or their varied religious experience, may therefore be properly classified as *traditional* or *nonmodern*, much less *non-Western*. Latin America has been part of the Western world from the very beginning, but of course it is the Iberian version of that world that set the tone and established the dominant institutional patterns. Latin America is nothing if not varied, and concepts like *tradition* and *traditional* are clearly inadequate for a continent that displays such accelerated urbanization; relatively high rates of literacy, education, and media penetration; and one of the largest and most dynamic economies in the world (Brazil).

The question is better phrased as one that addresses the specific ways in which religious change participates in—drawing strength, accelerating, and in some instances providing shelter from—the overall pattern of political, social, cultural, demographic, and economic transformation commonly conflated under the heading of "modernization and development." When "all that is solid melts into air,"[6] religion need not disappear (as classical secularization theory anticipated) but can itself change in ways that use the tools of modernity and mass communication to continue the core religious project, placing individual and proximate acts in contexts of ultimate significance and building meaningful communities, in a world that is very different from the one Columbus imagined he was finding when he searched for the Indies but landed in what came to be called America.

Notes

1. The crew for Columbus's first voyage was drawn from sailors of Palos de la Frontera.

2. As Ivan Illich memorably put it, "The less efficient the Church is as a power, the more effective She is as a celebrant of the mystery" (quoted in du Plessix Gray, 1969: 285).

3. Appleby points to three models of conflict transformation that flow from these positions, each the expression of a lived religious witness, each likely to produce its own distinct political or social consequences: *Spiritualist,* a self-authenticating Gospel mandate, an end in itself. Fostering dialogue among peoples is *the* Christian way of life. *Conversionists* seek to bring the world more in conformity with the reign of God in Jesus Christ, primarily by spreading the good news of salvation and, where possible, converting people to Christianity. *Liberationists* "seek to usher in a nonsectarian, inclusive order of social and economic justice, that they believe to be the *sine qua non* of lasting peace. . . . The cutting edge for liberationists is 'holistic community development,' an approach that entails paying close attention to social relations among community members of different religious, ethnic or tribal backgrounds; to their spiritual and psychological need and cultural trends, and to their material needs" (Appleby 2000: 277, 278).

4. Cf. Buruma 2010, which compares what the author calls Western, Oriental, and Enlightenment solutions to the problem of combining religion with democracy.

5. James Scott writes that "just as millions of anthozoan polyps create, willy-nilly, a coral reef, so do thousands upon thousands of individual acts of insubordination and evasion create a political or economic barrier reef of its own. It is largely in this fashion that the peasantry makes its political presence felt. And whenever, to continue the simile, the ship of state runs aground on such reefs, attention is usually paid to the shipwreck itself, and not to the vast aggregation of petty acts that made it possible" (Scott 1985: 36).

6. The phrase comes from Marx's description of the impact of capitalism on traditional life. See Berman 1982 for a stimulating discussion of the cultural aspects of modernity.

Acronyms

AMIA	Argentine Jewish Mutual Aid Association, Asociación Mutual Israelita Argentina
ANC	African National Congress
APRA	American Revolutionary Popular Alliance
ASE	Annuarium Estadisticum Ecclesiae
CCR	Catholic Charismatic Renewal
CEAS	Episcopal Commission for Social Action, Comisión Episcopal de Acción Social
CEB	ecclesial base community, comunidad eclesial de base
CEH	Commission on Historical Clarification, Comisión de Esclarecimiento Histórico
CELAM	Council of Latin American Bishops, Consejo Episcopal Latinoamericana
CEPLA	Latin American Evangelical Pentecostal Commission, Comisión Evangélica Pentecostal Latinoamericana
CIPAE	Committee of Churches for Emergency Help, Comité de Iglesias Para Ayudas de Emergencia
CLAI	Latin American Council of Churches, Consejo Latinoamericano de Iglesias
CLAR	Confederation of Latin American Religious Orders, Confederación Latinoamericana de Religiosos
CONADEP	National Commission on the Disappearance of Persons, Comisión Nacional Sobre la Desaparición de Personas
CONELA	Latin American Evangelical Fellowship, Confraternidad Latinoamericana Evangélica

CONEP	National Council of Evangelicals of Peru, Concilio Nacional de Evangélicos del Perú
CONFER	Confederation of Religious Orders of Peru, Confederación de Religiosos del Perú
COPACHI	Committee of Cooperation for Peace in Chile, Comité de Cooperación para la Paz en Chile
CORE	Congress of Racial Equality
CVR	National Commission on Truth and Reconciliation, Comisión de la Verdad y Reconciliación
DUP	Democratic Unionist Party
ELN	National Liberation Army, Ejército Nacional de Liberación
ERP	Revolutionary Army of the People, Ejército Revolucionario del Pueblo
FASIC	Protestant Foundation of Social Support of the Churches, Fundación de Ayuda Social de las Iglesias Cristianas
FIS	Islamic Salvation Front, Front Islamique du Salut
FMLN	Farabundo Martí National Liberation Front, Frente Farabundo Martí para la Liberación Nacional
FOR	Fellowship of Reconciliation
GIA	Armed Islamic Group, Groupe Islamique Armée
IURD	Church of the Universal Reign of God, Igreja Universal do Reino de Deus
MST	landless movement, Movimento Sem Terra
MSTM	Movement of Priests for the Third World, Movimiento de Sacerdotes para el Tercer Mundo
NGO	nongovernmental organization
PRB	Population Reference Bureau
SCLC	Southern Christian Leadership Conference
SERPAJ-AL	Service for Peace and Justice in Latin America, Servicio de Paz y Justicia–America Latina
SIDE	Secretariat for State Information, Secretaría de Informaciones del Estado
SIL	Summer Institute of Linguistics
VES	Villa El Salvador
WCD	World Christian Database

Bibliography

Acha, Elisabeth. 2006. "Todos Se Fueron, Nosotros Decidimos Quedarnos, Iglesia y Conflicto Armado Interno en Pucallpa." Pp. 77–156 in Cecilia Tovar, ed., *Ser Iglesia en Tiempos de Violencia*. Lima: CEP.

Adorno, Theodor. 1967. *Prisms*. Translated by Samuel and Shierry Weber. Cambridge: MIT Press.

Aguilar, Mario I. 2003. "Cardinal Raúl Silva Henríquez, the Catholic Church, and the Pinochet Regime, 1973–1980: Public Responses to a National Security State." *The Catholic Historical Review* 89 (4): 712–731.

———. 2006. "The Mesa de Diálogo and the Fate of the Disappeared in Chile, 1999–2000: National Forgiveness Without Political Truth." Pp. 41–56 in Iain S. Maclean, ed., *Reconciliation: Nations and Churches in Latin America*. London: Ashgate.

Ajami, Fouad. 1986. *The Vanished Imam: Musa al Sadr and the Shia of Lebanon*. Ithaca: Cornell University Press.

Algranti, Joaquín M. 2010. *Política y Religión en los Márgenes: Nuevas Formas de Participación Social de las Mega Iglesias Evangélicas en la Argentina*. Buenos Aires: Ediciones Ciccus.

Ammerman, Nancy Tatom. 1994a. "Telling Congregational Stories." *Review of Religious Research* 35 (4).

———. 1994b. "The Dynamics of Christian Fundamentalism: An Introduction." Pp. 13–17 in Martin Marty and R. Scott Appleby, eds., *Accounting for Fundamentalisms: The Dynamic Character of Movements*. Chicago: University of Chicago Press.

———. 1994c. "Accounting for Christian Fundamentalisms: Social Dynamics and Rhetorical Strategies." Pp. 149–170 in Martin Marty and R. Scott Appleby, eds., *Accounting for Fundamentalisms: The Dynamic Character of Movements*. Chicago: University of Chicago Press.

———. 1996. *Congregation and Community*. New Brunswick, NJ: Rutgers University Press.

Anderson, Leslie A. 2010. *Social Capital in Developing Democracies: Nicaragua and Argentina Compared*. New York: Cambridge University Press.

Annis, Sheldon. 1987. *God and Production in a Guatemalan Town.* Austin: University of Texas Press.

Anonymous. 1981. *Morir y Despertar en Guatemala,* Part 2, "Presencia de la Iglesia." Lima.

Appleby, R. Scott. 2000. *The Ambivalence of the Sacred: Religion, Violence, and Reconciliation.* New York: Rowman and Littlefield.

———. 2006. "What's in a Name? 'Fundamentalism' and the Discourse About Religion." Pp. 87–103 in James Boyd White, ed., *How Should We Talk About Religion? Perspectives, Contexts, Particularities.* Notre Dame: University of Notre Dame Press.

Archdiocese of Lima, Comisión Episcopal de Acción Social (CEAS). 1990. *La Iglesia Católica en el Campo Peruano en la Década del 80 Elementos para una Evaluación.* Lima: CEAS Departmento Campesino.

Archdiocese de São Paulo. 1998. *Torture in Brazil: A Shocking Report on the Pervasive Use of Torture by Brazilian Military Governments, 1964–1979.* Translated by Jaime Wright. Austin: University of Texas Press (translation of *Brasil: Nunca Mais*).

Argentine National Commission on the Disappeared. 1986. *Nunca Mas.* New York: Farrar, Straus and Giroux.

Arguedas Ramírez, Gabriela. 2010. "El Aún Tortuoso Camino Hacia la Emancipación." Presented at the meetings of the Latin American Studies Association, Toronto, Canada.

Arjomand, Said. 1995. "Unity and Diversity in Islamic Fundamentalism." Pp. 179–198 in Martin Marty and R. Scott Appleby, eds., *Fundamentalisms Comprehended.* Chicago: University of Chicago Press.

Arnson, Cynthia. 2011. Testimony Before the Senate Foreign Relations Committee, Subcommittee on the Western Hemisphere, Peace Corps and Global Narcotics Affairs, March 31, Washington, DC.

Austin, Diane J. 1981. "Born Again . . . and Again and Again: Comunitas and Social Change Among Jamaican Pentecostalists." *Journal of Anthropological Research* 37 (3): 226–246.

Avritzer, Leonardo. 2002. *Democracy and the Public Space in Latin America.* Princeton, NJ: Princeton University Press.

Ayres, Alyssa. 2007. "Religious Violence Beyond Borders: Reframing South Asian Cases." Pp. 105–121 in Linell E. Cady and Sheldon W. Simon, eds., *Religion and Conflict in Southeast Asia: Disrupting Violence.* New York: Routledge.

Barrett, David B., George T. Kurian, and Todd M. Johnson. 2001. *World Christian Encyclopedia: A Comparative Survey of Churches and Religions in the Modern World,* 2nd ed. Oxford: Oxford University Press.

Barrionuevo, Alexei. 2011. "A Child of War Discovers 'Dad' Is Parents' Killer." *New York Times,* October 9, p. 1.

Bartee, Wayne. 2000. *A Time to Speak Out: The Leipzig Citizen Protests and the Fall of East Germany.* London: Praeger.

Bastián, Jean Pierre. 1993. "The Metamorphosis of Latin American Protestant Groups: A Sociohistorical Perspective." *Latin American Research Review* 38 (2): 33–62.

———. 1997. *La Mutación Religiosa de América Latina. Para una Sociología del Cambio Religioso en la Modernidad Periférica.* Mexico Fondo de Cultura Económica.

Bayard de Volo, Lorraine. 2001. *Mothers of Heroes and Martyrs*. Baltimore: Johns Hopkins University Press.

Becker, David, Elizabeth Lira, Isabel Castillo, Elena Gómez, and Juana Kovalskys. 1990. "Therapy with Victims of Political Repression in Chile: The Challenge of Social Reparation." *Journal of Social Issues* 46 (3): 133–149.

Beinart, William, and Colin Bundy. 1987. *Hidden Struggles in Rural South Africa. Politics and Popular Movements in the Transkei and Eastern Cape, 1890–1930*. London: J. Currey.

Berman, Marshall. 1982. *All That Is Solid Melts into Air: The Experience of Modernity*. New York: Simon and Schuster.

Berryman, Philip. 1984. *Religious Roots of Rebellion: Christians in the Central American Revolutions*. Maryknoll, NY: Orbis Books.

———. 1987. *Liberation Theology: Essential Facts About the Revolutionary Movement in Latin America and Beyond*. Philadelphia: Pantheon.

———. 1995a. *Stubborn Hope: Religion, Politics, and Revolution in Central America*. Maryknoll, NY: Orbis Books.

———. 1995b. "Is Latin America Turning Pluralist? Recent Writings on Religion." *Latin American Research Review* 30 (3): 107–122.

———. 1996. *Religion in the Megacity: Catholic and Protestant Portraits from Latin America*. Maryknoll, NY: Orbis Books.

———. 1999. "Churches as Winners and Losers in the Network Society." *Journal of Interamerican Studies and World Affairs* 41 (4): 21–34.

Betances, Emilio. 2007. *The Catholic Church and Power Politics in Latin America: The Dominican Case in Comparative Perspective*. Lanham, MD: Rowman and Littlefield.

Bethge, Eberhard. 2000. *Dietrich Bonhoeffer: A Biography*. Minneapolis: Fortress.

———. 2005. *Friendship and Resistance: Essays on Dietrich Bonhoeffer*. Geneva: WCC Publications.

Blancarte, Roberto J. 2000. "Popular Religion, Catholicism, and Socioreligious Dissent in Latin America: Facing the Modernity Paradigm." *International Sociology* 15 (4): 591–603.

———. 2009. "The Changing Face of Religion in the Democratization of Mexico: The Case of Catholicism." Pp. 223–256 in Frances Hagopian, ed., *Religious Pluralism, Democracy, and the Catholic Church in Latin America*. Notre Dame, IN: University of Notre Dame Press.

Blondet, Cecilia. 1991. *Las Mujeres y el Poder. Una Historia de Villa el Salvador*. Lima: Instituto de Estudios Peruanos.

Blondet, Cecilia, and Carolina Trivelli. 2004. *Cucharas en Alto. Del Asistencialismo al Desarrollo Local: Fortaleciendo la Participacion de las Mujeres*. Lima: Instituto de Estudios Peruanos.

Boff, Leonardo, and Clodovis Boff. 1986. *Liberation Theology from Confrontation to Dialogue*. San Francisco: Harper and Row.

Bolce, Louis, and Gerald De Maio. 2007. "Secularists, Antifundamentalists, and the New Religious Divide in the American Electorate." Pp. 251–276 in J. Matthew Wilson, ed., *From Pews to Polling Places: Faith and Politics in the American Religious Mosaic*. Washington, DC: Georgetown University Press.

Bonhoeffer, Dietrich. 1959. *The Cost of Discipleship*. New York: SCM Press.

———. 1995. *Dietrich Bonhoeffer: Selected Writings* (edited by Edwin Robertson). London: Harper Collins Publishers.

Bonilla, Victor Daniel. 1972. *Servants of God or Masters of Men: The Story of a Capuchin Mission in Amazonia.* New York: Penguin.

Bonnin, Juan Eduardo. 2010. *Iglesia y Democracia. Táctica y Estrategia en el Discurso de la Conferencia Episcopal Argentina (1981–1990).* Buenos Aires Ceil-Piette, Informe de Investigación No. 24.

Borer, Tristan. 1998. *Churches and Political Action in South Africa.* Notre Dame, IN: University of Notre Dame Press.

Boyer, Peter. 2005. "A Hard Faith: How the New Pope and His Predecessor Redefined Vatican II." *New Yorker,* May 16.

Branch, Taylor. 1988. *Parting the Waters: America in the King Years, 1954–1963.* New York: Simon and Schuster.

———. 1998. *Pillar of Fire: America in the King Years, 1963–1965.* New York: Simon and Schuster.

———. 2008. *At Canaan's Edge: America in the King Years, 1965–1968.* New York: Simon and Schuster.

Brea, Jorge A. 2003. "Population Dynamics in Latin America." *Population Bulletin* 58 (1): 3–36.

Brienza, Hernan. 2003. *El Caso von Wernich. Maldito tú Eres, Iglesia y Represión Ilegal.* Buenos Aires: Editorial Marea.

———. 2007. *Camilo Torres: Sacristán de la Guerrilla.* Buenos Aires Capital Intelectual Colección Fundadores de la Izquierda Latinoamericana.

Brinks, Daniel. 2008. *The Judicial Response to Police Killings in Latin America.* Cambridge: Cambridge University Press.

———. 2010. "Violencia de Estado a Treinta Años de la Democracia en América Latina." *Journal of Democracy en Español* 2 (July): 10–27.

Broderick, Walter J. 2002. *Camilo Torres: Escritos Politicos.* Bogotá: El Ancora Editores.

Browning, Don, Bonnie J. Miller-McLemore, Pamela D. Couture, K. Brynolf Lyon, and Robert M. Franklin. 1997. *From Culture Wars to Common Ground.* Louisville: Westminster John Knox Press.

Bruce, Steve. 2009. *Paisley: Religion and Politics in Northern Ireland.* Oxford: Oxford University Press.

———. 2010. *Secularization.* Oxford: Oxford University Press.

Bruneau, Thomas C. 1974. *The Political Transformation of the Brazilian Catholic Church.* Cambridge: Cambridge University Press.

———. 1982. *The Church in Brazil: The Politics of Religion.* Austin: University of Texas Press.

Bruneau, Thomas C., and Warren E. Hewitt. 1992. "Catholicism and Political Action in Brazil: Limitations and Prospects." Pp. 45–62 in Edward L. Cleary and Hannah Stewart-Gambino, eds., *Conflict and Competition: The Latin American Church in a Changing Environment.* Boulder, CO: Lynne Rienner.

Brysk, Alison. 2000. *From Tribal Village to Global Village: Indian Rights and International Relations in Latin America.* Stanford: Stanford University Press.

———. 2004. "From Civil Society to Collective Action: The Politics of Religion in Ecuador." Pp. 25–40 in Edward L. Cleary and Timothy Steigenga, eds., *Resurgent Voices in Latin America: Indigenous Peoples, Political Mobilization, and Religious Change.* New Brunswick, NJ: Rutgers University Press.

Burdick, John. 1993. *Looking for God in Brazil.* Berkeley: University of California Press.

————. 2004. *Legacies of Liberation: The Progressive Catholic Church in Brazil at the Start of a New Millennium*. London: Ashgate.

Burdick, Michael. 1995. *For God and the Fatherland: Religion and Politics in Argentina*. Albany: State University of New York Press.

Burgerman, Susan. 2001. *Moral Victories: How Activists Provoke Multilateral Action*. Ithaca, NY: Cornell University Press.

Burity, Joanildo, and Maria Dos Dolores C. Machado, eds. 2006. *Os Votos de Deus: Evangelicos, Politica e Elecioes no Brasil*. Recife, Brazil: Fundacao Joaquim Nabuco.

Buruma, Ian. 2010. *Taming the Gods: Religion and Democracy on Three Continents*. Princeton, NJ: Princeton University Press.

Byrnes, Timothy A. 2001. *Transnational Catholicism in Postcommunist Europe*. Lanham, MD: Rowman and and Littlefield.

————. 2011. *Reverse Mission: Transnational Religious Communities and the Making of US Foreign Policy*. Washington, DC: Georgetown University Press.

Cáceres, Jorge. 1989. "Political Radicalization and Popular Pastoral Practices in El Salvador, 1969–1985." Pp. 103–148 in Scott Mainwaring and Alexander W. Wilde, eds., *The Progressive Church in Latin America*. Notre Dame, IN: University of Notre Dame Press.

Cady, Linell E., and Sheldon W. Simon, eds. 2007. *Religion and Conflict in South and Southeast Asia: Disrupting Violence*. New York: Routledge.

Caimari, Lila. 1994. *Peron y la Iglesia Católica Religión, Estado y Sociedad en la Argentina (1943–1955)*. Buenos Aires: Emece.

Camp, Roderic Ai. 1994. "The Cross in the Polling Booth: Religion, Politics, and the Laity in Mexico." *Latin American Research Review* 29 (3): 69–100.

————. 1996. *Crossing Swords: Religion and Politics in Mexico*. New York: Oxford University Press.

————. 2008. "Exercising Political Influence, Religion, Democracy, and the Mexican 2006 Presidential Race." *Journal of Church and State* 50 (1): 49–72.

Carter, Miguel. 1990. "The Role of the Catholic Church in the Downfall of the Stroessner Regime." *Journal of Interamerican Studies and World Affairs* 32 (4): 67–121.

————. 1991. *El Papel de la Iglesia en la Caída de Stroessner*. Asunción: RP Ediciones.

————. 2003. "The Origins of Brazil's Landless Rural Workers' Movement (MST): The Natalino Episode in Rio Grande do Sul (1981–84). A Case of Ideal Interest Mobilization." Oxford: University of Oxford Centre for Brazilian Studies, Working Paper Series CBS 43-2003.

————. 2010. "The Landless Worker's Movement and Democracy in Brazil." *Latin American Research Review* (Special Issue): 186–217.

————. 2012. *For Land, Love and Justice: The Origins of Brazil's Landless Social Movement*. Durham, NC: Duke University Press.

Carter, Stephen. 1993. *The Culture of Disbelief: How American Law and Politics Trivialize Religion*. New York: Anchor Books.

————. 2000. *God's Name in Vain: The Rights and Wrongs of Religion in Politics*. New York: Basic Books.

Casanova, José. 1994. *Public Religions in the Modern World*. Chicago: University of Chicago Press.

————. 2001. "Civil Society and Religion: Retrospective Reflections on Catholicism and Prospective Reflections on Islam." *Social Research* 65 (4): 1041–1080.

Castro Aguilar, Rosa. 2001. "Faith and Citizenship: Local Catholic Experiences in Peruvian Communities." Pp. 1–22 in Anna L. Peterson, Manuel A. Vásquez, and Philip J. Williams, eds., *Christianity, Social Change, and Globalization in the Americas.* New Brunswick, NJ: Rutgers University Press.

Catoggio, Maria Soledad. 2006. "Violencia, Censura, Gobierno y Castigo en el Caso de la Llamada 'Biblia Latinoamericana': Una Perspectiva Foucaultiana." *E Latina Revista Electronica de Estudios Latinoamericanas* 4 (14): 3–24.

————. 2008a. "Gestión y Regulación de la Diversidad Religiosa. Políticas de 'Reconocimiento' Estatal: El Registro Nacional de Cultos." Pp. 105–115 in Fortunato Mallimaci, ed., *Religión y Políitica Perspectivas America Latina Europa.* Buenos Aires: Biblos.

————. 2008b. "Movimiento de Sacerdotes para el Tercer Mundo y Servicios de Inteligencia, 1969–1970." *Sociedad y Religión* 17 (30–31): 171–189.

————. 2010. "Cambios de Hábito: Trayectorias de Religiosas Durante la Ultima Dictadura Militar." *Latin American Research Review* 45: 27–48.

————. 2011. "Contestatarios, Mártires, y Herederos: Sociabilidades Político Religiosos y Ascesis Altruista del Catolicismo Argentino en la Dictadura y la Pos Dictadura." PhD thesis, Universidad de Buenos Aires, Facultad de Sociología.

Chapman, Audrey. 2001. "Truth Commissions as Instruments of Forgiveness and Reconciliation." Pp. 257–277 in Raymond G. Helmick and Rodney L. Petersen, eds., *Forgiveness and Reconciliation: Religion, Public Policy, and Conflict Transformation.* West Conshohocken, PA: Templeton Foundation Press.

Chesnut, R. Andrew. 1997. *Born Again in Brazil: The Pentecostal Boom and the Pathogens of Poverty.* New Brunswick, NJ: Rutgers University Press.

————. 2003. *Competitive Spirits: Latin America's New Religious Economy.* New York: Oxford University Press.

————. 2011. *Devoted to Death: Santa Muerte, the Skeleton Saint.* New York: Oxford University Press.

Cleary, Edward L. 1989. *Paths from Puebla: Significant Documents of the Latin American Bishops Since 1979.* Translated by Philip Berryman. Washington, DC: US Catholic Conference.

————. 1992. "Evangelicals and Competition in Guatemala." In Edward L. Cleary and Hannah Stewart Gambino, eds., *The Latin American Church in a Changing Environment.* Lanham, MD: Rowman and Littlefield.

————. 2004a. "Shopping Around: Questions About Latin American Conversions." *International Bulletin of Missionary Research* 28 (2): 50–54.

————. 2004b. "New Voices in Religion and Politics in Bolivia and Peru." Pp. 43–64 in Edward L. Cleary and Timothy J. Steigenga, eds., *Resurgent Voices in Latin America: Indigenous Peoples, Political Mobilization, and Religious Change.* New Brunswick, NJ: Rutgers University Press.

————. 2007. *Mobilizing for Human Rights in Latin America.* Bloomfield, CT: Kumarian Press.

————. 2009. *How Latin America Saved the Soul of the Catholic Church.* Mahwah, NJ: Paulist Press.

———. 2011. *The Rise of Charismatic Catholicism in Latin America*. Gainesville: University Press of Florida.

Cleary, Edward L., and Juan Sepulveda. 1997. "Chilean Pentecostals: Coming of Age." Pp. 97–122 in Edward L. Cleary and Hannah Stewart-Gambino, eds., *Power, Politics, and Pentecostals in Latin America*. Boulder, CO: Westview.

Cleary, Edward L., and Timothy J. Steigenga, eds. 2004a. *Resurgent Voices in Latin America: Indigenous Peoples, Political Mobilization, and Religious Change*. New Brunswick, NJ: Rutgers University Press.

———. 2004b. "Resurgent Voices: Indians, Politics, and Religion in Latin America." Pp. 1–24 in Edward L. Cleary and Timothy J. Steigenga, eds., *Resurgent Voices in Latin America: Indigenous Peoples, Political Mobilization, and Religious Change*. New Brunswick, NJ: Rutgers University Press.

Cleary, Edward L., and Hannah Stewart-Gambino, eds. 1992. *Conflict and Competition: The Latin American Church in a Changing Environment*. Lanham, MD: Rowman and Littlefield.

———. 1997. *Power, Politics, and Pentecostals in Latin America*. Boulder, CO: Westview.

Coleman, James. 1990. *Foundations of Social Theory*. Cambridge: Harvard University Press.

Coleman, John A. 2003. "Religious Social Capital: Its Nature, Location, and Limits." Pp. 33–48 in Corwin Smidt, ed., *Religion as Social Capital: Producing the Common Good*. Waco, TX: Baylor University Press.

Coleman, Kenneth, Edwin E. Aguilar, José M. Sandoval, and Timothy J. Steigenga. 1993. "Protestantism in El Salvador: Conventional Wisdom Versus the Survey Evidence." Pp. 20–44 in Virginia Garrard-Burnett and David Stoll, eds., *Rethinking Protestantism in Latin America*. Philadelphia: Temple University Press.

Comaroff, Jean. 1985. *Body of Power, Spirit of Resistance: The Culture and History of a South African People*. Chicago: University of Chicago Press.

Comisión de la Verdad y Reconciliación, Peru. 2004. *Hatun Willakuy Versión Abreviada del Informe Final de la Comisión de la Verdad y Reconcilación*. Lima.

Comisión Episcopal de Acción Social (CEAS). 1990. *La Iglesia Católica en el Campo Peruano en la Década del 80. Elementos Para una Evaluación*. Lima: CEAS, Departamento Campesino.

Conaghan, Catherine. 2005. *Fujimori's Peru: Deception in the Public Sphere*. Pittsburgh: University of Pittsburgh Press.

Cotler, Julio. 1992. *Clase, Estado, y Nación en el Perú*. Lima: Instituto de Estudios Peruanos.

Cousineau, Madeleine. 1986. *Opting for the Poor: Brazilian Catholicism in Transition*. New York: Sheed and Ward.

———. 1995. *Promised Land: Base Christian Communities and the Struggle for the Amazon*. Albany: State University of New York Press.

———. 2003. "'Not Blaming the Pope': The Roots of the Crisis in Brazilian Base Communities." *Journal of Church and State* 45 (2): 349–365.

Cox, Harvey. 1995. *Fire from Heaven: The Rise of Pentecostal Spirituality and the Reshaping of Religion in the Twenty-First Century*. Reading, MA: Addison-Wesley.

———. 2009. *The Future of Faith*. New York: HarperCollins.

Da Costa, Nestor. 2003. *Religión y Sociedad en el Uruguay del Siglo XXI. Un Estudio de la Religiosidad en Montevideo.* Montevideo: CLAEH, Centro UNESCO de Montevideo.

———. 2009. "La Laicidad Uruguaya." *Archives de Sciences Sociales des Religions* 146 (April–June): 137–155.

Dahl, Robert A. 1971. *Polyarchy: Participation and Opposition.* New Haven: Yale University Press.

———. 2002. *How Democratic Is the American Constitution?* New Haven, CT: Yale University Press.

Dawkins, Richard. 2008. *The God Delusion.* New York: Mariner Books.

De Biasi, Martín. 2010. *Entre Dos Fuegos. Vida y Asesinato del Padre Mugica,* 2nd ed. Buenos Aires: Cooperativa de Trabajo Editora Patria Grande.

De Gregori, Carlos Ivan. 1985. *Sendero Luminoso I. Los Hondos y Mortales Desencuentros, II La Utopia Autoritaria.* Lima: Instituto de Estudios Peruanos.

———. 1989. *Que Dificil es Ser Dios. Ideología y Violencia Política en Sendero Luminoso.* Lima: El Zorro de Abajo.

De Gregori, Carlos Ivan, Cecilia Blondet, and Nicolás Lynch. 1986. *Conquistadores de un Nuevo Mundo. De Invasores a Ciudadanos en San Martín de Porres.* Lima: Instituto de Estudios Peruanos.

Deiros, Pablo. 1991. "Protestant Fundamentalism in Latin America." Pp. 142–196 in Martin Marty and R. Scott Appleby, eds., *Fundamentalisms Observed.* Chicago: University of Chicago Press.

Della Cava, Ralph. 1968. "Brazilian Messianism and National Institutions: A Reappraisal of Canudos and Joaseiro." *Hispanic American Historical Review* 48 (3): 402–420.

———. 1992. "Vatican Policy 1978–90: An Updated Overview." *Social Research* 59 (1): 169–199.

———. 1993. "Thinking About Vatican Policy in Central and Eastern Europe and the Utility of the Brazilian Paradigm." *Journal of Latin American Studies* 25 (2): 257–282.

Devoto, Fernando J. 2002. *Nacionalismo, Fascismo, y Tradicionalismo en la Argentina Moderna. Una Historia.* Buenos Aires: Siglo XXI Editora Iberoamericana.

Dodson, Michael, and Laura Nuzzi O'Shaughnessy. 1990. *Nicaragua's Other Revolution: Religious Faith and Political Struggle.* Chapel Hill: University of North Carolina Press.

Doimo, Ana María. 1989. "Social Movements and the Catholic Church in Vitória Brazil." Pp. 193–327 in Scott Mainwaring and Alexander W. Wilde, eds., *The Progressive Church in Latin America.* Notre Dame, IN: University of Notre Dame Press.

Donatello, Luis Miguel. 2008. "La Ultima Dictadura Militar Como Problema Teólogico Militar." Pp. 169–182 in Fortuanto Mallimaci, ed., *Modernidad Religión y Memoria.* Buenos Aires: Colihue Universidad.

———. 2010. *Catolicismo y Montoneros: Religión, Política y Desencanto.* Buenos Aires: Manantial.

Drogus, Carol Ann. 1990. "Reconstructing the Feminine: Women in São Paulo's CEBs." *Archives de Sciences Sociales des Religion* 71 (July–September): 63–74.

————. 1995. "The Rise and Decline of Liberation Theology: Churches, Faith, and Political Change in Latin America." *Comparative Politics* 27 (4): 465–477.

————. 1997a. *Women, Religion, and Social Change in Brazil's Popular Church.* Notre Dame, IN: University of Notre Dame Press.

————. 1997b. "Private Power or Public Power: Pentecostalism, Base Communities, and Gender." Pp. 55–75 in Edward L. Cleary and Hannah Stewart-Gambino, eds., *Power, Politics, and Pentecostals in Latin America.* Boulder, CO: Westview.

————. 1999. "No Land of Milk and Honey." *Journal of Interamerican Studies and World Affairs* 41 (4): 35–51.

Drogus, Carol Ann, and Hannah Stewart-Gambino. 2005. *Activist Faith: Popular Women Activists and Their Movements in Democratic Brazil and Chile.* University Park: Pennsylvania State University Press.

Drzewieniecki, Joanna. 2001. "Coordinadora Nacional de Derechos Humanos: Un Estudio de Caso." In *Cuadernos de Investigación Social.* Lima: Departamento de Ciencias Sociales Pontificia Universidad Católica del Perú, Cuaderno 17.

Dugger, Celia W. 2009. "Mugabe Aides Are Accused of Terror in Amnesty Bid." *New York Times,* April 10.

du Plessix Gray, Francine. 1969. *Divine Disobedience: Profiles in Catholic Radicalism.* New York: Vintage Books.

Durkheim, Emile. 2008. *The Elementary Forms of Religious Life.* Translated by Carol Cosman. New York: Oxford World Classics.

Eckstein, Susan. 2001. *Power and Popular Protest: Latin American Social Movements.* Berkeley: University of California Press.

Eickelman, Dale, and James Piscatori. 2004. *Muslim Politics.* Princeton: Princeton University Press.

Elorrio, Juan Garcia. 1967. "Bajo el Signo de Camilo," *Cristianismo y Revolución,* No. 4. Cited on p. 12 in Hernan Brienza, *Camilo Torres Sacristan de la Guerrilla.* Buenos Aires: Capital Intelectual Colección Fundadores de la Izquierda Latinoamericana.

Elshtain, Jean B. 2009. "Religion and Democracy." *Journal of Democracy* 20 (2): 5–17.

Embree, Ainslee T. 1994. "The Function of the Rashtriya Swayamsevak Sangh: Defining the Hindu Nation." Pp. 653–668 in Martin Marty and R. Scott Appleby, eds., *Accounting for Fundamentalisms: The Dynamic Character of Movements.* Chicago: University of Chicago Press.

Esquivel, Juan Cruz. 2009. "Cultura Política y Poder Eclesiástico. Encrucijadas para la Construcción del Estado Laico en Argentina." *Archives de Sciences Sociales des Religions* 146 (April–June): 41–59.

Falla, Ricardo. 2001. *Quiché Rebelde: Religious Conversion, Politics, and Ethnic Identity in Guatemala.* Translated by Philip Berryman. Austin: University of Texas Press.

Feinberg, Richard, Carlos Waisman, and Leon Zamosc. 2006. *Civil Society and Democracy in Latin America.* New York: Palgrave Macmillan.

Feitlowitz, Marguerite. 1988. *A Lexicon of Terror: Argentina and the Legacies of Torture.* New York: Oxford University Press.

Ferguson, Sam. 2007. "Priest Convicted in Argentine 'Dirty War' Tribunal." *Truthout Report,* October 10.

Ferrari, Lisa L. 2006. "The Vatican as a Transnational Actor." Pp. 33–50 in Paul Christopher Manuel, Lawrence C. Reardon, and Clyde Wilcox, eds., *The Catholic Church and the Nation-State: Comparative Perspectives*. Washington, DC: Georgetown University Press.

Fields, Karen. 1985. *Revival and Rebellion in Colonial Central Africa*. Princeton, NJ: Princeton University Press.

Fink, Christina. 2009. "The Movement of the Monks: Burma, 2007." Pp. 354–370 in Adam Roberts and Timothy Garton Ash, eds., *Civil Resistance and Power Politics: The Experience of Non-Violent Action from Gandhi to the Present*. New York: Oxford University Press.

Finke, Roger, and Rodney Stark. 2005. *The Churching of America, 1776–2005: Winners and Losers in Our Religious Economy*. New Brunswick, NJ: Rutgers University Press.

Fleet, Michael H., and Brian H. Smith. 1997. *The Catholic Church and Democracy in Chile and Peru*. Notre Dame, IN: University of Notre Dame Press.

Fonseca, Alejandro. 2008. "Religion and Democracy in Brazil: A Study of the Leading Evangelical Politicians, 1998–2001." Pp. 163–206 in Paul Freston, ed., *Evangelical Christianity and Democracy in Latin America*. New York: Oxford University Press.

Fox, Jonathan. 1996. "How Does Civil Society Thicken? The Political Construction of Social Capital in Rural Mexico." *World Development* 24 (6): 1089–1103.

———. 2004. "Empowerment and Institutional Change: Mapping 'Virtuous Circles' of State-Society Interaction." Pp. 68–92 in Ruth Alsop, ed., *Power, Rights and Poverty: Concepts and Connections*. Washington, DC: World Bank/UK Department of International Development.

Freire, Paulo. 1968. *Pedagogy of the Oppressed*. New York: Seabury Press.

———. 1974. *Education for a Critical Consciousness*. New York: Seabury Press.

French, Jan Hoffman. 2007. "A Tale of Two Priests and Two Struggles: Liberation Theology from Dictatorship to Democracy in the Brazilian Northeast." *The America* 63 (3): 409–443.

Freston, Paul. 2001. *Evangelicals and Politics in Asia, Africa, and Latin America*. Cambridge: Cambridge University Press.

———, ed. 2008. *Evangelical Christianity and Democracy in Latin America*. New York: Oxford University Press.

Friedmann, Elizabeth, and Kathryn Hochstetler. 2002. "Assessing the 'Third Transition' in Latin American Democratization: Civil Society in Brazil and Argentina." *Comparative Politics* 35 (1): 21–42.

Froehle, Bryan T. 1994. "Religious Competition, Community Building, and Democracy in Latin America: Grassroots Religious Organizations in Venezuela." *Sociology of Religion* 55 (2): 145–162.

———. 1997. "Pentecostals and Evangelicals in Venezuela: Consolidating Gains, Moving in New Directions." Pp. 201–226 in Edward L. Cleary and Hannah Stewart-Gambino, eds., *Power, Politics, and Pentecostals in Latin America*. Boulder, CO: Westview.

———. 2010a. "World Catholicism, Theological Associations, and the Future: Realities and Possibilities." Presented at the conference "The Changing Face of Global Catholicism: Implications for Theology and Theological Education," Chicago, De Paul University, Center for World Catholicism and Intercultural Theology.

————. 2010b. "The Emergence of Parish Leadership in the United States: Emerging Practices of Lay Leadership in Catholic Faith Communities." Presented at the conference "Parish Leadership by Laity: International Experiences and Perspectives on c. 517.2," Munster, Germany.

Froehle, Bryan T., and Mary L. Gautier. 2003. *Global Catholicism: Portrait of a World Church*. Maryknoll, NY: Orbis Books.

Gaffney, Patrick G. 1994. *The Prophet's Pulpit: Muslim Preaching in Contemporary Egypt*. Berkeley: University of California Press.

Garrard-Burnett, Virginia. 1998. *Protestantism in Guatemala: Living in the New Jerusalem*. Austin: University of Texas Press.

————. 2007. "Stop Suffering? The Iglesia Universal del Reino de Dios in the United States." Pp. 218–238 in Edward L. Cleary and Timothy J. Steigenga, eds., *Conversion of a Continent: Contemporary Religious Change in Latin America*. New Brunswick, NJ: Rutgers University Press.

————. 2010. *Terror in the Land of the Holy Spirit: Guatemala Under General Efraín Ríos Montt*. New York: Oxford University Press.

Gaskill, Newton. 1997. "Rethinking Protestantism and Democratic Consolidation in Latin America." *Sociology of Religion* 58 (1): 69–91.

Ghio, José Maria. 2007. *La Iglesia Católica en la Política Argentina*. Buenos Aires: Prometeo Libros.

Gifford, Paul, ed. 1995. *The Christian Churches and the Democratisation of Africa*. Leiden: E. J. Brill.

————. 1998. *African Christianity: Its Public Role*. Bloomington: Indiana University Press.

————. 2004. *Ghana's New Christianity: Pentecostalism in a Globalising African Economy*. Bloomington: Indiana University Press.

————. 2008. "Evangelical Christianity and Democracy in Africa: A Response." Pp. 225–230 in Terence O. Ranger, ed., *Evangelical Christianity and Democracy in Africa*. New York: Oxford University Press.

Gill, Anthony. 1998. *Rendering unto Caesar: The Catholic Church and the State in Latin America*. Chicago: University of Chicago Press.

Gillespie, Richard. 1984. *Soldiers of Perón: Argentina's Montoneros*. New York: Oxford University Press.

Gillfeather, Katherine. 1979. "Women Religious, the Poor, and the Institutional Church in Chile." *Journal of Interamerican Studies and World Affairs* 21 (2): 129–155.

Gilligan, Carol. 1982. *In a Different Voice: Psychological Theory and Women's Development*. Cambridge: Harvard University Press.

Goldman, Francisco. 2007. *The Art of Political Murder: Who Killed the Bishop?* New York: Grove Press.

Gómez, Ileana. 2001. "Building Community in the Wake of War: Churches and Civil Society in Morazán." Pp. 123–144 in Anna L. Peterson, Manuel A. Vásquez, and Philip J. Williams, eds., *Christianity, Social Change, and Globalization in the Americas*. New Brunswick, NJ: Rutgers University Press.

González, Ondina E., and Justo L. González. 2008. *Christianity in Latin America: A History*. New York: Cambridge University Press.

Gramsci, Antonio. 1971. *Selections from the Prison Notebooks*. New York: International Publishers.

Granovetter, Mark. 1973. "The Strength of Weak Ties." *American Journal of Sociology*. 78 (6): 1360–1380.

Guider, Margaret Eletta. 2006. "Reinventing Life and Hope: Coming to Terms with Truth and Reconciliation Brazilian Style." Pp. 111–131 in Iain S. Maclean, ed., *Reconciliation: Nations and Churches in Latin America*. London: Ashgate.

Gutiérrez, Gustavo. 1984. *We Drink from Our Own Wells: The Spiritual Journey of a People*. Maryknoll, NY: Orbis Books.

———. 1986. *Hablar de Dios Desde el Sufrimiento del Inocente. Una Reflexión Sobre el Libro de Job*. Lima: CEP-IBC (Centro de Estudios y Publicaciones, Instituto Bartolome de las Casas).

———. 1988. *A Theology of Liberation: History, Politics, and Salvation*, 15th ed. Maryknoll, NY: Orbis Books.

———. 1990. "Church of the Poor." Pp. 9–25 in Edward Cleary, ed., *Born of the Poor: The Latin American Church Since Medellín*. Notre Dame, IN: University of Notre Dame Press.

———. 1992. *En Busca de los Pobres de Jesucristo*. Lima: Instituto Bartolomé de las Casas.

———. 1993. *Las Casas: In Search of the Poor of Christ*. Maryknoll, NY: Orbis Books.

———. 1996. *¿Donde Dormirán los Pobres?* Lima: CEP (Centro de Estudios y Publicaciones).

———. 1998. *On Job: God Talk and the Suffering of the Innocent*. Maryknoll, NY: Orbis Books.

———. 2004. *Gustavo Gutiérrez Textos Esenciales. Acordarse de los Pobres*. Lima: Fondo Editorial del Congreso del Perú.

———. 2006. "La Opción Preferencial por el Pobre en Aparecida." *Paginas* 206 (August): 6–25.

Guzmán, German. 1968. *La Violencia en Colombia Parte Descriptiva*. Bogotá: Ediciones Progreso.

Haas, Liesl. 1999. "The Catholic Church in Chile: New Political Alliances." Pp. 43–66 in Christian Smith and Joshua Prokopy, eds., *Latin American Religion in Motion*. New York: Routledge.

Habermas, Jürgen, and Joseph Cardinal Ratzinger. 2006. *The Dialectics of Secularization: On Reason and Religion*. San Francisco: Ignatius Press.

Hadenius, Axel, and Frederick Uggla. 1991. "Making Civil Society Work, Promoting Democratic Development: What Can States and Donors Do?" *World Development* 24 (10): 1621–1639.

Hagopian, Frances, ed. 2009. *Religious Pluralism, Democracy, and the Catholic Church in Latin America*. Notre Dame, IN: University of Notre Dame Press.

Hallum, Anne Motley. 1996. *Beyond Missionaries: Toward an Understanding of the Protestant Movement in Central America*. Lanham, MD: Rowman and Littlefield.

Hansen, Thomas Blom. 1999. *The Saffron Wave: Democracy and Hindu Nationalism in Modern India*. Princeton, NJ: Princeton University Press.

Hanson, Eric. 1987. *The Catholic Church in World Politics*. Princeton, NJ: Princeton University Press.

Harding, Susan Friend. 2001. *The Book of Jerry Falwell: Fundamentalist Language and Politics*. Princeton, NJ: Princeton University Press.

Harris, Frederick. 1999. *Something Within: Religion in African American Political Activism*. New York: Oxford University Press.

———. 2003. "Ties That Bind and Flourish: Religion as Social Capital in African American Politics and Society." Pp. 121–138 in Corwin Smidt, ed., *Religion as Social Capital: Producing the Common Good*. Waco, TX: Baylor University Press.

Harris-Lacewell, Melissa. 2007. "From Liberation to Mutual Fund: Political Consequences of Differing Conceptions of Christ in the African American Church." Pp. 131–160 in J. Matthew Wilson, ed., *From Pews to Polling Places: Faith and Politics in the American Religious Mosaic*. Washington, DC: Georgetown University Press.

Hatch, Nathan O. 1991. *The Democratization of American Christianity*. New Haven, CT: Yale University Press.

Hayner, Priscilla B. 2002. *Unspeakable Truths: Facing the Challenge of Truth Commissions*. New York: Routledge.

Hedges, Chris. 2002. *War Is a Force That Gives Us Meaning*. New York: Anchor Books.

Hefner, Robert W. 2000. *Civil Islam: Muslims and Democratization in Indonesia*. Princeton, NJ: Princeton University Press.

———. 2007. "The Sword Against the Crescent: Religion and Violence in Muslim Southeast Asia." Pp. 33–50 in Linell E. Cady and Sheldon W. Simon, eds., *Religion and Conflict in Southeast Asia: Disrupting Violence*. New York: Routledge.

Hellman, John. 1981. *Emmanuel Mounier and the New Catholic Left, 1930–1950*. Toronto: University of Toronto Press.

Hellman, Judith. 1992. "The Study of New Social Movements in Latin America and the Question of Autonomy." Pp. 52–61 in Arturo Escobar and Sonia Alvarez, eds., *The Making of Social Movements in Latin America: Identity, Strategy, and Discourse*. Boulder, CO: Westview.

Helmick, Raymond G. 2001. "Does Religion Fuel or Heal in Conflicts?" Pp. 81–97 in Raymond G. Helmick and Rodney L. Petersen, eds., *Forgiveness and Reconciliation: Religion, Public Policy, and Conflict Transformation*. West Conshohocken, PA: Templeton Foundation Press.

Helmick, Raymond G., and Rodney L. Petersen, eds. 2001. *Forgiveness and Reconciliation: Religion, Public Policy, and Conflict Transformation*. West Conshohocken, PA: Templeton Foundation Press.

Henderson, Anne. 2003. *The Killing of Sister Irene McCormack: The Horrific True Story of the Execution of Sister Irene McCormack*. New York: HarperCollins.

Hewitt, William E. 1991. *Base Christian Communities and Social Change in Brazil*. Lincoln: University of Nebraska Press.

Hirschman, Albert O. 1984. *Getting Ahead Collectively: Grass Roots Experiences in Latin America*. Elmsford, NY: Pergamon Press.

Hitchens, Christopher. 2007. *God Is Not Great: How Religion Spoils Everything*. New York: Hachette Book Group.

Holzner, Claudio. 2011. "Mexico: Weak State, Weak Democracy." Pp. 83–110 in Daniel H. Levine and José E. Molina, eds., *The Quality of Democracy in Latin America*. Boulder, CO: Lynne Rienner.

Hong, Joshua Young-gi. 2008. "Evangelicals and the Democratization of South Korea Since 1987." Pp. 185–234 in Donald H. Lumsdaine, ed., *Evangelical Christianity and Democracy in Asia*. New York: Oxford University Press.

Htun, Mala. 2003. *Sex and the State: Abortion, Divorce, and the Family Under Latin American Dictatorships and Democracies*. New York: Cambridge University Press.

———. 2009. "Life, Liberty, and Family Values: Church and State in the Struggle over Latin America's Social Agenda." Pp. 335–364 in Frances Hagopian, ed., *Religious Pluralism, Democracy, and the Catholic Church in Latin America*. Notre Dame, IN: University of Notre Dame Press.

Hughes, Pedro. 2006. "Epílogo. Vivir la Fé en Tiempos de Violencia." Pp. 633–649 in Cecilia Tovar, ed., *Ser Iglesia en Tiempos de Violencia*. Lima: CEP (Centro de Estudios y Publicaciones).

Iannacone, Laurence R. 1995. "Voodoo Economics? Defending the Rational Approach to Religion." *Journal for the Scientific Study of Religion* 34 (1): 76–88.

Iannacone, Laurence R., Roger Finke, and Rodney Stark. 1997. "Deregulating Religion: The Economics of Church and State." *Economic Inquiry* 35 (2): 350–364.

Iannacone, Laurence R., and Rodney Stark. 1994. "A Supply Side Reinterpretation of the 'Secularization' of Europe." *Journal for the Scientific Study of Religion* 33 (3): 230–252.

Inglehart, Ronald. 2009. "Cultural Change, Religion, Subjective Well-Being, and Democracy in Latin America." Pp. 69–75 in Frances Hagopian, ed., *Religious Pluralism, Democracy, and the Catholic Church in Latin America*. Notre Dame, IN: University of Notre Dame Press.

Inglehart, Ronald, and Pippa Norris. 2004. *Sacred and Secular: Religion and Politics Worldwide*. New York: Cambridge University Press.

Ireland, Rowan. 1992. *Kingdoms Come: Religion and Politics in Brazil*. Pittsburgh: University of Pittsburgh Press.

———. 1999. "Popular Religions and the Building of Democracy in Latin America: Saving the Tocquevillian Parallel." *Journal of Interamerican Studies and World Affairs* 41 (2): 111–136.

Jenkins, Philip. 2002. *The Next Christendom: The Coming of Global Christianity*. New York: Oxford University Press.

———. 2006. *The New Faces of Christianity. Believing the Bible in the Global South*. New York: Oxford University Press.

Jerryson, Michael K. 2010. "Militarizing Buddhism: Violence in Southern Thailand." Pp. 179–209 in Jerryson, Michael K., and Mark Jurgensmeyer, eds., *Buddhist Warfare*. New York: Oxford University Press.

Jerryson, Michael K., and Mark Jurgensmeyer, eds. 2010. *Buddhist Warfare*. New York: Oxford University Press.

Johnson, Kirk. 2005. "Memory of Activist Sister Is Now Brother's Mission." *New York Times*, March 20.

Johnson, Todd M., and Kenneth R. Ross. 2010. *Atlas of Global Christianity*. Edinburgh: Edinburgh University Press.

Johnston, Douglas. 1994. "The Churches and Apartheid in South Africa." Pp. 177–207 in Douglas Johnston and Cynthia Sampson, eds., *Religion: The Missing Dimension of Statecraft*. New York: Oxford University Press.

———. 2001. "Religion and Foreign Policy." Pp. 117–128 in Raymond G. Helmick and Rodney L. Petersen, eds., *Forgiveness and Reconciliation: Religion, Public Policy, and Conflict Transformation*. West Conshohocken, PA: Templeton Foundation Press.

Johnston, Douglas, and Cynthia Sampson, eds. 1994. *Religion: The Missing Dimension of Statecraft*. New York: Oxford University Press.

Jones, Daniel, Anna Laura Azparren, and Luciana Polischuk. 2009. "Evangelicos, Sexualidad y Política. Las Instituciones Evangélicas en los Debates Públicos Sobre Unión Civil y Educación Sexual en la Ciudad Autónoma de Buenos Aires (2003–2004)." Pp. 193–248 in Juan Marco Vaggione, ed., *El Activismo Religioso Conservador en Latinoamérica*. Córdoba: Católicas por el Derecho de Decidir.

Jurgensmeyer, Mark. 2001. *Terror in the Mind of God: The Global Rise of Religious Violence*. Berkeley: University of California Press.

Kamsteeg, Frans H. 1998. *Prophetic Pentecostalism in Chile: A Case Study in Religion and Development Policy*. Lanham, MD: Scarecrow Press.

———. 1999. "Pentecostalism and Political Awakening in Pinochet's Chile." Pp. 187–204 in Christian Smith and Joshua Prokopy, eds., *Latin American Religion in Motion*. New York: Routledge.

Keck, Margaret E. 1995. *The Worker's Party and Democratization in Brazil*. New Haven, CT: Yale University Press.

Keck, Margaret E., and Kathryn Sikkink. 1998. *Activists Beyond Borders: Advocacy Networks in International Politics*. Ithaca, NY: Cornell University Press.

Kent, Daniel W. 2010. "Onward Buddhist Soldiers: Preaching to the Sri Lankan Army." Pp. 157–178 in Michael W. Jerryson and Mark Jurgensmeyer, eds., *Buddhist Warfare*. New York: Oxford University Press.

Kepel, Gilles. 1994. *The Revenge of God: The Resurgence of Islam, Christianity, and Judaism in the Modern World*. Cambridge: Polity Press.

———. 2002. *Jihad: The Trail of Political Islam*. London: I. B. Tauris.

———. 2003. *Muslim Extremism in Egypt: The Prophet and the Pharaoh*. Berkeley: University of California Press.

Kincaid, Douglas. 1987. "Peasants into Rebels: Community and Class in Rural El Salvador." *Comparative Studies in Society and History* 29 (3): 466–494.

King, Martin Luther, Jr. 1986. "Letter from Birmingham City Jail" (1963). Pp. 289–302 in Martin Luther King Jr., *A Testament of Hope: The Essential Writings and Speeches of Martin Luther King, Jr.*, edited by James W. Washington. New York: Harper Collins.

Klaiber, Jeffrey. 1992. "The Church in Peru: Between Terrorism and Conservative Restraints." Pp. 87–104 in Edward L. Cleary and Hannah Stewart-Gambino, eds., *Conflict and Competition: The Latin American Church in a Changing Environment*. Boulder, CO: Lynne Rienner.

———. 1998. *The Church, Dictatorships, and Democracy in Latin America*. Maryknoll, NY: Orbis Books.

Klich, Ignacio, ed. 2006. *Arabes y Judíos en América Latina Historia, Representaciones y Desafíos*. Buenos Aires: Siglo XXI Editores.

Kramer, Eric. 2005. "Spectacle and the Staging of Power in Brazilian Neo Pentecostalism." *Latin American Perspectives*, Issue 140, 32 (1): 95–120.

Kselman, Thomas. 1985. *Miracles and Prophecies in Nineteenth Century France*. New Brunswick, NJ: Rutgers University Press.

Kurtz, Marcus. 2004. *Free Market Democracy and the Chilean and Mexican Countryside*. New York: Cambridge University Press.

Lalive d'Epinay, Christian. 2009. *El Refugio de las Masas. Estudio Sociológico del Protestantismo Chileno*, 2nd ed. Santiago: Universidad de Santiago de Chile.

Lawrence, Bruce. 1986. *Defenders of God: The Fundamentalist Revolt Against the Modern Age.* San Francisco: Harper and Row.

Lehmann, David. 1990. *Democracy and Development in Latin America: Economics, Politics, and Religion in the Postwar Period.* Philadelphia: Temple University Press.

———. 1996. *Struggle for the Spirit: Religious Transformation and Popular Culture in Brazil and Latin America.* London: Polity Press.

Lernoux, Penny. 1982. *Cry of the People: The Struggle for Human Rights in Latin America—The Catholic Church in Conflict with U.S. Policy.* New York: Penguin Books.

———. 1994. *Hearts on Fire: The Story of the Maryknoll Sisters.* Maryknoll, NY: Orbis Books.

Levine, Daniel H. 1973. *Conflict and Political Change in Venezuela.* Princeton, NJ: Princeton University Press.

———. 1981. *Religion and Politics in Latin America: The Catholic Church in Venezuela and Colombia.* Princeton: Princeton University Press.

———. 1986. "Religion and Politics in Comparative and Historical Perspective." *Comparative Politics* 19 (1): 95–122.

———. 1988. "Assessing the Impacts of Liberation Theology in Latin America." *The Review of Politics* 50 (2): 241–263.

———. 1990a. "Considering Liberation Theology as Utopia." *The Review of Politics* 52 (3): 602–619.

———. 1990b. "How Not to Understand Liberation Theology, Nicaragua, or Both." *Journal of Interamerican Studies and World Affairs* 32 (3): 229–246.

———. 1992. *Popular Voices in Latin American Catholicism.* Princeton, NJ: Princeton University Press.

———. 1993a. "Constructing Culture and Power." Pp. 1–39 in Daniel H. Levine, ed., *Constructing Culture and Power in Latin America.* Ann Arbor: University of Michigan Press.

———. 1993b. "Popular Groups, Popular Culture, and Popular Religion." Pp. 171–225 in Daniel H. Levine, ed., *Constructing Culture and Power in Latin America.* Ann Arbor: University of Michigan Press.

———. 1994. "Goodbye to Venezuelan Exceptionalism." *Journal of Interamerican Studies and World Affairs* 36 (4): 145–182.

———. 1995a. "Protestants and Catholics in Latin America: A Family Portrait." Pp. 155–178 in Martin M. Marty and R. Scott Appleby, eds., *Fundamentalisms Comprehended.* Chicago: University of Chicago Press.

———. 1995b. " On Premature Reports of the Death of Liberation Theology." *The Review of Politics* 57 (1): 105–311.

———. 1996. *Voces Populares en el Catolicismo Latinoamericano.* Lima: CEP (Centro de Estudios y Publicaciones).

———. 2003. "Theoretical and Methodological Reflections About the Study of Religion and Politics in Latin America." Pp. 3–16 in Margaret Crahan, ed., *Religion, Culture, and Society: The Case of Cuba.* Washington, DC: Woodrow Wilson International Center for Scholars.

———. 2006a. "Pluralidad, Pluralismo, y la Creación de un Vocabulario de Derechos." *America Latina Hoy* 41 (December): 17–34.

———. 2006b. "Religión y Política en América Latina. La Nueva Cara Pública de la Religión." *Sociedad y Religión* 18 (26–27): 7–29.

————. 2006c. "Religious Transformations and the Language of Rights in Latin America." *Taiwan Journal of Democracy* 22 (December): 117–141.

————. 2008. "The Future as Seen from Aparecida." Pp. 173–190 in Robert Pelton, ed., *Aparecida Quo Vadis*. Scranton, PA: University of Scranton Press.

————. 2009a. "The Future of Christianity in Latin America." *Journal of Latin American Studies* 41 (1): 121–145.

————. 2009b. "Pluralism as Challenge and Opportunity." Pp. 405–428 in Frances Hagopian, ed., *Religious Pluralism, Democracy, and the Catholic Church in Latin America*. Notre Dame, IN: University of Notre Dame Press.

————. 2010. "Reflections on the Mutual Impact of Violence and Religious Change in Latin America." *Latin American Politics and Society* 52 (3): 131–150.

————. 2011. "Camilo Torres: Fe Política y Violencia." *Sociedad y Religión* 21 (34–35): 59–91.

Levine, Daniel H., and Phyllis Levine. 1994. "Unidos por la Fe en un Pueblo Organizado: Acción Comunitaria por la Salud Mental en Maracaibo." Pp. 72–91 in Juan Carlos Navarro, ed., *Organizaciones de Participación Comunitaria: Su Contribución en la Lucha Contra la Pobreza*. Caracas: Ediciones IESA.

Levine, Daniel H., and José E. Molina, eds. 2011. *The Quality of Democracy in Latin America*. Boulder, CO: Lynne Rienner.

Levine, Daniel H., and Catalina Romero. 2006. "Urban Citizen Movements and Disempowerment in Peru and Venezuela." Pp. 227–256 in Scott Mainwaring, Ana Maria Bejarano, and Eduardo Pizarro Leongómez, eds., *When Representation Fails: The Crisis of Democratic Representation in the Andes*. Stanford, CA: Stanford University Press.

Levine, Daniel H., and David Smilde. 2006. "The Catholic Church and the Chávez Government in Venezuela." *The Catholic Herald* (London) (September).

Levine, Daniel H., and David Stoll. 1997. "Bridging the Gap Between Empowerment and Power in Latin America." Pp. 63–103 in Susanne Hoeber Rudolph and James Piscatori, eds., *Transnational Religion and Fading States*. Boulder, CO: Westview.

Levine, Daniel H., and Alexander W. Wilde. 1977. "The Catholic Church, 'Politics' and Violence: The Colombian Case." *The Review of Politics* 39 (2): 220–249.

Lim, David S. 2009. "Consolidating Democracy: Filipino Evangelicals Between People Power Events, 1986–2001." Pp. 235–284 in David Halloran Lumsdaine, ed., *Evangelical Christianity and Democracy in Asia*. New York: Oxford University Press.

Lincoln, C. Eric, and Lawrence H. Mamiya. 1990. *The Black Church in the African American Experience*. Durham, NC: Duke University Press.

Loaeza, Soledad. 2009. "Cultural Change in Mexico at the Turn of the Century: The Secularization of Women's Identity and the Erosion of the Authority of the Catholic Church." Pp. 96–130 in Frances Hagopian, ed., *Religious Pluralism, Democracy, and the Catholic Church in Latin America*. Notre Dame, IN: University of Notre Dame Press.

Lodge, Tom. 2009. "The Interplay of Non-violent and Violent Action in the Movement Against Apartheid in South Africa, 1983–94." Pp. 213–230 in Adam Roberts and Timothy Garton Ash, eds., *Civil Resistance and Power Politics: The Experience of Non-Violent Action from Gandhi to the Present*. New York: Oxford University Press.

López, Darío. 1998. *Los Evangélicos y los Derechos Humanos: La Experiencia del Concilio Nacional Evangélico del Perú.* Lima: Ediciones Puma.

———. 2004. *La Seducción del Poder: Evangélicos y Politica en el Perú de los Noventa.* Lima: Ediciones Puma.

———. 2008a. "Evangelicals and Politics in Fujimori's Peru." Pp. 131–162 in Paul Freston, ed., *Evangelical Christianity and Democracy in Latin America.* New York: Oxford University Press.

———. 2008b. *El Nuevo Rostro del Pentecostalismo Latinoamericano.* Lima: Ediciones Puma.

Lowy, Michael. 1996. *The War of the Gods: Religion and Politics in Latin America.* London: Verso.

Lumsdaine, David H., ed. 2009a. *Evangelical Christianity and Democracy in Asia.* New York: Oxford University Press.

———. 2009b. "Evangelical Christianity and Democratic Pluralism in Asia: An Introduction." Pp. 3–42 in David H. Lumsdaine, ed., *Evangelical Christianity and Democracy in Asia.* New York: Oxford University Press.

Maclean, Iain S. 2006a. *Reconciliation: Nations and Churches in Latin America.* London: Ashgate.

———. 2006b. "Truth and Reconciliation: Hope for the Nations or Only as Much as Is Possible?" Pp. 3–40 in Iain S. Maclean, ed., *Reconciliation: Nations and Churches in Latin America.* London: Ashgate.

Maduro, Otto. 1970. *Revelación y Revolución Notas Sobre el Mensaje de Cristo y Sus Implicaciones Frente a la Necesitada Liberación de los Pueblos de América del Imperialismo y de los Capitalistas.* Merida, Venezuela: Ediciones del Rectorado, Universidad de los Andes.

———. 2005. *Religion and Social Conflicts.* Maryknoll, NY: Orbis Books.

Magne, Marcelo Gabriel. 2004. *Dios Está con los Pobres. El Movimiento de Sacerdotes para el Tercer Mundo. Prédica Revolucionaria y Protagonismo Social, 1967–1976.* Buenos Aires: Ediciones Imago Mundi.

Mainwaring, Scott. 1986. *The Catholic Church and Politics in Brazil, 1916–1985.* Stanford, CA: Stanford University Press.

———. 1989. "Grass-Roots Catholic Groups and Politics in Brazil." Pp. 151–192 in Scott Mainwaring and Alexander Wilde, eds., *The Progressive Church in Latin America.* Notre Dame, IN: University of Notre Dame Press.

Malkin, Elisabeth. 2010. "Many States in Mexico Crack Down on Abortion." *New York Times*, September 22.

Mallimaci, Fortunato. 1996. "Diversidad Católica en una Sociedad Globalizada y Excluyente: Una Mirada al Fin de Milenio desde la Argentina." *Sociedad y Religión* 14/15 (November): 72–99.

———. 2005. "Catolicismo y Política en el Gobierno de Kirchner." *América Latina Hoy* 41 (December): 57–76.

———. 2008a. *Modernidad, Religión, y Memoria.* Buenos Aires: Colihue.

———. 2008b. "Las Paradojas y las Multiples Modernidades en Argentina." Pp. 75–90 in Fortunato Mallimaci, ed., *Modernidad Religión y Memoria.* Buenos Aires: Colihue.

———. 2008c. *Religión y Política Perspectivas Desde América Latina y Europa.* Buenos Aires: Editorial Biblos.

————. 2009. "Catolicización y Militarización, Catolicismos y Militarismos: La Violencia y lo Sagrado en la Argentina del Terrorismo de Estado." Presented at Symposium on Katolische Kirche und Gewalt im 20 Jahrhundert, Westfalishche Wilhelms-Universität Munster, Germany, May 19–21.

Mallimaci, Fortunato, Humberto Cucchetti, and Luis Miguel Donatello. 2006. "Caminos Sinuosos: Nacionalismo y Catolicismo en la Argentina Contemporánea." Pp. 155–190 in Franscisco Colom and Angel Rivero, eds., *El Altar y el Trono: Ensayos Sobre el Catolicismo Iberoamericano*. Bogotá: Antropos.

Mallimaci, Fortunato, and Marta Villa. 2007. *Las Comunidades Eclesiales de Base y el Mundo de los Pobres en la Argentina: Conflictos y Tensiones por el Control del Poder en el Catolicismo*. Buenos Aires: CIEL/PIETTE/CONICET.

Mannheim, Karl. 1961. *Ideology and Utopia*. New York: Harcourt Brace and World.

Marius, Richard. 1985. *Thomas More: A Biography*. New York: Alfred A. Knopf.

Mariz, Cecilia. 1994. *Coping with Poverty: Pentecostals and Christian Base Communities in Brazil*. Philadelphia: Temple University Press.

Mariz, Cecilia Loreto, and Maria das Dores Campos Machado. 1997. "Pentecostalism and Women in Brazil." Pp. 41–54 in Edward L. Cleary and Hannah Stewart-Gambino, eds., *Power, Politics, and Pentecostals in Latin America*. Boulder, CO: Westview.

Martin, David. 1990. *Tongues of Fire: The Explosion of Protestantism in Latin America*. Oxford: Blackwell Publishers.

Martín, Juan Pablo. 2010. *El Movimiento de Sacerdotes para el Tercer Mundo. Un Debate Argentino*. Buenos Aires: Universidad Nacional del General Sarmiento.

Marty, Martin E., and R. Scott Appleby. 1992. *The Glory and the Power: The Fundamentalist Challenge to the Modern World*. Boston: Beacon Press.

————, eds. 1995. *Fundamentalisms Comprehended*. Chicago: University of Chicago Press.

Marzal, Manuel. 1988. *Los Caminos Religiosos de los Inmigrantes a la Gran Lima: El Caso de el Agustino*. Lima: Pontificia Universidad Católica del Perú, Fondo Editorial.

Matos Mar, José. 2005. *Desborde Popular y Crisis del Estado: Veinte Años Después*. Lima: Fondo Editorial del Congreso.

Mecham, J. Lloyd. 1934. *Church and State in Latin America: A History of Politico-Ecclesiastical Relations*. Chapel Hill: University of North Carolina Press.

Melucci, Alberto. 1988. *Nomads of the Present: Social Movements and Individual Needs in Contemporary Society*. Philadelphia: Temple University Press.

Mendoza-Boltelho, Martin. 2010. "Social Capital, Leadership, and Social Change." In Brady Wagoner, Erick Jensen and Julian Oldmeadow, eds., *Culture and Social Change: Transforming Society Through the Power of Ideas*. New York: Routledge.

Metaxas, Eric. 2010. *Bonhoeffer: Pastor, Martyr, Prophet, Spy*. Nashville: Thomas Nelson.

Micheo, Alberto. 1983. "Una Experiencia Campesina." *Revista SIC* (Caracas) 417.

Mignone, Emilio. 1988. *Witness to the Truth: The Complicity of Church and Dictatorship in Argentina*. Maryknoll, NY: Orbis Books.

Mitchell, Joshua. 2007. "Religion Is Not a Preference." *Journal of Politics* 69 (2): 351–362.

Mockabee, Stephen T. 2007. "The Political Behavior of American Catholics." Pp. 81–104 in J. Matthew Wilson, ed., *From Pews to Polling Places: Faith and Politics in the American Religious Mosaic*. Washington, DC: Georgetown University Press.

Moodie, T. Dunbar. 1974. *The Rise of Afrikanerdom: Power, Apartheid, and Afrikaner Civil Religion*. Berkeley: University of California Press.

Morello, Gustavo. 2003. *Cristianismo y Revolución. Los Origines Intelectuales de la Guerrilla Argentina*. Prologue by Horacio Crespo. Córdoba: Editorial de la Universidad Católica de Córdoba.

———. 2007. "Prólogo: Camilo y Argentina." Pp. 9–14 in Hernan Bienza, *Camilo Torres: Sacristán de la Guerrilla*. Buenos Aires: Capital Intelectua–Colección Fundadores de la Izquierda.

———. 2011a. "Catolicismos y Terrorismo del Estado en la Ciudad de Córdoba en los Setenta. El Caso de los Misioneros de la Salette." PhD thesis, Universidad de Buenos Aires, Facultad de Sociología.

———. 2011b. "Christianity and Revolution: Catholicism and Guerrilla Warfare in Argentina's Seventies." *Journal for Faith, Spirituality, and Social Change* (Winchester, UK), www.fssconference.org.uk/journal/index.htm.

———. 2011c. "El Terrorismo de Estado y el Catolicismo en Argentina. El Caso de los Misioneros de la Salette." In *Jahrbuch für Geschichte Lateinamerikas/ Anuario de Historia de America Latina*. Graz, Austria: Böhlau Verlag.

———. 2012. "Comunidad Política, Sociedad Civil, y Actores Religiosos. Un Caso de Articulación en Torno a la Defense de los Derechos Dumanos en la Argentina de los Setenta." *Latin American Research Review*, forthcoming.

Morris, Aldon. 1984. *The Origins of the Civil Rights Movement*. New York: Free Press.

Mujica Bermúdez, Luis. 2006. "A Grandes Problemas Pequeñas Soluciones: La Vida Cotidiana en Tiempos de Violencia. Una Respuesta Desde las Comunidades Cristianas." Pp. 211–236 in Cecilia Tovar, ed., *Ser Iglesia en Tiempos de Violencia*. Lima: CEP (Centro de Estudios y Publicaciones).

Munck, Gerardo. 2007. *Regimes and Democracy in Latin America: Theories and Methods*. New York: Oxford University Press.

Munck, Gerardo, and Jay Verkuilen. 2002. "Conceptualizing and Measuring Democracy: Evaluating Alternative Indices." *Comparative Political Studies* 35 (1): 5–34.

Muñoz, Hortensia. 2001. "Believers and Neighbors: Huaycán Is One and No One Shall Divide It." Pp. 87–104 in Anna L. Peterson, Manuel A. Vásquez, and Philip J. Williams, eds., *Christianity, Social Change, and Globalization in the Americas*. New Brunswick, NJ: Rutgers University Press.

Nagle, Robin. 1997. *Claiming the Virgin: The Broken Promise of Liberation Theology in Brazil*. New York: Routledge.

Navarro, Maryssa. 1989. "The Personal Is Political: The Mothers of the Plaza de Mayo." Pp. 241–258 in Susan Eckstein, ed., *Power and Popular Protest: Latin American Social Movements*. Berkeley: University of California Press.

Neuhaus, Richard John. 1984. *The Naked Public Square: Religion and Democracy in America*. Grand Rapids, MI: William Eerdmans.

Noll, Mark A. 2009. *The New Shape of World Christianity: How American Experience Reflects Global Faith*. Downers Grove, IL: Intervarsity Press.

Noone, Judith M. 1995. *The Same Fate as the Poor*. Maryknoll, NY: Orbis Books.

Norget, Kristin. 2004. "'Knowing Where We Enter': Indigenous Theology and the Popular Church in Oaxaca, Mexico." Pp. 154–186 in Edward L. Cleary and Timothy J. Steigenga, eds., *Resurgent Voices in Latin America: Indigenous Peoples, Political Mobilization, and Religious Change*. New Brunswick, NJ: Rutgers University Press.

O'Donnell, Guillermo. 2007. *Dissonances: Democratic Critiques of Democracy*. Notre Dame, IN: University of Notre Dame Press.

Olson, Laura R. 2007. "Whither the Religious Left: Religiopolitical Progressivism in Twenty-First Century America." Pp. 534–580 in J. Matthew Wilson, eds., *From Pews to Polling Places: Faith and Politics in the American Religious Mosaic*. Washington, DC: Georgetown University Press.

O'Neill, Kevin. 2010. *City of God: Christian Citizenship in Postwar Guatemala City*. Berkeley: University of California Press.

Oquist, Paul. 1978. *Violencia, Conflicto y Política en Colombia*. Bogotá: Biblioteca Popular Instituto de Estudios Colombianos.

Oro, Ani Pedro. 2006. "A Igreja Universal e a Politica." Pp. 119–148 in Joanildo A. Burity and Maria Dos Dolores C. Machado, eds., *Os Votos de Deus: Evangélicos, Politica e Eleições no Brasil*. Recife, Brazil: Fundacao Joaquim Nabuco.

Oro, Ani Pedro, and Pablo Semán. 2000. "Pentecostalism in the Southern Cone Countries: Overview and Perspectives." *International Sociology* 15 (4): 605–627.

Orsi, Robert. 2005. *Between Heaven and Earth: The Religious Worlds People Make and the Scholars Who Study Them*. Princeton, NJ: Princeton University Press.

Ortner, Sherry. 1995. "Resistance and the Problem of Ethnographic Refusal." *Comparative Studies in Society and History* 37 (1): 173–193.

Ottmann, Goetz Frank. 2002. *Lost for Words? Brazilian Liberationism in the 1990s*. Pittsburgh: University of Pittsburgh Press.

Oxhorn, Philip. 1995. *Organizing Civil Society: The Popular Sectors and the Struggle for Democracy in Chile*. University Park: Pennsylvania State University Press.

Pagnucco, Ronald, and John D. McCarthy. 1992. "Advocating Non Violent Direct Action in Latin America: The Antecedents and Emergence of SERPAJ." Pp. 120–150 in Bronislaw Misztal and Anson Shupe, eds., *Religion and Politics in Comparative Perspective: Revival of Religious Fundamentalism in East and West*. Westport, CT: Praeger.

Parker, Cristián. 1996. *Popular Religion and Modernization in Latin America*. Maryknoll, NY: Orbis Books.

———. 2005. "América Latina. ¿Ya no es Católica? (Cambios Culturales, Transformación del Campo Religioso y Debilitamiento de la Iglesia)." *América Latina Hoy* 41 (December): 35–56.

———. 2009. "Education and Increasing Religious Pluralism in Latin America: The Case of Chile." Pp. 131–181 in Frances Hagopian, ed., *Religious Pluralism, Democracy, and the Catholic Church in Latin America*. Notre Dame, IN: University of Notre Dame Press.

Pásara, Luis. 1989. "Peru: The Leftist Angels." Pp. 276–326 in Scott Mainwaring and Alexander Wilde, eds., *The Progressive Church in Latin America*. Notre Dame, IN: University of Notre Dame Press.

Pásara Luis, Nerna Delpino, Ricio Valdeavellano, and Alonzo Zarzar, eds. 1991. *La Otra Cara de la Luna. Nuevos Actores Sociales en el Perú*. Lima: CEDYS.

Paz, Nestor. 1978. *My Life for My Friends: The Guerrilla Journal of Nestor Paz.* Maryknoll, NY: Orbis Books.

Pelton, Robert, ed. 2008. *Aparecida Quo Vadis.* Scranton, PA: University of Scranton Press.

Perlman, Janice. 1976. *The Myth of Marginality: Urban Poverty and Politics in Rio de Janeiro.* Berkeley: University of California Press.

Perruzzotti, Enrique, and Catalina Smulovitz, eds. 2006. *Enforcing the Rule of Law: Social Accountability in the New Latin American Democracies.* Pittsburgh, PA: University of Pittsburgh Press.

Peterson, Anna L. 1997. *Martyrdom and the Politics of Religion: Progressive Catholicism in El Salvador's Civil War.* Albany: State University of New York Press.

Peterson, Anna L., Manuel A. Vásquez, and Philip J. Williams, eds. 2001a. *Christianity, Social Change, and Globalization in the Americas.* New Brunswick, NJ: Rutgers University Press.

———. 2001b. "The Global and the Local." Pp. 210–228 in Anna Peterson, Manuel A. Vásquez, and Philip J. Williams, eds., *Christianity, Social Change, and Globalization in the Americas.* New Brunswick, NJ: Rutgers University Press.

Pew Forum on Religion and Public Life. 2006. *Spirit and Power: A Ten-Country Survey of Pentecostals.* Washington, DC: Pew Research Center.

Pfeil, Margaret R. 2006. "Social Sin, Social Reconciliation." Pp. 171–189 in Iain S. Maclean, ed., *Reconciliation: Nations and Churches in Latin America.* London: Ashgate.

Philpott, Daniel. 2004. "The Catholic Wave." *Journal of Democracy* 15 (2): 32–46.

———, ed. 2006. *The Politics of Past Evil: Religion, Reconciliation, and the Dilemmas of Transitional Justice.* Notre Dame, IN: University of Notre Dame Press.

Piven, Frances Fox, and Richard Cloward. 1977. *Poor People's Movements: Why They Succeed, How They Fail.* New York: Vintage.

———. 1998. *The Breaking of the American Social Compact.* New York: Free Press.

Posel, Deborah, and Grame Simpson, eds. 2002. *Commissioning the Past: Understanding South Africa's Truth and Reconciliation Commission.* Johannesburg: Witwatersrand University Press.

Putnam, Robert. 1993. *Making Democracy Work: Civic Traditions in Modern Italy.* Princeton, NJ: Princeton University Press.

———. 2000. *Bowling Alone: The Collapse and Revival of American Community.* New York: Simon and Schuster.

Putnam, Robert, and David Campbell. 2010. *American Grace: How Religion Divides and Unites Us.* New York: Simon and Schuster.

Ranger, Terence. 1986. "Religious Movements and Politics in Sub Saharan Africa." *African Studies Review* 29 (2): 1–69.

———, ed. 2008a. *Evangelical Christianity and Democracy in Africa.* New York: Oxford University Press.

———. 2008b. "Introduction: Evangelical Christianity and Democracy in Africa." Pp. 3–36 in Terence O. Ranger, ed., *Evangelical Christianity and Democracy in Africa.* New York: Oxford University Press.

Ranly, Ernesto. 2003. *Los Religiosos en Tiempos de Violencia en el Perú Crónica y Teoría de la Non Violencia.* Lima: Confederación de Religiosos del Perú (CONFER).

REMHI (Recovery of Historical Memory Project). 1999. *Guatemala: Never Again!* Guatemala: ODHAD (Human Rights Office, Archdiocese of Guatemala).

Riesebrot, Martin. 1998. *Pious Passion: The Emergence of Modern Fundamentalism in the United States and Iran*. Berkeley: University of California Press.

Riofrio, Gustavo. 1991. *Lima: ¿Para Vivir Mañana?* Lima: CIDIAG/FOVIDA.

Robben, Antonius C. G. M. 2008. *Pegar Donde Más Duele: Violencia Política y Trauma Social en Argentina*. Buenos Aires: Anthropos Editorial.

Rodríguez, Patricia. 2009. "With or Without the People: The Catholic Church and Land Related Conflicts in Brazil and Chile." Pp. 185–224 in Frances Hagopian, ed., *Religious Pluralism, Democracy, and the Catholic Church in Latin America*. Notre Dame, IN: University of Notre Dame Press.

Rohter, Larry. 2005. "Peru's Catholics Brace for Fissures in Their Church." *New York Times*, May 8.

Romero, Catalina. 2009. "Religion and Public Spaces: Catholicism and Civil Society in Peru." Pp. 365–401 in Frances Hagopian, ed., *Religious Pluralism, Democracy, and the Catholic Church in Latin America*. Notre Dame, IN: University of Notre Dame Press.

———. 2010. "Entre la Tormenta y la Brisa: Desafíos al Catolicismo en América Latina." Pp. 229–243 in Catalina Romero and Luis Periano, eds., *Entre la Tormenta y la Brisa Homenaje a Gustavo Gutiérrez*. Lima: Fondo Editorial de la Pontificia Universidad Católica del Perú.

Romero, Oscar A. 1980. "The Political Dimension of the Faith from the Perspective of the Option for the Poor." Pp. 177–187 in *Archbishop Oscar Romero, Voice of the Voiceless: The Four Pastoral Letters and Other Statements*. Maryknoll, NY: Orbis Books.

———. 1985. *Voice of the Voiceless: The Four Pastoral Letters and Other Statements*. Maryknoll, NY: Orbis Books.

Roniger, Luis. 2009. *Antisemitism, Real or Imagined? Chávez, Iran, Israel, and the Jews*. Jerusalem: ACTA (Analysis of Current Trends in Antisemitism), Vidal Sassoon International Center for the Study of Antisemitism, The Hebrew University of Jerusalem.

Roy, Olivier. 2004. *Globalized Islam: The Search for a New Ummah*. New York: Columbia University Press.

Ruderer, Stephan. 2010. "Entre Religión y Política: El Vicariato Castrense en las Últimas Dictaduras de Chile y Argentina." Presented at meetings of the Latin American Studies Association, Toronto.

Rutagambwa, Elisée. 2006. "The Rwandan Church: The Challenge of Reconciliation." Pp. 173–189 in Paul Christopher Manuel, Lawrence C. Reardon, and Clyde Wilcox, eds., *The Catholic Church and the Nation-State: Comparative Perspectives*. Washington, DC: Georgetown University Press.

Ryback, Timothy. 1990. *Rock Around the Bloc: A History of Rock Music in Eastern Europe and the Soviet Union*. New York: Oxford University Press.

Saenz, Rogelio. 2005. "The Changing Demographics of Roman Catholics." Washington, DC, Population Reference Bureau, www.prb.org/Articles/2005/The ChangingDemographicsofRomanCatholics.aspx.

Sampson, Cynthia. 1994. "To Make Real the Bond Between Us All: Quaker Conciliation During the Nigerian Civil War." Pp. 88–118 in Douglas Johnston and Cynthia Sampson, eds., *Religion: The Missing Dimension of Statecraft*. New York: Oxford University Press.

Samson, C. Matthews. 2008. "From War to Reconciliation: Guatemalan Evangelicals and the Transition to Democracy, 1982–2001." Pp. 63–96 in Paul Freston, ed., *Evangelical Christianity and Democracy in Latin America.* New York: Oxford University Press.

Schober, Juliane. 2007. "Buddhism, Violence, and the State in Burma (Myanmar) and Sri Lanka." Pp. 51–69 in Linell E. Cady and Sheldon W. Simon, eds., *Religion and Conflict in Southeast Asia: Disrupting Violence.* New York: Routledge.

Schoenwalder, Gerd. 2002. *Linking Civil Society and the State: Urban Popular Movements, the Left, and Local Government in Peru, 1980–1992.* University Park, PA: Penn State University Press.

Scott, James C. 1985. *Weapons of the Weak: Everyday Forms of Peasant Resistance.* New Haven, CT: Yale University Press.

Scully, Timothy. 1992. *Rethinking the Center: Party Politics in Nineteenth- and Twentieth-Century Chile.* Stanford, CA: Stanford University Press.

Secretaria Status, Rationarium Generale Ecclesiae. Selected years. *Annuarium Statisticum Ecclesiae* [Statistical Yearbook of the Church]. Vatican: Libreria Editrice Vaticana.

Serbin, Kenneth. 2000. *Secret Dialogues: Church-State Relations, Torture, and Social Justice in Authoritarian Brazil.* Pittsburgh, PA: University of Pittsburgh Press.

Shane, Scott. 2011. "Killings Spotlight Anti-Muslim Thought in US." *New York Times,* July 25.

Sharp, Gene. 1973. *The Politics of Nonviolent Action,* Vol. 2: *The Methods of Nonviolent Action.* Boston: Porter Sargent Publishers.

Sherman, Amy. 1997. *The Soul of Development: Biblical Christianity and Economic Transformation in Guatemala.* New York: Oxford University Press.

Sigmund, Paul. 1990. *Liberation Theology at the Crossroads: Democracy or Revolution?* New York: Oxford University Press.

Sikkink, Kathryn A. 1993. "Human Rights, Principled Issue Networks, and Sovereignty in Latin America." *International Organization* 47 (3): 411–441.

———. 1996. "Nongovernmental Organizations, Democracy, and Human Rights in Latin America." Pp. 150–168 in Tom Farer, ed., *Beyond Sovereignty: Collectively Defending Democracy in the Americas.* Baltimore: Johns Hopkins University Press.

Sikkink, Kathryn A., and Carrie Booth Walling. 2006. "Argentina's Contribution to Global Trends in Transitional Justice." Pp. 301–324 in Naomi Roht-Arriaza and Javier Mariezcurrena, eds., *Transitional Justice in the Twenty-First Century: Beyond Truth and Justice.* New York: Cambridge University Press.

Silveira Campos, Leonardo. 2006. "De Politicos de Cristo. Uma Analise do Comportamento Politico de Protestantes Historicos e Pencostais no Brasil." Pp. 29–90 in Joanildo Burity and Maria Dos Dolores C. Machado, eds., *Os Votos de Deus: Evangélicos, Politica e Eleições no Brasil.* Recife, Brazil: Fundacao Joaquim Nabuco.

Smidt, Corwin, ed. 2003. *Religion as Social Capital: Producing the Common Good.* Waco, TX: Baylor University Press.

———. 2007. "Evangelicals and Mainline Protestants at the Turn of the Millennium: Taking Stock and Looking Forward." Pp. 29–52 in J. Matthew Wilson, ed., *From Pews to Polling Places: Faith and Politics in the American Religious Mosaic.* Washington, DC: Georgetown University Press.

Smilde, David. 1997. "The Fundamental Unity of the Conservative and Revolutionary Tendencies in Venezuelan Evangelicalism: The Case of Conjugal Relations." *Religion* 27 (4): 343–359.

———. 1999. "El Clamor por Venezuela: Latin American Evangelicalism as a Collective Action Frame." Pp. 125–146 in Christian Smith and Joshua Prokopy, *Latin American Religion in Motion*. New York: Routledge.

———. 2004a. "Contradiction Without Paradox: Evangelical Political Culture in the 1998 Venezuelan Elections." *Latin American Politics and Society* 46 (1): 75–102.

———. 2004b. "Popular Publics, Street Protests and Plaza Preachers in Venezuela." *International Review of Social History* 49 (supplement): 179–195.

———. 2004c. "Los Evangélicos y la Polarización: La Moralización de la Política y la Politización de la Religion." *Revista Venezolana de Ciencias Económicas y Sociales* 10 (2): 163–179.

———. 2007. *Reason to Believe: Cultural Agency in Latin American Evangelicalism*. Berkeley: University of California Press.

———. 2008. "Relational Analysis of Religious Conversion and Social Change: Networks and Publics in Latin American Evangelicalism." Pp. 93–111 in Timothy J. Steigenga and Edward L. Cleary, eds., *Conversion of a Continent: Contemporary Religious Change in Latin America*. New Brunswick, NJ: Rutgers University Press.

———. 2011. "Public Rituals and Political Positioning: Venezuelan Evangelicals and the Chávez Government." Pp. 306–329 in Martin Lindhart, ed., *Practicing the Faith: Ritual in Charismatic Christianity*. New York: Berghahn Books.

Smilde, David, and Daniel Hellinger, eds. 2011. *Participation, Politics, and Culture in Venezuela's Bolivarian Democracy*. Durham, NC: Duke University Press.

Smilde, David, and Coraly Pagan. 2011. "Christianity and Politics in Venezuela's Bolivarian Democracy: Catholics, Evangelicals and Political Polarization." Pp. 317–341 in David Smilde and Daniel Hellinger, eds., *Participation, Politics, and Culture in Venezuela's Bolivarian Democracy*. Durham, NC: Duke University Press.

Smilde, David, and Timothy Steigenga. 1999. "Wrapped in the Holy Shawl: The Strange Case of Conservative Christians and Gender Equality in Latin America." Pp. 173–186 in Christian Smith and Joshua Prokopy, eds., *Latin American Religion in Motion*. New York: Routledge.

Smith, Amy Erica. 2010. "The Bully Pulpit: Church Influence on Political Socialization in a Municipal Election Campaign in Brazil." Presented at meetings of the Latin American Studies Association, Toronto, Canada.

Smith, Brian H. 1982. *The Church and Politics in Chile: Challenges to Modern Catholicism*. Princeton, NJ: Princeton University Press.

———. 1990. *More Than Altruism: The Politics of Private Foreign Aid*. Princeton, NJ: Princeton University Press.

———. 1998. *Religious Politics in Latin America: Pentecostal vs. Catholic*. Notre Dame, IN: University of Notre Dame Press.

Smith, Christian. 1991. *The Emergence of Liberation Theology: Radical Religion and Social Movement Theory*. Chicago: University of Chicago Press.

Smith, Peter H. 2005. *Democracy in Latin America: Political Change in Comparative Perspective*. New York: Oxford University Press.

Smyth, Geraldine. 2001. "Brokenness, Forgiveness, Healing, and Peace in Ireland." Pp. 329–360 in Raymond G. Helmick and Rodney L. Petersen, eds., *Forgive-

ness and Reconciliation: Religion, Public Policy, and Conflict Transformation. West Conshohocken, PA: Templeton Foundation Press.

Sobrino, Jon. 2003. "A Theologian's View of Oscar Romero." Pp. 22–51 in Oscar Romero, *Voice of the Voiceless: The Four Pastoral Letters and Other Statements.* Maryknoll, NY: Orbis Books.

Sorel, Georges. 1999. *Reflections on Violence.* Cambridge: Cambridge University Press.

Staub, Ervin, and Lauria Ann Pearlman. 2001. "Healing, Reconciliation, and Forgiving After Genocide and Other Collective Violence." Pp. 205–227 in Raymond G. Helmick and Rodney L. Petersen eds., *Forgiveness and Reconciliation: Religion, Public Policy, and Conflict Transformation.* West Conshohocken, PA: Templeton Foundation Press.

Steele, David. 1994. "At the Front Lines of the Revolution: East Germany's Churches Give Sanctuary and Succour to the Purveyors of Change." Pp. 119–152 in Douglas Johnston and Cynthia Sampson, eds., *Religion: The Missing Dimension of Statecraft.* New York: Oxford University Press.

Steigenga, Timothy. 2001. *The Politics of the Spirit: The Political Implications of Pentecostalized Religion in Costa Rica and Guatemala.* Lanham, MD: Lexington Books.

———. 2004. "Conclusion: Listening to Indigenous Voices." Pp. 231–253 in Edward L. Cleary and Timothy J. Steigenga, eds., *Resurgent Voices in Latin America: Indigenous Peoples, Political Mobilization, and Social Change.* New Brunswick, NJ: Rutgers University Press.

———. 2005. "Democracia y el Crecimiento del Protestantismo Evangélico en Guatemala: Entendiendo la Complejidad Política de la Religión 'Pentecostalizada.'" *América Latina Hoy* 41: 121–138.

———. 2007. "The Politics of Pentecostalized Religion: Conversion as Pentecostalization in Guatemala." Pp. 256–279 in Timothy J. Steigenga and Edward L. Cleary, eds., *Conversion of a Continent: Contemporary Religious Change in Latin America.* New Brunswick, NJ: Rutgers University Press.

———. 2012. "Conversion and Politics: How Political Science 'Found Religion' and What Remains Lost in the Process." In Luis Rambo and Charles Farhadian, eds., *Oxford Handbook of Religious Conversion.* Oxford: Oxford University Press.

Steigenga, Timothy, and Edward L. Cleary, eds. 2007a. *Conversion of a Continent: Contemporary Religious Change in Latin America.* New Brunswick, NJ: Rutgers University Press.

———. 2007b. "Understanding Conversion in the Americas." Pp. 3–32 in Timothy J. Steigenga and Edward L. Cleary, eds., *Conversion of a Continent: Contemporary Religious Change in Latin America.* New Brunswick, NJ: Rutgers University Press.

Steigenga, Timothy, and Sandra Lazo de la Vega. 2012. "Indigenous Peoples: Religious Change and Political Awakening." In Virginia Garrard-Burnett and Paul Freston, eds., *The Cambridge History of Religion in Latin America.* New York: Cambridge University Press.

Stepan, Alfred. 2003. "The World's Religious Systems and Democracy: Crafting the 'Twin Tolerations.'" Pp. 213–253 in Alfred Stepan, ed., *Arguing Comparative Politics.* New York: Oxford University Press.

Stewart-Gambino, Hannah. 2005. "Las Pobladoras y la Iglesia Despolitizada en Chile." *América Latina Hoy* 41: 121–138.

Stokes, Susan. 1995. *Cultures in Conflict: Social Movements and the State in Peru.* Berkeley: University of California Press.

Stoll, David. 1982. *Fishers of Men or Founders of Empire.* London: International Work Group on Indigenous Affairs.

———. 1990. *Is Latin America Turning Protestant?* Berkeley: University of California Press.

———. 1993. *Between Two Armies: In the Ixil Towns of Guatemala.* New York: Columbia University Press.

Stoll, David, and Virginia Garrard-Burnett, eds., 1993. *Rethinking Protestantism in Latin America.* Philadelphia: Temple University Press.

Swanson, Tod D. 1994. "Refusing to Drink with the Mountains: Traditional Andean Meanings in Evangelical Practice." Pp. 79–98 in Martin Marty and R. Scott Appleby, eds., *Accounting for Fundamentalisms: The Dynamic Character of Movements.* Chicago: University of Chicago Press.

Tambiah, Stanley Jerava. 1976. *World Conqueror and World Renouncer: A Study of Buddhism and Polity in Thailand Against a Historical Background.* New York: Cambridge University Press.

———. 1992. *Buddhism Betrayed: Religion, Politics, and Violence in Sri Lanka.* Chicago: University of Chicago Press.

Tarrow, Sidney. 1994. *Power in Movement: Social Movements, Collective Action, and Politics.* New York: Cambridge University Press.

Tilly, Charles. 2007. *Democracy.* New York: Cambridge University Press.

Timmerman, Jacobo. 2002. *Prisoner Without a Name, Cell Without a Number.* Madison: University of Wisconsin Press.

Tocqueville, Alexis de. 1967. *Democracy in America,* Vol. 1. New York: Harper and Row.

———. 1990. *Democracy in America,* Vol. 1. New York: Vintage Books.

Toft, Monica Duffy, Daniel Philpott, and Timothy Samuel Shah. 2011. *God's Century: Resurgent Religion and Global Politics.* New York: W. W. Norton.

Torres, Camilo. 1964. "La Revolución Imperativo Cristiano" (September). Reproduced in Camilo Torres, 1968, *El Cura Que Murió en la Guerrilla.* Barcelona: Editorial Nova Terra.

———. 1965a. "Mensaje a los Cristianos" (published in *Frente Unido* 1, August 26, 1965). Reproduced on pp. 114–115 in Walter J. Broderick, ed., 2002, *Camilo Torres. Escritos Politicos.* Bogotá: El Ancora Editores.

———. 1965b. "Interview with Adolfo Gilly" (published in *Marcha,* Montevideo, June 4). Reproduced in Hernan Brienza, 2007, *Camilo Torres: Sacristán de la Guerrilla.* Buenos Aires: Capital Intelectual–Colección Fundadores de la Izquierda Latinoamericana.

———. 1965c. "Encrucijadas de la Iglesia en América Latina" (published in *ECO,* June 1965). Reproduced on pp. 247–250 in Camilo Torres, 1968, *El Cura Que Murió en la Guerrilla.* Barcelona: Editorial Nova Terra.

———. 1965d. "Carta a Mi Obispo" (June 24, 1965). Reproduced in Camilo Torres, 1968, *El Cura Que Murió en la Guerrilla.* Barcelona: Editorial Nova Terra.

———. 1965e. "Carta al Cardenal." Reproduced in Hernan Brienza, 2007, *Camilo Torres: Sacristán de la Guerrilla.* Buenos Aires: Capital Intelectual–Colección Fundadores de la Izquierda Latinoamericana.

———. 1968. *Camilo Torres: El Cura Que Murió en las Guerrillas.* Barcelona: Editorial Nova Terra.

Tovar, Cecilia, ed. 2006a. *Ser Iglesia en Tiempos de Violencia.* Lima: CEP (Centro de Estudios y Publicaciones).

———. 2006b. "Introducción." Pp. 15–36 in Cecilia Tovar, ed., *Ser Iglesia en Tiempos de Violencia.* Lima: CEP (Centro de Estudios y Publicaciones).

———. 2007. "Retomando el Camino de Medellín." La V Conferencia General del Episcopado en Aparecida. *Paginas* (Lima) 206 (August): 42–51.

Tovar, Teresa. 1990. "La Ciudad Mestizo. Vecinos y Pobladores en el 90." In Carmen R. Balbi, ed., *Movimientos Sociales Elementos para una Relectura.* Lima: DESCO.

———. 1991. "El Discreto Desencanto Frente a los Actors." *Paginas* 121 (October).

Turner, Victor. 1974. *Dramas, Fields, and Metaphors.* Ithaca, NY: Cornell University Press.

Tutu, Desmond. 1995. "Identity Crisis." Pp. 95–97 in Paul Gifford, ed., *The Churches and the Democratisation of Africa.* Leiden: E. J. Brill.

Vaggione, Juan Marco, ed. 2009a. *El Activismo Religioso Conservador en Latinoamérica.* Córdoba: Católicas por el Derecho a Decidir.

———. 2009b. "El Fundamentalismo Religioso en Latinoamérica. La Mirada de los/as Activistas por los Derechos Sexuales y Reproductivos." Pp. 287–319 in Juan Marco Vaggione, ed., *El Activismo Religioso Conservador en Latinoamérica.* Córdoba: Católicas por el Derecho a Decidir.

Vallier, Ivan. 1970. *Catholicism, Social Control, and Modernization in Latin America.* Englewood Cliffs, NJ: Prentice-Hall.

Van Cott, Donna Lee. 2000. *The Friendly Liquidation of the Past: The Politics of Diversity in Latin America.* Pittsburgh, PA: University of Pittsburgh Press.

———. 2007. *From Movements to Parties in Latin America: The Evolution of Ethnic Politics.* Cambridge: Cambridge University Press.

———. 2008. *Radical Democracy in the Andes.* Cambridge: Cambridge University Press.

Vásquez, Manuel, and Marie F. Marquardt. 2003. *Globalizing the Sacred: Religion Across the Americas.* New Brunswick, NJ: Rutgers University Press.

Vázquez, Luis. 2011. "Go and Make Disciples: Evangelization, Conversion Narratives, and Salvation in Puerto Rican Evangelical Salsa Music." PhD thesis, University of Michigan, Ann Arbor.

Verbitsky, Horacio. 1996. *Confessions of an Argentine Dirty Warrior.* New York: New Press.

———. 2005. *El Silencio: De Paulo VI a Bergoglio: Las Relacions Secretas de la Iglesia con la ESMA.* Buenos Aires: Editorial Sudamericana.

———. 2006. *Doble Juego: La Argentina Católica y Militar.* Buenos Aires: Editorial Sudamericana.

———. 2007. *La Iglesia en la Argentina: Un Siglo de Historia Política (1884–1983). Cristo Vence Tomo I, De Roca a Perón.* Buenos Aires: Editorial Sudamericana.

———. 2008. *Historia Política de la Iglesia Católica: La Violencia Evangélica Tomo II, De Lonardi al Cordobazo (1955–1969).* Buenos Aires: Editorial Sudamericana.

———. 2009. *Historia Política de la Iglesia Católica: Vigilia de Armas. Tomo II, Del Cordobazo de 1969 al 23 de Marzo de 1976.* Buenos Aires: Editorial Sudamericana.

Voas, David. 2009. "The Rise and Fall of Fuzzy Fidelity in Europe." *European Sociological Review* 25 (2): 155–168.

Walshe, Peter. 1983. *Church Versus State in South Africa: The Case of the Christian Institute*. Maryknoll, NY: Orbis Books.

———. 1991. "Prophetic Christianity and the Liberation Movement." *Journal of Modern African Studies* 29 (1): 27–60.

Warner, R. Stephen. 1988. *New Wine in Old Wineskins: Evangelicals and Liberals in a Small Town Church*. Berkeley: University of California Press.

———. 1993. "Work in Progress Toward a New Paradigm for the Sociological Study of Religion in the United States." *American Journal of Sociology* 98 (3): 1044–1093.

Weber, Max. 1948a. "The Social Psychology of the World Religions." Pp. 267–301 in Hans Gerth and C. Wright Mills, eds., *From Max Weber: Essays in Sociology*. London: Routledge and Kegan Paul.

———. 1948b. "Religious Rejections of the World and Their Directions." Pp. 323–362 in Hans Gerth and C. Wright Mills, eds., *From Max Weber: Essays in Sociology*. London: Routledge and Kegan Paul.

———. 1978a. *Max Weber: Selections in Translation* (edited by W. G. Runciman). Cambridge: Cambridge University Press.

———. 1978b. "The Concept of Following a Rule." Pp. 99–110 in W. G. Runciman, ed., *Max Weber: Selections in Translation*. Cambridge: Cambridge University Press.

———. 1978c. "Protestant Asceticism and the Spirit of Capitalism." Pp. 138–173 in W. G. Runciman, ed., *Max Weber: Selections in Translation*. Cambridge: Cambridge University Press.

———. 1978d. "The Soteriology of the Underprivileged." Pp. 174–191 in W. G. Runciman, ed., *Max Weber: Selections in Translation*. Cambridge: Cambridge University Press.

Wechsler, Lawrence. 1990. *A Miracle, a Universe: Settling Accounts with Torturers*. New York: Knopf Doubleday.

Weil, Simone. 1986. "The Iliad or the Poem of Force." Pp. 162–195 in Sian Miles, ed., *Simone Weil: An Anthology*. New York: Grove Press.

Wells, Ronald A. 2006. "Northern Ireland: A Study of Friendship, Forgiveness, and Reconciliation." Pp. 189–222 in Daniel Philpott, ed., *The Politics of Past Evil: Religion, Reconciliation, and the Dilemmas of Transitional Justice*. Notre Dame, IN: University of Notre Dame Press.

Wilde, Alexander W. 2011. "Human Rights in Two Latin American Democracies." In Katherine Hite and Mark Ungar, eds., *Human Rights Challenge of the Past/Challenge for the Future*. Washington, DC: Woodrow Wilson International Center for Scholars.

———. 2012. "A Season of Memory: Human Rights in Chile's Long Transition." In Katherine Hite, Cath Collins, and Alfredo Joignant, eds., *The Politics of Memory in Chile*. Forthcoming.

Willems, Emilio. 1967. *Followers of the New Faith: Culture Change and the Rise of Protestantism in Brazil and Chile*. Nashville: University of Tennessee Press.

Williams, Philip J. 1989. *The Catholic Church and Politics in Nicaragua and Costa Rica*. Pittsburgh, PA: University of Pittsburgh Press.

Wilson, Everett. 1997. "Guatemalan Pentecostals: Something of Their Own." Pp. 139–162 in Edward L. Cleary and Hannah Stewart-Gambino, eds., *Power, Politics, and Pentecostals in Latin America*. Boulder, CO: Westview.

Wilson, J. Matthew. 2007. *From Pews to Polling Places: Faith and Politics in the American Religious Mosaic*. Washington, DC: Georgetown University Press.

Wilson, Richard. 1991. "Machine Guns and Mountain Spirits: The Cultural Effects of State Repression Among the Q'eqchi' of Guatemala." *Critique of Anthropology* 11 (1): 33–61.

Wolford, Wendy. 2006. "Sem Reforma Agraria, Nao Ha Democacia: Deepening Democracy and the Struggle for Agrarian Reform in Brazil." Pp. 139–168 in Carlos Waisman, Richard Feinberg, and Leon Zamosc, eds., *Civil Society and Democracy in Latin America*. New York: Palgrave Macmillan.

Wooster, Henry. 1994. "Faith at the Ramparts: The Philippine Catholic Church and the 1986 Revolution." Pp. 153–176 in Douglas Johnston and Cynthia Sampson, eds., *Religion: The Missing Dimension of Statecraft*. New York: Oxford University Press.

Worth, Robert F. 2008. "Generation Faithful: Hezbollah Seeks to Marshal the Piety of the Young." *New York Times*, November 20.

Wuthnow, Robert. 1988. *The Restructuring of American Religion*. Princeton, NJ: Princeton University Press.

———. 1992. *Rediscovering the Sacred: Perspectives on Religion in Contemporary Society*. Grand Rapids, MI: William B. Eerdmans.

———. 1999. "Mobilizing Civic Engagement: The Changing Impact of Religious Involvement." Pp. 331–366 in Theda Skocpol and Morris Fiorina, eds., *Civic Engagement in American Democracy*. Washington, DC: Brookings Institution Press.

———. 2003. "Can Religion Revitalize Civil Society? An Institutional Perspective." Pp. 191–210 in Corwin Smidt, ed., *Religion and Social Capital: Producing the Common Good*. Waco, TX: Baylor University Press.

Yashar, Deborah. 2005. *Contesting Citizenship in Latin America: The Rise of Indigenous Movements and the Postliberal Challenge*. Cambridge: Cambridge University Press.

Zald, Meyer, and John D. McCarthy, eds. 1987a. *Social Movements in an Organizational Society*. New Brunswick, NJ: Transaction Books.

———. 1987b. "Religious Groups as Crucibles of Social Movements." Pp. 67–95 in Meyer Zald and John D. McCarthy, eds., *Social Movements in an Organizational Society*. New Brunswick, NJ: Transaction Books.

Zaret, David. 1985. *The Heavenly Contract: Ideology and Organization in Pre-Revolutionary Puritanism*. Chicago: University of Chicago Press.

Zirker, Daniel. 1999. "The Brazilian Church-State Crisis of 1980: Effective Non-Violent Action in a Military Dictatorship." Pp. 259–278 in Stephen Zunes, Lester Kurtz, and Sarah Beth Asher, eds., *Nonviolent Social Movements: A Geographical Perspective*. Oxford: Blackwell Publishing.

Zub, Roberto. 2008. "The Evolution of Protestant Participation in Nicaraguan Politics and the Rise of Evangelical Parties." Pp. 97–130 in Paul Freston, ed., *Evangelical Christianity and Democracy in Latin America*. New York: Oxford University Press.

Index

Abernathy, Ralph, 194(n29)
Abortion debate, 122
Accommodation, 22, 112
Accompaniment, liberation theology view of, 156
Accountability, 164, 167, 199, 222(n2)
Activism: academic study of, 40–41; pluralism threatening church control of public space, 104–105; religious, 66. *See also* Social movements
Adorno, Theodor, 221, 225(n18)
Advertising, religious, 49
Affiliation, religious, 55, 70(table)
Africa: political role of churches, 233–234
African American communities, 197, 232, 233, 238–240
African National Congress (ANC), 236
Afterlife, 200–201
Agenda of life, 223(n5)
Allende, Salvador, 110
American Revolutionary Popular Alliance (APRA; Peru), 142
AMIA, bombing of, Argentina, 191(n16)
Amnesty, 210, 219, 224(n10)
Anglicans, 66
Anomie, 84–85
Anticlericalism, 53, 93–94
Anti-Semitism, 191(n16)
Aparecida conference (2007), 19(box); autonomy and control as central issues, 95; mission and goals of, 6, 26–27,

81–83, 90(n13); missionary disciples as theme, 81; papal presence, 112
Apartheid state (South Africa), 234–236, 256(n4)
Argentina: AMIA, bombing of, 191(n16); anti-Semitism of the military, 191(n16); Catholic Action, 20–21; church defense of rights, 222(n1); church growth and installed capacity, 73(table); church role in conflict, 30(n7), 123, 166–167; coup, 19(box); failure of social movements, 14; history of democracy in Latin America, 99; impact of regime on religion, 261–262; kidnapping and disappearances, 190(n6); late twentieth-century return of democracy, 25; Mothers of the Plaza de Mayo, 184–185, 206; nonviolence strategy, 184–186; prosecutions of military and political leaders, 217–218; response to and impact of violence, 177–179, 180–184; retributive justice, 219–220; revolutionary inspiration, 23; truth commission, 210; violence in the name of faith, 171
Argentine Anti-Communist Alliance, 177
Armed conflict. *See* Civil wars; Conflict; Revolutionary periods
Assemblies of God, 66, 117
Augustine (Saint), 239

Tutu, Desmond, Archbishop (South Africa) 215, 235–236, 250–251, 256(n4)

Twin tolerations, 266

Ubuntu (community), 250–251

Ultimate ends, ethic of, 122–123. *See also* Weber

Unaffiliated population, 70(table)

United Front of the Colombian People, 171

United Nations: Salvadoran peace, 209

United States: Catholic Charismatic Renewal movement, 67–68; church-state separation, 34, 48; civil rights movement, 34, 147, 238–240, 248; congregations as social space, 158; continuing political impact of religious pluralism, 231–232; empowerment functions of religion, 155; faith and politics in African American communities, 197; fundamentalist belief in the contamination and corruption of politics, 106; international human rights networks, 205–206; Pentecostalism, 66–67; pluralism and secularization, 58–59; rescue of disappeared in Argentina, 183; Tocqueville's perception of religion in, 94–95, 125(n1); Vatican politics' influence in, 223(n5)

Urbanization, 56, 77–78, 84–85

Uruguay: history of democracy in Latin America, 99; late twentieth-century return of democracy, 25; secularism, 53

Utopian perspective, 129–130, 160(nn2,3)

Valech Commission (Chile), 212–213

Vallier, Ivan, 15, 41–43

Values: liberation theology, 37–40; qualitative analysis methods, 51–52; in a secularizing society, 56–57; societal need for basic values, 15

Vatican II, 19(box); defense of rights, 199; globalization and, 36; impact on Medellín conference, 22; propelling church involvement in democratic transition, 92; "signs of the times," 129

Venezuela: Christian Democratic anti-Left strategy, 20; church role in military

conflict and democratic transition, 108–109, 118–120; empowering social groups, 146; evangelical backing of Hugo Chávez, 114; religious agendas clashing with social movements, 161(n9); social capital formation, 154

Vicariates of Solidarity, 110, 111, 178, 180, 192(n19), 193(n26), 208, 211, 212

Victimization of churches, 166–170

Villa El Salvador, Peru, 139–140, 160–161(n6)

Violence, 2; alternative explanations, 164, 218; anti-Semitism of the Argentine military, 191(n16); Aparecida themes addressing, 81; church alliance with the poor, 24; church defense of rights, 195–196, 222(n1); death and disappearances of clergy, 61(n4); formation of human rights organizations, 138; global occurrences, 245; as impediment to Peru's popular movement, 142; institutionalization of, 6, 165; issues delineating reconciliation, 219–220; late twentieth-century decline in, 25–26; liberation theology, 38, 39–40; long-term consequences of, 167; mediation and peacemaking, 208–209; in the name of faith, 170–176; nonviolence strategy, 184–188, 193(n29), 248–249, 251; as part of daily life, 223(n7), 253–254; Protestant growth associated with, 25; Protestant view of Latin American politics, 92–93; reconciling theology with, 221–222; recovery as a right, 198–199; religious change and, 163–164, 166–170; reshaping religious-political relationships, 14; response in Argentina and Peru, 177–178, 180–184; response of church institutions, 164–166; rhythm and dynamic of, 167; ritualization of, 244–245; social movements emerging from, 188; theory of religion-violence connection, 243–249; types of, 189(n2); youth violence, 189(n3). *See also* Truth and reconciliation commissions

About the Book

Long assumed to be an unchanging and unquestioned bulwark of established power and privilege, religion in Latin America has diversified and flourished, while taking on new social and political roles in more open societies. How did this change occur? Why did churches in the region embrace new ideas about rights, sponsor social movements, and become advocates for democracy? Are further changes on the horizon? Daniel Levine explores these issues, uniquely situating the Latin American experience in a rich theoretical and comparative context.

Daniel H. Levine is professor emeritus of political science at the University of Michigan. His numerous publications include *The Quality of Democracy in Latin America* (coedited with José E. Molina), *Popular Voices in Latin American Catholicism*, and *Religion and Politics in Latin America: The Catholic Church in Venezuela and Colombia*.